# Social Interaction Systems

# Social Interaction Systems

## Theory and Measurement

## Robert Freed Bales

Transaction Publishers
New Brunswick (U.S.A.) and London (U.K.)

First paperback edition 2002

Copyright © 2001 by Transaction Publishers, New Brunswick, New Jersey.

This book is printed on acid-free paper that meets the American National Standard for Permanence of Paper for Printed Library Materials.

Library of Congress Catalog Number: 98-53727
ISBN: 0-7658-0872-2
Printed in the United States of America

Library of Congress Cataloging-in-Publication Data

Bales, Robert Freed, 1916-
    Social interaction systems : theory and measurement / Robert Freed Bales.
        p. cm.
    Includes bibliographical references.
    ISBN 0-7658-0872-2 (paper : alk. paper)
    1. Social interaction.   I. Title.

HM291 .B253   1999                                          98-53727
302—dc21                                                    CIP

Dedicated to the Memory of

Talcott Parsons, Gordon W. Allport,
Henry A. Murray, Clyde M. Kluckhohn,
Samuel A. Stouffer

Founders of
The Department and Laboratory of Social Relations
at Harvard, 1945–1972


From these ashes
I have dreamed
a Phoenix will arise.

## Maher's Ode on Bales's Law of Invariant Variability

There was a professor who lived on a hill
And I know for a fact that he's living there still
On human behavior for years he had mused
He went into it clear but came out confused.

For the books that he read and the lectures he heard
Stated findings quite dull or extremely absurd
And the more that he looked the less that he saw
'Til one day he thought, "I've discovered a law!"

In any experiment people confront
There are some who do one thing and others who don't
There are some who turn left and some who turn right
Some sit in the center quite frozen with fright.

Some turn up on time while others delay
There are some who refuse while others obey
Some press the wrong button and some press them all
Some prefer honey, some prefer gall.

So when findings appear, pray don't celebrate
It's twenty to one they won't replicate
In the next group of subjects the difference is hid
When it came to the crunch, some didn't, some did.

In Physics, proud wearer of Science's crown,
We can safely predict what goes up must come down
In Psychology, sadly, it's not the same case
The rockets we launch collapse on their base.

Here is my law, for woman and man,
In any assessment some can't and some can
Some couldn't, some could, some wouldn't, some would
The way the twigs are bent doesn't bias the bud.

Turn away from the mean, and examine the spread
Dim down the computer and switch on your head
Were it not for the variance where would we be?
If you can't make a t-test, you can't take a p.

Now this is a comfort, not grounds for complaint
Thank God for the fact that some are and some ain't.
From the data of variance pleasure derive
It's one of the things that helps us survive.

—Brendan A. Maher (1997)

# Contents

# List of Figures

# Preface

As social psychologists approach the end of the first century of our discipline there are still many who complain about its lack of integration. I believe that social psychologists now have the knowledge and experience to be able to realize a major new theoretical integration. I present here an introduction to a body of theory and methods addressed to the problem. The theory is the result of more than fifty years of my best intellectual efforts, with the collaboration of more others than I can name. It is based on widespread application in the field, as well as on extensive observation in the laboratory. In its application it produces data for further theoretical advance. My name for it is "social-interaction systems theory."

All of my research career I have been trying to achieve a more integrated view of the field of social psychology, with which I am primarily identified. I have felt that we must make a transition from an individually centered frame of reference (still the mainstream approach), to a larger framework centered on multiple-person systems of social interaction and their dynamics. Almost all of my work has been an attempt to give substance to that aspiration.

One of my revered mentors in the old Department of Social Relations at Harvard, Gordon Allport, used to try to provoke final action from graduate students who couldn't seem to stop their wandering research and get down to the final writing of their dissertations. "Time to put on the blinkers," he would say. "Time to sugar off!" His reference was to an old farm chore in New England—hitching up the horses and hauling in the sap to make maple sugar. (The blinkers on the head harness kept the horses' eyes looking straight ahead.)

The purpose of this book, at the time I actually began it, was to "sugar off"—to give a thoroughly boiled down extract of the body of theory and methods I have been working on for so many years. As I worked to "sugar off" it became oppressively clear that what I really wanted to produce was a *grand theory*, one that could be named quite simply: "Social Interaction Systems, Theory and Measurement." At the same time, I could not forget that some of my distinguished elder colleagues (in particular, Robert Merton and Morton Deutch) had earlier tried to send their colleagues this message: "Grand theory in sociology and social psychology is dead. We should work on theories in the middle range that tie directly to bodies of empirical data." I have tried to do this, and it well describes what I have done, but I have not been entirely able to restrain my aspirations to contribute to a future grand theory.

As a result, the theoretically well-prepared reader may sense that what he is reading is a parable, a story about homely things and events which is meant to have a more general meaning. On the simpler level, the reader will be introduced to a small-scale model in which all the parts are concrete and well defined. The model and procedures are easily usable for practical work with groups and individuals. But in my mind, the model seems to have a life of its own. It has changed my thinking. I think it has large-scale implications. Tentative answers are suggested to philosophical and methodological dilemmas that are still not resolved in the disciplines of social psychology and sociology. Grand-scale aspirations are barely concealed.

My attempts to deal with the problems of integration of social psychology and its effective utilization began with a period of frustration and disappointment with the concepts and methods available at the beginning of my graduate studies in 1938. (See Bales 1941; 1984a.)

My intuition told me that I needed to study social interaction by direct observation in order to cast further light on my problems. Early steps were devoted to the development of an observational method called *Interaction Process Analysis* (Bales 1950). From 1945 to about 1955, I used this method in the observation of initially leaderless problem-solving groups in the laboratory. I concentrated on building empirical norms for a set of four similar case-analysis problems. The intention was to employ the standard setting and the empirical norms in a further set of experimental studies. This setting was used for studies devoted to group size, time cycles, developmental trends, and a number of other emergent regularities in social interaction.

The importance of interpersonal conflicts in these groups, apparently conflicts about *values*, led to a factor-analytic study with my colleague Arthur Couch, who understood how to do factor analysis, as I did not. Our computer facilities at that time put a limit of 144 on the number of variables Couch could include in a factor analysis. Consequently, we culled exactly 144 maximally-varied verbal expressions of values (value statements) from over 800 such statements initially gathered from general literary sources, personality tests, anthropological reports, and from the earlier observations of the laboratory groups. The intercorrelated item clusters which emerged as orthogonal factors we then conceptualized as general value dimensions. We adopted these dimensions as the basis of a new method for the real-time observation and recording of value statements in the laboratory groups. The method was called *Value Content Analysis.*

Couch and I mounted an omnibus study of values and behavior, and as many other different kinds of measures as we could manage. The extensive number of intercorrelations the study produced turned out to be critical in my own theoretical development. We first measured with standard personality tests the initial personality characteristics of sixty Harvard undergraduates. They were then randomly assembled into "initially leaderless groups" of five members each, and were asked to discuss case-analysis problems and to perform several related problem-solving tasks. The instructions asked the assembled members to attempt to come to a group decision by the end of an hour. There were a number of sessions.

The two methods—*Interaction Process Analysis* and *Value Content Analysis*—were used for the direct observation of the interpersonal interaction. The following kinds of things were observed or measured: who initially chose to sit where around the discussion table; who addressed whom in what way, in what explicit time order; who made what kinds of value statements to whom; who made what kinds of value statements of opposing content; what interpersonal perceptions did each person have of each of the others; who liked and disliked whom; how did each of the participants guess that each of the others were rating and perceiving?

From a number of factor analyses that Arthur Couch made of the very large number of variables observed and measured in this study he completed his thesis (1960). I continued to study the complete tables of intercorrelations of each variable with every other variable. The main shape of the body of theory I now call social-interaction systems theory gradually emerged from this detailed study. It was described in my book, *Personality and Interpersonal Behavior* (Bales 1970).

By about 1955, I had abandoned my envisioned impersonal role of "experimental social psychologist." In fact, all of my studies in the early laboratory period had been more essentially "observational" than "experimental." I also abandoned the intention to proceed with a strictly experimental approach. Inspired partly by training in psychoanalysis, I came out from behind the one-way mirror of the group-observation laboratory and spent roughly the next thirty years in the study of what I called "academic self-analytic groups" in a classroom-laboratory setting.

These academic self-analytic groups, for the most part, were made up of Harvard undergraduates, usually about twenty-five in number, enrolled in a course that was regularly listed in the university course catalog. Actually it was a course that was strictly one of a kind. I played a very restrained role as leader-teacher. I made very occasional interpretations or interventions, but remained mostly silent. My role for several years was rather like that of the well-known Tavistock leader, a role which Wilfred Bion (1961) had originally modeled based on his understanding of Freud's psychoanalytic role as adapted to group therapy. But I gradually came to feel that trying to achieve effective group development and performance within the resulting "negative transference" (which inevitably developed) was doomed to take almost forever, and would surely fail with some, probably too many, of the more submissive students.

Thereupon I changed my approach to that of a basically friendly and democratic leader-teacher, whose intention was to improve the functioning of the group, but who chose to do it, mostly, by careful preparation of the course format, readings, occasional interpretations and comments on the discussions, formal observations of the discussions, systematic gathering of interpersonal perceptions and descriptions of members of each other, followed by feedback and group interpretation of members' current and changing perceptions of each other.

In this context, with the help of colleagues and students, I developed a method for the coding and computer-based analysis of the behavioral interaction of each participant toward each other, and at the same time, a classification of the accompanying value statements implicit in the verbal content of what each member said. The method was called *A System for the Multiple Level Observation of Groups* (Bales and Cohen 1979).

The method is a complex data-gathering instrument which leads by way of computations on ratings made by group members, to a graphic display called a *Field Diagram*. The Field Diagram shows the location of each member in a graphic *space* which represents value differences. The total plot of members' locations in the space often shows a pattern of several clusters, and a few isolates, which can be recognized by the members as a pattern of their relationships with each other.

Value differences and similarities among members are assumed to affect the way they interact with each other and gradually change. The plot is thus, in theoretical terms, a visual display of *dynamic system fields* presumably operating in the group. The Field Diagram, along with other summaries of the ratings, was used as feedback data to self-analytic-group members about their individual personalities and roles, their relationships, and their mode of operation as a group.

As an unanticipated bonus of this long-time technical buildup over many years in the laboratory classroom, it turned out that the twenty-six-item descriptive form used by group members to describe their perceptions of each other's behavior and their positions on value issues seemed to be almost exactly what was needed for practical applications in the field. The form for the description of values inferred from behavior, called *Individual and Organizational Values* (IOVAL), proved to be the bridge to widespread practical application in the field.

I have always felt the compulsion to ground my thinking in empirical data. The theory, the methods, and the data of this book are all completely defined in terms of practical measurements and operations in the real world. But the system as a whole is unavoidably large and complex. In order to proceed with some unity of empirical emphasis, I have focused on the attempt to understand certain unexpected features of a large body of data from business organizations, and still more specifically on findings concerning "effective leadership."

This body of data is the fruit of collaboration over the last fifteen years or so with my colleagues, Robert Koenigs and Margaret Cowen. In 1983, in anticipation of my academic retirement in 1986, we formed an organization intended to explore further the implications of my research and theory on groups and, at the same time, to provide consulting services. The organization is called the SYMLOG Consulting Group (SCG), and is now based in San Diego. We determined from the first that the organization would be self-supporting through consulting, rather than dependent on grants, but that it would nevertheless give a major emphasis to academically oriented research and theory (see Koenigs and Cowen 1988).

The acronym SYMLOG stands for "Systematic Multiple Level Observation of Groups" (Bales and Cohen 1979). The theory and methods of SCG are based mainly on my previous academic work in the study of small groups and leadership, and on Dr. Koenigs's experience and theory in organization development.

In the mid-1970s, Dr. Robert Koenigs joined me for a period of teaching and research in organization development at Harvard, and our long collaboration was formed at that time. By 1983, when we established SCG, I had pursued research on leadership and groups over a period of more than forty years in the Laboratory of Social Relations, and the Department of Psychology at Harvard. Dr. Koenigs's previous work had been done over a period of more than ten years as a member and consultant in the Center for Planned Change, an independent center for organization development originated by academics in psychology at St. Louis University.

In training one needs to be able to evaluate performance. Robert Koenigs early developed the conviction that group members' concepts of "effectiveness" provided a strategic criterion for detecting and defining the most important improvements needed. Together we devised the composite wording of the survey questions we have used with slight variations over a long period of research and practice (all questions focused on "values shown in behavior").

The data I shall utilize from the SCG data bank, with the collaboration of Robert Koenigs, are drawn from business teams and organizations in the United States, although by now (fifteen years or more from the formation of SCG) the network of approximately 400 SCG consultants is international in scope and data are accumulating from other countries and cultures. We have tested and validated translations for the rating items that are basic to the method into about twelve languages, and continue to add more, but there is not yet a large enough accumulation of data from other countries to be included here.

SCG has been self-supporting through consulting from the first. It is now a corporation in California. It is democratically controlled in part, with the participation of a growing number of associated active consultants spread out in a number of different countries. SCG maintains a regular APA-approved training program for certification of consultants and holds yearly meetings among consultants for quality control and scientific communication. SCG has assumed a permanent legal obligation to devote a part of its income to academic research and publication in social psychology. It has accumulated a large data bank for research dedicated both to practical development and theoretical social-psychological research. Research opportunities and technical help are offered to the academic community. My technical role in the organization is that of senior consultant for research and development.

The present book is part of the effort to bring the contemporary theory and methods of SCG to the attention of academic social psychologists. The book outlines the theory and methods and reviews the most important empirical studies from my early research, conducted primarily with colleagues and graduate students in the normal course of their academic careers.

Nearly all of the empirical studies in the academic part of my research were done in close collaboration with other colleagues, graduate student assistants, and a large aggregate population of undergraduates assembled into small groups year after year. They were all collaborators, of whatever academic rank. I am deeply indebted to them in all ways—for ideas, abilities, stimulation, work, and indispensable social support.

The early "leaderless" groups in the laboratory and, later, the "self-analytic" groups I observed for so many years had many apparent problems, which did not help them much, perhaps, but which gave me great theoretical help and additional insight. These groups did not run smoothly. Their members solved their problems in leadership and social relations as best they could, with minimal help (or minimal interference) from me. The emergent regularities and structures which they developed, the several different levels of variables which appeared to be important, and which I learned to measure, provided an early working model of the more mature and practically-implemented contemporary theory and its methods of analysis.

The work of SCG has been centered on value-based planned change and training in leadership, teamwork, and organization development. The settings have been mostly, but not solely, business organizations—in the United States, but substantial pieces of the data bank have also come from Canada, and nine Western European countries, including England. Data from South Africa, Australia, Japan, and a number of Pacific Rim countries are beginning to accumulate. Most of the work so far has been done using the English version of the instruments and feedback reports, but a number of non-English-speaking Pacific Rim countries are involved in translation projects in preparation for further work.

However, the implications I draw from the data are not meant to be confined to business contexts or to the cultural contexts of the United States. As a sociologist and social psychologist, I am concerned with understanding groups, organizations, and leadership in the broadest possible sense. I shall draw freely on summary findings from my own past studies with laboratory-based groups, as well as findings from contemporary business organizations.

The interpretations I shall make are meant to help understand better certain basic, and, so far as I can tell, universal features of social-interaction systems.

But general knowledge is not enough. Effective leadership must depend upon a sufficiently accurate understanding of the specific dynamics of the particular group, organization, and environment. Measurement can almost always improve the necessary understanding, and may be absolutely essential. Moreover, the focus on effective leadership serves more than a practical purpose. I have a deep conviction that we do not understand our general theory well enough until we are able to deal more effectively with the system about which we are theorizing.

It is clear that political conditions in some parts of the world, as well as substantial problems of language and cultural differences, make translation and use of the system difficult in some countries. Experience so far, however, indicates that the methods are rugged and the results are highly valued by the clients. Translations can be made and validated successfully. They are capable of producing data for crosscultural comparisons and for similar work in other cultures. Political conditions may provide the most difficult barriers to worldwide use, since the methods are only used if conditions are sufficiently democratic to support and protect individuals in the groups who provide data for use in feedback. Identification of individuals is always protected.

For the stimulus to "put on the blinkers" and try to "sugar off," I am particularly grateful to Paul Hare, the prime historian of research on small groups, who was an early Associate in the Laboratory of Social Relations, and has been a valued comrade in research and publication from the first. For the ability to finally get the present book into type and diagrams, I am grateful to Paul's daughter, Sharon Hare, also a social psychologist, and an associate of the SYMLOG Consulting Group.

My colleagues Robert Koenigs and Margaret Cowen, president and vice president of the SYMLOG Consulting Group, know my appreciation. Without their collaboration, the going organization, the training of consultants, the substantial results from the field would never have come into existence. The members of their team and the large number of consultants in the field who have supplied their know-how in the gathering and feedback of data to group members in business and organizational settings have completed the circle of theory, application, and new theory. I am also grateful to Irving Louis Horowitz, the editorial director of Transaction, who has given me much aid and comfort, not to speak of many postponements.

But my most important debt of appreciation is to my wife, Dorothy. For the last fifty-six years she has filled our lives with love and happiness. She has provided the intellectual support and musical companionship that has enabled me to do my best. I am very grateful to her.

Robert Freed Bales
Weston, Massachusetts
17 January 1998

# Part 1
# Theory and Methods

# 1

# Overview of the SYMLOG System

I begin with a reprint of an instructional booklet I have written for SYMLOG Consulting Group. The booklet is designed to introduce consultants and others to the methods and theories of the present system. The consultant's perspective is my preferred perspective for the formulation of the theory. This perspective is essentially similar to the perspective of a leader, or active participant, who wishes to improve or maintain the effectiveness of a specific system, and believes that strategic information about the system will help.

This perspective confronts the major practical and pragmatic problems, as well as the value dilemmas and ethical problems, involved in the application and in the further testing and development of the theory and methods. It brings many features into focus that might otherwise be ignored or lost to sight in more abstract theorizing. Academic theorists will see many familiar features in perspective and with operational definitions.

The booklet is meant to be as simple and concrete as possible. It presents a picture of a specific group with named members. It introduces the necessary language for talking about the group and similar groups, the individual members, the theories, and the methods in relation to each other. The following chapters of the book are designed to further explain and enlarge on the history and development of the various features. The present picture is designed to enable the reader to keep the various features of a complex system in a single global focus.

## Introduction

The SYMLOG System is a theory of personality and group dynamics integrated with a set of practical methods for measuring and changing behavior and values in a democratic way. It is designed for application in a specific group in its natural situation. The theory and methods are applicable to many kinds of groups and situations. Typically the purpose is to understand the group better in order to improve productivity and satisfaction. The theory and measurements indicate specific ways in which leaders and members can most

3

effectively act to encourage desirable changes in group performance and to reduce stress.

Applications include assessment of the teamwork and leadership potential of individuals for selection and training, the composition of groups and improvement of teamwork, leadership training, and the training of educators in a broad sense, including teachers, coaches, therapists, and other professionals who work primarily with people. The method also provides information and facilities for many kinds of fundamental and applied research in social psychology and sociology.

## What Does the Name *SYMLOG* Mean?

The name *SYMLOG* is an acronym for (1) SYstematic, (2) Multiple Level, (3) Observation of Groups.

### Systematic

The theory and methods provide ways for leaders and group members to measure and consider a more complete and strategic set of variables involved in their behavior and values than would otherwise be possible. The conceptual framework is fundamental, comprehensive, and well structured. The basic research has been conducted over a long period—more than forty years—by the author and his colleagues at Harvard University, and more than fifteen years in business teams and organizations in the United States and other countries. The methods are reliable, valid, and rugged over a broad range of conditions.

### Multiple Level

There are a number of methods of measurement for specific purposes. The various methods enable one to measure many aspects, or levels, of individual behavior, including the internal psychological aspects (perceptions, attitudes, values, concepts) as well as nonverbal behavior, overt behavior, and the value content of communication.

The methods for integrating the measurements enable one to obtain a higher level understanding of: (a) the internal dynamics of individual personalities; (b) the relationships of particular group members to each other; (c) the overall dynamic tendencies of the total group; and, (d) the effects of the broader organizational culture on the inner workings of the group.

### Observation of Groups

The findings on which the theory is based are the result of systematic observation of real groups. The research has concentrated on the ways in which individuals with different kinds of personalities affect each other in task-oriented groups. Measurements are based on practical observations. The most practical method in applications consists of ratings of the frequency of various kinds behavior and values, made by group members who know each other well.

An analysis of a group may be based on the perceptions of a leader, or single other member, if necessary. But reliability and validity are greatly improved if most or all of the group members contribute their observations. Observations by external observers can also be included. Corrections for individual biases or differences of perspective between different observers are built into the methods. Assessments of individuals for selection or training are always based on ratings by multiple observers.

## How Are the Observations Used?

All measurements are integrated and analyzed by the use of expert computer programs to produce graphic displays and written reports. If the members wish to share their information, they may see exactly how each of them sees the group. Or, if they wish, they may preserve any desired degree of confidentiality. Arrangements as to confidentiality and degree of detail of the data feedback to individuals and the group are made in advance.

An individualized *Report* is addressed to each group member. The Report may show how that individual sees each other member. It may show the way others see the individual, giving tentative suggestions as to the reasons he or she may be seen in the given way, and what changes might improve teamwork. A similar Report based on group averages is addressed to the group as a whole.

The methods of measurement are maximally compact and efficient as to time and effort required. In many cases the data may be gathered, processed, and printed into reports within the time constraints of a single meeting. Discussion of the reports usually takes place, after time for study, in subsequent group meetings, or in coaching sessions of individuals with consultants.

## Theoretical Background

SYMLOG theory is a comprehensive integration of findings and theories from psychology, social psychology, and sociology. It is unique in its breadth, its high degree of integration, and its practical implementation. It is a new *field theory* (Bales 1985).

As a field theory, SYMLOG takes effective account of the fact that every act of behavior takes place in a larger context, that it is a part of an interactive field of influences. The approach assumes that one needs to understand the larger context—personal, interpersonal, group, and external situation—in order to understand the patterns of behavior and to influence them successfully. The measurement procedures of SYMLOG are designed to measure the behavior patterns, the values, and their larger context.

## The Field Diagram

One of the major methods for integrating and drawing inferences from the measurements is the construction and analysis of the *Field Diagram*. The Field Diagram is a picture of a group that shows how individual members relate to each other and to the situation. Figure 1.1 presents an illustrative example.

The Field Diagram is a map. The location of each member is shown as a circle on the diagram, labeled with the member's code name. The circle in its

**FIGURE 1.1**
**An Example Field Diagram**

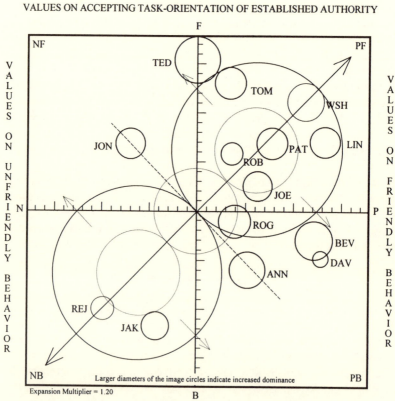

VALUES ON ACCEPTING TASK-ORIENTATION OF ESTABLISHED AUTHORITY

Larger diameters of the image circles indicate increased dominance

Expansion Multiplier = 1.20

VALUES ON OPPOSING TASK-ORIENTATION OF ESTABLISHED AUTHORITY

*Source:* © 1997 SYMLOG Consulting Group, San Diego, CA. Reprinted by permission.

particular location is called the *image* of the member. The circle size and location of the image in the field is based on the average of the way all members see the behavior and values of that member.

The Field Diagram shows two scales crossing the areas and intersecting in the middle. These are called *dimensions* (P-to-N and F-to-B on the diagram). The dimensions of the field are scales that are used as coordinates, against which the locations of images are plotted. Points on the scales are the frequencies with which individuals show one aspect or another of certain *bipolar behavioral characteristics*. A large amount of research indicates that at least three such bipolar characteristics are fundamental, and probably universal (thus always need to be taken into account):

1. Dominance versus Submissiveness;
2. Friendliness versus Unfriendliness; and
3. Acceptance versus Non-acceptance of Authority.

The frequency rates with which an individual behaves in each of these kinds of ways, or implies that a given kind of behavior is good or bad (makes evaluations or shows values in behavior), can be observed, rated as to frequency of occurrence, and located on a scale of frequency. These ratings are made by group members using a *Rating Form* shown as figure 1.2.

Each of the three dimensions is psychologically bipolar. The two ends of the dimension are evaluatively opposed to each other—if a person at a given time feels that a kind of behavior at one end is good, the kind of behavior at the other end is likely to be rejected as bad.

Thus, each *dimension* as shown on the Field Diagram really consists of two opposing directions. The middle of the diagram where the two scales cross is the zero point of both scales. Each dimension consists of two opposite directions—one direction from the zero point out to one extreme, and an exactly opposite direction from the zero point out to the other extreme.

Only two dimensions—Friendliness versus Unfriendliness, and Acceptance versus Non-acceptance of Authority—can be shown on the plane of the Field Diagram. But there are three dimensions of behavior to be portrayed. How is this inconvenience addressed?

Location in the first dimension, the Dominance versus Submissiveness of the individual, is not indicated by a scaled line on the diagram. Rather, it is represented metaphorically, by the *size of the image circle* standing for the member. A large image circle indicates that the individual is seen as Dominant; a small image circle means that the member is seen as Submissive.

The other two dimensions are represented directly on the plane of the Field Diagram as long lines with scale marks. The location of an image in one of the dimensions alone gives no information about its location on either of the other two dimensions. The two dimensions shown as scaled lines on the dia-

## FIGURE 1.2
## A Sample SYMLOG Consulting Group Rating Form,
## Individual and Organizational Values

Reflect on the work-related experiences you have had with the person you are about to rate. Whether you have worked closely with this person or have had only limited contact, keep your impressions of him or her in mind as you answer the question below. Not all parts of a descriptive items may seem to go together. *If any part applies, then use it as your guide.*

> In general, what kinds of values does this person show in his or her behavior?

**Descriptive Items—Individual and Organizational Values**

| | Rarely | Sometimes | Often |
|---|---|---|---|
| 1 Individual financial success, personal prominence and power | [ ] | [ ] | [ ] |
| 2 Popularity and social success, being liked and admired | [ ] | [ ] | [ ] |
| 3 Active teamwork toward common goals, organizational unity | [ ] | [ ] | [ ] |
| 4 Efficiency, strong impartial management | [ ] | [ ] | [ ] |
| 5 Active reinforcement of authority, rules, and regulations | [ ] | [ ] | [ ] |
| 6 Tough-minded, self-oriented assertiveness | [ ] | [ ] | [ ] |
| 7 Rugged, self-oriented individualism, resistance to authority | [ ] | [ ] | [ ] |
| 8 Having a good time, releasing tension, relaxing control | [ ] | [ ] | [ ] |
| 9 Protecting less able members, providing help when needed | [ ] | [ ] | [ ] |
| 10 Equality, democratic participation in decision making | [ ] | [ ] | [ ] |
| 11 Responsible idealism, collaborative work | [ ] | [ ] | [ ] |
| 12 Conservative, established, "correct" ways of doing things | [ ] | [ ] | [ ] |
| 13 Restraining individual desires for organizational goals | [ ] | [ ] | [ ] |
| 14 Self-protection, self-interest first, self-sufficiency | [ ] | [ ] | [ ] |
| 15 Rejection of established procedures, rejection of conformity | [ ] | [ ] | [ ] |
| 16 Change to new procedures, different values, creativity | [ ] | [ ] | [ ] |
| 17 Friendship, mutual pleasure, recreation | [ ] | [ ] | [ ] |
| 18 Trust in the goodness of others | [ ] | [ ] | [ ] |
| 19 Dedication, faithfulness, loyalty to the organization | [ ] | [ ] | [ ] |
| 20 Obedience to the chain of command, complying with authority | [ ] | [ ] | [ ] |
| 21 Self-sacrifice if necessary to reach organizational goals | [ ] | [ ] | [ ] |
| 22 Passive rejection of popularity, going it alone | [ ] | [ ] | [ ] |
| 23 Admission of failure, withdrawal of effort | [ ] | [ ] | [ ] |
| 24 Passive non-cooperation with authority | [ ] | [ ] | [ ] |
| 25 Quiet contentment, taking it easy | [ ] | [ ] | [ ] |
| 26 Giving up personal needs and desires, passivity | [ ] | [ ] | [ ] |

*Source:* © 1997 SYMLOG Consulting Group, San Diego, CA. Reprinted by permission.

gram are independent of each other. This is indicated by the fact that they cross each other at right angles in the middle of the diagram.

The meaning of the code letters at the ends of the dimensions can be understood by referring to the cube diagram shown as figure 1.3. The cube dia-

**FIGURE 1.3**
**SYMLOG Cube Diagram**

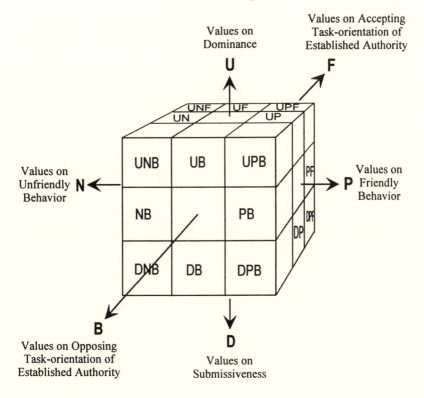

**Directions in the Physical Space Model**

Metaphorical names for the physical directions coordinated with names for describing the Value directions for Individual and Organizational Values

| | | | | |
|---|---|---|---|---|
| U | = | Upward | = | Values on Dominance |
| D | = | Downward | = | Values on Submissiveness |
| P | = | Positive | = | Values on Friendly Behavior |
| N | = | Negative | = | Values on Unfriendly Behavior |
| F | = | Forward | = | Values on Accepting Task-orientation of Established Authority |
| B | = | Backward | = | Values on Opposing Task-orientation of Established Authority |

gram is a model that shows the three dimensions as if they were the three dimensions of a physical space. The opposing directions are named as if the head of the viewer were placed in the exact center of the cube, looking toward

**FIGURE 1.4**
**Individual and Organizational Values, Listed by Number and Vector**

| | | |
|---|---|---|
| 1 | **U** | Individual financial success, personal prominence and power |
| 2 | **UP** | Popularity and social success, being liked and admired |
| 3 | **UPF** | Active teamwork toward common goals, organizational unity |
| 4 | **UF** | Efficiency, strong impartial management |
| 5 | **UNF** | Active reinforcement of authority, rules, and regulations |
| 6 | **UN** | Tough-minded, self-oriented assertiveness |
| 7 | **UNB** | Rugged, self-oriented individualism, resistance to authority |
| 8 | **UB** | Having a good time, releasing tension, relaxing control |
| 9 | **UPB** | Protecting less able members, providing help when needed |
| 10 | **P** | Equality, democratic participation in decision making |
| 11 | **PF** | Responsible idealism, collaborative work |
| 12 | **F** | Conservative, established, "correct" ways of doing things |
| 13 | **NF** | Restraining individual desires, for organizational goals |
| 14 | **N** | Self-protection, self-interest first, self-sufficiency |
| 15 | **NB** | Rejection of established procedures, rejection of conformity |
| 16 | **B** | Change to new procedures, different values, creativity |
| 17 | **PB** | Friendship, mutual pleasure, recreation |
| 18 | **DP** | Trust in the goodness of others |
| 19 | **DPF** | Dedication, faithfulness, loyalty to the organization |
| 20 | **DF** | Obedience to the chain of command, complying with authority |
| 21 | **DNF** | Self-sacrifice if necessary to reach organizational goals |
| 22 | **DN** | Passive rejection of popularity, going it alone |
| 23 | **DNB** | Admission of failure, withdrawal of effort |
| 24 | **DB** | Passive non-cooperation with authority |
| 25 | **DPB** | Quiet contentment, taking it easy |
| 26 | **D** | Giving up personal needs and desires, passivity |

*Source*: © 1997 SYMLOG Consulting Group, San Diego, CA. Reprinted by permission.

F (for Forward). From this perspective, the physical directions are used to stand metaphorically for the psychological directions of the value and behavior space.

The rater completes a response to each of the twenty-six items for each image rated. As the rater considers each item, the item functions as a kind of *directional probe* into the rater's complex global perception of the person or concept being described, called the *Image*. Since all major directions in the value and behavior space are thus probed and measured, a very fine-grained description of the rater's perceptions of the Image is obtained. The twenty-six "directions" are also called *vectors* and can be symbolized by twenty-six arrows pushing out from the center of the large cube. The correspondence between each of the value items, listed in their standard order, and its value "direction" out from the center of the large cube is shown in figure 1.4.

## Dominance versus Submissiveness

The rating received by an individual in this dimension represents the prominence, status, power, and personal influence that the individual is seen by the rater to have in relation to other group members.

In figure 1.1 the circles representing TED, BEV, and ANN are larger than those of the other group members. Of these, TED's circle is the largest, which indicates that he is perceived by the group as the most dominant member. ROB and DAV have the smallest circles, meaning that they are seen as the most submissive members of the group.

Dominant members may be high participators, probably extroverts; they may also show a tendency to impose their views on the group. The more submissive members are typically seen as quiet, passive, or introverted. However, the full meaning of an image size or location cannot be understood from its location in any single dimension. The other two dimensions must be considered at the same time.

## Friendliness versus Unfriendliness

Values on Unfriendly Behavior are shown on the left side of the diagram, and Values on Friendly Behavior, on the right side. An image on the left side of the diagram is often associated with behaviors and values perceived to be self-interested and self-protective, while images on the right side tend to be associated with behaviors and values perceived as equalitarian, cooperative, or protective of others.

In figure 1.1 the image labeled with the name of LIN is farthest toward the right or friendly side. Thus, LIN is seen as the friendliest person in the group. JON and JAK have images on the unfriendly side of the diagram. They are probably perceived as self-centered and individualistic.

(These descriptions, of course, are wholly inadequate except as code words. Detailed descriptions of the behavior and values that raters typically associate with given locations on the Field Diagram are included in the feedback reports, along with some suggestions as to possible reasons for the behavior, and its effects on teamwork.)

## Acceptance versus Non-Acceptance of Authority

In the most general SYMLOG framework the term *authority* is understood in a very broad sense. It refers to a group environment of more or less organized social restraints and constraints, widely recognized to have some kind of legitimacy.

As diverse examples, one may cite: customs, group norms, and work demands; rules of rationality; methods of reality testing; evaluations of efficiency; norms of ethics and morality; written rules, laws, and regulations; as well as, the orders of persons appointed or elected to positions of authority. There are many other examples.

Some restraints that have a quality of authority are widely accepted, some are not. Some of the restraints are rejected, or are not even known about by some individuals. Those restraints that are accepted by an individual are felt as a part of the conscience.

In order to make the items most appropriate in a given context, the wording of some of the items used in rating, and the wording of the dimensional title itself, are adapted (by research) to the specific type of group and setting. (See Bales, Koenigs, and Roman 1987.)

In figure 1.1, the wording for the dimension marked F-to-B is adapted for work groups or teams in organizations of various kinds: *Values on Accepting the Task-Orientation of Established Authority* versus *Values on Opposing the Task-Orientation of Established Authority*. The *task-orientation of established authority* means essentially the rules and procedures that have been set up by authorities, immediately external to the working group, who will evaluate the performance of the group.

Figure 1.2 shows the SYMLOG Consulting Group rating form used in organizational settings. The items on this form describe Individual and Organizational Values. The items describe values shown in behavior rather than simply behavior. (Another form is available which describes behavior.)

In spite of the adaptation of items, ambiguities remain. There are always several layers or sources of authority for teams in organizations (indeed for groups of any kind). These various sources and kinds of authority may conflict with each other in specific cases. The F-to-B dimension describing attitudes toward authority, although critically important, is unavoidably complex and ambiguous in its meaning. It is necessary in some cases to specify in the rating instructions the source of authority intended. If necessary, separate ratings are made for separate sources of authority.

However, there is a simplifying factor. Many persons develop a generalized trait or tendency to accept or reject authority in a global way. This quality of behavior is usually visible to others, and is often the basis of the rating.

Figure 1.1 shows TED and TOM close to the F extreme of the F-to-B dimension, indicating that they are perceived by others to have a high commitment to established authority, and to the task as defined by authority. TED's values are perceived by others to be neither friendly nor unfriendly—his image circle is on the line dividing the friendly side of the diagram from the unfriendly side. TOM's values are seen to be similar to TED's with regard to acceptance of authority, but to be somewhat friendlier.

In contrast, ANN and JAK are seen on the B side of the dimension, ANN on the friendly side and JAK on the unfriendly. The locations of these images on the B side of the dimension mean that these members are either seen as unconcerned with the task at hand, or as opposing the work, to some degree, as it is currently defined by authority.

Because ANN's values are seen as more friendly, and less opposed to authority than JAK's, it is likely that she is more concerned with managing interpersonal needs within the group and may be trying to soften the requirements of authority in order to avoid conflict in the group. JAK's image is on the unfriendly side of the space, and toward the extreme in the B direction, indicating that the members feel he is obstructing the progress of the group by focusing attention on himself and disrupting the group's work.

### How Image Locations Are Derived

The location of a member image on the Field Diagram is derived from the average rating the member receives from all of the raters, on each of the three dimensions. There are twenty-six items on the rating form; each item is designed to measure a specific direction out from the center of the three-dimensional space that can be constructed to portray the three independent dimensions. The three-dimensional SYMLOG space is graphically visualized with the aid of the cube model.

Figure 1.3 shows this model as a perspective drawing of a large cube divided into smaller cubes. The cube model is a metaphorical spatial representation of the three dimensions of the SYMLOG space, all seen at once. The six main directions out from the center are indicated by arrows, identified by the code letters U, D, P, N, F, and B. The arrow pointing upward is labeled U and the code letter stands for the direction of Dominance. The arrow pointing downward is labeled D. This code letter stands for the direction of Submissiveness.

The twenty-six items measure not only these six main directions, but also the intermediate directions between them. Each of the twenty-six directions is represented by a specific small cube. (The small cube in the very center of the large cube represents the origin, or beginning point, of all the directions, and is not itself treated as a direction.)

One can imagine directional arrows coming out from the center of the large cube through the center of each of the small cubes. Each of the small cubes is labeled with a combination of the code letters that identifies its relation to the six main directions. Thus, the intermediate direction between the main directions U, P, and F is labeled UPF. The intermediate direction between P and B is labeled PB, and so on, all around the cube.

Each direction stands for the evaluative location in the space of a specific kind of value, identified by the content of the corresponding item on the rating form. The items with the code names attached are shown in figure 1.4. The code preceding each item identifies the small cube in the cube diagram to which it corresponds. The location of the small cube, in turn, identifies the direction in the space that the item is designed (and known by research) to measure.

The method of deriving the summary location of an image in each of the three dimensions can now be specified very simply. Three choices for indicating frequency ratings are provided on the form. The following numerical weights are assigned to them: *Rarely* = 0, *Sometimes* = 1, and *Often* = 2.

To obtain the final location of an image in the Dominance-versus-Submissiveness dimension, all the frequency ratings of the items with a code name containing the letter U are added together; all of the ratings for items with a code name containing the letter D are added together; and the summary rating for the direction D is then subtracted from the summary rating for the direction U.

The location for each of the other two dimensions is obtained in an exactly parallel manner: the summary ratings for N are subtracted from the summary ratings for P to obtain the location on the P-N dimension, and the summary ratings for B are subtracted from those for F to obtain the location in the F-B dimension. The computer program which makes these computations is called the "vector engine," since when the final location of the image in the three-dimensional space is determined, this location also determines the direction and length of the vector from the center of the space to the final location of the image.

## Rating Questions

When members of a group make a given set of ratings, using the twenty-six descriptive items, they are responding to a carefully formulated *rating question*. A rating question is always included at the top of the rating form to specify what the rating is about, that is, what question should be in the mind of the rater, to which the rating itself on each item is an answer. The following question is standard:

> In general, what kinds of values does this person show in his or her behavior? (The Self is always included among the persons rated.)

This particular question is designed to indicate the *actual* behavior of the individual. Group members may also be asked to rate the kind of behavior they feel would be ideal for a particular member in order to be most effective:

> In general, what kinds of values would be ideal for this person to show in order to be *most effective*?

An *ideal* is treated as a concept. In addition to ratings about actual persons, raters are usually asked to make ratings of several important concepts. The locations of these images help in understanding the meaning of the Field Diagram, or its implications for change:

1. *Wish.* In general, what kinds of values do you *wish* to show in your own behavior, whether or not you are actually able to do so?
2. *Reject.* In general, what kinds of values do you tend to *reject*, either in yourself or in others?
3. *Expect.* In general, what kinds of values do you *expect* others will rate you as showing in your behavior?
4. *Most Effective Leader.* In general, what kinds of values does the *most effective leader* of a task-oriented team you have known show in his or her behavior? (Alternatively, the question may be asked about most effective member, team, a particular role, etc.)

The group whose Field Diagram is presented in figure 1.1 also rated the concepts *wish* and *reject* (indicated on the diagram by the circles labeled WSH and REJ).

## Group Dynamics

The design of the Field Diagram is a representation of a total theoretical space in which all possible types of behavior and values in groups can be represented. This spatial framework is called, metaphorically, the *group space*.

Within this theoretical space of all possible behaviors an actual group generates an actual moving *field of forces*. In the concrete sense, the forces exist in the psychological pressures exerted by the behavior of each member on each of the others. The overt behavior is perceived and interpreted by each individual in a somewhat different way. An underlying field of images, meanings, evaluations, and motivations is aroused in the mind of each. Thus, much of the relevant behavior in the field of forces does not show on the surface, but goes on psychologically in the minds of the members.

As group members react to each other with further behavior and communication, their motivational similarities and conflicts produce a systematic amplification, damping, and shaping of the total group-average field, both at the level of visible behavior and at the underlying level of psychological meanings. The *group average Field Diagram*, by its higher level integration of many levels of the behavior and values of all the group members over a significant span of time, makes it possible to see a visual representation of the unique overall tendencies of the total field of forces. Figure 1.1 is actually a group average Field Diagram. For example, TED's location is the average of the way he is rated by all the other members.

The clusters, separations, and general constellation of the images located in the group average Field Diagram often tend to produce a strong impression in the mind of the viewer that unseen forces have been operating systematically to produce the observed overall pattern. The clues given by these patterns make it possible to infer many additional tendencies not evident on the surface, or not previously recognized.

The SYMLOG theory of group dynamics highlights and clarifies these cues, and so provides further help in interpretation. The body of theory that attempts to describe and explain the most frequently found general patterns of images, is called the *theory of polarization and unification*. This body of theory is implemented concretely through an instrument called the *Overlay*.

The Overlay is equally useful in analyzing the constellations of images on a much broader level than the relationships of individuals in a work group. The Field Diagram may be one showing groups within an organization, or the images of concepts having to do with the overall culture of an organization, or even over a still larger population of persons, provided they are in communication and interaction.

The same theory, essentially, applies over many kinds of systems of human interaction, but the dynamic forces and processes act with more time delays and barriers to communication as the population grows larger.

*The Overlay*

The Overlay, applied to a constellation of member and concept images within the bipolar dimensions of the group space, brings to life the theory of polarization and unification. The Overlay is shown in figure 1.1, superimposed over the constellation of images. It consists of a design showing two large circles tangent to each other; a long line passing through their centers and tipped with arrowheads pointing in opposite directions at the ends; a long dashed line; dotted circles within the large circles; and arrows in dotted lines leading out of the large circles. The long solid line tipped with arrows is called the *Line of Polarization*.

The Overlay is movable as a whole design—in practice, it may be actually drawn on a sheet of transparent plastic and placed physically over the constellation of images on the Field Diagram. It may be tentatively moved around in search of the location that seems best to match and contain the major clusters of images within one or both of the two large circles. It can be used in this way in a search for the systematic underlying pattern of forces that could have acted on the image locations to produce the clustering, separation of clusters, and other features of the image constellation.

Cutting through the middle of the Line of Polarization, between the two large circles, there is a long dashed line that is drawn at right angles to the Line of Polarization. This is called the *Line of Balance*.

The design or pattern of the Overlay represents the SYMLOG general theory of group dynamics. The theory has been arrived at inductively from extensive studies of many live groups in action, but it is also supported by a multitude of less general theories and particular facts. The way it is fitted over the clusters and constellation of images on the Field Diagram of the particular group represents the application of the general theory to the particular group. Every group has many unique features, but the deviations from the most general pattern also give valuable information and clues as to unrecognized factors.

Whether the particular fit chosen is the best or most useful one is always open to question. Its implications are never regarded as the final truth, but rather as a source of hypotheses, a set of clues to be explored further in discussion. Group members often help to choose the fit that best agrees with their more intimate knowledge of the group, or that seems to give them new insight. The picture of the group that comes into focus when the Overlay is well placed on the diagram is usually so recognizable and provocative of discussion that very little additional information needs to be added.

Given a hypothetical fit, the ways in which member images relate to each part of the Overlay are then explored to test whether the implications fit further facts, including, perhaps, facts that have been overlooked or suppressed, or facts of unrecognized strategic value. The following paragraphs describe the main features of the Overlay and some of the possible implications.

*The Line of Polarization*

The theory assumes that human beings generally have a tendency, in their own individual minds, to separate the self-image as far as possible from the images of things they consider *bad* and to identify the self-image with the images of things they consider *good*. The tendency to separate the bad as far as possible from the good is called *polarization*. The opposition in direction of the arrows at the ends of the Line of Polarization on the Overlay represents this tendency. The good direction from the point of view of the individual is called the *Reference Direction*, the bad one is called the *Opposite Direction*.

The result of this tendency acting on many images is to produce an underlying polarized field of perception in the mind of the individual that tends to bias the perception of images—the good images are seen as even better, and the bad ones are seen as even worse.

At the same time, according to the theory, there is a tendency to bias one's perception in such a way as to draw the good images as closely together as possible into a more compact cluster around the self-image. And similarly, there is a tendency to draw the bad images as closely together as possible into a bad cluster, so that they may be dealt with psychologically as one simple cluster. This tendency, whether at the good pole, or at the bad pole, is called the tendency toward *unification*. (The term unification does not necessarily refer to the unification of the group as a whole.)

Each of the two large circles on the Overlay represents a tendency toward unification of the images in its cluster. If there is a central image that exerts an attraction on the other images in the cluster, or best exemplifies the attractive values, it is supposed that the resulting underlying field of forces will tend toward a circular form around the center of attraction.

If these assumptions are sound, then the attracting tendency will be expected to become weaker as distance from the center increases. There is evidence to support this. This weakening of the attraction is represented in the design of the Overlay by dividing the area of each of the large circles into two parts. A smaller dotted circle is inscribed within the larger circle. This smaller circle is called the *Inner Circle*. It represents the area of strongest attraction. The surrounding area is called the *Marginal Area*. It represents the area of weaker attraction.

*Fitting the Overlay to the Field*

There is evidence that, on the average, the *wish* image of an individual is quite close to an idealized self-image. The two images are usually quite close to each other in the field, with the self-image not quite so far out toward the extreme edge of the diagram as the *wish* image. It is known that both the self-image and the *wish* image tend to exert an attractive influence on the location of other images sufficiently close to them; that is, these images seem to set up an underlying unifying field, or perceptual bias, in the mind of the individual. The given individual tends to see images close to the *wish* image (or the self-image) drawn together in a more compact cluster than other individuals, on the average, see the same images. For these reasons it is usually a promising start toward a suggestive fit of the Overlay, to locate it so that the good end of the Line of Polarization passes through the center of the *wish* image.

It is also known that on a Field Diagram showing the perceptions of an individual, the *reject* image is usually quite close to the Line of Polarization in the Opposite Circle. Its location is essentially the mirror location of the *wish* image—the logical opposite of the *wish*. (The group-average location of the *reject* image of the group shown in figure 1.1 is also very close to the mirror-image location of the group-average *wish*.)

In fact, this tendency toward precise opposition is so strong (even though individuals vary somewhat) that over a large population of individuals, if the Line of Polarization is fitted between the *wish* and *reject* images, it passes almost precisely through the midpoint of the diagram.

Thus, on the average, if the Overlay is fitted so that its midpoint exactly coincides with the midpoint of the Field Diagram, and the reference end of the Line of Polarization is rotated so that it passes through the center of the *wish* image, it may be predicted that the opposite direction will pass through the *reject* image.

This is a very useful prediction, since deviations of the *reject* image from the expected location may yield another less obvious prediction, namely this: if the *reject* image is observed to be on the unfriendly side, but very far distant from the Line of Polarization on that side, this deviation may indicate that the rater(s) may have had in mind a rejected or threatening image (an image not necessarily included among the identified images) that strongly attracts negative feeling and so draws the *reject* image out of its regular mirror location.

## The Reference Group, Core Group, and Marginal Members

One of the large circles on the Overlay is called the *Reference Circle*, and the other is called the *Opposite Circle*. When the Reference Circle is placed on the friendly side of the Field Diagram, with the reference end of the Line of Polarization passing through the average *wish* image, and the center of the Overlay is made to coincide with the center of the Field Diagram, the main cluster of member images is usually found within the Reference Circle. This is the case in figure 1.1 (although the scatter of images in this group is greater than usual).

If there is another cluster of member images, it is likely to be located within the Opposite Circle. Only the image of JAK and the *reject* image are found there in figure 1.1.

Members whose images fall within the boundary of the Reference Circle are predicted to be attracted and mutually reinforced enough by proximity to the group-average location so that they are relatively unified, but perhaps not strongly so. They are expected to be similar enough, in spite of differences, to be held together in a cooperative cluster by skilled leadership. This group is called the *Reference Group*. In the group portrayed in figure 1.1 the reference group would include PAT, ROB, JOE, TOM, LIN, and ROG.

Unless there are great differences among the members of the reference group as to where they individually place their *wish* images, it is supposed that the average location of the *wish* image tends to exert an influence as a major reference point, a point of comparison, for most of the members. Because it is located by an averaging process, the average *wish* image location tends to identify a middle-of-the-road, or compromise, value position that in a democratic vote might well be the actual point of highest preference—the winning position. Members close to it are expected to have a position of strategic influence in initiating and maintaining group norms.

If there is a cluster of images sufficiently compact and so located as to fall within the inner circle, the dotted circle shown on the Overlay in the center of the Reference Circle, this is treated as a prediction that these members are psychologically unified strongly enough to form a cooperative subgroup (the *Core Group* or *Inner Core*) with little feeling of internal conflict. In the illustrative group, the core group would include only PAT, JOE, and ROB.

If some members of the reference group are located in the marginal area, the area outside the inner circle, but still inside the Reference Circle, it is predicted that their psychological relationship to the members of the core group is also marginal—they are attracted, though somewhat weakly, to the members of the inner core, and in return, they may be accepted, although regarded with some feeling of conflict by the core members. They may be called *Marginal Members*. In the illustrative group, TOM, LIN, and ROG are marginal members of the reference group.

If the marginal members are on opposite sides of the inner circle (as TOM, LIN, and ROG are) they are likely to feel considerable conflict. They are too far apart in their values to cooperate easily, and are held together, if at all, by their relationships to the members of the inner core. One or more of the core group, a member such as PAT, may be able to provide the effective mediating leadership to hold them together. On the other hand, there is no guarantee of this. PAT's position in the middle simply highlights a potential for the strategic exercise of leadership.

Members in the marginal area are in danger of polarizing against each other and dividing the reference group into two factions. The small dotted arrows on the Overlay, originating in the marginal area and passing over into the *Outside Area*, symbolize this tendency and locate two of the most usually opposed directions. These arrows locate what is called the *Lateral Line of Polarization*, at right angles to the primary Line of Polarization (the long Line of Polarization previously described). The dotted arrows are called *Lateral Polarization Arrows*. (These are found on the Opposite Circle also.)

TOM appears to be in imminent danger of leaving the reference group, or of being rejected and pushed out of it. TED is definitely outside the reference group and is probably polarized against BEV and DAV, who appear outside the border of the Reference Circle in the PB direction.

## Opposition Subgroup

In the most effective teams there are usually no member images in the Opposite Circle at all, but in some groups isolated member images may be found there. In the cases of the most severe group conflict, there may be a cluster of images within the Opposite Circle. A single member is called an *Opposition Member*; a cluster may be called an *Opposition Subgroup*. If the subgroup has a leader, that person is called the *Opposition Leader*. If there are any group members in the Opposite Circle, members in the reference group tend to reject those members, and vice versa. This process of mutual rejection is called *Group Polarization*.

Members in the opposition subgroup are usually not simply innocent victims but have shown behavior and values that have played a major part in a process of group polarization. Although the opposition members may be called a subgroup, they typically do not cooperate easily with each other and may even be polarized among themselves. Unification of images in the Opposite Circle is a tendency more usually found in the Field Diagrams of individuals than in group-average diagrams.

Members in the reference subgroup may try in many ways to change members in the opposition subgroup, but their attempts are often futile. If the struggle goes on long enough, the members of the reference subgroup tend to give up and discontinue any further attempts to include the opposition members.

*Line of Balance*

The Line of Balance is the long dashed line between the Reference and Opposite Circles. It marks the dividing line, the no-man's land, between the two sides in a polarized struggle. It indicates to which of the main subgroups an image is closest. However, the values and behavior of members who are isolated from the reference or opposition groups may be so different from the members of either of these groups that the isolates may not try to join either group, or may not be accepted if they do try. The isolates near the Line of Balance tend to be kept at a distance. JON, in figure 1.1, is in this location.

In a dynamic sense, the two ends of the Line of Balance define a potential alternative Line of Polarization. This alternative polarization, if strongly activated, can neutralize and take the place of the usual polarization. Because of this dynamic potential, there are two potential roles in the group—*Scapegoat* and *Mediator*—toward which isolates may be drawn, or into which they may be forced. (Clusters of members in outside positions may be called *third-party subgroups*, and they also may be potential scapegoats or mediators.)

The alternative polarization is most likely to be activated if the isolates near the Line of Balance are relatively dominant and also far out toward one end of the line or the other. The potential presumably increases as their location is closer to the Line of Balance, and as conflict between the reference group and the opposition group grows more severe. They may be drawn into one of these roles by their own motivation, or they may be unwittingly and unwillingly forced into the role by the emotionally loaded feelings and actions of other members.

1. *Scapegoats.* If there is a polarized struggle in progress and feelings are high, an isolated member, or third-party subgroup, may attract negative feeling from both main conflicting subgroups, and so become a scapegoat, blamed and attacked by both sides. The risk is more pronounced for isolates rated by others on the unfriendly side of the Field Diagram. In the group shown in figure 1.1, JON would be in this position if there were a

significant opposition subgroup, although JON is neither very dominant, nor very far out.

2.  *Mediators.* A member whose image is located midway between the two opposed subgroups, on the friendly side of the field, on or near the Line of Balance and far out toward the end of the Line of Balance, has a potential opportunity to become a mediator. In the illustrative group, ANN is a possible candidate, although she is not very far out. Such a member may be able to identify with both sides, feel similar to both, and so attract positive feelings from both.

If a member in this position sees the opportunity to take the initiative, and is sufficiently dominant, and skillful, he or she may provide critical help by mediating between the two sides. This is more likely to occur if the candidate is located on the friendly side of the field, but sometimes a person seen on the unfriendly side may function as a mediator. It even happens, sometimes, that the same person or third-party subgroup acts as both scapegoat and mediator.

## The Swing Area

The dotted circle in the center of the Overlay is the *Swing Area.* It encloses an area between the Reference Circle and the Opposite Circle, lying partly within the marginal area of each. Members whose images are located in this area can be likened to the swing vote in a political election: they may swing to one side to support one subgroup on a given issue and then support the other subgroup on a different issue. On any given issue it is very uncertain which way they may go, if either way. ROG (figure 1.1) is in the Swing Area, and is a marginal member of the reference group.

Submissive members whose images fall in this area often feel stuck. In other words, they may be in so much conflict as to whether to move in one direction or the other that they cannot move at all. They tend not to attract much attention and may, in fact, want merely to sink out of sight because they are unable to resolve their conflict. Other members in this area may be very visible, even dominant, but give ambiguous cues as to whether they are friendly or unfriendly and whether or not they are oriented to the group tasks. Still other members found in the Swing Area may simply be indifferent.

## The Leader-Mediator

The role of a leader-mediator (not necessarily the formal leader) within the group is of special interest because this role is found in so many good teams and is often crucial. Effective teams that endure over time do not often manifest the extremes of polarization, subgrouping, isolated members, potential scapegoats, and so on, which have been described above. However, even very effective teams often have a mild tendency toward polarization.

In most effective work groups, most of the members' images are found in or near the upper right-hand quadrant—the friendly, task-oriented area in which members accept the established authority and direction of the group. Usually, most of the reference group is found within this quadrant. The group-average *wish* image is often found near the center of the quadrant.

However, there is a very common tendency for one or a few of the members to diverge from the reference-group cluster and move in a more task-oriented but unfriendly direction so that they approach, or pass over, the boundary of the Reference Circle. In the Field Diagram shown in figure 1.1, TED has already passed over the border in this direction (if he was ever inside), and TOM appears to be approaching the border.

At the same time, one or a few of the members may diverge from the center of the cluster and move in the friendly and less task-oriented direction. In figure 1.1, LIN has moved into the marginal area on the extremely friendly side; BEV and DAV seem to have passed over the border of the Reference Circle in the PB direction.

This kind of divergence from the group-average *wish* location (a lateral polarization) is often related to the demands of formal roles within the group (technical demands for structure and control, in the F and NF directions, versus human relations demands, in the P and PB directions). This distinction is recognized in most of the well-known theories of leadership.

Lateral polarizations formed along this axis are usually not as severe as those formed along the primary Line of Polarization, but they have a dangerous potential of suddenly becoming more extreme. This is probably the most characteristic kind of polarization in task-oriented groups. If such a polarization is not mediated or resolved effectively, it can become a threat to both group productivity and group satisfaction.

When such a polarization begins to form, a skillful leader-mediator can play a crucial role in keeping the two people or factions from diverging too far from each other. In the illustrative group, PAT appears to be in a position to help the group in this way because PAT's image is about midway between those of TED and BEV, indicating values somewhere in between the two and probably including some elements of both locations. Bargraphs of PAT's values, compared to those of TED and BEV, would help in locating the more specific values on which there is convergence.

However, in order to be successful, a mediator needs to be sufficiently dominant and skillful; able to understand and communicate the needs and priorities of the differing members to each other, and to find compromises; or better yet, to activate values and wishes pointing to higher-order goals that satisfy the needs of both factions.

### The SYMLOG Bargraph

In order for an individual (or a group) to understand the reasons why a particular image appears in a given location on the Field Diagram, or to think

## FIGURE 1.5
### Bargraph: Average of Ratings on All Group Members

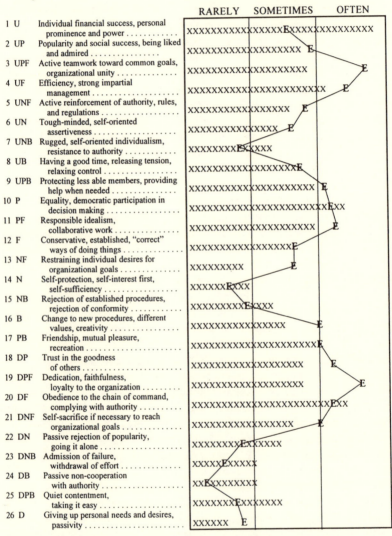

Type: P      Final Location: 2U  4P  2F        the bar of X's = the average rating on each item
Ratings: 132                                   E = the *optimum* location for most effective teamwork

| | | RARELY | SOMETIMES | OFTEN |
|---|---|---|---|---|
| 1 U | Individual financial success, personal prominence and power . . . . . . . . . . . | XXXXXXXXXXXXXXXXXEXXXXXXXXXXXXX | | |
| 2 UP | Popularity and social success, being liked and admired . . . . . . . . . . . . . . | XXXXXXXXXXXXXXXXXXXX E | | |
| 3 UPF | Active teamwork toward common goals, organizational unity . . . . . . . . . . . | XXXXXXXXXXXXXXXXXXX E | | |
| 4 UF | Efficiency, strong impartial management . . . . . . . . . . . . . . . . . . | XXXXXXXXXXXXXXXXXXXXXXXXX E | | |
| 5 UNF | Active reinforcement of authority, rules, and regulations . . . . . . . . . . . . . . | XXXXXXXXXXXXXXXXXXX E | | |
| 6 UN | Tough-minded, self-oriented assertiveness . . . . . . . . . . . . . . . . . | XXXXXXXXXXXXXXXXX E | | |
| 7 UNB | Rugged, self-oriented individualism, resistance to authority . . . . . . . . . . | XXXXXXXXEXXXXX | | |
| 8 UB | Having a good time, releasing tension, relaxing control . . . . . . . . . . . . . . | XXXXXXXXXXXXXXXXXXXXXXE | | |
| 9 UPB | Protecting less able members, providing help when needed . . . . . . . . . . . . . | XXXXXXXXXXXXXXXXXXXX E | | |
| 10 P | Equality, democratic participation in decision making . . . . . . . . . . . . . . | XXXXXXXXXXXXXXXXXXXXXXXXXXXXEXX | | |
| 11 PF | Responsible idealism, collaborative work . . . . . . . . . . . . . . | XXXXXXXXXXXXXXXXXXXXX E | | |
| 12 F | Conservative, established, "correct" ways of doing things . . . . . . . . . . . . . | XXXXXXXXXXXXXXXXXXXXE | | |
| 13 NF | Restraining individual desires for organizational goals . . . . . . . . . . . . | XXXXXXXXX E | | |
| 14 N | Self-protection, self-interest first, self-sufficiency . . . . . . . . . . . . . . . . | XXXXXXEXXX | | |
| 15 NB | Rejection of established procedures, rejection of conformity . . . . . . . . . . | XXXXXXXXXEXXXX | | |
| 16 B | Change to new procedures, different values, creativity . . . . . . . . . . . . . . | XXXXXXXXXXXXXXXXX E | | |
| 17 PB | Friendship, mutual pleasure, recreation . . . . . . . . . . . . . . . . . . | XXXXXXXXXXXXXXXXXXXXXXE | | |
| 18 DP | Trust in the goodness of others . . . . . . . . . . . . . . . . . . . . | XXXXXXXXXXXXXXXXXXX E | | |
| 19 DPF | Dedication, faithfulness, loyalty to the organization . . . . . . . . | XXXXXXXXXXXXXXXXXXX E | | |
| 20 DF | Obedience to the chain of command, complying with authority . . . . . . . . . | XXXXXXXXXXXXXXXXXXXXXXXXXXXEXX | | |
| 21 DNF | Self-sacrifice if necessary to reach organizational goals . . . . . . . . . . . . | XXXXXXXXXXXXXXXXXX E | | |
| 22 DN | Passive rejection of popularity, going it alone . . . . . . . . . . . . . . . . . | XXXXXXXXEXXXXXX | | |
| 23 DNB | Admission of failure, withdrawal of effort . . . . . . . . . . . . . . | XXXXXEXXXXX | | |
| 24 DB | Passive non-cooperation with authority . . . . . . . . . . . . . . . . | XXEXXXXXXXX | | |
| 25 DPB | Quiet contentment, taking it easy . . . . . . . . . . . . . . . . . | XXXXXXXEXXXXXXX | | |
| 26 D | Giving up personal needs and desires, passivity . . . . . . . . . . . . . . . . . . . | XXXXXX  E | | |

*Source*: © 1997 SYMLOG Consulting Group, San Diego, CA. Reprinted by permission.

sensibly about how to change, it is important to know more specifically on what values and what behaviors the raters were focusing. What is needed for this purpose is an item-by-item profile of the ratings actually received, which may be compared to some known reference profile with desired characteristics.

The SYMLOG Consulting Group (SCG) *Bargraph* (figure 1.5) provides this kind of comparison. The items shown on the Bargraph are the same as those used on the rating form, figure 1.2. The length of the line of Xs following each item indicates the average rating received by members of the group in response to that item. The frequency intervals used in the original rating—Rarely, Sometimes, and Often—are shown at the top of the columns to enable a qualitative interpretation of the meaning of the length of the row of Xs.

The Bargraph also shows an *Effectiveness Profile* drawn as a vertical zigzag line connecting the letter E on each line of Xs with each succeeding letter E down the list of items. The letter E locates the frequency that surveys have indicated is most effective for each item.

SCG has asked for ratings in surveys based on various questions, such as "the most effective leader you have actually known" (or most effective member, etc.) from leaders and members of a large number of groups in a wide variety of organizational settings. An effectiveness profile represents the average frequency rating given on each item in answer to an effectiveness question over a large population of representative raters.

The profile of the *most effective* locations in figure 1.5 is shown as the vertical zigzag line. It shows a series of three regularly projecting and receding wavelike forms of high and low frequencies as it passes down the set of items. The observed regularity of these forms is an indication of the validity of the items—that they are measuring the directions they were designed to measure.

These three regular waves are the theoretically expected result of the order in which the items have originally been arranged. The items follow one another in the order of a step-by-step sequence of directions that sweeps around the cube model of directions (see figure 1.3) in a counterclockwise direction three times: at first around the upper level of small cubes, then around the middle level, and finally around the lower level.

It can easily be seen by comparison whether the row of Xs summarizing the ratings made on the actual behavior of the members of the group for a given kind of value is longer or shorter than the location indicated on the effectiveness profile—that is, whether a given kind of behavior or values has been attributed to actual members more or less frequently than the "most effective" frequency.

Figure 1.5 displays the group-average ratings from the group shown in figure 1.1. The solid vertical profile is the SCG proposed "Optimum Value Profile." It can be seen that the group shown is quite far from the best it might be. Many values fall short of the profile research shows to be "optimum," and some are over the "optimum" frequency. Bargraphs are also made for the ratings received by each individual member.

The SCG "optimum" profile shown in figure 1.5 is a composite of average ratings for most effective images over various groups and situations. A particular group or some members of it will probably disagree with some aspects of any effectiveness profile that may have been chosen for comparison. The purposes of a particular group, or its particular situation, may indeed require a somewhat different profile. Nevertheless, by making a comparison between their own ratings and a well chosen normative profile, any group can be in a better position to discuss and decide the way they want their group to function.

### Conclusion: Changing a Group's Performance

Study of the individual and group-average Field Diagrams, the implications of the Overlay, the Bargraphs, and the analysis and interpretations offered by the written reports, can produce remarkable increases in both direct knowledge and new insights. Leaders and members alike begin to see strategic ways to help the group move towards improved relationships and better performance.

The most effective, productive, and satisfied groups show characteristic patterns in their Field Diagrams and Bargraphs. Movement toward these optimum patterns can be taken as the goal of efforts to change. The Field Diagrams are most useful in throwing light on the group dynamics; the Bargraphs are most useful in indicating more specifically how to change.

The roles of group members and the values of organizational significance can be changed. They are much easier to change than the deeper personality characteristics of group members. One of the great secrets of successful change is that it may be easier to change the whole interdependent constellation of roles and values than to change them one at a time. Roles and organizational values are interdependent—the successful movement of each one is dependent upon the supporting movement of others.

A general transformation can be encouraged in many cases by open group discussion to which all members contribute. The probability of effective change is increased by carrying the discussion to the point of explicit decisions and commitments to modify behaviors.

1.  SYMLOG can contribute greatly to the satisfaction and productivity of group members.
2.  It provides a data-gathering procedure which permits a thorough assessment of teamwork.
3.  It enables leaders and members to visualize and talk about the group in an effective way.
4.  It provides a theoretical framework by which they can better understand their group and particular member relationships.
5.  It gives many clues and suggestions as to what changes could improve teamwork.
6.  It gives a way to monitor and maintain progress by periodic repetitions of the procedure.

## Note

This is one of a series of articles on leadership and effective teamwork distributed by SYMLOG Consulting Group. All rights reserved. No portion of this article may be reproduced for any purpose without the express written permission of the distributors. Research in application in business groups, surveys for the development of norms, and the actual implementation of the computer programs are contributions of the SYMLOG Consulting Group. The development of the basic theory and background research are presented in Bales (1950, 1970, 1980, 1985), Bales and Cohen (1979), and Bales, Koenigs, and Roman (1987).

SYMLOG Consulting Group is prepared to cooperate fully with academic researchers in all kinds of basic research on theory and methods. SYMLOG Consulting Group provides a number of observational and rating methods which allow a group member to receive computer-generated reports based on the actual perceptions others have of each member of the group. Reports are obtained only through consultants trained and certified by the SYMLOG Consulting Group. Consultants offer a number of different kinds of programs to clients.

For information, visit the SYMLOG website (www.SYMLOG.com) or contact SYMLOG Consulting Group, 18580 Polvera Drive, San Diego, CA 92128, USA; phone 619-673-2098; fax 619-673-9279.

# 2

# Dynamic Fields in Social Interaction Systems

The previous chapter, taken together with Appendix A (which will be introduced in detail in chapter 5), presents a theoretical model of a three-dimensional, bipolar space of intercorrelations. Measured variables are located in the space according to how strongly they are correlated with each other, negatively as well as positively, in each of the three bipolar dimensions. The correlations are computed over the sample size of individual participants in each study, either as the makers of ratings, or as the receivers of ratings. Hence the correlations reflect covariation in the ups and downs of pairs of "traits," or elements associated with differences between one individual and another.

Each participant as seen on the average by others is distinguishable in his or her location. This location may change over time to some extent, but acts of one participant may nevertheless be more or less predictably linked in their effects and partial causes to the acts of other participants. The main directions and strengths of intercorrelations probably tend to be maintained within the specific network of communication that exists between real people in moderate spans of real time, interacting within a definable and bounded geographic space.

The intercorrelations between individuals tend to be generated and maintained because the acts and perceptions of the interacting individuals are "causally" connected with each other as events in a time-ordered series. A change in any one element tends to be followed by changes in others. The causal relationships vary from direct to indirect, from high to low, from simple to complex, from unidirectional to circular or recursive, and so on.

The present model of the relationships of variables of the social-interaction system (represented by the correlations of measured variables with the theoretical vectors in the intercorrelation space of Appendix A) is a theoretical construct. But, the model purports to reflect and represent a real-world set of probable causal relationships between the acts of participants in an intact group, or an organization, over some time span of its empirical existence.

In plain language, we say that individuals tend to develop *roles* in groups. A social-interaction system is a set of individuals whose actions and reactions come to constitute a particular patterned set of roles. But the concept "role" is a very blunt conceptual instrument. And so, of course, is the concept "system." I want to be able to describe the general features, and then the unique departures from the general, of particular individuals and the particular group by *explicit measurement*.

The SYMLOG measurement system, as explained in chapter 1, can be used to produce a Field Diagram, a flat projection of the three-dimensional intercorrelation space. The Field Diagram shows the large three-dimensional cube (figure 1.3) as seen from the top, with the eye placed at the terminating arrowhead of Vector 1 U, looking straight down along the U-D dimension to Vector 26 D. The whole intervening space of the cube diagram, from U to D, is compressed for the Field Diagram so that what we see is only a two-dimensional figure, with the two dimensional scales, P-N and F-B, intersecting in the middle.

The square Field Diagram is a way of showing, by the location of image circles on *one flat plane*: (1) the dynamic forces at work in the "interpersonal interacting process" in which the results of real-time sequences are indicated by distances between the images; (2) the three-dimensional bipolar factor-analytic space in which two of the dimensions, P-N and F-B, are denoted by the unitized scales intersecting in the middle of the field; (3) all directions of the porcupine spines of the twenty-six vectors, although the twenty-six are reduced to the eight that are visible on the P-N-by-F-B plane.

### Individual Members as Parts of the System

It is possible with the SYMLOG measurement system to locate the group-average perception of a group member, for instance, a member who has been assigned the code name TED. Figure 2.1 shows a Field Diagram representing an intact group I knew well. This group was one of my academic self-analytic groups, which met three times a week for a full term. An extended case study of the group, detailing the way in which each of the members saw the self and each of the other members may be found in *SYMLOG* (Bales and Cohen 1979).

In figure 2.1, the members of the group are represented by their three- or four-letter code names. Each member has been rated by all the others, and their locations in the three-dimensional cube have been computed by the vector engine, explained later. Since their locations in the U-D dimension have been compressed for the Field Diagram, the information about the relative dominance of each member is shown by the size of the circle representing each one. There is a standard scale (not shown here) of circle sizes which runs from quite small circles to fairly large ones. Smaller images, such as the one for TINA at 3D, stand for locations in the Downward, or more submissive, direction of the scale, and large images, such as the one for MOOS at 8U, stand for locations in the Upward, or more dominant, direction of the scale.

**FIGURE 2.1**
**Group Average Field Diagram of a Self-analytic Group**

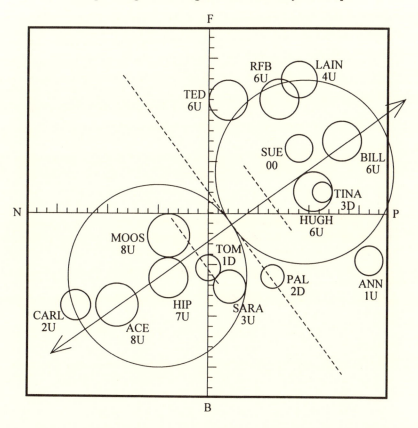

The Field Diagram facilitates a number of tentative predictions about TED, as a person, and his relationships to other members in the group. These predictions, or inferences, are possible because: (1) the Field Diagram is simply a visually flattened view of the complete three-dimensional cube; (2) the cube is simply a geometric representation of the location of the twenty-six vectors in the intercorrelation space; (3) the intercorrelation space of Appendix A contains a large amount of research-based information about how particular measurable variables have been correlated with each of the twenty-six vectors in past groups; and (4) TED's location in the Field Diagram allows us to estimate to what vector he is nearest.

On the Field Diagram of figure 2.1, it appears that TED is very close to the F vector on the flat plane. The size of his image, 6U, indicates some noticeable dominance. As a rough guess, the way he probably appears to other members of the group, on the average, may be described by some of the items on the list for Vector 4 UF in Appendix A. On the list of correlated variables for the Vector 4 UF in the intercorrelation space, the following descriptive items are given this vector: "an assertive business-like manager;" and "values efficiency, strong impartial management."

These descriptive items have been found to be correlated positively with certain other kinds of characteristics of the individuals rated as answering the description, such as: tends to be high on observed behavior on the IPA category *Gives Suggestion*; "Makes others feel that he rates them high on *Individualism*;" "Initiates value statements advocating *Group Loyalty and Cooperation*." An example of the kinds of value statements that persons of this kind tend to make is the following: "Good group members should accept criticisms of their points of view without argument, in order to preserve a harmonious group." From my experience with TED in the group, I feel the characteristics cited above pretty well capture his image as I saw it.

The item descriptions of each of the value vectors, as one reads the complete set of twenty-six in Appendix A, are helpful in visualizing the intercorrelation space of relationships between the variables, and the common-sense reasons for the intercorrelations. The reader can usually identify more or less easily with the reactions of other members of a group who might be confronted with the pronouncement of a generalized value statement, or kind of behavior, by a specific member of the group.

For example, imagine the reaction to the following value statement from the list for Vector 4 UF, TED's vector: "A group cannot get their job done without voluntary cooperation from everybody!" In most cases, surely, each of the other members who are addressed with such a value statement would tend to think immediately of the kind of effect the value would have upon him or her as a group member if the value statement, as worded, were actually realized or implemented. Other members might think: What does he mean *voluntary* cooperation? From *everybody*? Just *who* would implement it? And *how*? What *kind of person* would make such a self-contradictory statement? What does it actually mean *in practice*? Is it *acceptable*? Why or why not? How shall *I* reply? What do I think of *TED* for making it?

For a group participant to make any one of the twenty-six kinds of value statements represented in the intercorrelation space in real interaction would surely tend to bring to mind various images, good or bad to the hearer. The statement's threatening or promising effects on the hearer's self-image and on the hearer's social position in the group, whatever it may be, are immediately brought into question. The hearer's own values are typically brought into play and mobilized in relation to the image that comes to mind.

## The *Object* to Be Rated Is an *Image* in the Mind

The picture in the mind aroused by the identification of the object to be rated is called an *Image*. The term *Image* places emphasis on the fact that the image in the mind is not the real thing—it is a mental representation that stands for some real thing. The real thing is called an *object*.

The rating form names and identifies the object, or concept, that is to be rated. At the top of the rating form, a rating question is posed. Here are several rating questions as examples:

In general, what kinds of values do *you* actually show in your behavior?

In general, what kinds of values would be ideal for you to show in order to be *most effective*?

In general, what kinds of values do you *expect* others will rate you as showing in your behavior?

In general, what kinds of values do you tend to *reject*, either in yourself or in others?

In general, what kinds of values does this person show in his or her behavior?

A list of the nineteen rating questions for which data are analyzed in the present book is given in Appendix B.

It is assumed that the object (TED) has already been transformed in the rater's mind by experience into a mental perception, or a concept, which we call by the general term *Image*. The object has already been evaluated, probably many times, and somewhat differently from time to time, so that it has many related meanings in different contexts. The image of the object that is recalled and rated is thus complex. It is assumed that the object has many possible *meanings* according to context. This is why the prefix "In general" is always used. It is assumed, and even emphasized, that the rater cannot know directly what values are in the mind of another person, but must base his or her rating on inferences from the values that the person seems to "show in behavior."

It is also assumed that the group member, as a rater, is able to consider the image of the object in the light of his or her concept of each of the value vectors, that is, *all* of the twenty-six value vectors, one after the other. The theory also assumes that the concepts and evaluations that different raters have of the same value vector are different to some degree from rater to rater. The same words, appearing in a vector description, do not mean exactly the same thing to different raters.

From the researcher's point of view, the object rated is a "cognitive-evaluative image" in the mind of the individual group member. It is attached, it is assumed, by mental associative ties, along with many other images more or less like it, to a semi-consolidated summary "value" (an abstraction). More indirectly, this image is attached to a whole personal system of values. It is formulated in the categorizations and other features of the native language (for example, English, German, Japanese) in terms of which it is expressed, and in terms of which the rater thinks of its meaning. The method actually attempts to measure the reactions to only twenty-six carefully worded abstractions as test probes. But it is assumed that a value description as a test probe also is attached to, or mentally associated with, many other more or less similar images, as well as to other values and the language of the culture in the minds of individuals.

The present system of measurement confines its scope to values about what individuals think or believe social relationships should, or should not, be under different circumstances, and about how the "self" and "others" should, or should not, act in various circumstances. Nevertheless, the position assumed in the present theory is that there are inevitable conflicts in the mind of every individual as to what *should* be. Further, it is assumed that no individual can avoid having values and, from time to time, acting upon values that conflict with each other, although most people probably assume that their values *should* be consistent with each other.

### Value Conflict Is Endemic

Untold efforts (such as in prayer), in every culture and every day, are made by individuals in attempt to deal with the dilemma that violation of some of one's values, some of the time, and in some unavoidable circumstances, seems to be inevitable. In fact, on some occasions, a kind of disapproved behavior is thought to be justified, though perhaps unfortunate, and is approved by other values that one also holds. This dilemma, of course, is an ancient ethical, religious, and theological problem.

The present theory may be thought to be heretical from the point of view of many people who think hard and earnestly about these problems, and feel strongly about them. The present theory holds that certain very important conflicts in our values about social relationships are not accidental; they are "systemically generated." They are produced, to some degree, and are shown, with some frequency, by the normal and unavoidable operation of any social-interaction system.

Each value description on the value rating form is countered by another with which it conflicts. The twenty-six values on the rating form are meant to be a compact specification of the values that are always relevant and operating in the minds of participants to some extent in any social-interaction system. What is variable is not *whether* these values will be found represented in the system, but the frequency *with which* they are shown, and *to which* objects they are associated. That is, *what are their more concrete meanings?*

Certain conflicts of values are *built in* to the nature of social-interaction systems. They are built in partly by our biological inheritance, which prepares us with the tendencies and capabilities to act in conflicting ways at different times as a consequence of what has been necessary to the biological survival of our species in the course of evolution. At the same time, these conflicts are built in partly by the systemic nature of social interaction and social relationships.

Drives, which Freud treated as the contents of the blind (unconscious) biological Id, are regarded, in the present theory, as a rudimentary but nevertheless cognitively structured set of values. That is, drives are presumed to be prepared genetically to "recognize" or be "tripped off" by their biologically significant objects, and the human brain is prepared to deal with them consciously and rationally, given maturation. Drives with their cognitive steering mechanisms are rudimentary values. The rudimentary cognitive structures by which the objects of drives are recognized are, surely, to some extent "wired in," although maturation may also be necessary. The drives of the Id are not blind. The drives are inconsistent with each other, in part, because the inconsistencies have been, and still are, preconditions to survival in social relationships in the evolution of our species.

Some social relationships are hostile to the survival of some individuals. The differentiations between persons are emergents of biology and systems of social interaction. The differentiations are inevitably asymmetrical, to some extent, concerning who receives the primary advantages and who is disadvantaged. In the present theory, these asymmetries, and the accompanying conflicts of values between individuals and subgroups, are regarded as inevitable in their tendencies to emerge and create problems. But the asymmetries are assumed to be open to modification, minimization, and counterbalancing in many ways. For example, modification may occur through intellectual and rational processes, or through social arrangements and controls in the development of culture as it evolves. Yet counterbalancing is predicated on sufficient understanding of the sources of the problems and the ability of the adaptive and innovative processes to deal with the demands of the external environment.

It is impossible in the context of the present book to elaborate the possible heresies underlying the assumptions of the present system. But it seems only fair to point out that they may make it hard for the theory to gain acceptance in social psychology, as well as in the general society. Similar heretical problems may have made it especially difficult in the history of social psychology to deal earlier with the measurement of values and to recognize that values exist in every individual in dynamically oppositional systems.

Contributors to the development of social psychology may have found it easier to suppose that values are, or can be, implicitly consistent with each other. Linked with the supposition of consistency is the idea that values are externally justified moral teachings, the wisdom of which, if subscribed to sufficiently broadly, should control behavior. In the present view, values are a constitutive part of real behavior; they are not externally imposed, nor superimposed upon more "primitive" behavior; and the conflicts are built in.

A value is a high-order abstraction in the mind of the individual, to be sure, but it is *real* as an existent psychological structure. Important values are *real* psychological "traits" in the individual mind. These traits are *real* residual results of *real* past experiences. They influence behavior at less abstract levels whether the individual thinks about "values" or not.

Sometimes, but only in some cases, huge amounts of thought have gone into the development of the individual's value system. In contrast, for some values and for some individuals, the degree of abstraction is not very high. Not much thought has been addressed to the value as a value and its consistencies or conflicts with other values. But whether the particular value or the whole system of values has been highly intellectualized, it is assumed to be an important characteristic of the individual's mental, motivational, and cognitive-evaluative set, as it actually exists. It is not easy to change by moral admonition or in any other intended way.

A value, in most cases, is assumed to have a very general tendency to remain more or less constant. In this respect, it is a trait-like entity. Most of the values in the minds of individual participants in intact groups are assumed to be highly motivated. They represent the channeling of fundamental biologically based motivations as they have been modified and given direction in the individual personality by learning, practice, and experience, perhaps particularly by traumas and the social-interaction contexts of traumas, both as victims and witnesses. Alternatively, and also very likely, they have been deeply influenced and may have become "fixated" by impressively satisfying and gratifying experiences (Bales 1980).

The values of essentially all individuals have probably been modified by some degree of intellectual elaboration and probably, in most cases, by concern for the care and enhancement of the current self-picture, and for the longer term "survival" of the self in some essential sense. Across the whole spectrum of human experience, individuals differ to the extent of deadly extremes, homicidal or suicidal, as to which values and which modes of realization they have accepted and come to believe are most important for their essential survival. They differ in their perceptions and concepts of what is "out there" in the situation, in their memories as to what has happened in the past, and in their visualizations as to what is possible in the future.

## Vector Descriptions for the Rating Form

At the time TED was rated, a rating form with twenty-six items describing types of *behavior* was used. Each member of the group was asked to rate how frequently, in general, TED actually showed behavior that the rater felt was exemplary of each of the twenty-six item descriptions.

*Behavior Items*

In my original formulation of the twenty-six vectors I conceived them to be value vectors (Bales 1970). The value titles I gave them then are still appropriate, and are included as the major titles in Appendix A. But a form based on behavior descriptions promised to be helpful in feedback to group participants. With the aid of my colleague, Stephen Cohen, in the 1970s I developed a behavior rating form which measures the twenty-six vectors of the behavior rating space with suitable behavioral descriptions. Using factor analysis and other statistical tests in a very carefully designed study, Cohen checked the item locations in the space, their reliability, and validity (reported in Bales and Cohen, 1979).

The study was conducted using video clips of dyadic encounters of members of the "Loud family" (a well-known candid television series of the time). The video clips were collected and analyzed separately by Myron Wish (1976) and his colleagues at Bell Laboratories. Cohen and I selected items from Wish's analyses and further refined them, with the aid of Cohen's study. The resulting behavior items, which we recommended for further use, are included as part of the title of each of the twenty-six vectors in Appendix A.

*Value Items*

A demand for item phrasing that was less concrete arose from later work in the 1980s with business organizations. SYMLOG Consulting Group (SCG) needed a way for members to be able to describe their evaluative pictures not only of individual group members but also of whole organizations, or various subgroups, such as teams or departments. Additionally, we wanted to discover how group members felt about various concepts, such as "what kinds of values would be ideal for the most effective operation of the group."

In 1983, drawing on the experience in organization development of Robert Koenigs and Margaret Cowen, and with their advice, I developed another form for the measurement of *values* in the organizational context. It is called the form for *Individual and Organizational Values*, or IOVAL. Figure 1.2 shows the wording of the items, each a description of a *value*. The wordings of the items on this form are also shown in Appendix A for each of the twenty-six vectors in the intercorrelation space.

As a part of the procedure for selecting and formulating these items, I assumed that the kinds of values most relevant to the functioning of social-interaction systems across the broadest spectrum of variation would be values which codify and represent the many more concrete forms of behavior most relevant to the social and human relationships of group members and subgroups of them. Values of this kind are very general attitudes about what these social relationships *ought* to be, or *ought not* to be. But items on the rating form are carefully worded to avoid implications of *ought* or *ought not*. These implications are added intuitively by the individual rater and are deduced later by the researcher from the general patterns of the answers.

Although the wording of the IOVAL form was shaped with business groups in mind, I attempted to make it as widely applicable to all kinds of groups and organizations as possible, and as "unprejudiced" in its wording as I could. So far as I was able, I worded each description in a way that I expected would not only be highly correlated with the desired vector, but also would be neither too strong nor too weak in its wording. Additionally, I designed the item wording to be ambiguous enough so that persons who opposed the value, as well as those who favored it, could interpret it as expressing their own attitude against, or for, the values in the value area tapped.

The practical need to develop the IOVAL form, with item descriptions of values, proved to be fortuitous. The effort to develop the form forced me toward a more generalized conceptualization and recognition of the critical and strategic place of values and value statements in the dynamics of human social-interaction systems. The experience suggested that value systems as whole interactive systems could actually be compared across a wide variety of groups and settings, perhaps even across cultures.

## The Vector Engine for Locating Images in the Field

The method by which responses on a rating form are converted to vectors in the intercorrelation space was described in chapter 1. Here I use the metaphor of the *vector engine* to explain the procedure in more detail. The responses to a rating question are judgments of the frequency with which the Image is associated with each of the twenty-six items.

I have assumed that a response of "always" as a rating of frequency with which a value is shown in behavior is likely to be unrealistic, and that a response of "never" is also probably unrealistic. Hence, these alternatives are not offered as possible ratings. The ratings, and the numerical values assigned for the computation model are only three: *Often* = 2, *Sometimes* = 1, or *Rarely* =0.

This very short scale may be controversial among social psychologists, who nearly always use more intervals in their scales. But the three-interval scale is desirable for a number of reasons. It is the basis of the standardized metric scale that is necessary for all computations concerning the location of an Image in the space. Experience indicates that the three-interval scale is quite adequate to bring out the similarities and differences that are theoretically and practically important, but this is open to argument. Research is needed.

The cube diagram (figure 1.3) shows that there are nine small cubes on each of the six sides of the large cube. For example, on the top, or U side, there are nine small cubes, each of which has a code name containing the letter "U": U itself, UP, UPF, UF, UNF, UN, UNB, UB, and UPB. The single letter that is found in these various combinations (in this case, "U") is called a "single-letter vector-component direction." The vector engine recognizes the single-letter component directions, one letter at a time only—not the complete two- or three-letter code names.

Each of the nine cubes on a given side of the large cube, for example the P side, will have received a rating of 2, 1, or 0 from a single rater. It is possible, though not likely, that a single rater might have thought that the Image rated was so tremendously Friendly and Positive in all of the nine different ways described by the item descriptions associated with the P side, that the infatuated rater could have assigned a rating of 2 (Often) to each of the nine different value descriptions.

The secret of understanding the way the vector engine works is to know that it does not try immediately to compute the final vector corresponding to the final location of the image in the three dimensions acting simultaneously. Rather the engine is set to compute so that it only recognizes the single-letter vector components, one letter at a time (like a dog that has been trained to sniff luggage for only one specific drug at a time).

To find the location of the image on the P-N scale for example, the engine starts sniffing for "P" and sorts out all nine single-letter P components (regardless of any other single letters that may also be contained in the two- or three-letter code names). The single-minded engine totals the frequency scores the rater has assigned to each of the nine vectors, as if all nine of the P-side vectors measure P equally directly (although we know that only the central vector on the P side measures P directly). In a similar fashion, for the N side, the vector engine would also amass all nine single-letter N components.

Then, since the theory assumes that the sum of the values on the N side function psychologically to work against the sum of the values in the P side, the final step is to compute the difference between the P sum and the N sum. Whichever of the two sums is greater determines the direction of the P-N scale final location, either on the P side or on the N side, or precisely in the middle if the two sums are equal.

For the remaining two of the three bipolar scales, one for each dimension of the three-dimensional space, the engine computes the final location in a way exactly parallel to the way it found the location on the P-N scale. The location of the image on the P-N and F-B scales is used to plot the location of the image on the plane of the Field Diagram. The location of the image on the U-D dimension, it will be remembered, is represented by choosing a circle of the right size from the U-D scale of circles, and plotting that size of image circle on the Field Diagram. In short, the vector engine computes the final vector of the image and classifies it as most closely associated with one and only one of the twenty-six named vectors in the intercorrelation space (Appendix A).

In the measurement system, the intercorrelation space is actually a sphere with a radius of eighteen units. For example, for the P-N dimension, the whole bipolar scale is thirty-six scale units in length, with a precise midpoint at which the vector direction is null. In order to come out with a P-side total of eighteen, all P ratings would have to be 2 and all N ratings would have to be zero. This is not likely. If, for example, the N total were nine, the P total would have to be more than nine in order to have a final scale location of greater than zero on the P side.

Ambivalence on a given dimension is overcome for sure only if the location on one end of the bipolar vector is nine or more. Accordingly, I take it as a rule of thumb, that two images on a Field Diagram separated by less than nine units may be close enough to be drawn toward each other by some unifying tendency. If they are separated from each other on any one of the three dimensions by more than nine units, ambivalence is increasingly unlikely, and rejection may lead toward greater separation, that is, polarization of the two images in relation to each other.

The outer boundary of the intercorrelation space and the cut-off distance for attraction are portrayed in the Value Area Overlay for the Field Diagram, seen as figure 2.9 and described later. Using the Overlay, the researcher can easily formulate hypotheses about the tendencies of images to unify or polarize.

## The Bargraph Profile, Another Perspective on Patterns in the System

The final location of an Image produced by the vector engine provides a single resultant vector as the representation of the Image, a gestalt for the Image. Another way to consider an Image is to examine its twenty-six constituent vectors. The framework for such an examination is the SYMLOG Bargraph.

The Bargraph is a vertical profile showing the average frequency rating that has been received on each of the twenty-six value descriptive items for the Image rated. The frequency "bar" for each item is represented by a row of Xs. Each bar of Xs may be compared with a point on the zigzag line offered by SCG as *optimum* "for most effective." The bars are made up of Xs so that departures from the Optimum profile can be counted by the viewer.

Because the vectors that make up the Bargraph are related to each other, as illustrated in the cube diagram (figure 1.3), the twenty-six bars taken together may be considered as a *profile*, with identifiable patterning characteristics. A Bargraph comparing TED's profile of received ratings from other group members with the Optimum profile is shown in figure 2.2. (For this illustration I have actually substituted a made-up Bargraph which fits my memory of TED

## FIGURE 2.2
### Bargraph of the Average of Ratings by Group Members on TED

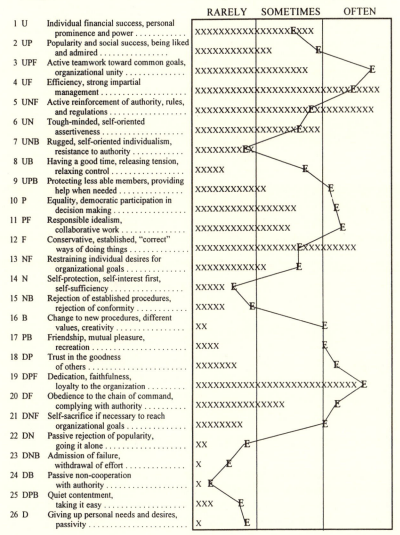

Type: UF    Final Location: 6.0U  1.9P  10.6F    the bar of X's = the average rating on each item
Ratings: 15                                      E = the *optimum* location for most effective teamwork

| | | RARELY | SOMETIMES | OFTEN |
|---|---|---|---|---|
| 1 U | Individual financial success, personal prominence and power . . . . . . . . . . . . | | | |
| 2 UP | Popularity and social success, being liked and admired . . . . . . . . . . . . . . . | | | |
| 3 UPF | Active teamwork toward common goals, organizational unity . . . . . . . . . . . . . | | | |
| 4 UF | Efficiency, strong impartial management . . . . . . . . . . . . . . . . . . | | | |
| 5 UNF | Active reinforcement of authority, rules, and regulations . . . . . . . . . . . . . . | | | |
| 6 UN | Tough-minded, self-oriented assertiveness . . . . . . . . . . . . . . . . . | | | |
| 7 UNB | Rugged, self-oriented individualism, resistance to authority . . . . . . . . . . . | | | |
| 8 UB | Having a good time, releasing tension, relaxing control . . . . . . . . . . . . . . . | | | |
| 9 UPB | Protecting less able members, providing help when needed . . . . . . . . . . . . . . | | | |
| 10 P | Equality, democratic participation in decision making . . . . . . . . . . . . . . . | | | |
| 11 PF | Responsible idealism, collaborative work . . . . . . . . . . . . . . | | | |
| 12 F | Conservative, established, "correct" ways of doing things . . . . . . . . . . . . . | | | |
| 13 NF | Restraining individual desires for organizational goals . . . . . . . . . . . . . | | | |
| 14 N | Self-protection, self-interest first, self-sufficiency . . . . . . . . . . . . . . . . | | | |
| 15 NB | Rejection of established procedures, rejection of conformity . . . . . . . . . . . | | | |
| 16 B | Change to new procedures, different values, creativity . . . . . . . . . . . . . . | | | |
| 17 PB | Friendship, mutual pleasure, recreation . . . . . . . . . . . . . . . . . . . | | | |
| 18 DP | Trust in the goodness of others . . . . . . . . . . . . . . . . . . . . . | | | |
| 19 DPF | Dedication, faithfulness, loyalty to the organization . . . . . . . . | | | |
| 20 DF | Obedience to the chain of command, complying with authority . . . . . . . . . | | | |
| 21 DNF | Self-sacrifice if necessary to reach organizational goals . . . . . . . . . . . . . | | | |
| 22 DN | Passive rejection of popularity, going it alone . . . . . . . . . . . . . . . . . . | | | |
| 23 DNB | Admission of failure, withdrawal of effort . . . . . . . . . . . . . . | | | |
| 24 DB | Passive non-cooperation with authority . . . . . . . . . . . . . . . . . | | | |
| 25 DPB | Quiet contentment, taking it easy . . . . . . . . . . . . . . . . . | | | |
| 26 D | Giving up personal needs and desires, passivity . . . . . . . . . . . . . . . . . . . . | | | |

*Source*: © 1997 SYMLOG Consulting Group, San Diego, CA. Reprinted by permission.

and which, by computation, produces a location of an image on the Field Diagram that is close to that of TED.)

The main feature of both TED's profile and the Optimum profile is the tendency for item endorsements to follow a pattern of three peaks, with the most highly endorsed items, usually UPF, PF, and DPF, marking the apex of each peak. More will be said later about the compelling quality of these three items. For now, it is important to note that the Bargraph, like the Field Diagram, provides a visual frame for understanding the myriad influences on an Image and its interrelationships.

### Empirical Evaluative Norms for Displays

More than a million sets of twenty-six ratings of various perceptions, concepts, and issues have been gathered by SCG consultants using the IOVAL form. Extensive research mining these data has made it possible, over many years of cumulative efforts, to compile a picture of the perceptions of persons and concepts of "ideal for most effective." An average pattern of such ratings can be estimated. I call such a picture an "empirical evaluative norm." The SCG Optimum value profile for the Bargraph is a prime example. Such a picture also exists for patterns on the Field Diagram. Standardized distributions, like these norms, make possible comparison of any present Bargraph or Field Diagram with norms that are both averages of large bodies of data, and theoretically rationalized expectations of *optimum* patterns.

I derived the Optimum profile for the Bargraph from the addition of a number of real average profiles based on adequately large sample sizes. Some profiles dealt with actual conditions and others with ideal. Samples were composed of leaders and individuals who were team members, but not in a formal leadership position.

In the course of developing the Optimum profile, I detected differences between what leaders consider to be ideal for members and what members consider to be ideal for themselves. The differences were not great but they were evident. This is a highly significant fact for the general theory of social-interaction systems. It tends to imply that there is no single basis from which the ideal values of individual members and the values of leaders representing the organization can be deduced. The title of the IOVAL rating form actually takes into account this discrepancy. The twenty-six items it describes include both *individual* and *organizational* values. I resolved the dilemma simply, and maybe crudely, in estimating the Optimum profile by averaging the different profiles, item by item, giving equal weight to each.

SCG research has discovered that there is widespread agreement, even crossculturally, on the precise relative frequencies with which the twenty-six values need to be shown in behavior in order to be "most effective" or "ideal" for teamwork and organizational purposes (see also chapter 9, "The Mystery of *Most Effective* Values"). The reasons for this finding need to be considered very carefully, since it seems to be theoretically important, as well as a hopeful finding. The locations of the numerous ratings on Images of effectiveness tend to cluster, in a bell-shaped curve, around a certain point on the UPF vector, *Active teamwork toward common goals, organizational unity*.

Perhaps the profile of values on which raters approach consensus is idealistic, in the sense of "unattainable." Perhaps these frequencies are what the organizational theorist Chris Argyris (1964) calls "espoused" values. Perhaps they are not realistically expected to be strictly adhered to, as contrasted with the frequencies that are actually found.

Where did the detailed frequencies of a profile that so many different group members can agree on come from? Could it be that the relative frequencies represent some kind of emergent system-generated "reality"? If so, what kind of reality? Could it be that over a long trial-and-error process of evolution there has been a drift in the culture toward answers to value questions which really are the "best" comparative emphasis among persistently conflicting values? Could it be that all the possible departures from this empirical profile point in so many different directions that none of the alternative positions is capable of commanding majority agreement? (I am talking about the "fittest" values, not individuals.)

There are many indications that the ideal frequencies of the twenty-six Individual and Organizational Values on the Bargraph Optimum profile are a realistic working residue of aggregate past experiences of the great majority of individuals, over many different circumstances. The theory holds that the frequencies shown on the Optimum profile are in fact attainable for the average of the group as a whole. As a goal for the longer run, the frequencies represent a standard that is conducive to greater effectiveness of the group and hope for survival of the system.

For the consultant's work with individual group members, I have composed a computer-assembled, customized *Report*, a detailed analysis of how the individual, as a group member, has been rated by the other participants, on the average, using each of the twenty-six value categories. This Report on a Bargraph, addressed to an individual, comments on the implications for group effectiveness of each of the twenty-six average ratings received. In many cases, the Report gives some advice with explanations as to how the individual might modify behavior or values in order to improve his or her acceptability and effectiveness in the eyes of the other raters.

Participants in feedback groups usually, and properly, want to know the source and justification for the SCG Optimum profile shown on the Bargraph. It can be given to them in a detailed memorandum, but they are often satisfied to postpone their full acceptance of the one offered as *optimum*, and proceed with the understanding that the profile is presented as a place to begin, to be used simply as a basis of comparison and discussion. The consultant attempts to make clear that he or she expects the participants will indeed be questioning what is optimum for them as they read the reports they receive.

Participants understand that they will be explaining their ratings to each other in small discussion groups, where each may ask other members, if they wish, why they have been given the ratings on the Bargraph that they have actually received. These discussions are held in small subgroups to minimize possible embarrassment about more public disclosure. The small groups try to determine whether departures from the SCG Optimum profile do indeed pinpoint real "problems." If not, they may discuss and take into account what changes in the profile they feel would be preferable for them. It is relevant to report that I do not know of any cases where serious changes in the Optimum profile have been suggested.

### Patterns on the Field Diagram Reveal New Information

The total set of interacting influences in the social-interaction system, and in each individual personality, is assumed to create, or activate, a dynamic field of values and value conflicts and congruences in the minds of participants. The patterns of the locations of the images on the Field Diagram represent our picture of the real system field for a particular group and Image. The theory deals with the different patterns of location of images in real observed system fields, what they mean, what they tend to predict, and how they will probably change under different conditions.

The same group under different conditions will change the pattern of the system field of the locations of its group members. By changing the focus of attention to a different Image, a leader, a researcher, a consultant, or any group member can influence the kind of group decision that is likely to form. In old-fashioned language, "rhetoric" is the term given to the intentional injection of imagery in order to influence the outcome of a discussion, or broader process of social evaluation on some issue. The injection of a "red herring" in a discussion, if it succeeds in diverting the discussion, is an example. Or a "brilliant idea" that catches on might be another example.

In the language now popular in the theory of complex systems, it can be said that we can "perturb the system" in different ways. One way is by the injection of a new image into the communication, an image that commands attention. As researchers or consultants we perturb the existing system in different ways by asking for ratings of different kinds of Images, as illustrated by the rating questions given earlier. Each rating question will produce a different pattern on the Field Diagram. Each Image potentially separates group members and unifies them in different ways, and produces different isolates.

In natural conditions, changes in the Images that are called to attention by necessities for group decision may come about through the appearance of new external threats, the appearance of more threatening internal divisions, by mobilization of attention to ideal conceptions of the future, by changes in the meaning of socially important persons or objects, by the deliberate injection of particular kinds of images into the discussion by individuals, and so on. Particularly striking examples are jokes that "hit the point," and suddenly collapse the tension among many, or most, of the group members.

The very operations of measuring the Images of socially important objects by the same system, and bringing them together in a single graphic plot showing their comparative locations in the same theoretical reference dimensional space, creates a pattern on the Field Diagram that is more than a "scatter" of unconnected images. Thanks to the integrative power of the human visual apparatus and the human brain, one feels that he "sees" an emergent *pattern of distribution* of the images, which could not have been known or hardly imagined without the measurements and the plotting.

The measuring and plotting operations have created new information for the viewer or interpreter: more exact information about where individual members stand and about relationships and potential relationships between members. The new information is almost certainly more inclusive of all members than has been available before, and hence more information about more relationships has also been made available. Much of the information revealed about relationships probably has not existed as information previously in the mind of the viewer. This may be true of most of the members, as well.

The publicly unrecognized struggles and emerging organization, or reorganization, of the underlying forces of evaluation, the attractions and repulsions among members, the unintentional giving and receiving of nonverbal cues, and the outcomes of private interactions of members in smaller outside groups have become recognizable in a visual pattern of images that tend to appear as clusters, with separations of clusters and individual member images in isolated locations. The distribution over the whole Field Diagram is typically not a random scatter, although it probably has some random elements.

If there are enough circle images on the Field Diagram, one sees some variety of a pattern of *unification* and *polarization*. Figure 2.1, seen earlier, illustrates such a pattern in a small intact group, one of my self-analytic groups. One feels impelled to conclude that the visible pattern must be the result, in part, of "dynamically organizing and reorganizing" effects of social interaction. The personality elements involved, may have "existed" in some potential sense before, but their coming into prominence and their dynamic effect at a particular time may be due to the public "unlocking" of previously unrecognized information about values of approval and disapproval.

It has been my experience that even in my own ratings of the participants of an intact group of which I have some knowledge, new information comes to attention, and new insights are likely as to what is probably going on that has been missed earlier. The practical usefulness of the method of rating and plotting on a Field Diagram is not confined to those situations where information is obtained from the participants themselves. The method can be used alone by the leader of a group to improve his or her own information, even though other members do not rate. Although different participants (including leaders or researchers) bias the available information in different ways, usually related to their positions in the group or their values, the probability is that each participant can make some contribution to the composite "truth," that is, the emergent overall pattern.

The average ratings received by individual members showing the way they are perceived by others, as in figure 2.1, are of great value. Experience indicates that the feedback reports to individuals, are often recognized by the members who receive the reports as unexpectedly perceptive. Sometimes they are felt to be valid even beyond what the persons rated had supposed others could know about them. There are also exceptions, cases where individuals recognize that they have been very wrong in their expectations as to how others actually view them. However, this is not common. The reconsideration of serious misperceptions on the part of individuals in such cases is a powerful incentive to change.

Usually when individuals are shown to be in socially undesirable locations, they have already known this, and have rationalized and justified it in various ways. In feedback sessions conducted with serious purpose, it is the analysis of these rationalizations by other participants that provide the best opportunities for change.

It seems to me that this account of what is going on in the formation and change of dynamic system fields becomes much more plausible and understandable when it is recognized that each personality includes a whole system of multiple values, and that these already existing values exert influence on each other in conflicting as well as cooperating ways in the individual's own mind. The same may be said for the norms and the average value system of the total group. Like the individual personality, the total group, or social-interaction system, is complex with regard to dynamic relationships among the values involved. In all cases, the processes of organization and reorganization depend upon communication and new information from members in the system. Unfortunately, communication is typically imperfect and general public knowledge of the state of affairs tends to lag behind the actual changes that are taking place in more remote or less interactive parts of the system.

## Composing Groups, Based on Patterns of Field Dynamics

The pattern tendencies toward polarization and unification have practical implications for the selection and composition of members for new teams. The majority of members in intact groups in our population are typically located toward the PF pole; and the minority of members, or more isolated individual members, are typically located toward the NB pole. The self-analytic group shown in figure 2.1 has more members around the NB pole than is usual, and more than desirable in a work team. Below are some reasonable inferences relevant to the composition of new groups. Let us treat the group of figure 2.1 as an "assessment group," assembled for the purpose of selecting members for a new group.

BILL, as an example of a candidate for a newly composed group, is in the PF quadrant of the assessment group. He is located far to the Positive side of the intercorrelation space. This suggests that BILL would likely be an accepted majority member of a newly composed group. Additional facts to be presented later about the Value Area Overlay suggest that BILL's values would likely lead other group members to rate him in such a way as to place him on the Liberal Teamwork Side of the Most Effective Teamwork Core but not quite in the Core proper (refer to figure 2.9). In a business team his placement might prevent him from being a task-oriented leader, although he might well be a social-emotional leader. BILL was the most admired student leader of the majority in the group, although he lacked somewhat in dominance as a possible candidate for leadership in a newly composed business team. His image circle is not large, compared to that of ACE, for example.

On the contrary, if, like ACE in the assessment group, a candidate's average assessment ratings received were in the NB quadrant of the Field Diagram, he or she would likely be in a minority if placed in a newly composed business team, and might be rejected, at least to some degree. ACE, in my group, although he was a first-year student in the business school, declared that he was actually going to the business school "to learn how to rip off the capitalistic system!"

CARL, ACE's coalition partner in the NB quadrant, appeared to be close in his values to a passive philosophical anarchist. CARL and ACE stuck together in a coalition most of the time for the sake of making trouble, but at the same time they harbored a barely suppressed distrust of each other. On one occasion CARL rose from his chair and made a joking attempt to choke ACE, who fell off his chair and hastily retreated because he thought CARL was serious in his attack. (CARL was considerably larger and stronger then ACE.)

ACE and CARL sometimes formed a coalition with HIP and MOOS, in order to make life as miserable as possible for TED, whom they regarded as an impossibly naive authoritarian. It was their self-appointed mission to increase his sophistication. This conflict represented a line of polarization running from their UNB location toward the UF or UNF location occupied by TED as they saw him. TED had no active supporters in the group. He made overtures to SUE and TINA with remarks in favor of feminism, but they spurned his efforts. He was too far toward the authority-oriented side to appeal to them.

The separations between clusters of images on a Field Diagram are assumed to be due to value conflicts between the members of the two or more clusters.

The conflict between clusters is assumed to be aggravated by the tendencies within each cluster for the members to form coalitions with each other in order to oppose members in other clusters or distant locations. The continuous process of interaction is assumed to tend to make individuals more fully informed and aware of the values represented by each individual in each cluster.

There may be attempts on the part of some individuals to reconcile the conflicts. PAL, in the group shown in figure 2.1, was a friendly young woman who apparently could not make up her mind which subgroup she wanted to be with. She tended to shuttle back and forth between the two subgroups when they retired to separate locations for what might be called "caucuses" during the breaks. (The group met as a whole for two hours running, with a short break after the first hour, during which members could assemble separately or wander at will among a number of other locations.)

Thus social interaction within the group as a whole tends to consolidate and aggravate in restless movement the pattern of distribution of images. This kind of process is sometimes called "self-organization" in the current theory of complex systems. In our case, the term for the whole process might better be called dynamic "organization" or "reorganization," since we need the term "self" to refer to the self-image of each individual.

There has been little exploration as yet of the use of assessed profiles of individuals to predict the tendencies and relationships of individuals in new deliberately composed groups. I would predict, as a beginning, for example, that two individuals assessed in separate assessment groups would tend to move closer to each other or further away in their Field Diagram locations in a newly composed group in proportion to the correlation, positive or negative, between their two assessed profiles.

The spatial model and the measurement of the location and dynamic relations of images in the space appear to offer the possibility of models that predict, at least to some extent, the fundamental dynamics of social interaction in whole *systems*, or fields of different patterns, rather than as atomistic collections of individuals without context.

The group-average diagram of the locations of persons, such as figure 2.1, constitutes a picture of a "field" of influences and attempts to influence, a set of relationships between individuals in social interaction. Many of these relationships are partially unresolved and unstable, or probably still moving in certain directions at the time members make ratings of each other. If the ratings are not of each other as persons, but of an Image such as "most effective" values, essentially the same thing may be said. The dynamic elements in relationships are not persons in the direct concrete sense, but values held by persons about the Image. The Field Diagram and the other displays to be described below enable the experienced analyst to make certain predictions about what is going on beneath surface awareness, or potentially may go on, prior to the surfacing of overt conflicts and coalitions.

## Patterns in the Fields of Large Samples

When the number of images on the Field Diagram is small enough, as in figure 2.1, one can read the diagram and make inferences about the specific individuals and their relations. This is essentially a clinical or case-oriented procedure. In contrast, when the number is large, but especially when the raters are not members of a single intact group, the images represent a "population" of raters, and the interpretive approach needs to differ.

The SCG data bank on intact groups is large enough so that individual responses can be drawn randomly to create samples of 1000, or larger. Such large samples are made up of individuals randomly selected from intact groups, such as "teams" in organizations, or sometimes as random or designed samples from a whole organization.

In the samples from intact groups, the ratings are influenced by the constellation of Images being rated and their associations in the minds of the raters. Typically, respondents have rated images of the *self, other team members*, and concepts, such as the values they *wish* to show, and the values they tend to *reject*, either in themselves or others. The unique local situation of the individual rater as a group member, the possible reactions of those other individuals to the ratings they receive, and the situations and tasks of the group have presumably also been in the mind of the rater.

The samples of 1000 individual raters that I am about to show are random selections of the ratings of individuals who are members of intact groups that are probably roughly comparable to each other, but the members selected are from many different intact groups and probably do not know each other. The individual raters in these kinds of samples are not directly comparable to a population of completely unconnected persons from all kinds of situations, such as a randomly chosen sample for a national poll. Nor are the results quite the same as they would be if the sample included the responses of *all* members of each of a large sample of intact groups.

A pattern of images on a Field Diagram showing a large number of images (such as 1000) typically consists of one or perhaps two areas of relatively more dense clustering. In intact interacting groups the factors which tend to produce more dense clustering of images are similarities of persons in the way they evaluate the specific Image brought to their attention by the rating question.

Clustering is evidence of tendencies toward *unification* (within clusters) and *polarization* (between clusters). In an intact group some initial degree of clustering (which existed before measurement) is assumed probably to have been modified by interaction so that, within particular clusters, the felt attractions of members have been increased to some extent by their attempts to persuade each other to modify their values, or modify the meanings of particular values toward even greater similarity. The tendencies to form coalitions in order to better resist opponents in other clusters are also assumed to have played a part, at least in some cases. No doubt there have been other tendencies toward shortening the distances within clusters and separating the clusters further from each other.

Although the Field Diagram distributions of 1000 randomly selected raters are not the reactions of persons who are members of the *same* intact interacting group, all of the raters in fact are members of intact interacting groups in business contexts, and so probably have been subjected to unifying and polarizing tendencies of a roughly similar kind in their different intact groups. Insofar as the intercorrelations of variables tend to be roughly similar from one intact group to another, it seems plausible that the samples of 1000 on different Images, such as *wish* and *reject*, give clues about the general clustering and polarizing tendencies that are found in similar form in small intact groups as well.

### The Polarity of *Wishes* and *Rejections*

The Field Diagram in figure 2.3 shows the distribution of locations of the images of *wish* (WSH) as rated by each of 1000 randomly selected members of intact groups in answer to the following question:

> In general, what kinds of values do you *wish* to show in your own behavior, whether or not you are actually able to do so?

A comparable Field Diagram in figure 2.4 shows the locations of the images of *reject* (REJ) as rated by each of 1000 raters of an independently selected random sample. Respondents rated the following question:

> In general, what kinds of values do you tend to *reject*, either in yourself or in others?

In comparing these two Field Diagrams one is immediately struck by the almost complete contrast in the locations of the two kinds of images. The *wish* images are located mostly in the PF (Positive, Forward) quadrant of the field, while the *reject* images are located mostly in the diagonally opposite quadrant, the NB (Negative, Backward) quadrant. The implication is that most of the raters have a strongly polarized internal value system.

It is true that due to our sampling method we are tapping this information from two different populations of 1000 each, but in fact each individual in both samples has been asked to rate both *wish* and *reject*. We know from examination of the ratings of single individuals that, with almost no exceptions, each single individual tends to show the polarization. The negative correlation of the *wish* and *reject* profiles for a single individual is so dependable, in fact, that it may be taken as one of the criteria for a valid set of ratings by an individual.

**FIGURE 2.3**
**Scatterplot Field Diagram of 1000 Ratings on**
*Values that You Wish to Show in Your Own Behavior* **(WSH)**

VALUES ON ACCEPTING TASK-ORIENTATION OF ESTABLISHED AUTHORITY

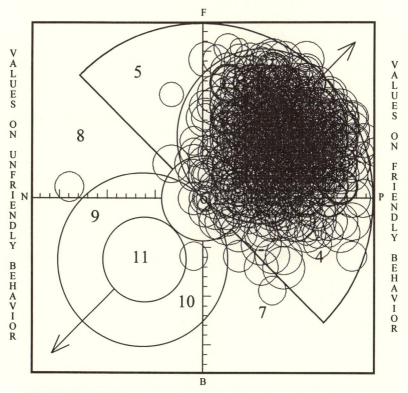

VALUES ON OPPOSING TASK-ORIENTATION OF ESTABLISHED AUTHORITY

*Source*: © 1997 SYMLOG Consulting Group, San Diego, CA. Reprinted by permission.

The near oppositional symmetry of the two patterns suggests that, on the average, most individuals tend to internally polarize their *wishes* and *rejects* more or less diagonally in a straight line across the two dimensions of the space, more or less intersecting the center of the total field. But it is also apparent that individuals differ from each other very considerably in the direction of their lines of polarization across the field. The total range in the angle of separation of the lines of polarization is probably more than ninety degrees.

This broad range might suggest that if a researcher were to select a random sample of ten or so individuals from a similar business population of 1000

**FIGURE 2.4**
**Scatterplot Field Diagram of 1000 Ratings on**
*Values that You Tend to Reject* **(REJ)**

VALUES ON ACCEPTING TASK-ORIENTATION OF ESTABLISHED AUTHORITY

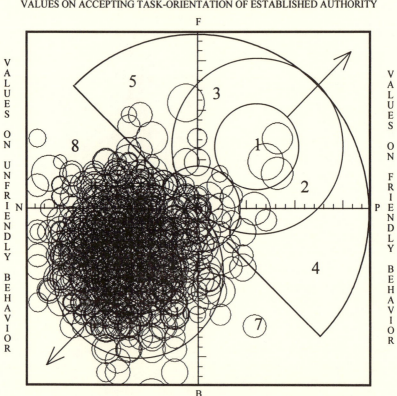

VALUES ON OPPOSING TASK-ORIENTATION OF ESTABLISHED AUTHORITY

*Source*: © 1997 SYMLOG Consulting Group, San Diego, CA. Reprinted by permission.

and assemble them into a single intact working team, the chances of built-in personality-based polarized conflicts would be high. There is a feature of these distributions, however, which would tend to improve the chances that such a randomly assembled team could work together.

This feature is the fact that each of the two Field Diagrams may be viewed as a "density plot" in which the most dense area is roughly in the middle of the range of the angles of separation between the lines of polarization. The distribution across the range of more than ninety degrees, described above, actually thins out to more scattered images toward the edges of each large cluster. More simply stated, the *wish* images tend to show a central tendency in density, with the most dense area in the PF direction. Similarly, the *reject* images show a plot with a more dense center quite close to the NB direction.

The implication is that most of the individual lines of polarization between *wish* and *reject* images are fairly close to the PF-NB Line of Polarization. Actually the average *wish* image is located a little toward P from PF. And the average *reject* image is a little toward N from NB. This symmetry deserves comment, but for the moment I shall emphasize the more important point that the main polarization existing in the minds of the greater number of group members runs from roughly the PF direction to its opposite in the NB direction.

Thus a random sample of ten individuals to compose a single intact group from a population of 1000, taking into account that the general *wish* versus *reject* polarization is PF versus NB, might not look so unpromising. It might well look more promising than the self-analytic group I have shown earlier as figure 2.1. The main line of polarization in this group was a startlingly strong polarization between a majority of members in the PF quadrant of the field and a minority of members actually in the NB quadrant.

One must remember that the images on the rejected end of the Line of Polarization in the minds of individual members of a given group are not necessarily the images of *group members*, as they were in my self-analytic group shown in figure 2.1. They may be images of any kind of threat. The images on the NB end in the diagram for *reject* images (figure 2.4) are in fact the images of rejected *values*, not actual group members. Other than problematic group members such as CARL or ACE in my self-analytic group, there are of course an unlimited number of other kinds of objects or concepts or states of being which might be evaluated by most people as located in the NB direction: sickness, famine, flood, death, and any number of different kinds of threats from outside the group, including competitors or other groups.

Figures 2.5 and 2.6 are the Bargraphs for *wish* and *reject* computed from two independent randomly drawn samples of 1000 raters each from the SCG data bank. The Bargraph for *wish* is computed from the same rating data as the Field Diagram for *wish*, which has been shown above as figure 2.3. The Bargraph for *reject* is computed from the same rating data as the Field Diagram for *reject*, shown above as figure 2.4.

The normative profile, the SCG Optimum, is shown as a vertical zigzag line on the *wish* Bargraph. The normative *reject* profile is shown in similar fashion on the *reject* Bargraph. By visual inspection alone it can be seen that the negative correlation between the two observed profiles is extremely high. Even though they are based on independently selected samples, they are almost exact mirror images, as one would hope. The profile of the *reject* image is strongly and negatively correlated with the profile of the *wish* image ($r = -.98$). The high

## FIGURE 2.5
### Bargraph of 1000 Ratings on *Values that You Wish to Show in Your Own Behavior* (WSH)

Type: UPF   Final Location: 3.4U  8.0P  5.5F
Ratings: 1000

the bar of X's = the average rating on each item
E = the *optimum* location for most effective teamwork

|  |  | | RARELY | SOMETIMES | OFTEN |
|---|---|---|---|---|---|
| 1 | U | Individual financial success, personal prominence and power . . . . . . . . . . . | | XXXXXXXXXXXXXXXXXEXX | |
| 2 | UP | Popularity and social success, being liked and admired . . . . . . . . . . . . . . . | | XXXXXXXXXXXXXXXXXXXXXXEXXX | |
| 3 | UPF | Active teamwork toward common goals, organizational unity . . . . . . . . . . . . . | | XXXXXXXXXXXXXXXXXXXXXXXXXXXXXXXXXXEX | |
| 4 | UF | Efficiency, strong impartial management . . . . . . . . . . . . . . . . . . | | XXXXXXXXXXXXXXXXXXXXXXXXXXXXXXXXEXXX | |
| 5 | UNF | Active reinforcement of authority, rules, and regulations . . . . . . . . . . . . . . . | | XXXXXXXXXXXXXXXXXXXXXE | |
| 6 | UN | Tough-minded, self-oriented assertiveness . . . . . . . . . . . . . . . . . . | | XXXXXXXXXXXXXXXXXXXXE | |
| 7 | UNB | Rugged, self-oriented individualism, resistance to authority . . . . . . . . . . . | | XXXXXXXXXE | |
| 8 | UB | Having a good time, releasing tension, relaxing control . . . . . . . . . . . . . . . | | XXXXXXXXXXXXXXXXXXXXXEXXXX | |
| 9 | UPB | Protecting less able members, providing help when needed . . . . . . . . . . . . . . | | XXXXXXXXXXXXXXXXXXXXXXXEXXXX | |
| 10 | P | Equality, democratic participation in decision making . . . . . . . . . . . . . . . . | | XXXXXXXXXXXXXXXXXXXXXXXXXEXXXX | |
| 11 | PF | Responsible idealism, collaborative work . . . . . . . . . . . . . . | | XXXXXXXXXXXXXXXXXXXXXXXXXXXEXXXX | |
| 12 | F | Conservative, established, "correct" ways of doing things . . . . . . . . . . . . . | | XXXXXXXXXXXXXXXXXXE | |
| 13 | NF | Restraining individual desires for organizational goals . . . . . . . . . . . . . | | XXXXXXXXXXXXXXXXXXXEXX | |
| 14 | N | Self-protection, self-interest first, self-sufficiency . . . . . . . . . . . . . . . . | | XXXXXXXE | |
| 15 | NB | Rejection of established procedures, rejection of conformity . . . . . . . . . . . | | XXXXXXXXXXEX | |
| 16 | B | Change to new procedures, different values, creativity . . . . . . . . . . . . . . | | XXXXXXXXXXXXXXXXXXXXXXXEXXXXX | |
| 17 | PB | Friendship, mutual pleasure, recreation . . . . . . . . . . . . . . . . . . | | XXXXXXXXXXXXXXXXXXXXXXEXXX | |
| 18 | DP | Trust in the goodness of others . . . . . . . . . . . . . . . . . . . . . | | XXXXXXXXXXXXXXXXXXXXXXXXEXXXX | |
| 19 | DPF | Dedication, faithfulness, loyalty to the organization . . . . . . . . | | XXXXXXXXXXXXXXXXXXXXXXXXXXXXXXXE | |
| 20 | DF | Obedience to the chain of command, complying with authority . . . . . . . . . | | XXXXXXXXXXXXXXXXXXXXXXXXXE | |
| 21 | DNF | Self-sacrifice if necessary to reach organizational goals . . . . . . . . . . . . . | | XXXXXXXXXXXXXXXXXXXXXEX | |
| 22 | DN | Passive rejection of popularity, going it alone . . . . . . . . . . . . . . . . . . | | XXXXXXXXXEx | |
| 23 | DNB | Admission of failure, withdrawal of effort . . . . . . . . . . . . . . | | XXXXXEX | |
| 24 | DB | Passive non-cooperation with authority . . . . . . . . . . . . . . . . . . | | XXE | |
| 25 | DPB | Quiet contentment, taking it easy . . . . . . . . . . . . . . . . . . | | XXXXXXXEXXX | |
| 26 | D | Giving up personal needs and desires, passivity . . . . . . . . . . . . . . . . . . . . | | XXXXXXXXXE | |

*Source*: © 1997 SYMLOG Consulting Group, San Diego, CA. Reprinted by permission.

## FIGURE 2.6
### Bargraph of 1000 Ratings on *Values that You Tend to Reject* (REJ)

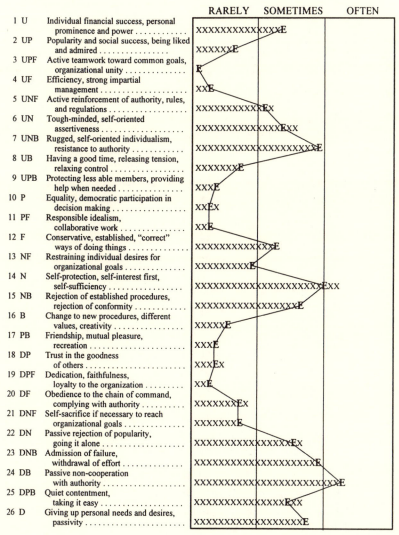

Type: DN   Final Location: 2.3D 7.2N 4.4B     the bar of X's = the average rating on each item
Ratings: 1000                                 E = the *optimum* location for most effective teamwork

negative correlation is real, not artifactual. It tends to be true of every individual rater who rates both Images, but occasionally there are cases where an individual, or a group average, shows a high rating on both *wish* and *reject* on a particular item. This is presumably an indication of ambivalence on a given value, and is of great diagnostic interest. The possibility of discovering significant ambivalence is the reason for constructing the separate profile for *reject*.

It will be noticed that the *reject* Bargraph for the sample of 1000 agrees almost exactly with the normative *reject* profile, which I have composed from previous samples, with only an X-unit, or two, of difference for a few values. The *wish* Bargraph for the sample of 1000, however, differs from the normative Optimum profile on a number of value descriptive items. (The SCG Optimum profile, as described earlier and explained in greater detail in chapter 10, is based on images of *effective* for leaders and members in work settings.)

A discrepancy of at least four X-units between a Bargraph frequency for the *observed* Image and the normative optimum frequency gives an indication of significant departures. According to this rule for significant departures, the *wish* Bargraph for this sample of 1000 is high on endorsement of the following items:

  8 UB    *Having a good time, releasing tension, relaxing control*
  9 UPB  *Protecting less able members, providing help when needed*
 10 P     *Equality, democratic participation in decision making*
 11 PF   *Responsible idealism, collaborative work*
 16 B     *Change to new procedures, different values, creativity*
 18 DP   *Trust in the goodness of others*

These value descriptive items seem to fit the impression most people probably have of the way in which *wishes* might well depart from the values one might consider "most effective." The *wish* tends to be more idealistic. The implication is that the SCG Optimum value profile is working as expected to tell us what is distinctive about the particular Image, *wish*.

### The *Current Culture* of American Business Organizations

How the members of American business organizations view the *current culture* of their organization is a matter of considerable practical interest. Figure 2.7 is a Bargraph for the *current culture*, based on a random sample of 1000 responses to the following rating question:

> In general, what kinds of values are *currently* shown in the culture of your organization?

The difference between the Bargraph for the *current culture* (CUR) and the Bargraph for the *wish* Image (WSH) is certainly provocative. Perhaps the

**FIGURE 2.7**

**Bargraph of 1000 Ratings on *Values that Are Currently
Shown in the Culture of Your Organization* (CUR)**

Type: F    Final Location: 0.5U  0.8P  4.5F       the bar of X's = the average rating on each item
Ratings: 1000                                      E = the *optimum* location for most effective teamwork

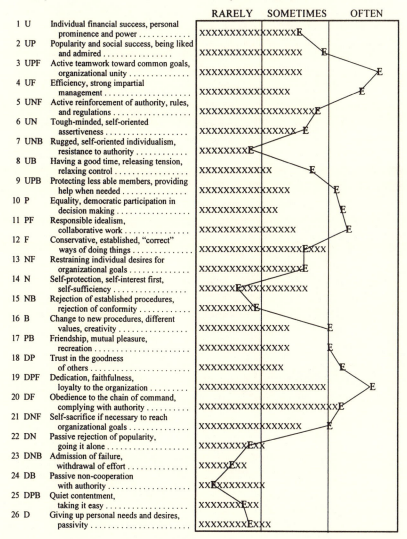

| | | RARELY | SOMETIMES | OFTEN |
|---|---|---|---|---|
| 1 U | Individual financial success, personal prominence and power . . . . . . . . . . . | | | |
| 2 UP | Popularity and social success, being liked and admired . . . . . . . . . . . . . . . | | | |
| 3 UPF | Active teamwork toward common goals, organizational unity . . . . . . . . . . . . . | | | |
| 4 UF | Efficiency, strong impartial management . . . . . . . . . . . . . . . . . . . | | | |
| 5 UNF | Active reinforcement of authority, rules, and regulations . . . . . . . . . . . . . . . | | | |
| 6 UN | Tough-minded, self-oriented assertiveness . . . . . . . . . . . . . . . . . | | | |
| 7 UNB | Rugged, self-oriented individualism, resistance to authority . . . . . . . . . . . | | | |
| 8 UB | Having a good time, releasing tension, relaxing control . . . . . . . . . . . . . . . | | | |
| 9 UPB | Protecting less able members, providing help when needed . . . . . . . . . . . . . | | | |
| 10 P | Equality, democratic participation in decision making . . . . . . . . . . . . . . . | | | |
| 11 PF | Responsible idealism, collaborative work . . . . . . . . . . . . . . | | | |
| 12 F | Conservative, established, "correct" ways of doing things . . . . . . . . . . . . . | | | |
| 13 NF | Restraining individual desires for organizational goals . . . . . . . . . . . . . | | | |
| 14 N | Self-protection, self-interest first, self-sufficiency . . . . . . . . . . . . . . . . | | | |
| 15 NB | Rejection of established procedures, rejection of conformity . . . . . . . . . . . | | | |
| 16 B | Change to new procedures, different values, creativity . . . . . . . . . . . . . . | | | |
| 17 PB | Friendship, mutual pleasure, recreation . . . . . . . . . . . . . . . . . . . . | | | |
| 18 DP | Trust in the goodness of others . . . . . . . . . . . . . . . . . . . . . | | | |
| 19 DPF | Dedication, faithfulness, loyalty to the organization . . . . . . . . | | | |
| 20 DF | Obedience to the chain of command, complying with authority . . . . . . . . . | | | |
| 21 DNF | Self-sacrifice if necessary to reach organizational goals . . . . . . . . . . . . . | | | |
| 22 DN | Passive rejection of popularity, going it alone . . . . . . . . . . . . . . . . . | | | |
| 23 DNB | Admission of failure, withdrawal of effort . . . . . . . . . . . . . | | | |
| 24 DB | Passive non-cooperation with authority . . . . . . . . . . . . . . . . . | | | |
| 25 DPB | Quiet contentment, taking it easy . . . . . . . . . . . . . . . . . | | | |
| 26 D | Giving up personal needs and desires, passivity . . . . . . . . . . . . . . . . . . . . | | | |

deviations of the *wish* profile are compensations for values which are neglected or suppressed in the current culture of the environing organization as a whole. Both the *wish* profile and the *current culture* profile depart from the normative SCG Optimum profile and they depart in opposite directions.

Comparison of the Bargraph to the SCG Optimum profile, using the four-X-unit rule, shows that nearly all of the discrepancies indicated are problems of "deficiency." There are two value items, however, which are markedly *high* in their frequency of endorsement:

14 N    *Self-protection, self-interest first, self-sufficiency*
24 DB    *Passive non-cooperation with authority*

An indication of the importance of these two value areas as widespread "problems" appears also in the Bargraph for *reject* (figure 2.6), which shows these two values to be the most frequently rejected, or disapproved. The "individualism" of the culture of American business is a part of its international reputation, of course. These two values indicate two of the ways in which American business culture probably differs most markedly from the cultures of emerging business economies, for example in Southeast Asia.

Business leaders in these East Asian parts of the world are reported by Charles Hampden-Turner (1997) to be eager to emulate American and Western European ways of doing business, but notably, they tend to reject the values of "individualism" in favor of values of a new variety of pattern I will call "communalism," in combination with government sponsorship and cooperation. The values shown on the *current culture* Bargraph (figure 2.7) as most seriously *deficient* in the culture of American business organizations might well be called "communalistic," at least in the sense of a higher value on group solidarity within the organization, and probably in the real community outside the organization as well. The East-West competition which seems to be intensifying between individualism and communalism in business cultures makes me wonder, which will prove to be more "effective" in the real long-time sense?

Figure 2.8 is the Field Diagram of the distribution of the perceptions of the same 1000 raters of the *current culture* of the organizations in which they work. It is plain that many of the raters see the Image as located on the Negative side of the space. It can also be seen that the great majority of them see the Image as located in the Forward half of the space.

It is instructive to compare the Field Diagram of figure 2.8 with those of *wish* and *reject*, figures 2.3 and 2.4. Although there is considerable overlap between the location of the *current culture* images and the *wish* locations, there is also what I will call a considerable "ominous" overlap between the *current culture* images and the *reject* image locations.

As social-psychological analysts, we need a theory that will enable us to assess the significance of particular patterns of distribution of plotted images on Field Diagrams in terms of their implications for the value system of the

**FIGURE 2.8**
**Scatterplot Field Diagram of 1000 Ratings on *Values that Are***
***Currently Shown in the Culture of Your Organization* (CUR)**

VALUES ON ACCEPTING TASK-ORIENTATION OF ESTABLISHED AUTHORITY

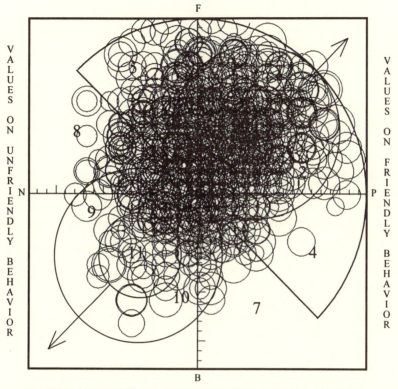

VALUES ON OPPOSING TASK-ORIENTATION OF ESTABLISHED AUTHORITY

organization as a whole over the longer time run, and by implication, for the most effective functioning of the more inclusive social-interaction system or surrounding community. The Value Area Overlay, discussed below, is such a theory.

**The Value Area Overlay, A Key to System Problems**

It is not hard to imagine that the locations of the images of the members of the small self-analytic group shown in figure 2.1 suggest two conflicting subgroups. This was indeed the case. The Overlay inscription of the two large circles which are strung together by a diagonal arrow-tipped line theoretically identifies the two subgroups. This inscription is called the *Polarization-Unification Overlay*. At the time I studied this self-analytic group, the Overlay was "fitted" to the patterned constellations of the images in the particular group as a method of best representing the real field which was created by the interaction of the members.

The idea of the Overlay is that images representing similar values will be located relatively close to each other on the Field Diagram, and that images representing opposite and conflicting values will be located far from each other. Each image will have been "propelled," as it were, by the vector engine (a mathematical scoring procedure) to just the coordinates shown on the Field Diagram and to be shown in the right sized circle. In principle, the ratings received by the Image may cause it to be propelled to a location anywhere in the global space.

Since the mid-1970s, when the self-analytic group shown in figure 2.1 met, the Overlay has been enhanced to function as an empirically based *normative* pattern of distribution, representative of the patterns of images of "most effective" found most frequently in large business populations. It is now called the *Value Area Overlay*. It is appropriate as a basis of comparison in the analysis of specific groups, and for the analysis of the differential distribution of ratings of group members of specific Images, such as *wish*, *reject*, *self*, and the like.

Figure 2.9 shows the design of the Value Area Overlay, which may be placed over any actual plotting of a pattern of rated Images on the Field Diagram, for example in the Field Diagrams of *wish*, *reject*, and *current culture* (figures 2.3, 2.4, 2.8). It represents a theory of the relationship of different areas of values to each other and their effects on the overall effectiveness of the pattern of Images.

According to the theory, when the profile rating of an Image by a group member has been converted into a single location in the intercorrelation space, it is henceforth to be treated for theoretical purposes as a vector, that is, as a live force in the total dynamic field. It is visualized as "pushing out" from the center of the field in the direction of a certain set of values. All of the values represented by the Image have been taken into account and reduced to a single vector, with specific direction and force. Henceforth the vector is treated in a social-psychological way as a "political actor" in a field of other similar actors. The images which represent the actors on the Field Diagram thus represent a kind of "activated political spectrum." Thus, I have chosen to name the parts of the Value Area Overlay with terms that carry political connotations.

The Value Area Overlay divides the Field Diagram plane into a set of eleven Areas, each with a name suggesting the value orientation of an individual, or a subgroup, or a subdivision of a large population. The locations of the Areas, closer to or further away from a normatively assumed "most effective" loca-

**FIGURE 2.9**
**The Value Area Overlay**

VALUES ON ACCEPTING TASK-ORIENTATION OF ESTABLISHED AUTHORITY

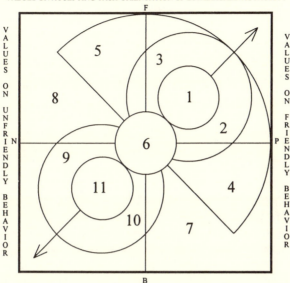

VALUES ON OPPOSING TASK-ORIENTATION OF ESTABLISHED AUTHORITY

**Meaning of the Areas**

| | |
|---|---|
| 1 | Most Effective Teamwork Core |
| 2 | Liberal Teamwork Side |
| 3 | Conservative Teamwork Side |
| 4 | Group-centered Wing |
| 5 | Authority-centered Wing |
| 6 | Swing Area |
| 7 | Libertarian Fringe |
| 8 | Individualistic Fringe |
| 9 | Anti-group Opposition |
| 10 | Anti-authority Opposition |
| 11 | Radical Opposition Core |

*Source*: © 1997 SYMLOG Consulting Group, San Diego, CA. Reprinted by permission.

tion, give the basic rationale for the names. The Overlay is primarily used by the social-psychological interpreter for further theoretical descriptions and analyses. For a given set of ratings of an Image specified by the rating question, the plotted locations, distributed in different Areas in different densities, allow the interpreter to relate the probable conflicts and cooperation of individuals to each other, and to estimate their outcome in relation to one final normative focus concerning the degree of "effectiveness."

*The Focus of the Overlay Is the Effective Core*

The Field Diagram in figure 2.10 shows a striking empirical display. The diagram is based on the responses from 1000 randomly drawn members of intact groups to the following rating question about a member of their group who is about to depart for a workshop on leadership:

> In general, what kinds of values would be *ideal* for this person to show in behavior in order to be *most effective*?

The person the members are rating is likely (but not necessarily) already the leader of their group.

The most astonishing thing to me about the pattern on the Field Diagram of *ideal* (IDL) is its compact unification, compared, for example, to that of the *current culture* (figure 2.8). It is true that there are some images floating around outside the large circle on the Value Area Overlay but they are few and not far separated from the most unified cluster. The pattern for *ideal* is fairly similar to the pattern for *wish* (figure 2.3) but actually the pattern for *ideal* is more compact and symmetrical. Most of the plotted image circles for this Image lie inside the Reference Circle of the Value Area Overlay (Areas 1, plus 2, plus 3).

The densest portion of the pattern seems circular in form, and is centered approximately on the center of the Reference Circle. Computations not shown here indicate that the distribution fanning out from every side of the central point of the cluster is very close to a normal bell-shaped distribution in each of the three dimensions of the space. (Technically, this kind of distribution is called a trivariate normal distribution.) The exact center of the two-dimensional cluster shown on the plane of the Field Diagram is not at the center of the whole field, but rather on a vector nine units out in the exact PF direction.

On the plane surface of the Field Diagram, the outer boundary of all vectors in all of the locations on the plane surface is a large enclosing boundary circle with a radius of eighteen units. This outer boundary is shown visually on the Value Area Overlay only around the perimeter of the more effective PF-centered half of the field. It extends around the NB-centered half of the field as well, of course, but I omit it on the Overlay inscription in order to place the visual emphasis on the PF half.

What is going on in a social-psychological sense to produce this distribution? The answer is not simple, and I am not sure I understand it all, but one thing seems very likely. Although two preferred value Vectors, P and F, are both acting at the same time, they are not producing two clusters of images,

FIGURE 2.10

**Scatterplot Field Diagram of 1000 Ratings on *Values that Would Be Ideal for this Person to Show in Behavior in Order to Be Most Effective* (IDL)**

VALUES ON ACCEPTING TASK-ORIENTATION OF ESTABLISHED AUTHORITY

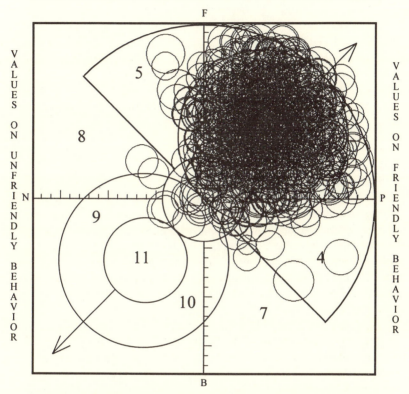

VALUES ON OPPOSING TASK-ORIENTATION OF ESTABLISHED AUTHORITY

*Source:* © 1997 SYMLOG Consulting Group, San Diego, CA. Reprinted by permission.

one for each vector. Rather, they are producing a convergence of image density at an angle half way between the two. It is as if there were a point of balance there that might well be called an "attractor," in the language of the theory of complex systems. It is as if the concept "ideal for most effective" requires a balanced combination of the values of the F vector and the P vector. The cluster is roughly circular and seems to have its own center of gravity, as if the images within it exerted an attractive influence on each other in some mysterious way. I say "mysterious" because the persons who each contributed one image to this cluster did not interact with each other. What then produced the circular form, so exactly centered? (The answer to this will take longer. I will take up the problem in chapter 10, "The Mystery of *Most Effective* Values.")

I believe that in the case of an intact group, such as a team, where "attraction" is something that can be psychologically felt by real participants, the convergence of the attraction of each of the two potentially orthogonal vectors into a single convergent PF direction can assume a kind of psychological reality in itself, as a value of visualized cooperation between legitimate leadership and somewhat differently located members. Such a combination would have real advantages as applied to task problems and group-maintenance problems, as well. The large PF cluster in an intact group does tend to be unified, but only partially unified. It has an F task-oriented half, and a P group-oriented half.

I assume that members on opposite edges of such a PF cluster in an intact group do in fact tend to conflict with each other on occasion, or at least to feel ambivalent about each other. The attractions that hold them together, even if only barely, are the added advantages of cooperation of a friendly group working on externally visualized task problems, the solutions to which are relevant to effective adaptation and survival in the external environment.

The advantages of a coalition among the PF members in opposition to threats in the rejected half of the space may also be very significant. The tendency toward rejection would be expected to apply to all of the Areas to the NB side of the NF-PB line of separation (part of Area 6, and Areas 7, 8, 9, 10, and 11). The edge of the circle made up of Areas 1, 2, and 3 is my guess as to the location where rejection tends to overcome the attraction of the PF cluster.

On the Value Area Overlay (figure 2.9) the large circle in the PF area of the Field Diagram, occupied by the main cluster of images of *ideal* in figure 2.10, is divided into three Areas. The region labeled on the Overlay as Area 1 is called the *Most Effective Teamwork Core*. This Core Area is circular and is chosen to be nine Field Diagram units in radius for reasons of maximizing the probability of mutual acceptance of members in that Area, as suggested above. The Area to the P side (Area 2) is called the *Liberal Teamwork Side*. The Area to the F side (Area 3) is called the *Conservative Teamwork Side*. Thus a degree of difference between the two Sides is recognized and expected, but the tendency to be drawn toward one centrally placed attractor is also recognized, or postulated.

It is one thing for the images to be drawn toward the center of the PF quadrant. It is another thing for members in the two Side Areas to avoid being drawn toward a degree of differentiation in the U, or P, or F directions. For members it is often difficult to remain within the unifying influence of the central attractor values, the UPF, PF, and DPF values (see Appendix A). Areas 1, 2, and 3 also contain the potentially conflicting values of dominance versus submission. All members of the PF cluster, in short, hold values of some diversity and are under different realistic concerns that also pull them toward the three more separated orthogonal vectors—U, P, and F. In fact, even within Area 1, the Most Effective Teamwork Core, conflict arising from value differences does not altogether disappear. Potential conflict is only moderated toward some minimum, at best.

When one considers that the raters in their self-pictures (see figure 2.11) are much more highly differentiated than the narrow constraints outlined by the borders of the central Core, one may realize, with dismay, that to shape one's values in such a way as to be actually rated so as to fall in the Core, among the high-density aggregation there, likely requires a considerable number of individuals to accept onerous constraints.

Considered in this way, one may begin to see that even the Most Effective Teamwork Core is possibly an area of rather tense and tenuous coalitions between members who are pulled at the same time in various diverse value directions, especially if they have roles as representatives or leaders of more diverse subgroups within the total system.

Leaders who attempt to hold to the middle-of-the-road position (although this position may be socially approved by the majority over all, and is also politically strategic) can become the target of blame from every side for failing to be fully devoted to each diverse interest. If the main part of the total group is too strongly polarized along an NF-PB Line of Polarization (analogous to the Republican versus Democratic Line of Polarization), middle-of-the-road leaders may find it impossible to maintain sufficient power and popularity to survive. A division of the leadership into a coalition between two somewhat separated leaders, a task leader toward the F side and a social-emotional leader toward the P side, is a possible, and probably a fairly common, way of easing the strain and instability of the leadership role.

*The Secondary Line of Polarization Suggests Conservative-Liberal Conflict*

The major *Line of Polarization*, it will be remembered, extends diagonally across the field from NB to PF. Perpendicular to this Line of Polarization is another long line extending from NF to PB. I have called this the *Secondary Line of Polarization*. In groups which actually are most effective, I have assumed, the major Line of Polarization will tend to be the most powerful, and the images will be relatively unified toward the PF end. But not all groups are most effective, by any means. In some groups the Secondary Line of Polarization (NF-PB) may be very powerful, and in fact may become the major polarization. A major division of group membership between Authority-centered (Area 5) and Group-centered (Area 4) coalitions can essentially paralyze PF movement, especially if the Swing Area is heavily populated. This is the "classic" conservative-versus-liberal polarization. Unfortunately, once

**FIGURE 2.11**
**Scatterplot Field Diagram of 1000 Ratings on**
*Values that You Actually Show in Your Behavior* **(SLF)**

VALUES ON ACCEPTING TASK-ORIENTATION OF ESTABLISHED AUTHORITY

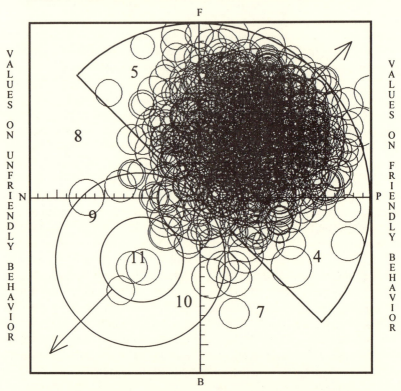

VALUES ON OPPOSING TASK-ORIENTATION OF ESTABLISHED AUTHORITY

*Source*: © 1997 SYMLOG Consulting Group, San Diego, CA. Reprinted by permission.

underway, it tends to be reinforced from each extreme and may proceed to polarize further until it becomes politically crippling and economically insupportable.

The Secondary Line of Polarization, running between NF and PB (omitting the Swing Area), is regarded as the extreme cut-off line between the PF half of the field and the NB half of the field. Within the PF half of the field there may be some prospect of bringing in all, or most, of the members located there to contribute to movement in the PF direction, or at least not to interfere too drastically. To achieve such movement, middle-of-the-road leadership will need to find a way to reconcile, or neutralize, the extreme differences between conservative and liberal members in their aspirations to realize maximum movement in their preferred directions, NF versus PB.

There are several approaches which have been taken, though they may be of varying degrees of ethical appeal. The most appealing, probably, but also hard to achieve in real substance, is leadership which is able to present unusually effective ways to solve problems of survival by successful innovation or creative adaptation to the demands of the external environment.

Conflict between conservative and liberal extremes will surely be relieved if major densities of group membership can be attracted to the Most Effective Core and the two adjacent Side Areas. By overlapping and linked coalitions reaching out in both the NF and PB directions, pathways of influence may be built to reach the more extreme members of the Authority-centered Wing and the Group-centered Wing. Part of this dragnet, or interlinked-chain approach for unifying diverse preferences may involve interest trading and more effective distribution of assets and rewards. If this is possible, it is likely to require some reduction in the differences of status and power among group members. This will please the more liberal members, but will be resisted by the more conservative.

It will nearly always be tempting for leadership to increase unification by a build-up of polarization vis-à-vis rejected group values, and images of threats. As rejected images, these are usually located by member ratings somewhere in the NB quadrant, but may be located anywhere to the NB side of the NF-PB line of division. If these rejected images include a subgroup of members, this may develop into full-blown prejudice. Prejudice and its consequences are extremely undesirable developments, not only ethically and morally, but in terms of many crippling effects on the system as a whole and its ability to achieve socialization and social development of new and existing minority members. The damaging effects may be slightly delayed but are sure to come and sure to be a curse, even over generations, if the system lasts that long.

### The NB Half of the Space Is Far from Effective

Images on the NB side of the space, to the left of the Secondary Line of Polarization extending from NF to PB, are assumed to be out of the range of attraction of the Most Effective Teamwork Core. Instead, each such image is potentially attracted to other images on the NB side, according to how similar the values of the other image are to its own profile of values. The inscriptions of the named Areas on the NB side are symmetrical to those on the PF side, but opposite in their potential orientation to the images on the PF side. Thus, opposite the Most Effective Teamwork Core on the PF side, on the NB side there is Area 11, called the *Radical Opposition Core*. The value profiles of the images in the Radical Opposition Core indicate opposition to established authority, the tasks required by authority, and conventional values in general. At the same time, persons whose images are placed in Area 11 tend to reject group-oriented, equalitarian, and friendly values. In the political spectrum of the historical past, the persons whose values lie in this Area have been revolutionaries, anarchists, and other "extremists," from the conventional point of view.

Although such persons may have common interests in the overthrow or exploitation of the ongoing system, and so may form coalitions in furtherance of these interests, they are not well equipped in terms of values, as a rule, to maintain their own leadership, their own rules, and their own group solidarity. Nevertheless, the members and the values of the Radical Opposition Core are assumed to have an attraction for other individuals whose values are tending toward either the N or the B directions, or both.

It is assumed that the Radical Core will attract members whose value profiles are in the areas adjacent to it: Area 9, the *Anti-group Opposition*, and Area 10, the *Anti-authority Opposition*. On the Field Diagram for values that are *rejected* (figure 2.4), it is evident that there is a middle area of greater density, but it is not precisely centered in the Radical Opposition Core. The major *reject* cluster extends into Area 9, Anti-group Opposition, and is not sharply defined. It is not clear whether this distribution represents a system tendency that will be found in many other cases. I have no hypothesis to suggest. But the imbalance in relation to Area 10, Anti-authority Opposition, is so marked that it seems to demand an explanation. The most dense area is well situated to counterbalance the *wish* cluster, which shows a tendency to spread into Area 4, the Group-oriented Wing (see figure 2.3).

Area 7, the *Libertarian Fringe*, has been very thinly populated in nearly all the Field Diagrams that I have seen. It represents a profile of values that is unconventional, opposed to authority, and yet has friendly attitudes toward others on the friendly side. Where I have seen it, it appeared to be associated with developmental immaturity on the part of the members who have these values. In one self-analytic group in my experience, it was represented by a kind of juvenile gang, led by a "tomboy," a robust likable female leader who was very intelligent, rode a motorcycle, and joked with the guys. She had formed a friendship with a talented and very likable male who also rode a motorcycle. In the group, they formed a coalition to promote a little rowdy fun, and had several followers. (It turned out, however, that Steve, the male member of the coalition, was actually a "closet" UPF type, just on his way up.)

Area 8, the *Individualistic Fringe*, is quite densely populated in the Field Diagram of *current culture* (figure 2.8). The Individualistic Fringe is adjacent to the Authority-centered Wing, but the profiles of members who are represented there are further toward the Unfriendly side, on the average, and presumably they are out of the reach of any attraction to the PF members of the space. Area 8, the Individualistic Fringe, is adjacent to Area 9, the Anti-group Opposition. In general, the persons whose profiles are in Areas 8 and 9, the Individualistic Fringe and in the Anti-group Opposition, tend to be feared and rejected by members in Area 4, the Group-centered Wing, and also rejected by members in Area 7, the Libertarian Fringe.

### Area Densities in the Field of *Current Culture*

In the total system, the density of images in the various Areas of the Value Area Overlay tells a large-scale story about the probable overall effectiveness and probability of survival of the total group or system in the longer run. The relative density in a given Area, in plainer words, indicates the relative number of members who can be expected for the time being, to work toward, or to impede, movement (decision making and action) in the direction of most effective operation. Thus the relative densities of the different Areas affect the prospect of longer-term survival of the group as a whole.

In order to get a better grip on the varying densities of different Areas and the implications of relative differences, the number of images of each type in each of the Areas may be counted and arrayed against norms based on experience. Figure 2.12 shows an example of what is called the *Value Area Density Chart*. It gives, in tabular form, the results of a complete count of the images found in each of the eleven Areas in the total field. The counts for each Area are also subdivided according to degree of dominance or submissiveness.

The Chart presents the SCG Optimum norm for the eleven Areas and the three levels of dominance, which appear as row and column totals. The values for the SCG Optimum are standardized to the sample size of the data being displayed. The SCG Optimum norms for the Area Density Chart, were empirically determined as follows. I added together and averaged a number of such Charts (cell by cell) for Images that had an "ideal" character in the way the rating question was phrased. I tried to balance the special emphasis of each type of Image by the addition of the charts of others which tended to counterbalance it.

The designation "H" after a number means that a *t*-test between the norm and the count indicates a significant difference, and that the number counted is *high* compared to the SCG Optimum. Similarly, an appended letter "L" means that the number counted is *low*. These discrepancies are very relevant in estimating whether sufficient strength of leadership is available in the particular distribution, whether too many members feel themselves in subordinate or passive roles, and the probability and probable causes of dissatisfaction and desire for change in the total system.

The Value Area Density Chart in figure 2.12 (used here mainly for illustration of the Chart) is computed from the ratings on the *current culture* (CUR) shown in figure 2.8. The highly dispersed nature of the images in this Field

**FIGURE 2.12**

**Value Area Density Chart for the Scatterplot Field Diagram of 1000 Ratings
on *Values that Are Currently Shown in the Culture of Your Organization* (CUR)**

**Size and Number of Images Observed in Each Scatterplot Overlay Area Compared
with Number Expected***

Name of Image: CUR                                                        H = High
Total image circles in scatterplot: 1000                                  L = Low

| Area Number and Name | Size of Images | | | Comparison | |
|---|---|---|---|---|---|
| | Dominant (large) | Mid-size (mid) | Submis-sive (small) | Total in Area | Norm (scaled to N) |
| 1  Most Effective Teamwork Core | 60 L | 108 L | 32 | 200 L | 469 |
| 2  Liberal Teamwork Side | 26 L | 33 L | 13 | 72 L | 213 |
| 3  Conservative Teamwork Side | 45 L | 115 H | 44 H | 204 | 219 |
| 4  Group-centered Wing | 4 L | 8 | 6 H | 18 | 19 |
| 5  Authority-centered Wing | 26 H | 57 H | 30 H | 113 H | 20 |
| 6  Swing Area | 50 H | 126 H | 43 H | 219 H | 64 |
| 7  Libertarian Fringe | 1 H | 2 H | 2 H | 5 H | 1 |
| 8  Individualistic Fringe | 8 H | 27 H | 21 H | 56 H | 1 |
| 9  Anti-group Opposition | 12 H | 20 H | 16 H | 48 H | 1 |
| 10  Anti-authority Opposition | 9 H | 8 H | 9 H | 26 H | 1 |
| 11  Radical Opposition Core | 8 H | 23 H | 8 H | 39 H | 1 |
| Totals observed: | 249 L | 527 H | 224 H | 1000 | |
| Norms expected: | 531 | 415 | 53 | | |

* The norm, or *expected* number, for each cell of the table has been computed as a percentage of the total N of a large normative population. For easier comparison with the raw numbers of the *observed* data set, each percentage has been applied to the total N of the data set to obtain an *expected* raw number for the cell. Comparison of the *observed* with the *expected* then permits a statistical judgment of the *observed* number as *high* (H), *low* (L), or *normal*. Those cells that are *high* or *low* are marked H or L. However, the *normative* numbers are displayed on the table only for the cells showing the *Total in Area*.

*Source*: © 1997 SYMLOG Consulting Group, San Diego, CA. Reprinted by permission.

Diagram makes it evident that one needs a general theory of the dynamic characteristics of the disparate Areas and their different relations to the normative pattern of a total field characteristic of "most effective," in order to read its potential meanings.

Since the total number of images in the Field Diagram is 1000, the numbers in the Chart may be read as percentages simply by putting a decimal point in front of the last digit. Verbal description in terms of percentages, rather than raw numbers, allows a more immediate meaningful comparison between systems or between Images for a given system.

In the *current culture* Field Diagram (figure 2.8), there are many images located outside the PF-NB polarization. Compared with the Value Area Overlay normative distribution for the Field Diagram, the Areas called *Authority-centered Wing* and *Individualistic Fringe* are highly overpopulated in this Field Diagram. In contrast, the Areas called Most Effective Teamwork Core and Liberal Teamwork Side are significantly underpopulated.

A glance down the Area Density Chart on the *current culture* in figure 2.12, compared to the SCG Optimum shows a rather discouraging picture. The density in the Most Effective Teamwork Core for the *current culture* of the organization is *low*, at about 20 percent, as compared to the SCG Optimum of about 47 percent. The density of *dominant images* in the Core Area also turns out to be *low*. These two facts together seem to indicate an unfortunate perceived weakness of leadership in a critical area of functioning in the business populations with which SCG has worked. We do not know, unfortunately, whether the business groups most likely to become clients for SCG consultation are among those which are functioning well, middling, or poorly. My guess is "middling."

The Liberal Teamwork Side in the *current culture* Chart is notably *low* in density, with a density of 7.2 percent compared to the SCG Optimum of 21.3 percent. (The SCG Optimum is based, it will be remembered, on the ratings of concepts of "ideal for effectiveness" in comparable business populations.) The Conservative Teamwork Side in the *current culture* Chart is about normal in density. But, the Authority-centered Wing is markedly *high*, with a density of 11.3 percent compared to the SCG Optimum of 2.0 percent. The Swing Area is markedly *high*, with a density of 21.9 percent, compared to the SCG Optimum of 6.4 percent. All of the rest of the Areas on the NB side of the NF-PB line of division, those which show opposition to movement in the PF direction in one form or another, are significantly *high*. The column for Dominant images shows that the *current culture* density in all of these Areas is *high*. In other words the most dominant images tend to be found in the Areas most distant from the Areas associated with greatest "effectiveness." This is a set of facts that leaders in business organizations may find disturbing.

The Area Density Chart is also useful for indications of surpluses or deficits in dominance or submissiveness. Totals for *Size of Images*, along with the SCG Optimum, or expected norms, are shown along the bottom row of the Chart. The number of Dominant images, over all Areas is markedly *low*, at 24.9 percent compared to the SCG Optimum of 53.1 percent. But, all of the Areas on the opposition half of the field, moving counterclockwise from the Authority-centered Wing to the Libertarian Fringe, are *high* compared to SCG Optimum norms. Insofar as dominance is connected with leadership, the PF half of the field shows deficits, except for the Authority-centered Wing, while the NB opposition half of the field shows surpluses. Over all Areas, the relative density of submissive images is markedly *high*, at 22.4 percent compared to the SCG Optimum of 5.3 percent.

### Differences in Value Area Density Profiles of Images

The Table of Comparative Area Density Profiles (figure 2.13) gives the average distribution across the eleven Value Areas for a number of different Images. All numbers in the cells have been converted to percentages, although the sample size was the same for all observed Images: 1000 randomly selected rating sets from the total relevant SCG data-bank population. The SCG data bank contains comparable data for other Images. The average *rating* profiles on the twenty-six items for nineteen Images are shown in Appendix C. The density profile for the normative SCG Optimum (OPT) is shown at the extreme right of the table.

Several features of the comparative array of Image Area Densities in figure 2.13 may be noticed. The density in Area 1, associated with optimum leadership and effective teamwork, declines as we pass from left to right across the Images in the table. The SCG Optimum Value Area Density Profile (OPT) compares quite favorably with the profile for *ideal* for most effective (IDL) but is balanced a little more evenly between the Liberal Teamwork Side and the Conservative Teamwork Side. For both the *ideal* and the SCG Optimum profiles, the density in the Most Effective Teamwork Core approaches 50 percent of the total number of images in the system (specifically, 47 percent).

The density percentages for the Liberal Teamwork Side and the Conservative Teamwork Side are about equal to each other in the SCG Optimum profile, the *ideal* (IDL), and the *effective* (EFF) profiles. The two Sides together tend to sum to about 43 percent, a little less than the density of the Most Effective Teamwork Core (47 percent). Thus, in the profiles that tend to approximate the SCG Optimum, the Core in combination with the Two Sides together (the PF cluster) tend to account for about 90 percent of the total density of the whole field.

There are a number of facts of social-psychological interest that may be gleaned from figure 2.13. Only a few can be cited here. The ratings of the *self* (SLF) (figure 2.11) are worth comment in view of the early frame of reference centered on the "self" and "situation." The densities of ratings of the *self* in the Most Effective Teamwork Core and in the Liberal Teamwork Side are *low* compared to the comparable densities in the ratings of *wish* (WSH). The situation of the *self* in business organizations, on the average, appears to be difficult. Self-perceptions show *high* density in all the Areas of the NB oppositional half of the space, and *high* density as well in the Authority-centered Wing of the space as compared to other Areas in the PF half of the space. However, the Image of the *self* in the Authority-centered Wing is hardly that

**FIGURE 2.13**

**Table of Comparative Area Density Profiles Showing the Percentage of the Total Number of Images in Each of the Value Areas of the Field**

| Value Area | Percentages in each Area from Charts of various Images | | | | | | | | |
|---|---|---|---|---|---|---|---|---|---|
| | IDL | EFF | WSH | MEL | SLF | EXP | OTM | REJ | OPT |
| 1 Most Effective Teamwork Core | 47.1 | 45.6 | 44.7 | 42.5 L | 37.4 L | 35.7 L | 28.7 L | .3 | 46.9 |
| 2 Liberal Teamwork Side | 19.2 | 23.3 | 32.7 H | 23.5 H | 18.6 L | 17.8 L | 13.9 L | .4 | 21.3 |
| 3 Conservative Teamwork Side | 22.4 | 21.4 | 11.2 L | 20.2 | 23.0 | 20.0 | 20.3 | .4 | 21.9 |
| 4 Group-centered Wing | 2.2 | 1.6 | 5.2 H | 3.5 H | 2.5 | 3.3 H | 3.6 H | .2 | 1.9 |
| 5 Authority-centered Wing | 1.5 | 2.5 | .6 L | 3.6 H | 3.8 H | 5.2 H | 9.1 H | .4 | 2.0 |
| 6 Swing Area | 7.3 | 5.4 | 5.0 L | 6.4 | 12.3 H | 12.0 H | 15.3 H | 8.5 | 6.4 |
| 7 Libertarian Fringe | .1 | .0 | .3 H | .0 | .4 H | .4 H | .5 H | 1.0 | .1 |
| 8 Individualistic Fringe | .1 | .0 | .2 H | .2 H | .4 H | 1.9 H | 2.5 H | 6.1 | .1 |
| 9 Anti-group Opposition | .1 | .0 | .0 | .1 | .7 H | 1.3 H | 2.9 H | 31.3 | .1 |
| 10 Anti-authority Opposition | .0 | .1 | .1 | .0 | .4 H | 1.0 H | 1.2 H | 9.3 | .1 |
| 11 Radical Opposition | .0 | .1 | .0 | .0 | .5 H | 1.4 H | 2.0 H | 42.1 | .1 |

Questions for codes:

*In general, what kinds of values ...*

IDL   would be *ideal* for this person to show in order to be *most effective?*

EFF   would be ideal for you to show in order to be *most effective?*

WSH   do you *wish* to show in your own behavior, whether or not you are actually able to do so?"

MEL   does the *most effective leader* of a task-oriented work team you have known show in his or her behavior?"

SLF   do *you* actually show in your behavior?"

EXP   do you *expect* others will rate you as showing in your behavior?"

OTM   does this person show in his or her behavior?" (other team members)

REJ   do you tend to *reject*, either in yourself or in others?"

*Source:* © 1997 SYMLOG Consulting Group, San Diego, CA. Reprinted by permission.

of an authoritarian manager with clout. Rather, the *self* in this Area tends to show, on the average, the characteristics of a submissive follower. This Area, as well as all of the other Areas on the Negative and Backward Sides are significantly *high* in submissive (small) images (see also the Field Diagram in figure 2.11).

The table in figure 2.13 indicates that the raters do not *expect* (EXP) to be seen in a flattering way by their teammates. On the contrary, and in particular, their *expect* images show a relatively *high* density in the Anti-group Opposition Area, and even in the Radical Opposition Core. The absolute numbers are not high, but they do indicate some turning away from aspirations to move in optimum directions toward greater effectiveness.

*Other team members* (OTM) are seen in even more socially undesirable and problem-generating ways. The most socially undesirable perceptions, short of the *reject* Image itself, are of the *current culture* (CUR). It may be that the well-known tendency to project undesirable traits onto other persons and objects is operating, and is shown more strongly toward objects the further they are felt to be from the *self*.

### The Dynamically Organizing System Field as a Whole

The pattern of measurements of the locations of particles or parts of any densely interconnected system of variables and their movement over time may be seen from a perspective *outside* the system as a dynamic "field." The smoke patterns around a model airplane in a wind tunnel give a picture of the aerodynamic field. The curly tracks made by subatomic particles as they pass through the cloud chamber of an atom smasher may be said to give a picture of a dynamic "field" of subatomic forces as they unfold in the minuscule span of time that can be captured in their passage through the cloud chamber.

The importance of an interactive gestalt, or "field" of influences, has been recognized in various ways in the history of social psychology. It was recognized in principle in an early emphasis on the "situation" or the "total situation," especially in the sociological literature (Small 1905; Thomas and Znaniecki [1918–20]1958; Znaniecki 1925; Parsons 1937; Bales 1941). In Lewin's field theory the gestalt emphasis was recognized not only in the concept of the "life space," but also in the concept of "feedback," as having a guiding and modifying influence on the continuing ongoing processes of behavior. Gestalts are "temporal" as well as "spatial."

In the social-interaction system—the mental processes of individuals and their social interactions with each other—the space of relationships between values and associated variables is assumed to be so densely packed that if one were able to measure them all, the intercorrelations would be like a thick "soup." The variables which make up the soup are closely interconnected and acting upon each other back and forth so rapidly that, taken together, the dense network constitutes a patterned whole that can be pictured as a "field."

The "field" represented on a Field Diagram of elements or images in a social-interaction system is assumed to be a manifold of dynamic elements, each of which tends to "move" in a given direction in the space, and to influence each of the others to some degree. These restlessly moving elements, through their many influences, qualifications, and feedbacks on each other, tend to shape and alter the locations in the space of each other. The shape often assumes a more regularly formed and powerfully preemptive pattern, such as a symmetrical pattern of two opposed clusters or clouds of elements, each cluster made up of relatively similar elements, but the two clusters are made up of relatively polarized elements. This process of sorting out and otherwise changing relations among the elements, as noted before, is often called "self-organization" in the current theory of complex systems.

The Images with which we are concerned are assumed to be complex. Each Image contains elements (internal dynamic vectors) which we represent as twenty-six contending forces. The rated profile of the Image represents our estimate of the relative strengths of these contending forces, vis-à-vis each other. The images within an individual's mind are assumed to interact with each other and to develop a complex organization of polarizations between clusters and unifications within clusters of images.

When individual personalities interact with each other in social interaction, complexity is greatly increased. But the fundamental tendencies toward polarization and unification between and within subgroups persist. Individuals are assumed to be "drawn toward each other" in cooperative relationships, in proportion to the size of the positive correlation of their value profiles. Within clusters so produced, over time in continued interaction, there are tendencies to modify certain of the values of individuals within a cluster toward greater similarity, on the average. At the same time, individuals whose profiles are different enough to produce a negative correlation between them tend to be "repelled" from each other toward overt conflict in proportion to the size of the negative correlation.

As the ceaseless adjustment and readjustment proceeds, the total field tends to develop a pattern of polarized subgroups, or areas of relative similarity, within which subgroups can develop. If, by unfortunate combinations of personalities, there are too many negative correlations between the values of enough of the individuals, a more or less complete polarization of the whole group may develop.

In real situations of social interaction the underlying processes seem to organize themselves spontaneously and often surprisingly fast into discernibly patterned "dynamic system fields." Often the patterned overall results are not very clearly foreseen by the individuals involved. Individual selves and self-conceptions become dynamically interlocked with each other into unintended and poorly understood larger system fields of influences and constraints from which the individuals involved may find it difficult to escape. Typical rationalizations set in ("I didn't know it was loaded," "I didn't know what I was getting into," "I didn't know it was wrong or illegal," "Everybody else was doing it," "It was my duty, I was only following orders").

From the point of view of each of the participants, what is happening to the self sometimes cannot be adequately described or understood. What goes on in the "situation" is so complex that neither the participants nor the observers can keep track of it. "Systemic" processes set in, like chemical reactions in process, involving many elements, developing and influencing each other at different rates, at both more microscopic and more global levels, often without individual awareness, understanding, and without effective decision and control by any of the individuals involved.

Dynamic fields in personalities and in social-interaction systems can be called "self-organizing." But it should not be forgotten that real "selves," that is, individual personalities, are providing the motive power and making the decisions in both individual personalities and in social-interaction systems composed of different personalities. Since real psychological selves are important constituent parts of our kinds of systems, the meaning of the term "self-organizing" is ambiguous. For this reason, I suggest that it may be better not to use this term in the context of social-interaction systems. Some descriptive term such as "dynamically reorganizing" (of the specific system) may be preferable.

When a multitude of selves are involved, all influencing each other through an imperfect communication network, the overall uniformities of movement and the shape of the resulting moving constellation may not be traceable to particular identifiable individuals. The influence of some particular individuals may be obvious for a while, but the track of their specific influence may soon become untraceable, like a drop of vanilla in a bowl of cake batter. When an individual feels that his or her influence is unrecognizable and untraceable, an important pattern of restraints and encouragements that are ordinarily present is removed, and a different pattern of values may come forward out of suppression. Similarities among enough individuals in the emerging pattern of previously suppressed or restrained values may then lead to crowd action, manifestations of the so-called "group mind," and other similar breaks with "normal" behavior.

Each individual, in our kind of theoretical system, remains intact as a "part." But the local "situation" he or she faces when many persons are involved is made up of incomplete impressions of the larger-scale constellations of attitudes, values, and meanings, as they change around the self and give the self a changed local situation. The effect on the self may be powerful, and may give additional urgency to move in one direction or another. The tracks of this movement, in turn, are merged with many others as the process goes on.

## Regularities Reduce Complexity

The unlimited number of features of the real object of study—an actual social-interaction system—makes it literally impossible, of course, to recognize and measure all of the variables which might be relevant. One must try to make a strategically chosen sample give as much information as possible. The problems of constructing the kind of model necessary are very similar in a formal way to the problems of constructing models for weather forecasting. One must repeat the measurement procedure for many fields and many systems in the search for regularities and differences. In fact, the actual field of relationships changes according to many conditions, and is unique in many respects for each system one may study.

It is my belief that the search for regularities can pay off in scientific understanding because the strongest and most dependable relationships between the empirically different variables must be those which are generated, or systemically impelled, by similar internal dynamic processes of the whole system and each of its parts, which can be recognized as inherent or inevitable intercorrelations within any social-interaction system. In short, all social-interaction systems, I believe, are cognate and comparable to each other in certain of these systemic respects. Social interaction, wherever and whenever it occurs, even in very short temporary encounters, tends to generate a number of close and rapid feedbacks between particular mental and behavioral processes which then hang together and develop further into complicated relationships as a "dynamically organizing," and reorganizing, "system" so long as the interaction continues.

Even the smallest and most temporary set of social interactions tends to have such systemic tendencies. Every crystallized social-interaction system is a *fractal* part of all the larger and longer-lasting group systems of which it is a part. Each fractal part has system characteristics which are similar to, and partially generative of, all the larger group, organizational, and societal systems of which it is a part. Every social-interaction system is "self-similar" to the larger of such systems in which it is embedded, and all of its constituent subsystems are self-similar to each other and to it. Every such system, the larger, the intermediate, and the smaller, is unique in many respects, but they all have in common certain "systemic" elements and necessities, repeated over and over at each level of size.

Many of the systemic relationships that may be seen in small systems (small interacting groups, for example) have more complex counterparts in larger and more richly developed social systems of which they are a part. In looking at small-group studies, one needs to evaluate each generalization with the possibility in mind that the relationships that seem obvious and easy to understand at the small-group level may in fact be much more general in their implications. The relationships may be the emergents which are found as symbolic extensions, or even complete institutions, in larger systems. I suggest that the key to the fractal similarities between small and larger systems, the key which most comprehensively and understandably reveals the similarities, is the intercorrelation space of variables, broadly considered in terms of its many metaphorical extensions (see Appendix A).

## Vector Orthogonality Indicates Trouble in an Intact System

The psychological and social relationships among mental Images—perceptions, values, concepts, the pictures group members have of each other as persons—can be described in terms of their particular measured locations in the three dimensions of the theoretical space. The directions and degrees of their similarities and differences can be computed from their locations relative to each other. Some mental Images are positively correlated with each other, and are relatively close together in the intercorrelation space, and in the Field Diagram. Other mental Images are negatively correlated with each other, and are relatively far from each other, on opposite sides of the intercorrelation space, and the Field Diagram.

Psychologists utilizing factor analysis have repeatedly discovered, and lost sight of, parts of a global factor space defined by three bipolar dimensions of behavior and values. The studies have dealt with very different levels or aspects of behavior and perceptions, such as affects, fantasies, connotations of concepts, social attitudes, values, value statements, ideologies, nonverbal behavior, overt behavior, personality traits, perceptions of persons, and more. These factor-analytic studies will be reviewed in chapter 5. The very diversity of these domains is perhaps a part of the reason why the intercorrelation space of intact social-interaction systems has not been generally recognized as the natural framework for describing interpersonal behavior, value fields, and the relationships of differentiated and complex individuals within them. In particular studies, the factors have been found at different rotations in the intercorrelation space, and have not always been recognized as bipolar. Nor are they most typically orthogonal to each other in real, intact, operating groups.

Factor-analytic orthogonality of the three dimensions in the correlations of variables and values in real intact groups is not an optimal condition. In intact interacting groups orthogonality of the three main dimensions of social differentiation and social evaluation is symptomatic of widespread trouble—trouble in each of the three dimensions. My own interpretations of data, primarily from the SCG data bank, strongly imply that *if* the three positive ends of the Vectors called U, P, and F actually were found by factor analysis to be orthogonal in a specific *actually interacting* group, their orthogonal separation from each other would indicate a very threatening degree of conflict and disorganization in the values and relationships of the participants involved.

Statistical orthogonality of the three main dimensions in actual factor analyses is most likely to be found, I suspect, under one or more of the following conditions.

1.  The ratings are ratings of the meanings of the items themselves (that is, the items are concepts current in the language, rather than in the live evaluative perceptions of actual persons or things in a particular intact group).

2.  The number of descriptive items or concepts which have been collected and included as a population of items for factor analysis is very large, so that items of opposite meaning are more apt to be included.

3.  A minimal number of item descriptions have been preselected on conceptual or empirical exploratory grounds, as in the case of IOVAL, and have been arranged, as I have done with the cube diagram, to provide for the representation of opposites and similars, and to equalize the possible chances for endorsement or rejection of each of the items as applied to the reality involved.

4.  The rating judgments are made by raters who are unattached to each other, and perhaps unknown to each other. These can be called "unrelated-rater populations." The raters are not rating or choosing the acceptability of the items as characteristics of the members of intact groups to which they, as raters, belong. They are not describing their own values as directly applied to each other as members of the specific intact group. They do not have to live with the unpleasant results of over-differentiation in the ratings, or over-representation of the frequencies of negative or socially undesirable traits made in their own group. They do not have a coordinated bias toward the social desirability of the ratings they make. They do not have a bias encouraging them to make everything fit together as harmoniously as possible in the face of inquisitive outsiders.

I should point out that the makers and inventors of circumplexes of items and of factor-analytic and vector models, of whom I am one, are influenced by the last set of conditions described above. The makers of these instruments select the population of items and the populations or intact groups as the sources of data from which they construct their instruments. As a rule, they are not acting as ordinarily involved members of intact groups of the persons they study. They are not describing their evaluations of their own group members, or the values or traits that they actually think are desirable or undesirable in an intact interacting group to which they belong. They are trying to make instruments which will detect and display useful evidences of the traits and problems with which they have to deal, mostly one by one, as professional outside experts, and not as fellow group members.

This does not mean, of course, that members of intact groups, attempting to report how things actually are in their groups, always tend to report optimal conditions. This is definitely not the case. In any real intact social-interaction system, there are always pressures toward development of non-optimal behavior, such as competition for resources, personality differences in values, demands from the environment, and so on. These pressures and many others, tend to separate the U, P, and F vectors from positive correlations with each other and toward orthogonality, or even negative correlations with each other. Orthogonality of the three dimensions in an intact group is a bad sign for survival. In an actually interacting intact group, separation of the U, P, and F vectors which goes so far as to show actual right-angle orthogonality, or even further separation, is a visualized condition that raises the hair on the back of my neck.

## Conditions for Optimum Effectiveness

I believe that if one is trying to reach *optimum* effectiveness, which I take to mean a high probability of survival of the system *as a whole in the longer run*, then the three main vectors—U, P, and F—need to be brought into positive correlations with each other. Serious tendencies toward actual orthogonality of the three dimensions U-D, P-N, and F-B in an intact group, or toward negative correlations, as already mentioned, are indications of internal conditions that are anything but effective.

Of course many intact groups, probably most of them in fact, operate at a lower than optimum level of effectiveness and are still found to be surviving. But I think that a strong case can be made that the optimum condition is at least a moderate positive intercorrelation of the three main vectors—U, P, and F. Group members in business organizations, on the average, strongly agree with this position in their ratings as to what would be "ideal" for their operation in the future. In contrast, their ratings show, on the average, that the actual current culture of their organization or team is far from ideal.

Put plainly, in any system or group most effective operation is possible only to the extent that the following semi-coalitions can be established:

1.  The individuals who hold power and have the resources can be brought to lend their support and cooperation to those who are making task-oriented efforts and truly have the abilities to solve the problems of the group tasks (positive correlation of the U and F vectors);

2.  Those individuals whose main concern is the maintenance of relatively greater equality and group solidarity can be brought into cooperation with the individuals who work at task-oriented efforts (positive correlation of the P and F vectors); and

3.  The majority coalition of the whole group can be coordinated by a competent leader, or a set of cooperating leaders, who has been given legitimate authority and power (positive correlation between the U, P, and F vectors).

It is only by approximating this combination of members, their values, and their interactions that the group can be most effective in the long run in optimizing satisfaction, productivity, and in strengthening its prospects of survival.

These conditions of convergence can be clearly defined and seen on the Field Diagram of the present measurement and display system. If the conditions are met, one can see a pattern consisting of a unified cluster of images of members in the PF quadrant of the field, with the distribution or density pattern thinning out toward the edges, and with the mean of its bell-shaped density distribution in the *ideal* location in the Value Area Overlay on the Field Diagram.

In this density pattern, the area covered by images on the design of the Value Area Overlay is circular in its two-dimensional form. The distribution is contained almost fully by the Most Effective Teamwork Core and the two adjacent Side Areas, the more liberal and the more conservative. This essentially circular area on the plane of the Field Diagram, centered on the PF vector, defines the area I imagine to be a normally distributed degree of differentiation of values among individual members, generally consistent with the highest level of effectiveness that realistically can be expected.

All departures of images toward locations more distant on the Field Diagram, or more dominant, I believe, are damaging to effectiveness. Even the degree of separation of images to be found within the trivariate normal distribution around the effective teamwork area is disruptive, I assume, but the disruption and rejecting tendencies are not so strong that they cannot be countered by the mutual attraction afforded by interaction with others who are sufficiently similar in values and in need of cooperative relations. The most important kinds of departure from the optimum conditions can be clearly identified on a Field Diagram in various different forms of more scattered, irregular, polarized, or unbalanced patterns of images.

The conditions or part processes that generate problems for the system as a whole also can be seen in singularly marked departures of Bargraph profiles from the frequencies of value endorsement shown by the SCG Optimum. When an Image that has been rated with the Optimum-profile frequencies of the twenty-six vectors is propelled by the vector engine to its resultant single location on the Field Diagram, the image circle is located precisely in the center of the cluster on the Value Area Overlay called the Most Effective Teamwork Core. The two tests of optimum contribution to effectiveness—a close fit of the member images within the circular area in the PF quadrant in the pattern shown on the Field Diagram and a close fit to the Optimum profile on the Bargraph—are consistent with each other. In mathematical terms, they are two versions of the same thing.

My hypotheses that these two tests define the most effective patterns for social-interaction systems in general would be empirically testable hypotheses, except for two major caveats. The first caveat is the need to find and study all such systems, in order to test the hypotheses most convincingly. The second caveat is the need to find and apply a generally acceptable external criterion of "effectiveness," or "survival" in the long run. It is obvious that neither of these criteria can be fully satisfied.

But it will be possible to find, in continued practical work with teams and organizations, that singular and identifiable departures from the ideal or optimum patterns specified do reliably identify conditions of system operation that members will identify as "problems" they wish they could fix. And, (in hard-to-find conditions) it will be possible to find that approximations of the "most effective ideal" pattern tend to predict "external" criteria of effectiveness (see for example, Hogan 1988; Bachman 1988).

The ideal normative patterns indicate clearly the directions in which change would plausibly make for greater effectiveness, as members, *on the average over all members*, perceive it. The fact that the ideal patterns are empirically derived, that they consist in a constellation of balances and counterbalances of values that are measurable and achievable, rather than in a set of ideologically maximized deductions from one overly simple set of premises, surely will appeal to many. It is also a plus, in my opinion, that the ideal patterns have the property Aristotle recommended as "the golden mean." The theory definitely predicts that over-conformity, or extreme attempts to achieve virtue, are not *optimum*, at least in the longer run.

# Part 2
# Values

# 3

# The Centrality of Values

For some time sociologists have been trying to find ways of tying together more effectively what is known about small groups and what is known about larger groups, organizations, and complete societies. "Micro-systems" and "macro-systems" are believed to be somehow similar in important ways. But how can groups so disparate in size and in so many other ways be comparable?

I use the term "social-interaction systems" as a very general name for groups of all kinds and sizes. I believe that wherever actual social interaction continues over substantial time, certain behavioral, mental, and social processes tend to emerge and need to be studied together. These processes have regularities and patterns of interdependence (mutual shaping of each other) which almost require them to be treated as parts of a "system." These "systemic" characteristics are recognizably similar over a large range of group sizes.

Social-interaction systems of all sizes, even those as small as two persons, develop and change in ways that tend to elude individual intentions and attempts at control. Something like Adam Smith's "invisible hand" seems to be at work in developments, both desired and undesired, that emerge and persist in many aspects of social relationships. Nonetheless, it appears to me that intentional attempts to introduce changes in more desirable directions can only succeed on a substantial scale by understanding and harnessing these systemic processes.

Very central to groups of all sizes and kinds, as I see it, is that their internal processes and dynamics are represented, propelled, and regulated by concepts and urgencies in the minds of their members that behavioral scientists call "values" (C. Kluckhohn 1954). Thus, all social-interaction systems, irrespective of their size, include "values" as major organizational foci for cooperation and conflict and as sources of dynamic processes and change. Essentially the same may be said of values as they interact with each other in the mental processes of individual personalities.

I think it may turn out to be true that the most *efficient* way of representing the most important features of a group of almost any kind, and probably of most personalities, is by measurement of the degree and extent of acceptance or rejection of certain very general mental attitudes, called "values." The measurement of values can be an efficient approach because many, if not most, of the more important concrete kinds of social behavior as remembered in the mind and projected in expectations are represented cognitively in more brief and condensed form as "values."

The kind of values I have in mind are complex, higher-order mental processes. A "value" is a process of "evaluating." It is a mental process in the mind of an individual that relates perceptions, images, fantasies, and concepts to each other. When the person is involved in social interaction with other persons the mental process includes meanings that refer simultaneously to a set of mental images in the individual's mind and to corresponding events in the group.

The mental process I call a value also has a physiological and behavioral reality in the body of the person; the process of evaluating calls forth a mobilization of energy and a conscious feeling in the individual. A value in action is a mobilization of physiologically based motives and instinctual tendencies, but at the same time those underlying motives are oriented to action by a set of emotionally toned cognitive generalizations and images of the self and others in the mind of the individual about the way things *should* go in social behavior.

A value formulates at a mental level the image of a direction and pattern of intentional behavior more or less clearly worked out in the mind. The pattern is formulated as a set of intentions for the self and expectations of others. One's values are felt to be justified. They are felt to be part of a larger and more extensive structure of other values, which are also felt to be justified and which demand to be maintained.

This already very complex mental process is backed up still further by a readiness to feel moral indignation if the intention is frustrated, or if others do not act as the value prescribes. A value involves some visualization or conception of the self as acting in some justified way in relation to some other individual or group, and as *receiving* approval from some source for so acting. Seeing that the value is realized in behavior by both self and others is felt by the person who harbors it to be necessary to maintain an acceptable self-picture and acceptance of others.

No doubt there are important individual and developmental differences in complexity, but I assume that even quite young persons come into new situations of social interaction with values already extensively formed and organized. In the evaluative processes of most adults, mental images of the many concrete forms of social behavior that have not yet actually materialized are already visualized and expected.

For example, a value may well include assumptions and expectations that there will be some kind of role for the self, that there will be some development and maintenance of status differences, that there will be some kind of leadership, some division of labor, some differentiation of social roles, that some other individuals will not comply, and others may deviate from the values the individual approves, that there will be cooperation and conflict between leaders and their subgroups, and so on. In brief, the process of "evaluating," is an interior mental picturing of the external "drama" of social interaction as it *should* go from the point of view of the evaluating individual.

Most treatments of values in the literature do not describe a value as an evaluative mental and physiological process that is so complex. Nor do most treatments include so many disparate aspects, so extensively and intimately tied together, as the description I have given. Perhaps I have gone too far. Nevertheless, serious efforts to put together the results of research, in spite of the fact that the various approaches are seriously fragmented, amply demonstrate that values do exist as mental processes something like those I have described. The processes are complicated, and participants in groups inevitably evaluate, more or less completely, essentially all aspects of their lives, alone and together.

### Value Consistencies and Inconsistencies

Values are *mental* parts of the system, that is, they are attitudes and evaluative concepts, often formulated in terms of explicit beliefs, located in the minds of individuals. Each individual has values in some form or other as part of his or her own personality and social identity. All individuals tend to use these mental abstractions in efforts to control and justify their own behavior and to exert influences over other individuals.

The variegated total of values active in a given group may be considered to constitute a "value system." It should be recognized as a "system" because, as time goes on, its conflicting and cooperating parts tend to change and consolidate their relationships to form patterns. In most cases, the interdependence tends to form, willy-nilly, a larger, more simply patterned "whole." That whole I call a "dynamic system field." It is in motion and it is patterned.

The parts of a dynamic system field, that is, the different values, and the different persons who harbor them, are typically constrained in one way or another by circumstances and compelled to work upon each other. In shorter time periods they change each other, repeatedly. Over longer time periods small changes accumulate and certain larger patterns emerge. Occasionally big switch-overs and chaotic episodes of "thrashing about" occur. The more durable patterns of cooperation and conflict which evolve, in part unwittingly, turn out to be important determinants of success in problem solving, in longer term effectiveness, and may even ultimately affect the survival of the group.

Different kinds of shifts in acceptability and emphasis of the pattern of values occur in order to address the problems and demands of different situations. When the situation shifts, the relative emphasis and center of gravity of the person's internal value system also tends to shift to some extent, sometimes to a major extent. For example, at particular times, notably in times of severe threat, the relative emphasis and center of gravity of the individual's total value system tends to shift. In times of war, as we know, even gentle persons learn to kill, although some will not. And some normally restrained warriors become vicious in actual battle conditions. Under stress, some values that are ordinarily disapproved or rejected come to the fore as acceptable.

At any given time, conflicting or rejected aspects of the value system tend to be rationalized away or concealed, even from one's own conscious awareness. Values, which by their nature are vague, abstract, and general, even at their clearest, may acquire quite different meanings under stress. The concrete meanings and applicability may even completely reverse their usual sense of meaning.

The evaluations that different individuals naturally make are bound to conflict with each other, at least to some extent. Evaluations ("values") interact, support, and conflict with each other in the communication of individuals in groups, and a similar struggle goes on as well within the mental processes of each individual.

The values that exist as very general attitudes within each person's head have implications for other values in the same person's head. Some of the values tend to deny the desirability of others, even though they all continue to exist in some strength in the same mind and to contend with each other. They tend to be drawn or propelled into various more or less consistent clusters in the person's mind, according to various kinds of similarity or mutual consistency, as seen by that person.

Consistency among values in the same individual is not to be taken for granted. For example, most persons who think of themselves as democratic tend to harbor some authoritarian tendencies in addition to their anti-authoritarian tendencies. The same is true of persons regarded as authoritarian. One can hardly name a real person widely regarded as an authoritarian who does not attack other persons or agencies in authority, and whose values in short, are in part anti-authoritarian. Autocratic authoritarians often have, or think they have, some democratic values. They often believe that what they recommend is good for the group as a whole. The same is true of rebels. Many persons who think of themselves as anti-authoritarian rebels nevertheless tend to be autocratic if they act as leaders in their revolutionary subgroup. At the same time they may well think of themselves as champions of the oppressed, and in this sense may see themselves as democratic.

In spite of the mixtures and logical inconsistencies, whatever cluster of values is relatively accepted by a person at a given time tends to imply, or to compel, a relative rejection of other clusters. Relatively rejected values do not simply cease to exist in the person's mind. They tend to remain as parts of the same personality, but in reduced strength, or more heavily resisted, than before they were rejected. Although reduced in strength, rejected values (in the same way as accepted values) tend to be drawn or propelled toward each other into semi-consistent clusters of values that support or reinforce each other.

All of us tend to harbor conflicting clusters of values in our personalities. The values within each cluster hang together to some extent (they are positively intercorrelated) and repel the values in other clusters. None of us is compacted simply of values that are all consistent with each other.

The presence of value inconsistencies suggests that almost everybody is of at least two or three minds about almost everything of any real social importance. This phenomenon could be called a "law of universal social ambivalence." The fact that we cannot help holding on to conflicting sets of values, and are at least a little ambivalent about almost all of them, is surely one of the reasons that unexpected systemic processes set in among us when we try to get along with each other, and why unforeseen systemic repercussions sometimes elude our best efforts at reasonable control. Previously rejected values, if the "interpersonal chemistry" is just so, tend to break out and defeat our best efforts.

Almost any group of persons who become engaged in actual real-life interaction for any length of time will find that value conflicts emerge, both with regard to problems they face in their external environment and with regard to their relationships with each other. Quite within the normal range of individual differences, randomly chosen individuals are likely to disagree to some extent, often to a disruptive extent, on which values are good and bad, and on what priorities should be given to which values with regard to their particular group and situation.

The different priorities given by different participants to important values influence strongly the overt system of interaction, even though many of the values have not been made public in the group, and may even be concealed. These values have as their content particular preferred resolutions of differences among the members concerning how they feel and what they believe is "right" about features of the group.

## Selection Criteria for a Value Schedule

It is not very useful for present purposes to try to define the term "values" in the most general abstract sense for academic or philosophical purposes. The present approach concentrates on values concerned with social interaction. For "values concerned with social interaction" the present theory presents a finely tuned and detailed *working solution* of the problems of measurement posed by great variety and multiplicity, even in this more restricted realm of values. I believe it is a solution that will help in the development of a general theory of social-interaction systems. But it took me years of labor and refinement to discover and recognize it, and to articulate it for practical use.

The solutions I offer were not arrived at by deductive thought alone. I do not think the necessary elements for a working model can be created simply by deduction from some philosophical base of major premises no matter how appealing it may be. Many of the solutions I propose were the result of patient systematic research of many cumulative empirical studies, most of them by direct observation of actual groups, measurement of their values, and attempts to influence relationships and processes within them for the better, through feedback and interpretation of members' own observations. Some aspects of the working solution were lucky discoveries. Others required something like invention. In any case, the classification of critically important values, the modes of measurement, the most useful categories and intervals for aggregation of the data, the analyses and implications which I present, are not necessarily obvious. Nor can the problems and solutions be explained in a few words. A number of separable and non-obvious parts and elements are necessary to a real working solution.

An unimaginably complex constellation of values must be subject to drastic reduction and selection of the variables that are actually to be measured in order to discover any workable approach for describing and understanding the most important aspects of a social-interaction system. The selection must be representative of the most critically important variables, whatever that may mean in the given case.

My working assumption is that the most critical kinds of values will be found to focus on emergent features of the system. These center around the nature and control of various aspects of the social-interaction process itself, as it takes place among the participants. Thus, the most critical values concern dynamic relationships. The emerging features of the group, sometimes called aspects of group "structure," tend to include regularities such as: differential status among the members, division of labor among different roles, the emergence of different contenders for leadership representing quite different values, legitimate and illegitimate sources of authority, the sources and impact of power, subgroups holding different values, the relative balance of power among subgroups and its effects on overall group solidarity, and so on. (These features are implicit in the content of the limited set of value variables to be measured, but they are explicit in visible form on the Field Diagram.)

The same schedule of the most important values to be measured should serve to describe both the critically important features of personality and the critically important features of larger social-interaction systems.

The schedule of values to be measured will need to contain representative exemplars of the most important conflicting values, as well as those that are reinforcing. The priorities given to different values by the different participants, the degrees of consensus and disagreement on the various emerging aspects of the group are regulators of the way the interaction continues. Pre-existing and emerging value priorities strongly affect the group's prospects of success in further respects such as problem solving, productivity, effectiveness, and so on. Having an opposite for each value is important in contributing to validity and reliability in measuring the particular behavioral content of the value. Also, it is important as a method for determining the fewest number of distinct items required for a comprehensive schedule of values.

Item phrasing needs to be sufficiently ambiguous such that serious evaluation is required by users of the item system. If there is something like a "law of universal social ambivalence," as suggested earlier, it has strong implications for the way in which the actual items for an instrument to measure values need to be worded in order to measure properly. Items must not be worded so strongly in favor of some particular values that normally ambivalent human beings are unable to endorse them. Nor must they be so self-evidently fated to be rejected that hardly anybody could accept them.

The number and content of values involved in social interaction is far too great and varied to be measured in total. A representative and compact way is required to portray the distributions of the most critically important values. A number of factor analyses reported in the literature give clues as to the critical dimensions to be sampled, although they have not yet generally been recognized to bear on the problems at issue here. The factor-analytic data, properly put together, justify the delineation of a limited and definable set of value variables for measurement, values that are highly likely to become actively problematic in almost any social interaction that is continued over substantial time. Some of the relevant factor analyses and the implications will be discussed in chapter 5, "The Intercorrelation Space."

The values included in the present method of measurement are designed, on the basis of empirical data drawn mostly from factor-analytic studies, to be a representative set. The distributions of intensity, frequency, and more specific meanings of these values among different members and subgroups, are among the most important things a leader or a theorist needs to know in order to understand the major features, the directions, and the relative power of the converging and contrary dynamics under way in the group. The theory prescribes certain ways of aggregating the data in order to display the most important information about the existing and probably emerging patterns.

The process of identification and selection of items to most efficiently and accurately represent the total relevant population of values is absolutely critical to the kind of further synthesis and analysis that the present system makes possible. The choice of values selected for the limited list of twenty-six items and the precise wordings of the descriptions are the result of a long process of research and development, which will be described in detail in the following chapters. The selection of the items is the heart of the mathematical intercorrelation model that enables the researcher-consultant to see the overall pattern of the effects of the many particular values on each other, and the most probable patterns of conflict and cooperation of group members with each other.

Without a very good simplifying theory that allows one to select the most critically important variables for measurement and interpretation, the concept of a "value system" is almost useless for practical purposes. However, I believe that it is possible to measure and describe most of the "critically important" differences in value priorities among participants within the limited, systemically relevant, and interdependent set of twenty-six value variables. The critically important differences in priorities constitute the central foci of cooperation and conflict in a particular group. I propose that it is possible, in principle at least, to draw a practically small sample of types of values, strategically chosen, that will adequately represent the values most likely to be important in the self-organizing dynamics of most social-interaction systems, large as well as small.

The patterns become visible in a specific kind of analysis which places individuals and clusters of them in a "dynamic system field pattern" portrayed on a Field Diagram. Information so aggregated and systematized is critically important in trying to plan and anticipate the probable "effectiveness" of attempted leadership. In this sense, the limited set of measured variables I am about to propose may be called a set of "critically important values."

### Instruments for a Working Solution

Instead of trying to develop further a fundamental rationale, I propose simply to present the working instruments which are the end result of my efforts and then by degrees to explain later how they got to be that way. In brief, the working instruments are the rating form for collecting data, the diagrams for display of analysis, and the empirical evaluative norms for interpretation of displays.

A standard IOVAL rating form consisting of my strategic set of twenty-six value descriptors is used for all SCG studies (see figure 1.2). Using this form, persons, groups, or types of action can be described in terms of the particular values they exemplify. Comparable descriptions are gathered to represent the different points of view of the participants in the group concerning individual members, the group as a whole, its policies, its current culture, a personal or group desired future, and so on. The data profiles on these various objects of perception and evaluation are used for feedback and consultation, and subsequently amassed in the data bank.

A general name is needed to refer to the "object focus" that group members, as raters, describe by their ratings. The general name for this focus is *Image*. An Image, for example, might be the "self-image," a rating of the *self*. On the IOVAL rating form, a rater responds to a carefully worded question which specifies the Image. For the *self* Image, the question reads as follows:

In general, what kinds of values do *you* actually show in your behavior?

In answering this question, the rater considers each of the twenty-six items in turn and makes a rating of the frequency with which the value descriptor is appropriately associated with the focal Image. The rater gives an answer by choosing an estimate of the frequency: *Rarely, Sometimes,* or *Often.*

Usually more than one question is posed and the rater responds to all twenty-six items for the first question before moving to the next question and again considering the set of twenty-six items. Other typical questions concerning self-perceptions include:

> In general, what kinds of values do you *wish* to show in your own behavior, whether or not you are actually able to do so?

> In general, what kinds of values do you tend to *reject*, either in yourself or others?

Questions may be asked about specific other group members, the group as a whole, or other larger social systems. Appendix B shows a list of nineteen such rating questions for which large samples of data exist in the SCG data bank.

To obtain a Bargraph, sets of ratings of a single Image by a group of raters are averaged. Figure 3.1 shows a Bargraph of average ratings of *other team members* (OTM). The raters were members of work teams in which all members knew each other well. All individuals rated each other in answer to the following question:

> In general, what kinds of values does this person show in his or her behavior?

From a parent population of 24,376 rating sets, a sample of 1000 was drawn randomly.

The Bargraph in figure 3.2 shows the average of 1000 ratings from similar business groups to a different question, again posed for each of the other team members:

> In general, what kinds of values would be *ideal* for this person to show in behavior in order to be *most effective*?

The differences of the ratings of *other team members* (figure 3.1) and *ideal* to be most effective (figure 3.2) are notable.

The Bargraphs in figures 3.1 and 3.2 illustrate that different values are endorsed (or said, in effect, to be characteristic of the Image) with quite different frequencies. The frequencies are widely different for different value items in some cases. For example, on the Bargraph of *other team members* (OTM), Item 20 DF—*Obedience to the chain of command, complying with authority*—is endorsed as an appropriate description for the Image of a teammate with an average frequency in the *Often* interval. On the other hand, Item 24 DB—*Passive non-cooperation with authority*—shows an average fre-

**94    Social Interaction Systems**

**FIGURE 3.1**

**Bargraph of 1000 ratings on *Values that this Person
Shows in His or Her Behavior* (OTM)**

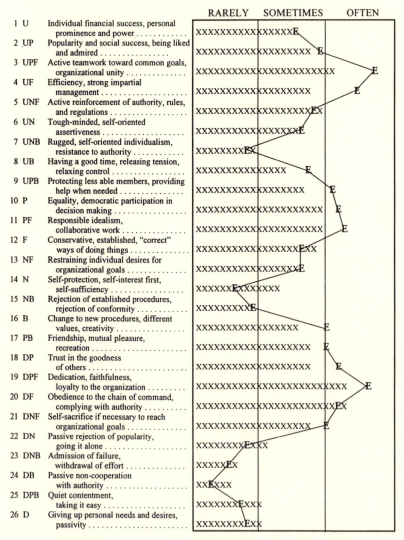

*Source*: © 1997 SYMLOG Consulting Group, San Diego, CA. Reprinted by permission.

**FIGURE 3.2**

**Bargraph of 1000 Ratings on *Values that Would Be Ideal for this Person to Show in Order to Be Most Effective* (IDL)**

Type: PF    Final Location: 2.7U 6.6P 6.9F

Ratings: 1000

the bar of X's = the average rating on each item

E = the *optimum* location for most effective teamwork

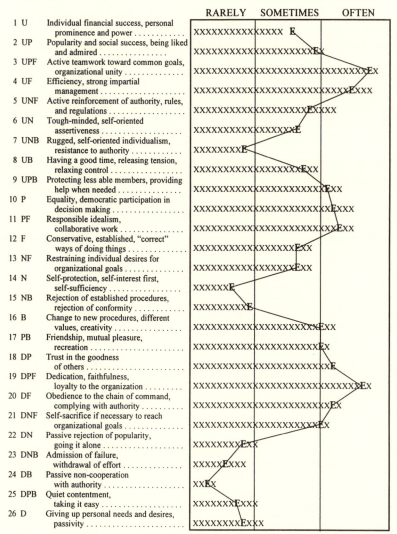

|  | | | RARELY | SOMETIMES | OFTEN |
|---|---|---|---|---|---|
| 1 | U | Individual financial success, personal prominence and power | | | |
| 2 | UP | Popularity and social success, being liked and admired | | | |
| 3 | UPF | Active teamwork toward common goals, organizational unity | | | |
| 4 | UF | Efficiency, strong impartial management | | | |
| 5 | UNF | Active reinforcement of authority, rules, and regulations | | | |
| 6 | UN | Tough-minded, self-oriented assertiveness | | | |
| 7 | UNB | Rugged, self-oriented individualism, resistance to authority | | | |
| 8 | UB | Having a good time, releasing tension, relaxing control | | | |
| 9 | UPB | Protecting less able members, providing help when needed | | | |
| 10 | P | Equality, democratic participation in decision making | | | |
| 11 | PF | Responsible idealism, collaborative work | | | |
| 12 | F | Conservative, established, "correct" ways of doing things | | | |
| 13 | NF | Restraining individual desires for organizational goals | | | |
| 14 | N | Self-protection, self-interest first, self-sufficiency | | | |
| 15 | NB | Rejection of established procedures, rejection of conformity | | | |
| 16 | B | Change to new procedures, different values, creativity | | | |
| 17 | PB | Friendship, mutual pleasure, recreation | | | |
| 18 | DP | Trust in the goodness of others | | | |
| 19 | DPF | Dedication, faithfulness, loyalty to the organization | | | |
| 20 | DF | Obedience to the chain of command, complying with authority | | | |
| 21 | DNF | Self-sacrifice if necessary to reach organizational goals | | | |
| 22 | DN | Passive rejection of popularity, going it alone | | | |
| 23 | DNB | Admission of failure, withdrawal of effort | | | |
| 24 | DB | Passive non-cooperation with authority | | | |
| 25 | DPB | Quiet contentment, taking it easy | | | |
| 26 | D | Giving up personal needs and desires, passivity | | | |

*Source:* © 1997 SYMLOG Consulting Group, San Diego, CA. Reprinted by permission.

quency in the *Rarely* interval. The values tapped by the two items are directly opposed to each other in the intercorrelation space so it is to be expected that the two items will show frequencies toward the opposite ends of the scale.

Each value item in the set of twenty-six has such an opposite, as will be discussed in more detail in chapter 5, "The Intercorrelation Space." Thus, for example, the description for Item 1 U reads *Individual financial success, personal prominence and power*, whereas its diametrical opposite, Item 26 D, reads *Giving up personal needs and desires, passivity*. Item 10 P reads *Equality, democratic participation in decision making*, whereas its diametrical opposite, Item 14 N, reads *Self-protection, self-interest first, self-sufficiency*. Item 12 F reads *Conservative, established, "correct" ways of doing things*, whereas its diametrical opposite, Item 16 B, reads *Change to new procedures, different values, creativity*.

No doubt, the psychologically relativistic nature of the judgment of frequency used for all ratings, on all the value items, and on all the Images rated is important. The meaning of the vague descriptive term *Often* is surely different for values that have high optimum frequencies (such as Item 3 UPF) than for items that have low optimum frequencies (such as Item 24 DB). The meaning of *Rarely*, *Sometimes*, and *Often* must also be very differently adjusted in the rater's mind depending on the item. Research on these problems is needed, but the practical method works very well indeed.

Very likely too, the constrained three-interval scale is important. This constrained scale prevents single individuals from recording very strong responses. This in turn tends to deemphasize the variability within the value system of particular individuals, and places the emphasis rather on the relative proportion of individuals in the group who assign the given rating.

How does one tell what Images are necessary to ask about? The theory does not specify what Images are necessary in order to best sample the "most critically important" aspects of the system. Although this could be regarded as a fatal flaw, experience has told us a great deal about what Images are almost always important to ask about in preparation for discussion on problems of the system.

The real leverage comes, not from a theoretical closure on a definitive schedule of Images, which must be covered in the rating process, but from the fact that the *same* value items are used to describe (evaluate) all Images. As one views the value profile of one Image after another—the "wished for" compared with the "rejected," the current "actual" compared to what is believed to be "most effective," one leader compared to another, one subgroup compared to another—the similarities and contrasts inexorably build up a picture of the holistic aspects of the system, its conflicts as well as its convergences. The evidences of conflicts and convergences throw light on critically important dynamics. This is the knowledge that gives real intellectual and practical leverage for influencing the current processes of change.

In fact, it appears that the IOVAL instrument provides a general-purpose *method* of attitude measurement for making *final outcome evaluations* of particular Images of particular individual personalities, cultures, social structures, issues in relation to the situation, and so on.

## The *Estimated* Optimum Profile for the Bargraph

It will be noticed that a zigzag vertical line is shown on the Bargraph. This profile is called the *estimated* Optimum value profile, or the normative profile. The "E" stands for "Estimate of Effective," which is used in SCG consulting. The Optimum profile is empirically derived from respondents' concepts of "Most Effective." The actual basis I have proposed for computation of the normative Optimum profile also takes account of additional moderating elements, as described in chapter 10, "Can There Be an *Optimum* Value Profile?"

The location of the "E" on the normative profile, to which the length of a bar representing an observed frequency may be compared, differs for most of the twenty-six value items. The whole Optimum profile, taken as a vertical pattern, shows three fairly regular "waves" of increasing and decreasing frequency.

These three waves appear as a result of several facts. First, in real group operation, as group members typically recognize, if all the values on the list were shown in behavior with equal frequency, the system could not possibly be "most effective." The values which appear to raters to be most conducive to effectiveness (as can be seen in figure 3.2) are endorsed with higher frequencies than values that are believed to be less effective.

Second, the value items were written and arranged in an explicit theoretical order on the list of twenty-six. The order was expected to predict more or less closely the frequencies of endorsement they would likely receive, on the average. The order exemplifies the pattern of intercorrelations the value items typically show in factor analyses of various types of Images in various types of groups, as will be explained in chapter 5.

What does "optimum" mean in the present context? I want it to mean a profile of values that minimizes the "problems" likely to be encountered in the normal functioning of the group who has provided the ratings. Such problems will be recognized and identified as undesirable by a majority of the members of the group.

Indication of a problem is a deviation of the observed frequency from the normative Optimum frequency. How much deviation may be regarded as significant? In a statistical sense, this depends upon the kind of Image rated, the size of the parent population, the size of the sample, and so on. But these important factors do not remain the same from one application to the next. In consultation there is never enough time to deal with all the data. What is needed for practical application is a simple rule of thumb for noting obvious departures from the normative profile.

My rule of thumb is to consider an item frequency different from the norm if it is four or more Xs distant from the E, whether below or above. The single criterion is applied even though the value items have widely different average frequencies. This single criterion for the size of deviation from the normative profile proves to be adequate for practical purposes, over the complete range of Bargraph profiles we normally see. The same size of deviation seems to detect what the majority of members of the system are apt to regard as "problems."

Application of the four-X-departure rule to the Bargraph on *other team members* (figure 3.1) indicates that only one item is above the norm: Item 14 N, *Self-protection, self-interest first, self-sufficiency.* The average frequencies for the following items are below the norm:

| | | |
|---|---|---|
| 3 | UPF | *Active teamwork toward common goals, organizational unity* |
| 4 | UF | *Efficiency, strong impartial management* |
| 9 | UPB | *Protecting less able members, providing help when needed* |
| 16 | B | *Change to new procedures, different values, creativity* |
| 18 | DP | *Trust in the goodness of others.* |

The deviations all appear to point to deficiencies in showing values members regard as desirable ingredients of effective teamwork. It is not hard to imagine that these various departures are connected with each other.

The working hypothesis I have offered for a practical test of "non-optimality" is that a four-X deviation from the E location indicates a "problem." I do not really expect perfect confirmation, but experience so far strongly supports the working hypothesis in the contexts of American business with which SCG has had contact. The estimated Optimum value profile is eminently fitted to use as a norm in practical assessment and feedback of results to individuals, teams, and organizations in American business contexts.

For other cultural contexts, we have had some relevant experience that demonstrates the applicability of the norm, if the translation and validation of the value descriptors has been well done. It is likely, however, that there will be cases where deviations will be interpreted by group members as indicating cultural differences, which they do not necessarily regard as "problems," and in some cases they may regard the differences as "virtues." In such cases, the estimated Optimum profile is useful as a basis for comparing and understanding important cultural differences.

## An Unexpected Convergence toward Effectiveness

Although it was not clearly anticipated, it turns out, as an empirical finding, that in spite of different conditions in different groups, and over many different environmental situations, there is a strong and regular convergence of raters' judgments of what frequencies of the various twenty-six values are "most effective."

There is an unexpectedly precise but still puzzling pattern of underlying meaning of "most effective." It is shown in the remarkably high frequency of certain values on the profile of relative frequencies over the twenty-six variables for the Image of *ideal* for "most effective" (figure 3.2). And it is also shown in the precise mean location and the surrounding bell-shaped curve of density of images of "most effective" on the Field Diagram (see figure 2.10). These puzzling results and their possible implications are discussed in chapter 9, "The Mystery of *Most Effective* Values."

The precision and unexpected regularity of this pattern is one of the most important findings of the study. The interlocking links by which it appears to come about seem to me to throw unexpected light on one of the traditionally puzzling problems of sociology, namely, what are the more detailed fundamental processes and their linkages by which a workable degree of overall "order" is developed and maintained in social systems?

Experience as well as theory about what raters mean by the concept of "most effective" has essentially confirmed for me the hypothesis that for practical purposes, the very same Optimum profile is not only appropriate, but gives critical leverage in understanding Bargraphs and Field Diagrams of all the different kinds of Images for which we normally obtain ratings. Thus, the same normative Optimum profile can be used for the whole range of kinds of Images, irrespective of group size, types of group, personality differences, different roles, and so on.

How can it be the case that the same normative profile and the same criterion of deviation seems appropriate for all Images? I think this is true because the value items, in their content and in their level of abstraction, in fact do formulate standards of evaluation that are highly related to members' concepts of "effectiveness." Concepts of "effectiveness" seem to be close to concepts of "favorable final outcome" for the system as a whole.

## Values and Emergent Features of the System

The heart of the present theory of social-interaction systems is the set of methods for identifying and measuring the set of potentially most critically important values that are typically involved in such a process. With the ability to measure these values one can begin to identify and understand the various kinds of self-organizing patterns that tend to appear and change over time.

It is important to emphasize that, according to the theory, the total pattern is largely the result of such "self-organizing" processes. The pattern tends to emerge whether or not any specific individuals intend for it to do so, and often in spite of their intentions. Individual decisions and acts of leadership can influence the development of the total pattern to some extent, particularly in smaller groups, but individual efforts always operate within a dynamic system context.

The twenty-six individual values measured in the present system do not operate simply as individual values, apart from the prominent features of the overt interaction system. Rather, the values and the overt behaviors are intercorrelated both positively and negatively. In certain kinds of situations the values seem to sort themselves out into several subsets. There will appear to be some mutually supporting values within a given subset, but in many cases the subsets will conflict with each other. The pattern of apparently supporting and opposing subsets will be different to some extent for each group.

As communication goes on in second and third meetings of a newly assembled group it begins to become more clear which persons hold which values. Persons who sense that they hold a sufficiently consistent subset of values begin to form a semi-unified cluster, or subgroup. Opposing individuals begin to form one or more subgroups. As time goes on, these subgroups may begin to meet "outside" the regular meeting place, in intermissions, after and before regular meetings.

As persons agree and disagree with each other and try to solve their problems, internal and external, a "self-organizing" tendency of the whole "system" is revealed. A *polarization* of two (or often three) *semi-unified clusters* of the values, and persons holding them, begins to assume more definite shape. Individuals begin to find their places within the subgroup in which the members seem most similar in values to themselves as individual personalities.

Participants in the system, leaders as well as members, often have a poor cognitive grasp of what is going on throughout the total system. The pattern is "spread out," "decentralized," "not yet assembled," and nobody is in a position to see it very well. The particular values that are most visibly involved are hardly ever the whole story. More and different values may be involved than are immediately visible. They are distributed unevenly and in unknown strengths over a number of different persons, perhaps scattered in different subgroups. There are potential leaders prepared to lead in different directions who emerge into visibility only over a span of time.

In the ever-recurring processes of social interaction, individuals are essentially forced by the circumstances of their interaction and environmental constraints into roles of reciprocal and oppositional value directions by the nature of their involvement in the same dynamic social-interaction system.

The interactional roles, by degrees, are organized over time into more explicitly formulated values which survive beyond the life of all particular groups as a part of the larger culture, and are detailed further into perceived personality traits of individuals based on their behavior. The nature of the empirical regularities of behavior which appear to be the source are described in detail in chapters 6, 7, and 8. The hypothesized nature of the process of cultural evolution, and its effect on the values of social desirability and undesirability ascribed to personality traits, are discussed in chapter 9.

## Correlation Patterns between Value Items

In research on a particular Image, such as *self*, over large varied populations, on the average, some values are closely related to each other. For example, consider Items 12 F and 13 NF (on the Bargraph). Values on Item 12 F—*Conservative, established, "correct" ways of doing things*—seem to most people to be quite similar to those on Item 13 NF—*Restraining individual desires for organizational goals.* Sometimes raters even complain that they cannot tell the difference between these two items (or some other pairs of items, particularly those in consecutive positions in the list). The values of Items 12 F and 13 NF are "allied," but separated (at an angle of about forty-five degrees) because they were selected and designed to be partly correlated. In survey studies they are positively correlated with each other, though not perfectly. The people who recommend the first are quite likely also to recommend the second, but the second has an added implied Negative element that distinguishes it from the first.

Other values are more or less directly opposite in meaning from these particular ones. For example, the values of Item 16 B—*Change to new procedures, different values, creativity*—seem contrary to the values of Item 12 F—*Conservative, established, "correct" ways of doing things.* Values for Items 16 B and 12 F are "polarized," that is, "negatively correlated" with each other. The persons who recommend the values of the first item are quite likely to reject the values of the second, and vice versa.

The values of Item 16 B—*Change to new procedures, different values, creativity*—have their own allies, for example, the values of Item 17 PB—*Friendship, mutual pleasure, recreation.* In survey studies value Items 16 B and 17 PB tend to be positively correlated, though there is a degree of separation between them. This relationship that has been built in intentionally by selection and design of the items.

Still other values just seem to be "different" from the most obviously polarized pairs, maybe because they are concerned with an unrelated aspect of social relationships. In research studies, on the average, over large heterogeneous populations, Item 10 P—*Equality, democratic participation in decision making*—turns out to be neither correlated with Item 12 F, on conservatism, nor with Item 16 B, on change to new procedures. In statistical language, 10 P can be said to be "zero correlated" with 12 F, and also zero correlated with 16 B. But this is only true for some groups. (As noted in chapter 2, it is definitely not optimum in an intact group for the values concerning friendliness [10 P] to be "orthogonal" to the values concerned with conservative task-oriented behavior [12 F].)

Item 10 P—*Equality, democratic participation in decision making*—has its own diametrical opposite, namely Item 14 N—*Self-protection, self-interest first, self-sufficiency.* In survey studies, generally, 10 P is negatively correlated with 14 N. This means that persons who are likely to accept and recommend Item 10 P are likely to reject 14 N, and vice versa. Values on 10 P and 14 N can be said to be "polarized." This value difference, of course, is likely to affect the relations of members of a group who happen to disagree on these values, and these conflicts are likely to interfere with optimum performance.

Research using the IOVAL instrument shows that there are some persons who are not very good at understanding why certain values are negatively correlated to each other, or why others are positively correlated with each other, or why still others are zero correlated over large heterogeneous populations. They put certain values together in certain ways in their own minds, and keep other values apart in ways that are uncharacteristic.

Most people, of course, do not see the relationships of their values to each other in terms of statistical measures of relationship of the kind we are using, like positive and negative correlations. They see things in ways that are more or less peculiar to their own personalities, or to what seems to them to be necessary for the optimum functioning of their particular intact group, in a way that "seems right" to them. Compared to the statistical correlations over broad heterogeneous populations between particular values, many individual persons seem to be "biased" to some significant degree in one way or another. Some unrecognized biases may actually be helpful in the particular intact group. But others may be unwittingly harmful.

Some persons find it very difficult to understand how others can see values related in a way so different from their own way of seeing them. There are strongly motivated reasons for this in the individual personalities but the reasons are not simple to understand. And it is not simple to try to help some such individual persons understand why their perceptions are so different, or to change them.

What are the reasons for the correlations, oppositions, and alternatively, the lack of predictable relationships (zero correlations) between particular values and clusters of values that are found? I deliberately selected and carefully worded the twenty-six value items to fairly represent the three different main dimensions of differences in values conceived to be theoretically at right angles to each other. Then I formulated value wordings for all of the exactly intermediately spaced intervals.

I made the selections only after extensive exploration. There are a number of factor-analytic studies of the ways in which values differ in real social, economic, political, cultural, religious, and philosophical life in the United States and other countries. My own researches, which were as broad and variegated as I could make them at the time, began in the mid-1950s. The problems of how to describe values and their empirical relationships to each other are not at all new. But I think it has not been realized how much convergent evidence there is about the average factor structure of many apparently diverse kinds, perched around in many places in the literature. And the ways in which the various analyses fit together into one coherent pattern is not obvious. I review a part of this evidence in chapter 5, "The Intercorrelation Space."

The ways in which values correlate with each other influence the relationships group members form as time goes on. Subgroups tend to form of persons who have similar interests. This is likely to put them into conflict with other subgroups of members who have opposing interests. Values concerned with social relationships are not based strictly on "ideas" or on "logic" or on abstract "justice." They are based on the differentiated places of individuals and subgroups in the *total* system of social relationships as they have developed and continue to change over time.

It is no real puzzle, then, that the correlational relationships between values differ (as they do) according to the Image that one asks about. Images tap different interests. The Image means somewhat different things to different people because individuals and subgroups are different from each other in their values and have different places in the total system of social relationships.

Moreover, the correlation pattern for one group differs to some extent from the pattern for any other for any given Image rated. It is not literally accurate to talk, as I may have appeared to do above, as if there were one "true" set of allied values and their dependable opposites. What I have said above about what "research shows" as to the correlations between particular values—positive, negative, or zero—is only roughly and relatively true, on the average, over many individuals, many groups, many Images, and over widely varied populations. The empirical regularities I have reported above as to "what research shows" vary to a considerable extent from group to group.

A given correlation pattern is actually a set of statistical measures of the consensus and dissent among a particular group of raters, and the subgroups of raters, concerning their values and their evaluations of a particular Image in particular time and place. We know in advance that the raters are not likely to understand exactly the same thing as to what "the Image" or "the issue" is. And we fully expect that they will show at least some disagreement about it, and maybe a lot.

## Values Constitute *Real Live* Systems

I designed the value items in IOVAL to be systematic measurement "probes," that is, strategically distributed sampling probes for research, appropriate to reach into essentially all important parts of the total space of similar and conflicting values concerned with social relationships, as these values exist in individual minds, and as they are embodied in social norms. I chose and designed the number and distribution of the items to probe the maximally separated areas in the space of value differences.

For purposes of making a good model for sampling I took care to try to reach into all the intermediate directions that are just half way between the major "orthogonal" dimensions (those three bipolar dimensions which are maximally separated). In addition (for purposes of economy and efficiency of measurement) I limited the number of probes to the minimum necessary. The number twenty-six is the minimum required to do the job. These questions are discussed in detail in chapter 5.

The probes are intended to tap into all parts of the value space and reveal the varying particular dynamic shapes or cluster patterns of "real live systems" of values. In the literature it has hardly been recognized that there actually is such a thing as a real, living, self-organizing, interacting, dynamic, global patterning of values, existing within the mental content of each individual person, and within each viable social-interaction system.

In general, the aim in studying personality traits with factor analysis has been to discover what is the minimum number of trait clusters (factors) that behave as independent or orthogonal factors in a statistical factor-analytic space. But the search has often stopped at that point, and researchers have felt satisfied when they have found some minimum number of independent factors.

A personality test is typically constructed to represent each one of the factors. Each factor may be conceptualized separately as a sort of freestanding independent variable. The interactive (nonlinear and contextual) *interdependence* of factors which may be discovered in real intact social-interaction systems of multiple individuals interacting over multiple periods of time has not been generally recognized and explored. The factors have not been related to each other as if they were interacting variables in a dynamic system.

The present theory explicitly assumes that personality-trait factors, such as the presently well-known *Big Five* (Costa and Widiger 1994), really acquire their content and properties from the fact that the factors are all aspects of the same kind of system-generated source. That source is the generic nature of social-interaction systems. So far as I know, there is no theory comparable to the present one in these respects.

The operative source of the orthogonal factors, in my opinion, is the natural emergence of a minimal number of major interactive dimensions of differentiation of behavior of individuals in relation to each other. This emergence occurs again and again, whenever a newly assembled group of people begins to interact. These dimensions are the three represented by the "value space" and the dimensions of the Field Diagram of the present theory. Since each of the three dimensions of the value space is bipolar, and since the vector toward each of the poles is a "direction" in the space, there are six such vectors or directions in the value space.

According to my analysis on the basis of content, the Big Five personality factors account for five of the six vectors in my space. The sixth vector of my space is implicit as the opposite pole of the dominance factor of the Big Five, as its submissive pole. The Big Five might alternately be called the "Big Six Personality Vectors."

Values can be regarded as higher-order organizations of personality traits, combined with attitudes of approval and disapproval towards them. The problems of how and why the personality traits tapped by personality tests interact together as a dynamic system has hardly been visualized as a set of problems of systemic significance.

## Why Do Some Values Tend to Conflict with Others?

Real living values, both as they exist in individual minds and as subgroup social norms, function as *justifications* for the motivated actions of certain persons toward other kinds of persons whom they feel are different from themselves. Conversely, reciprocal and contrary values function as *defenses* of persons who may have been victimized or exploited, against those who have treated them badly.

I want to emphasize, since I do not want to be mistaken for a Marxist, that I am not talking at this point, about *permanent "social classes"* of dominators and victims. I am talking about each of us, as individuals in single episodes of interaction, where we are propelled, almost by definition, into reciprocal roles that may be contradictory to each other as well as cooperating. Any one of us plays different roles in different episodes and relationships. Any one of us, to varying extents, harbors all of the kinds of conflicting values at issue among the twenty-six measured by IOVAL.

Sometimes we find ourselves in the role of dominant initiators of actions that we anticipate may not be well received, and feel we need "justifications." At other times we find ourselves in the relatively more submissive role of reactors to the possible depredations of others, and feel we need "defenses." From long and varied experience we are all well supplied with the psychological needs for both justifications and defenses, although we are certainly significantly different from each other in the proportions of the mix.

In any given social encounter, even a short-term encounter, what is good for the goose may not be good for the gander. What is good for an individual who is dominant in that particular encounter, who is highly motivated and needs to talk a lot in order to deal with the problem under discussion, may not be good for others, on whom he or she inflicts the domination. What is good for an individual who may benefit directly from solution of a given problem in relation to the environment, because he or she has ownership of the resources and most directly receives the rewards of a given solution, may not be good for others, who do not own or possess the resources required and may not receive a fair share of the rewards. What is good for an individual who is accepted and popular in a solidary group or subgroup may not be good for an individual who is not well accepted as a valued member, and in fact may be rejected.

# 4

# A Factor Analytic Approach to Values

Arthur Couch, my closest friend and colleague for a number of years in the mid-1950s, was later Assistant Professor and Assistant Director of the Laboratory of Social Relations. He came to do research with me from the laboratory of Launor Carter at the University of Rochester. Unknown to me, Carter (1951) and Couch and Carter (1952) had been pursuing a line of research very similar to my experimental studies of initially leaderless groups, using factor analysis.

Art was deeply impressed with the researches of Adorno and colleagues (1950) on the authoritarian personality, its various forms and correlates, and the *F Scale* which resulted. I, in turn, had been impressed by many quarrels in my experimental groups centering around values, particularly values concerning "authority." (No doubt these values were emphasized by the content of the cases which I had prepared for discussion in my experimental groups, and probably by the fact that they were "leaderless" to begin with.)

Art and I embarked on an ambitious study of values. We intended to make the population of value statements included in our study as broad and varied as we possibly could, in preparation for further studies of values in live interaction.

In the informal account of our study which follows, I indicate some of the principle findings, but take a number of detours to comment on the significance of the findings, and the significance of the experience itself for my later theoretical approach. I am deeply indebted to my experiences with Art, and to the transformation of my way of thinking by factor analysis, to which he introduced me. The original research was done in the mid-1950s, to build instruments for our own use, and was not published until much later (see Bales and Couch 1969).

## Obtaining the Items for a Test of *Values*

Given our very broad aim, one obvious way to obtain items was to listen to actual discussions and record statements that seemed to be promising. We obtained a substantial number of items in this way. The criteria for recognizing a promising item were not rigid, nor entirely clear, but so far as we could define them, we were looking for verbal statements with the following properties: (a) length of about one sentence; (b) declarative in form, apparently made with the desire of eliciting an agreement or disagreement from some other person; (c) the subject of which is some general class of objects, new instances of which might be found in the present or other discussions; and (d) predicate of which declares or implies that some general class of orientations, attitudes, or actions should be accepted as normatively binding on both the person who makes the statement and whoever agrees to it. Many examples will be found in Appendix A of the present book.

We assumed that a value statement in the concrete interaction context is a statement of an existing norm, presumed to bind more than one person, or a proposal for a new norm. Often both the person who made the statement and the one who agreed (or disagreed) seemed to expect that any agreement would be referred to as a justification for another more particular statement, or a specific suggestion, to be made later in the interaction. Sometimes it may have been clear to both participants what the more specific implication was and who would be required to do what if it were accepted, but often it was not clear.

It seems easier to identify the issues involved in defining a value statement if one approaches the problem in a real context of social interaction. Many points of ambiguity are forced to attention when the value statement is initiated in face-to-face interaction. For example, it appeared that a reaction to a written value statement differed from a value statement offered and reacted to in a group. It is not at all the same thing to react to a value statement on a written test, taken alone, as it is to state it in a group.

Couch reported, for example, that in his previous studies of authoritarian values and leadership he had expected individuals who scored high in advance on the F Scale to appear subsequently as more or less dominant and negative authoritarian leaders in the leaderless groups. To his surprise, the high scorers on the F Scale often appeared to be smiling, attractive, and cooperative members (probably close to Vector 11 PF in the intercorrelation space of my own system. See Appendix A.) On the same paradox, I remember that my mentor Gordon Allport was somewhat embarrassed and puzzled by the fact that prejudice seemed to be correlated somehow with religious conservatism in his studies of values.

If persons are asked, out of an interaction context, to endorse written value statements, it can hardly be clear to them who makes the statement, about whom it is made, to whom it applies, what specific action is implied by the predicate, who will perform what action toward whom, if the statement is accepted, and the like. When subjects are asked to respond to value statements on a questionnaire, most if not all of these issues are unclear. It is not surprising that some subjects refuse to answer on some items, or express irritation in such a vague context. Incidentally, the instructions Couch and I used on the printed form left the possibility of no answer on a given item as a legitimate response.

The surprising thing, perhaps, is the degree to which most respondents, including ourselves, as we found, are willing to fill in the missing context by projection, and respond with some degree of agreement or disagreement. Most existing personality tests, of course, depend on this willingness. Many of the items in standard personality tests contain elements appropriate for a values inventory. But my experience indicates that we may be badly self-deceived about the kinds of values the endorser of an item on a written self-descriptive personality test may actually initiate or endorse in the real process of interaction in a specific intact group. The intact group, of course, has a current dynamic structure of social relationships that makes particular demands, and gives special meanings to the value statements.

### Sources of Items

Once launched on the venture of exploring the domain of value statements, our aim became one of obtaining representation of as many different value areas as we practically could. We canvassed a number of sources and obtained, either directly or by slight extension and rewording, a pool of 872 items. We cannot claim that our sample was random, or systematic. It was simply as large and varied as we were able to make it at that time. It is relevant to note that a large project called the *Study of Values*, accompanied by a seminar with the participation of the senior members of the Department of Social Relations, was a prominent focus of interest at about the same time.

We began with a pool of 163 items culled from remarks made by our subjects. The Allport-Vernon-Lindzey *Study of Values* (Allport et al. 1951) provided the ingredients for eleven items, some from each of its value types. A classification of ideologically oriented value statements relevant to small groups, worked out earlier by Bales (1950: 172–6), provided thirty items. A questionnaire used in anthropological studies at the time by Florence Kluckhohn (1950) and collaborators, based on her classification of value orientations, provided the material for sixteen items. Charles Morris's questionnaire, *Ways to Live* (Morris 1956: 15–8), used in his cross-cultural studies and worked out with classical philosophical and religious issues prominently in view, was a rich source of 120 items. An unpublished questionnaire by Gibson Winter (1952) on values relative to participation in groups furnished sixteen items. Pitirim Sorokin's description of various types of cultural mentality in his *Social and Cultural Dynamics* (Sorokin 1937) provided the source for forty-six items. All of the authors just named were more or less explicitly concerned with values and with the problem of types or classes of values.

Various scales associated with, or inspired by, the *Authoritarian Personality* studies provided items, including the thirty-item F Scale in its entirety

(Adorno et al. 1950: 260). Twenty-six items were obtained from various scales by Levinson on ethnocentrism and minorities (Adorno et al. 1950: 103–50). Twelve items were obtained from his *Religious Conventionalism Scale* (Adorno et al. 1950: 208–21). Forty-two items were obtained from Levinson and Huffman's *Traditional Family Ideology Scale* (Levinson and Huffman1955). Twelve items were obtained from the Couch-Goodrich *Militant Radicalism Scale* (Couch and Goodrich 1952). Nine items were obtained from an unpublished dissertation by Edward Jones (1953).

Another rich source was Henry Murray's lists of sentiments, associated with various personality needs, in his *Explorations in Personality* (Murray 1938). These lists furnished 119 items. Raymond Cattell's *Sixteen Personality Factor Questionnaire* (Cattell, Saunders, and Stice 1951) was the source, by rewording and extension, of eighty-seven items. And, the *Thurstone Temperament Schedule* (Thurstone 1949) provided eighty-five items.

### Preliminary Reduction in the Number of Items

Working partly deductively from a classification of "system problems" utilized in other connections by Parsons and Bales (Parsons et al. 1953a) and partly inductively from the pool of items, we set up a temporary framework of sixteen classes. This framework provided a means of grouping items for comparison and editing. Near duplicates were eliminated; key words and phrases from separate items were combined into single items. By these and similar means the total number of items was reduced to 252, which were printed for administration under the title, "The Value Profile."

The Likert response form was used. The six response categories, together with the numerical values later assigned to them for computation were: (1) Strongly Disagree, (2) Disagree, (3) Slightly Disagree, (5) Slightly Agree, (6) Agree, (7) Strongly Agree. A weight of (4), that is, a mean value, was assigned to those cases where the subject failed to respond.

### The Sample

I confess that at the time of this study I was not very sensitive to the fact that a factor analysis yields, among other things, a set of statistical measures describing the population of the particular sample. In my original innocence I thought of the population of respondents primarily as a kind of neutral test tube for determining "the" relationships of the test items to each other. The real thing of interest was "the" way in which the items were related to each other in some vaguely apprehended eternal world. The sample we actually used was certainly not optimum, and probably in itself brought the values of authoritarianism and anti-authoritarianism into particularly violent confrontation in the minds of raters.

For example, around eighty respondents were obtained from Bennington College (notably liberal at the time), and a similar number from among officer candidates at Maxwell Air Force Base (not notably liberal, so far as I know!). The main part of the sample consisted of Harvard undergraduates, obtained by an advertisement in the college newspaper. They were paid for their time in answering the questionnaire. In addition to Harvard undergraduates, a small sample of faculty members from the Department of Social Relations, graduate students, and Radcliffe undergraduates filled out the questionnaire. The total from the Harvard area was 388. The total number of respondents was 552.

This sample, though decently large, was made up of several rather different cultural groups. And who knows of what, if anything, it was representative? However, it was probably not too bad for the assessment of value differences between students of college age in this country in the 1950s. We did not even try to face up to the difficult problems of class, race, and ethnic differences, to say nothing of cross-cultural differences. On the other hand, we gratefully took items from tests that had been used to some extent cross-culturally, notably those of Morris, Kluckhohn, and Allport-Vernon-Lindzey. We did the best we could. A few of our items no doubt must have sounded a little too much like the original Navaho, and others might have come from the Koran, or Confucius, not to mention Nietsche.

## Item Analysis

Two devices were used for further reduction of the 252 items to a number small enough for a factor analysis. First, the distribution of answers on each item was used to weed out items which did not discriminate between subjects in our population. Items on which nearly everybody agreed or disagreed were dropped. Less than 20 percent of the endorsements on either side of the midpoint of the scale was the approximate criterion for dropping an item.

This is not to say that such items did not express values, nor that such values were unimportant, but simply that we wanted a test that would differentiate respondents in our groups from one another. The factor-analytic space we were actually exploring was not the space of reactions to all value statements, but the space of those on which people in the small groups we were about to study were most apt to differ in their reactions.

Critics today concerned about the contrast between consensus-oriented sociology and conflict-oriented sociology might point out that we were implicitly (though not self-consciously) setting the stage for a general theory of value systems in which value conflicts were taken as the baseline. I think this is true. However, after all explorations and adjustments had been made (by about 1983), the value content of the twenty-six vectors of the contemporary values test instrument (IOVAL) are distributed as evenly as possible over the surface of a spherical space, and the possibilities of a preponderance of cooperative relationships is exactly the same as the possibility of a preponderance of conflict.

After reduction, the items remaining were grouped again according to the sixteen-category classification, and the sixteen separate matrices of correlations of each item with each other item in its group were computed. The examination of these correlations enabled us to locate clusters and familiarize ourselves with the character of each item in its local context of related items. In the final reduction we tried to include clusters, or at least pairs of intercorrelated items, to represent all the positions we could identify, and tended to drop items which too closely duplicated an already adequately represented cluster, or at the other extreme, items that were completely uncorrelated with any others.

The final set contained 143 items, plus one score based on the total of seventeen items included from the original thirty-item F Scale, as a marker variable. The 144 variables were intercorrelated, and the resulting matrix was factor analyzed by the Thurstone complete-centroid method (1947). In general, for reasons of logical inference, we preferred to deal with orthogonal factors, and orthogonality was always preserved in rotations.

### The Factor Structure

A set of tables containing the list of items, means, variances, centroid and rotated loadings, will be found in the paper as originally published. Only a few individual items will be discussed here to illustrate the structure of the factor space. Four orthogonal factors were found. All four factors, and a number of the combinations of them, can be measured reasonably well with the items available.

Factor I we called "Agreement with Value Statements in Favor of Acceptance of Authority." This factor was almost squarely on the well-known cluster usually called "authoritarianism." Our marker variable, total F Score, had a loading of .90 on Factor I. The best item, "Obedience and respect for authority are the most important virtues children should learn," was loaded .76 on Factor I and had essentially a zero loading on the other three factors.

Factor II was bipolar. We called it "Agreement with Value Statements in Favor of Need-determined Expression versus Value-determined Restraint." The best item, which had a loading of .62 and was almost pure, stated, "No values can be eternal: the only real values are those which meet the needs of the given moment." Another good item was more specific about needs: "Let us eat, drink, and be merry, for tomorrow we die!" The content of the items indicate that aggressive as well as sexual impulses were classed together with appetites.

Factor III we called "Agreement with Value Statements Favoring Equalitarianism." The best item, with a loading of .57, was: "Everyone should have an equal chance and an equal say." Factor III in our analysis was uncorrelated with Factor I. Equalitarianism, in our population, was not the opposite of acceptance of authority, but was statistically independent of it. It may have been positively correlated for some subgroup of persons, and negatively correlated for some others, and zero correlated for still others.

Factor III, agreement with equalitarianism, was also independent of Factor II, agreement with value statements favoring need-determined expression. The value statement in which a positive value is placed on both is illustrated by the item: "Society should be quicker to adopt new customs and throw aside mere traditions and old-fashioned habits." Apparently, the person who agrees feels that "society" in some general equalitarian sense of all individuals has the right to "throw aside" (an expressive gesture) "mere traditions" (conservative ways).

A negative value placed on need-determined expression (that is, a positive value placed on value-determined restraint) in combination with a positive value on equalitarianism is illustrated by the item: "There are no human problems that love cannot solve." "Love," in this connection, presumably means the ascetic, altruistic kind, and this kind of love is presumably usually associated with restraint.

Factor IV we called "Agreement with Value Statements Favoring Individualism." The item which best represented this factor reads: "It is the man who stands alone who excites our admiration." Another item associated with the individualistic factor read as follows: "What this country needs most, more than laws and political programs, is a few courageous, tireless, devoted leaders, in whom the people can put their faith." For some respondents the correlation between this item and Factor I, acceptance of authority, may have been positive, for others, it may have been negative. In any case, the overall correlation was zero.

The individualistic factor was related in special ways to quite a number of items. For example, an item negative to authority, but still individualistic is the item: "Whoever would be a man, must be a nonconformist." Combinations of individualism with need-determined expression have a somewhat different flavor, for example: "Love action, and care little that others may find you rash." On the other hand, the combination of individualism with value-determined restraint, the opposite end of Factor II, is represented by the item: "One should aim to simplify one's external life, and moderate those desires whose satisfaction is dependent upon physical or social forces outside of oneself."

There is a kind of individualism which is negative to equalitarianism, for example: "To be superior, a man must stand alone." However, agreement with individualism and agreement with equalitarianism are not always incompatible. The following item (from Charles Morris) was fairly well loaded on both factors: "The rich, internal world of ideals, of sensitive feelings, of reverie, of self-knowledge, is man's true home."

## Choice of Rotation

The rotation chosen for reference in interpreting the factors is, of course, a matter of conceptual convenience, the more so as the space is filled out with items and does not show any simple structure. For our conceptual purposes, the proper basis of comparison of factor analyses with each other is the nature of the space, that is to say, the fullest possible population of intercorrelations of items to each other, positive, negative, and zero correlations. The factors, however they are chosen by a particular rotation, are only a summary description of the statistical relations to each other of the population of items chosen for the study over the population of the sample of respondents.

Different rotations will give different perspectives for description. One of the reasons for disagreements on the theoretical level, and the multiplication of classification schemes, is that, in the absence of data which represent the space as essentially filled out with many items, or the choice of a particular population of respondents, undue emphasis may be attached to what amounts to a particular rotation, or a particular factor, or even a particular conception of the whole space and the relationship of factors within it.

## The Observation Method: Value Content Analysis (VCA)

One of the most important results of this early factor analysis was that it enabled us to formulate a compact and understandable set of four categories for use in real-time observation and classification of the value statements made by group members in their interactions with each other. The categories were conceptualized as factors in a factor space, and particular value statements by group participants were classified by their location in the space: on, near, or between two or more factors. The VCA scoring was done by Gene Kassebaum and analyzed for his dissertation (1958). The general findings are reported by vector in Appendix A.

VCA was of great importance to me in the eventual development of social-interaction systems theory because it made possible an immediate classification and recording of the value content of statements made by a specific group participant at the same time that the overt behavior (usually "gives opinion") was classified and recorded by *Interaction Process Analysis* (or IPA, described in chapter 7). The group member originating a value statement and the person to whom the statement was addressed were recorded. (The group as a whole was also a possible alternative communication target.) The reply (usually, "agrees" or "disagrees") and the oppositional value statement, if any, were also recorded. Thus a record was made of the member who made the reply, and a value-content classification was made of the reply. It was possible later to determine the place of any recorded value statement in the time sequence and how many acts it required.

These features of the real-time observation system made it possible to correlate directly the contents of value statements initiated and opposed by specific persons with other aspects of their personalities, and with their places in the overall social-relationship context. If one thinks as I do, that the interaction "system" at the most microscopic level has, as its first-hand concrete substance, the "action" of one individual followed by the "reaction" of some other, on the basis of the values they ascribe to each other, then the identification of persons in the process, and the other characteristics observed in VCA, are directly relevant.

By the use of VCA in real-time observation along with Interaction Process Analysis, "values" are brought down to earth and anchored to the specific contending persons and their specific "bones of contention." Values no longer "float in the air" as a vaguely assumed or ascribed general characteristic of a group, or as a "group atmosphere," or as a "group mentality." As a third-person observer, one can hardly assume a "consensus" over all members when one conceptualizes an interaction system as having a "value system." It becomes clear that the concrete substance of a "value system" must be recognized as a pattern of interchange of many different kinds of values of different members in different social locations in conflicting and cooperating relationships with each other. It becomes painfully clear that "the group" or "the organization" in concrete reality is a set of interacting individual persons, subgroups, majorities, minorities, and individual isolates. It sometimes may be the case that most of the group may be in practical consensus, but only sometimes, and even on these occasions the consensus is usually only partial, not complete.

In the early days of "group dynamics," when therapists such as Wilfred Bion (1961) reported addressing their groups with interpretations that lumped all participants together, by saying "the group is" (doing or feeling so and so, such as "pairing" or "in flight"), the hair on the back of my neck always bristled in indignation as I read Bion's interpretation. In my self-analytic groups I was always attuned to individual differences and interaction between different individuals and different value positions. I always made a point of looking for dissidents whenever a majority seemed to be forming. And, I nearly always found them, even if there was only one of them, back in a corner or looking longingly toward the door, showing nonverbal signs of disagreement and alienation. My interventions quite often called attention to the apparent discomfort of particular individuals or subgroups, and brought them into the interaction.

VCA was employed for real-time observation in the large omnibus study conducted for Arthur Couch's dissertation (1960). I also participated in this study as mentor and IPA observer. I restudied all the data from the intercorrelation tables as part of the background for my book, *Personality and Interpersonal Behavior* (1970).

## The Twenty-six Vector Intercorrelation Space

The intercorrelation space of twenty-six vectors is explained and discussed at length in the following chapter. A long and detailed listing of correlates of the twenty-six vectors of the intercorrelation space, as I have reconstructed and collected them, will be found in Appendix A. Although it is a long list, it is only a sample, a bare beginning, of what might be reconstructed from a careful study of the factor-analytic literature. I believe it will be found to be fairly representative and enlightening about what the intercorrelations of variables might be in a broader study, a more carefully researched model over a large population of intact groups.

I alone must take responsibility for putting together into one patchwork composite picture the results of many separate factor analyses, as if the relationships found in many different analyses can be metaphorically matched or patched together and used to characterize a single theoretical social-interaction system, and one theoretical intercorrelation space.

Couch (1960) produced six separate factor analyses for his dissertation. However, he did not put the factor analyses all together as I have done to characterize a single theoretical three-dimensional space, nor did he assemble the intercorrelations as if they were all results and partial evidences of a single theoretical generalized social-interaction system. He might or might not agree with what I have done.

My method of synthesis for the general model consisted of visually overlaying a transparency of the locations of all items in each particular factor analysis onto a single meta-theoretical visual factor-analytic field of three orthogonal factors. (This meta-theoretical visual field is what the Field Diagram as a framework for examining plotted data on a set of intercorrelations actually is.) On the Field Diagram of the present system, the factors, for convenience, are always graphically portrayed as dimensional scales, P-N and F-B, orthogonal to each other on the face of the Field Diagram. Items, that is, variables, that are correlated with each of the orthogonal reference axes, are plotted in positions on, near, and between the orthogonal factors.

The retrospective fitting of one Field Diagram to another by visual rotation can be done without much difficulty when each of the particular factor analyses contains enough relevant items to show and identify the three orthogonal individual factors as clusters, and when all factors of the particular factor analysis can be seen to approximately match in value content. The key to a match in content can be obtained by converting the location of each variable into its appropriate vector, as shown in the cube diagram (figure 1.3). The implied value content seems to me to be the most general frame of reference within which the items of domains of very different concrete content can be seen to have something important in common.

In order to have maximum confidence in this procedure, one needs to have a large number of maximally different variables, a large number of raters, and the fit needs to be reasonably good. One needs to be able to assume that all of the variables are indeed measurements from the same type of social-interaction system, that is, from groups of a similar type, such as a representative sample of intact groups where the variables have in fact been in active interaction in each of the groups, or where the individual members who are differentiated on the variables have had an opportunity to interact within the specific group. Fortunately for future research, the SCG data bank has comparatively large numbers of intact groups which meet these requirements, but only, of course, for certain variables having to do with ratings using value items or behavior description items.

It is important to know and to be able to take into account that, outside of the work connected with my own research, very few of the factor studies on which one may draw for suggestions were performed on data from the full membership of actually-interacting intact groups of raters. If the raters are simply a large population of individuals who are not involved with each other as members of an intact interacting group, I suspect that one is likely to find a closer approach to orthogonality of the main factors than in intact and effective groups. Luckily, however, if one has a firm enough grasp of the value content of the factors, they can be recognized even though they may be partially correlated with each other in the particular population one is studying. In intact groups, as I shall attempt to show in chapter 9, positive intercorrelations of the Vectors U, P, and F, are to be expected, *to the degree that the group is actually effective.*

My methods of overlapping the existing factor analyses were artistic and inexact. They may be questioned in many respects, and I hope they will be. But the end results, in my opinion, and to my great satisfaction, have turned out to be a viable and robust system, in practice as well as in theory. A very large collection of findings on groups and leadership from many separate studies over a period of more than fifty years of research, stretching from the laboratory to a large variety of groups in contemporary real-life situations are put in order and in organic relationship to each other by their interrelationships in the conceptual model of the generalized social-interaction system.

The integration reached would have been impossible I think, for me at any rate, except by something like this retrospective visual method of overlaying factor-analytic fields of variables or plots of variables of particular studies, one on top of the other, on a meta Field Diagram where the main dimensions U-D, P-N, and F-B are shown as orthogonal for purposes of reference (see chapter 6).

The intercorrelations of variables with particular vectors of the twenty-six vector space shown in Appendix A are not presented as firmly established, nor as expected to be always the same. Neither should specific intercorrelations between particular items be expected to be always the same. The intercorrelations do and must vary over a range, depending upon the issues and Images to which the members of the system are presently reacting.

Variations from an empirically derived Optimum norm, or an empirical average of ideal norms, are the principle means of gaining information about the problems of operation in the particular system studied, and are outstanding features in the feedback that the consultant is able to return to the members. The intercorrelations, even within a normal range of variation around the designated "optimum" locations, are presented as tentative and subject to continuing revision, according to results of current research and reexamination of the large untapped literature.

# 5

# The Intercorrelation Space

It has been my experience that an entirely new level of understanding of social interaction is provided by the factor-analytic concept of a global intercorrelation space of variables such as different kinds of interpersonal behavior, values, and perceptions of the different kinds of individual persons, all interacting and affecting each other in different ways and for different reasons within the same small group over the same limited time span, the span of an hour's meeting, for example.

In order to visualize the reality and, as I believe, the necessity of the concept of a social-interaction system, one needs some ordinary but thoughtful experience in the observation of individuals in interaction, and some imagination, since much that is important is not visible because it is suppressed in the minds of participants, and does not show overtly until later. It is not easy to visualize a great many behavior variables of a number of different individuals getting themselves organized, without appointed leadership and without any agreed-upon overall intention as to how they should be organized. It is often an apparently unorganized or even a disorganized process.

In order to get a real-life flavor of the way in which variables are related to each other and why, one can be helped by examples of the concrete variables that have actually been measured at the small-group interaction level under the conditions of initially leaderless groups. Leadership is one of the concrete aspects of organization, and it is very helpful to see how it arises.

### The Interpersonal Interactive Bubble of Process

The "interpersonal interactive bubble of process" is a metaphorical phrase. The "bubble" I am talking about is what I think of now as the small "living cell" of social-interaction systems. But its unique importance is that a great deal of it can be seen with the "naked eye," at least over the time span of a complete session of a small-group meeting to make a group decision. I originally called the time periods within a bubble "phases in group problem solving." That description refers to phases within a complete meeting. But there are little bubbles within larger bubbles, within the bubble of any complete group meeting.

Both a living cell and a bubble have an inside and an outside. To speak of "phases in group problem solving" is to recognize and describe, in part, the internal content of the cell, what goes on within the cell. To speak of a "bubble of process" is to recognize, or to imagine, the existence of a boundary, or cell wall. Much ordinary social interaction is made up of one bubble after another, and actually, one bubble within another.

The interpersonal interactional process within the cell wall, or bubble, has a beginning pause at a time of entry, and it has an end, or a pause at a time of exit. The obvious beginning in a meeting is the first period, when people arrive and begin with small talk and friendly behavior. But there is also another type of more minor beginning, one that occurs as a smaller bubble in the midst of the longer process of the meeting as a whole. This more minor kind of beginning is the *resumption* after a minor ending which has just occurred. This minor ending is a stopping place, or a pause, in the longer process. One can also see (and hear) the signs of this ending boundary. Often it is marked by a sudden burst of laughter. The final ending of the process is the ending of the meeting. The signs of this are obvious. The sign indicating that the meeting is about to come to an end is often, but not always, a period of joking and laughing.

By calling the bubble a "living cell" I mean to suggest that the content of the bubble (phases in group problem solving) is a section of real process that, in fact, and at the same time, is a microscopic social-interaction system. It is a complete cell also in the sense that it includes its own "DNA." That is, it carries and modifies a pattern of mental expectations in the minds of the participants. The pattern propagates succeeding systems like itself. Memories of earlier experience in the minds of participants carry forward in time the residues of unresolved problems and the seeds left by previous process. Like the living cell which contains its own DNA, the bubble contains and modifies a system of structured memories. It is both a progenitor, a generating source, and a constituent part of an indefinitely expanding fractal series of larger social-interaction systems.

Can all this be seen with the naked eye? The answer is obviously "no." I include the criterion of observation by the naked eye in my metaphor because I want to anchor my search (for the origins of the systemic elements of the theoretical social-interaction system) on the everyday common-sense level of what can be observed in a specific interacting group, and in identifiable periods of time in real processes of social interaction.

First-hand observation tends to reduce the semantic vagueness and ambiguity of the more abstract concepts that are necessary for representing the real system as a generalized theoretical system. The description and understanding of larger and more complex systems requires concepts that are more generalized and more abstract. But they are also necessarily more vague, and to me it is crucial to be able to get rid of semantic vagueness. I believe strongly in a method for acquiring and applying knowledge where the variables can be observed, where they can be operationally defined and measured, placed in the theoretical model, and then followed by inferences from the general abstract theoretical model back down to concrete actions where they can be tested in practice.

What I actually want to suggest, by the metaphor of a bubble of process, is that the beginning and ending marks of the boundary of the bubble can be observed with the naked eye and that the inside of the bubble can be seen as a series of interconnected interaction phases in real time. The series of phases has a beginning and an end as a period of real time in a given intact group.

The opening and closing of the bubble has a *dynamic* explanation, or total system-relevant explanation, whether or not it solves a particular intellectually identified "problem" with which it starts. The bubble is only a problem-solving process in a very ambiguous sense. Its unity is not necessarily a unity of cognitive consistency or rational choice of alternative means to a single pre-visualized end, the solution of the ostensible problem, or a group decision. Its unity and whatever predictability of sub-processes and phases it may have, is its encapsulation of a time-constricted period of total system operation during which an underlying tension of suppressed reactions builds up to a point of discharge. Laughter is the discharge.

The awareness of the repetitive occurrence of these bubbles of process was the first concrete generalization that I was able to extract from my observations. I was aided by what Bacon called an "instrument and help" which I invented for the purpose: the "interaction recorder," a machine which provided a moving paper tape on which I could note down the occurrence of specific types of acts at the time they occurred, who performed them toward whom. From the tape, I could reconstruct a graphic record of the ups and downs of a timeline connecting each act to the next. The ups and downs on the tape were meaningful, and intended to be so, because I had placed the categories of acts on a vertical list in a hypothetical order as to when on the timeline in a bubble they would have their peaks and their troughs. All this will be described in more detail in chapter 6.

The bubble, as a period of time of variable length, is marked by a beginning, or entry into the bubble, and an end, or exit from the bubble. A complete given group meeting may be regarded as a bubble, but later inspection of the tape from the interaction recorder will show that this large bubble is likely to be further subdivided into a few, or many, smaller bubbles completed in a shorter time by the occurrence of specific signs to be described below. The signs can be seen by the naked eye, and heard, since laughter is the typical ending sign. The bubbles prove to be of different lengths in time, some short, some long, like beads or capsules of variable sizes on a string of time.

To understand the similarity of all bubbles, each of which has both an overt and an implicit, or covert, mental content, it helps to be familiar with the concept of "fractals." Often the meeting as a whole can be seen as one large bubble that is "fractally similar" to many other meetings of other groups. But it is also similar in form to each of the smaller bubbles that appear within it. The description I give below best characterizes the whole meeting as one large bubble. But in time-ordered reality one can still identify similar small bubbles within the large one. The small bubbles are similar to the large bubble of the whole meeting, but the small ones are more abbreviated in every respect with regard to overt content. In the small bubbles much more is "implicit," that is, present mentally in the minds of the participants, but not expressed verbally at that time. The suppressed content comes out overtly later, or can be elicited by interview or questionnaire.

To my mind, seeing and understanding the fractal similarity between the small bubbles and the large ones is the essential secret of understanding how "micro" systems give rise to, and are related to, more "macro" systems. This is a problem that is actively under discussion as I write, especially among social psychologists on the sociological side. Micro systems and macro systems of social interaction, in particular, are similar in their overall system dynamics. The similarities may be sensed by reading Appendix A, "The Intercorrelation Space."

### A Typical Meeting as I Have Observed It

In the following description of a typical meeting I deliberately mix together the patterns of the smaller and the larger scales, as if they were all the same length, and I use the terminology of beginnings and endings appropriate to the bubble metaphor applied to the length of a complete meeting. The description sounds a little like one of Kipling's "just-so" stories: "How the elephant got his long trunk." My description has a little of a mythical flavor. "It never did happen exactly like this. This is a story for children." The story is at the same time both artificially simplified and artificially exaggerated.

The case described below is essentially true and strongly empirically based. It is divided into five phases of group process. While I am telling this just-so story, I am trying to provide background, in terms of concrete time-ordered events, for future discussions of the formal model and the formal language of my theory of social-interaction systems in the most general sense.

1. The first phase of a meeting is typically a period of friendly behavior when the participants first gather for the meeting. The content of what they are talking about might be described as "small talk and social knitting" in preparation for a session of more focused problem-solving work.

2. Next, the friendly interaction tends to give way to a pause and a focusing of group attention on a "problem." The problem may be the "work" of the group, or of the particular meeting. The early part of this work phase may

be marked by high rates of giving and asking for information, building up the background of the information needed to work on the problem. Low or reluctant participators may be drawn in by asking them for information, or opinion.

3. Then what follows, in most cases, is a period of work on the problem as first defined, or on other problems which make their way into attention. This phase of relatively neutral work is usually marked by rising rates of giving opinions, supporting information, and suggestions (actions), interspersed with agreement and disagreement (reactions).

4. At some point signs of a startle reaction and change of expression and attention may be seen on the faces of a number of the participants. The group is then launched into a more emotionally loaded fourth phase. This phase may be precipitated by a remark or incident, perhaps a more explicit far-out value statement which is a little shocking for some participants in its implications of the unusual intensity of underlying emotion and impending interpersonal conflict. The interpersonal conflicts that ensue may then become the problems that the group deals with, although in most cases they are not defined by the participants in the same cool problem-solving language as before. This interpersonal conflict phase is marked for the "naked eye and the outstretched ear" of the observer by further increases in rates of opinion, more generalized value statements, more disagreement, more unfriendly behavior, more showing tension, more open antagonism, and more withdrawal of some of the participants.

Some of the conflicts of the fourth phase are likely to seem to be embedded in the original problem. Other conflicts seem to be embedded in the differences in personality and character, that is, the value differences with which the participants began their interaction and which they are now beginning to show. The playing out of these conflicts often tends to escalate in emotional ways, at times to be chaotic, sometimes to be caught in circular interpersonal interlocks between participants, sometimes to change unpredictably. Sometimes it appears to verge on an intensity that could in some cases be traumatic for some or many of the participants.

5. A breaking point of some kind may then appear, perhaps a joke or a dramatic bit of humor, and a terminating phase sets in. One may expect, over a variegated population of intact groups, two kinds of terminal phases, successful and unsuccessful.

In the relatively successful case, repeated joking and laughing sets in. The content and sense of the jokes usually reflects, often at a fantasy level, the conflicts that the group has just been through. The period of joking and laughing may be prolonged. Its length and apparent intensity is probably a fair measure of the seriousness of the conflicts and the disturbances of self-picture and social position that the participants have experienced in the preceding phases. The end of the joking and laughing may be considered to mark the end of the particular bubble of process at the meeting length of scale.

In a less successful outcome, some, maybe many or most, bubbles of process at the meeting level of length in certain groups or in certain circumstances do not have a positive ending but persist in negative behavior and interpersonal conflict until the process is terminated lamely by some equivalent of giving up or disbandment.

If the meeting does not terminate, the new beginning of another bubble of interpersonal interactional process is typically marked by the appearance of a pause, a shift of bodily position to a more dignified posture, and the resumption of more friendly behavior again.

### Merging Bubbles

Putting bubbles with both positive and negative outcomes together and calling this hybrid stretch of process a "bubble" puts an emphasis on the cell wall, the container, rather than on the contents. The rationale of merging the two types of cells or bubbles is that all real systems have a mixture of positive and negative endings. For clinical or consulting use, we want to set our empirical norms for diagnosis of the problems of the system itself at an average cutting point where departures on one side of the norm will point toward relative success, and departures on the other side of the norm will point toward relative failure.

The metaphor of the "bubble," now a varicolored mixture of success and failure, is meant to suggest a spherical container which I want in later sections of this chapter to compare to the spherical form of the intercorrelation space of the social-interaction system. This comparison is intended to suggest that the space within the boundaries of the bubble contains the microscopic prototypes of all of the kinds of events which give rise to the correlations of the intercorrelation space (see Appendix A).

If enough bubbles are compared from enough intact groups, *and if* all the bubbles are somehow added together as if they were all instances of the same kind of real social-interaction process of the same time length, *and if* we include observations of such bubbles of process from many large and varied populations of participants, *then* the average tendencies, and the correlations of variables with each other over the total population of participants in the processes of the real bubbles, will demonstrate and put into understandable order all of the varieties of differentiation and conflicts in relationships that characterize social-interaction systems in general.

The bubbles of process are actually of different time lengths, specialized in various ways, and appear in different contexts. Thus, in order to generate a single more complete and clear picture, one must observe and record what goes on in many bubbles, and combine them, perhaps adding one over another. Merging the bubbles would seem to require some kind of "renormalization" or standardization of the dimensions of each so that they are all of the same size before adding them together. But the theory of dynamic social-interaction systems emphasizes the similarity of all bubbles. The theory says that, in spite of their differences, they are all samples of essentially the same thing: a process, partly overt and partly implicit or covert, in which certain kinds of dynamic relationships tend to form between the variables which interact within each bubble. Adding the bubbles together in some way brings into sharper focus the interconnections between the variables of the real processes. The merged view overcomes the problem of there being some processes which are missing in any one bubble, or present but suppressed and not seen with the naked eye.

Perhaps the procedure of adding together in some way the records of the correlations of variables within many bubbles of process after some kind of "fractal renormalization" of the time spans can be thought of as somewhat similar to the procedure in astronomy of adding many telescopic photographs together in order to get one composite picture with greater detail. Night after night, we can imagine, the same telescope is aimed at the same dim remote star in order to build up a picture of its light spectrum and its dark lines. Each of the pictures is taken through some interference. Each picture captures just a little light, but many exposures, laid one on top of another, build up a stronger and more comprehensive coverage of the spectrum of light and its unique dark lines coming from the same dim star. The pictures can be added together and the composite picture that results shows more detail than any one of them can.

Calling small, naturally-marked time periods of the real interpersonal interaction a "bubble of process" is meant to underline the fact that a span of time is required for the interaction of the variables we regard as parts of the system to show themselves and to reach their characteristic closure. The processes contained within the bubble require a certain amount of time to run their course and react to the feedback of each on each of the others. Unless one observes the interaction of the intact group for a sufficiently long period of time, or observes many groups, and then adds them together in some appropriate way, one cannot see the whole spectrum of dynamic relationships.

In short periods many of the relevant processes which take place in the minds of different participants are suppressed. Or they may appear, but in a very minor way, in some cases. They are not overt, or not obvious enough and thus are not seen with the naked eye. The intercorrelation space assumes a time span. The intercorrelated variables it describes are actions and reactions of a number of persons to each other and this takes time. Each bubble of process has some similarities to the merged picture, but also probably has some important differences from any other. Only a part of the process can be overt at a given time, because of the time restrictions that are inevitable in carrying on understandable communication, while the rest of the implicit part of the process is held in suppressed form in the mental states of the participants.

The periodicity of phases of joking and laughing, and the exaggerated non-verbal but active behavior which marks the final phase of the interaction process, just before exit from the bubble, is plain and convincing evidence that much of the rise and fall of intensity in the interaction of variables in the minds of the various participants is inevitably suppressed in the normal process. Getting through the bubble to its termination is inevitably a battle, to some degree, about something, or more accurately, about a whole system of things.

I suggest, on the basis of long experience with self-analytic groups, that if the participants are not unduly hampered, and if the observations cover a long-enough span of time, the suppressed elements generally tend to emerge into overt, visible form, though not completely in any given case. But in any case, evaluative questionnaires, such as those with prepared rating questions (see Appendix B) which elicit ratings of mental Images in terms of values, can add a tremendous amount of order and coverage to what can be understood even by long-time observation with the naked eye. One logical way to learn about what has been suppressed, or at least some of it, is for the researcher-consultant to feed back the results of the survey to the participants. Additional meanings of the facts are then typically elicited or provoked, discussed, reevaluated, and amplified still further.

Explanations of why an individual's values are what they are will surely be found, for the most part, in the experiences the individual has gone through in social interaction. All of these experiences have taken place in specific interpersonal interactive bubbles of process, the main features of which remain in the memory. The dimensions of differentiation of the individual's system of values are strongly influenced, or created, by the differentiation of interactive behavior in the particular bubbles and battles the individual has gone through. Values can be regarded as codified generalized residues, reactions, counteractions. These include sometimes deceptive maneuvers and attempts to control interactive processes with others in the future so that they will be more likely, as the individual sees it, to go in the way they "should," in the hope of eventual future survival of some kind. But individuals are very different from each other in their mental constructions as to what will promote their survival and why.

One more feature of the bubble metaphor may be exploited to make a point (before the bubble bursts). It is that the bubble has a *boundary of applicability*. The actual context the individual employs for reading the *meaning* of an experience is not an unlimited expanse of possible meanings. The experience that is left in memory as a potent image, both on the group and individual levels, has a boundary around it, as an experience, as the memory of an emotionally loaded encounter, and as the nucleus of a value or a set of values.

This is especially important in cases where the experience is traumatic. These are the memories that Roger Brown has called "flashbulb memories." They are apt to be vivid pictures of the recognition of threats to survival, and may also give definition to the kind of behavior that will henceforth be defined as necessary to "survival." They may tend to make certain values supremely important to be realized as compared to all other values.

Just where the boundary of applicability of the relevant situation is placed is a part of the *meaning* of the value. The meaning of the value is the concrete translation of "how it ought to have gone," or "what it is necessary to do for the self to survive." The boundary as to "who is involved" and "how they are to be dealt with" may be placed very close to the self-image and perhaps one definite other person in some cases. Or, it may be pictured in such a way in memory that the boundary of the bubble and the meaning of the value in application is drawn around a subgroup from the total intact group. Or the boundary may be drawn around the group as a whole in relation to some aspect of the outside environment. In fact one may visualize a whole series of concentric circles, or boundaries, which may extend outward so far as to include all mankind.

In any case, the particular boundary, which is placed around the relevant situation in the memory image, is likely to confine and make more specific the application of whatever values it may have made salient. The boundary may mark a "cut off" between the area within which important values apply and are taken seriously and an excluded area beyond in which the values are no longer applicable. Such boundaries constrain the contexts for the meanings of values. With a shift in context, the meanings of values are sometimes radically transformed under the pressure of traumatic effects or threats in real life. This familiar idea is described sometimes as the "relativity of values," or as "situational ethics."

Traumatic or stressful situations may tend to reinstate the defenses that trace to specific situations, that is, social-interaction contexts where, for the particular individual, the convictions as to what is necessary for his or her survival were originally crystallized. Important interaction situations may tend to leave memories which constrict the boundaries within which the derivative values apply. Or perhaps in other situations, the boundaries may be expanded and the meanings of important values may be redefined.

If there is anything new and suggestive to the present phrasing of the way in which values are acquired and modified, that is, in the midst of real interpersonal interactive bubbles of process, it is that recognizing their empirical origins, their great variability, and their close relationship to individual convictions as to what is necessary for survival may help us to understand how the "switch-over" is so often made from a more inclusive boundary to a more constricted one, or vice versa.

## A Scaffolding for the Intercorrelation Space

The cube diagram (figure 1.3) is a blueprint for the inside of the space of what I have just called the "bubble." It illustrates in terms of physical space the three bipolar dimensions of the theoretical model and the angular directions of each of twenty-six vectors of departure from the center of the space. I use the cube diagram because it provides an easily visualized picture of three orthogonal dimensions: Upward-Downward (U-D), Positive-Negative (P-N), and Forward-Backward (F-B). The three dimensions account for six of the twenty-six vectors in the space. The remaining twenty are named using two- and three-letter codes derived from the six primary vectors.

Mathematically inclined readers may want me to acknowledge that there is no way for all twenty-six vector intersections derived from a cube and intersecting a spherical surface to be exactly equally spaced from each other. This is true. A sphere, after all, is a three-dimensional object, and although one can rotate it to any orientation in order to look at it, the fact that the measurement procedure assumes three orthogonal dimensions prevents equal spacing of all vectors.

My interpretive operations essentially ignore this problem, and assume for practical purposes that the twenty-six vectors are equally spaced and are given equal weights in the measurement system. Cohen (Bales and Cohen 1979) gives the actual angular separations of each vector from each other vector. He recommends a weighting system to give the three-dimensionality greater recognition, but I am doubtful that it is better than the assumption of equal spacing and equal weighting that I use for my vector engine.

The three dimensions of the cube actually represent three orthogonal factors, each of them bipolar, in a mathematical model of a factor-analytic space. Theoretically, the factor-analytic space is a *spherical* space, like the metaphorical bubble. The sides of the large cube can be thought of as the sides of a large box which completely encloses the sphere. Thus in each of the eight corners of the box, there is a corner of space left over. This is "non-system space," out of the reach of the vectors.

The sphere has an exact mathematical center. The radius of the factor-analytic space, of which it is a model, is defined by the maximum correlation (either 1.00 or −1.00) of any two measured variables. The global interior space is also called the intercorrelation space. A large collection of intercorrelated variables located in this space is included in Appendix A.

Each of the twenty-six named vectors is a part of the mathematical model of the system which is used in various ways. Vector mathematics is a body of mathematical theory used to represent the result of combining the effects of a number of forces pushing or pulling in different directions and acting upon each other within the space at the same time.

Thus far, I have offered three different visualizations of the space and what goes on in it (systemic connections). They all refer to the same space. The first is the "interpersonal interactional bubble of process" that can be seen (partly) by the naked eye in real time. The second is the cube diagram of figure 1.3, a geometric model to provide names and directions for the vector theory of the way different "forces" combine to influence each other and lead to an outcome. The third is the spherical model of the three-dimensional, bipolar factor-analytic space that can be used to incorporate correlational data and meanings from previous factor analyses. The three visual models serve to introduce the terminology used in this chapter to describe the findings from a number of different factor analyses and to show how they can be fitted together as pictures of the relationships of variables in the same theoretical space. My real aim is to be able to talk about each vector specifically and about the relationships of vectors to each other.

In factor-analytic language, vectors which point in directions that are close to each other, such as Vectors U and UP, are said to be positively correlated with each other. Vectors which point in opposite directions, such as Vectors U and D, are negatively correlated with each other. Vectors that have neither a positive nor negative relationship are said to be zero-correlated. In the factor-analytic model, for example, the Vectors U, P, and F are zero-correlated, or "orthogonal" (at right angles to each other in the physical space).

## Appendix A Contains the Empirical Heart of the Theory

A fourth tool for exploring the relationships of variables to vectors in the present theory is a series of lists in Appendix A called the *Intercorrelation Space*. Each of the lists corresponds to one of my twenty-six vectors. These twenty-six vectors constitute a minimal definitive framework of *classes* of variables according to how they are predicted to affect other variables, and how they are predicted to be affected by those other variables in real social interaction.

My orientation of the dimensions, vectors, and variables is based closely on the interpersonal-behavior space, according to congruence as seen by observers. The orientation I show is the one which matches the kind of values that observers and group members tend to attribute to other persons, on the basis of what those others say (and probably also on the way they seem to behave) in an interacting group. The group members to whom the values are attributed do not always agree that their values are correctly seen and it seems quite apparent that motivated distortions are common on the part of both parties to the interaction. In fact, persons quite often believe their values are misunderstood, and they are often observed to behave in ways that are inconsistent with the values they profess. The two spaces, that of interpersonal behavior and that of attributed values seem to be isomorphic.

Appendix A is based principally, but not entirely, on the large study conducted by Couch and myself for his dissertation (Couch 1960) and on my own further consolidation and coordination of the data with the vector classes of the present model from the detailed tables of factor loadings in a number of different factor analyses by Couch (Bales 1970). The omnibus study of the late 1950s included a very large number of variables. In the original design of the study many variables which were expected to be "socially undesirable" were included, as well as many expected to be "socially desirable" (on this variable see Hare, Hare, and Koenigs 1996).

My earlier studies of social interaction (using IPA) provided a considerable number of kinds of observed variables for the large study, measures both of acts initiated and acts received. The factor analysis of values, described earlier in chapter 4, provided recognizable factors that made it possible to classify value statements made in the course of live interaction, and relate them to the specific persons who initiated them and toward whom. A number of standard personality tests of the participants were included. A number of interpersonal perception measures and measures of liking and disliking were included.

Couch and I wanted to study the intercorrelations of as many of these kinds of variables as possible when measured in the same group or set of groups. We accepted the handicap that the number of variables was so large that some unreliable correlations would appear by accident. The number of subjects we were able to manage was quite small (only sixty in all). Any good statistician would complain that we had far too few subjects and far too few groups to be able to get reliable information on the huge number of variables we wanted to relate to each other. We knew that very well, but we accepted the handicap for the sake of a first look at the territory. The number of variables was also far too large to include in a single factor analysis, given our computer capability at the time. Our solution was to divide the data in such a way as to be able to do a number of smaller factor analyses.

Appendix A incorporates many variables from many different studies into a single classification system, which moves around the intercorrelation space in the sequence of my twenty-six value vectors. Variables, such as the scores of individuals on a particular personality test, for example, Thurstone's test of Dominance, can be *interpolated* into the space of the present theory by careful examination and theoretical inferences. This is demonstrated for the observations of Value Content Analysis (VCA) in Appendix A. To be inserted in Appendix A, a variable must have been a part of a previous actual factor analysis that showed at least three approximately orthogonal dimensions analogous in content to the three that are part of the present theory (U-D, P-N, and F-B).

This sort of insertion on the basis of inference can be done by explicit mathematical procedures if the actual factor loadings are available, or it can be done by an artistically guided fitting of a graphic plot of item locations in relation to the three factors. If the orthogonal factors of the factor-analytic space seem to be the three of the present system, or if the factors discovered can be rotated to a satisfactory match to the present three, then the vector engine (described in chapter 2) of the present system can convert those factor loadings into a location of the variable in the theoretical three-dimensional social-interaction-system space. From the location of the variable in the orthogonal three-factor space, the vector engine can determine its vector attributes, and then determine what the closest vector is in the present system of vectors.

If these conditions are met, items from past factor analyses can be incorporated and the data brought to bear on the general theory. We can form a hypothesis that the relations between variables that the earlier analyses show to be connected are somehow closely connected with the general tendencies characteristic of social-interaction systems. A very large amount of published data remains to be explored in the case of the present theoretical space. I shall demonstrate this procedure for a number of different factor analyses later in this chapter.

I assembled the picture I present of the three dimensions and twenty-six vectors in Appendix A partly by matching across separate factor analyses and intercorrelation tables on the basis of marker variables and some risky inferences. For these reasons, I do not include actual numerical correlations or factor loadings and I do not make strong claims about the replicability of all the relationships I report. In fact, it is clear by now that, in principle, the whole shape of the intercorrelations in the space must be expected to shift to some degree according to the specific group and many other conditions. The set of relationships will change systematically from groups operating at near optimum, and groups which fail to reach optimum. My principal aim is to present a glimpse of the holistic network of interconnections which make up a social-interaction system.

Appendix A provides a summary of concrete variables and their relationships, but in order to make it yield maximum insight, one needs to be able to visualize actual persons, and to visualize their discrete acts directed toward each other in direct interchanges of action and reaction, distributed over time. One needs to see what kinds of acts follow what kinds of preceding acts, who initiates what kinds of acts, who follows whom in person-to-person interchanges. One needs to be curious as to what general features of the organization of interpersonal relations will tend to emerge, why, when, and how rapidly.

A systematic overview of this everyday level of process, and in particular an overview of the more regularized outcomes that tend to emerge, was completely lacking in the literature of the early part of the century. These deficiencies were probably due, at least in part, to the lack of first-hand experience in the observation of social interaction. Below I attempt to give some flavor, in metaphorical terms, of some of my own experiences and thoughts derived from first-hand observation in the initially leaderless problem-solving groups with which I began my research. These were not precisely my thoughts at the time. They reflect my perspective looking back from 1997 to 1947 or thereabouts.

## A *Field* of Value Judgments

The value space appears to me to be an accumulated result of persons' attempts to rationalize and make normative the kinds of judgments they make about the interpersonal behavior of others with whom they have been in inter-action, and those they have witnessed. However, formulated values may be-come relatively independent of one's own behavior for various reasons. Value concepts and value judgments are inherently abstract and vague: they are passed on through socialization and learned directly through language, they are used in various polarized struggles between subgroups and are defen-sively used in the psychic economy of individual personalities.

With a little study of Appendix A, the nature of the main "forces" repre-sented by the vectors may be intuitively understood, I believe. The main mea-surable forces are "values" and "value judgments"—emotionally loaded motivational tendencies to act in this way or that toward other individuals, and to react to actions of others according to the value significance of their actions.

Values are intuitively understood in the present theory as broad internal motivations that tend to impel behaviors of the individual who is committed to them in given directions that the actor believes tend to satisfy or realize the particular kind of value. Action impelled by values of any of the twenty-six classes of values selected for the present system inevitably, it seems to me, have implications for other persons with whom one is engaged in interaction, and almost inevitably evoke a reaction in others, although different reactions in different persons. One can hardly act in *any* way in a social-interaction context without giving cues to others as to what values are in one's mind. These social actions and reactions, seen and evaluated in turn, are motiva-tional driving forces within individuals which, in the course of social interac-tion, tend to assume the regularities of a "system."

Reading the description of a value vector in Appendix A may bring to mind a particular person. Pictures of persons one knows, or knows about, are bound to pop into one's mind. This is no accident, of course. There are per-sons, it seems, who emphasize a particular small set of values so dependably in what they say and do that they become stereotypes, and almost personify the values in the eyes of others.

The theory assumes that in a given person's mind, in fact in the minds of all of the persons involved, *all* of the values represented by the twenty-six vector titles (Appendix A) do in fact tend to be present and activated to some degree, and to interact, oppose and strengthen each other, and qualify each other in the process of evaluating and making decisions. It is assumed that all twenty-six kinds of values potentially make a difference in any given deci-sion and are intuitively brought to bear in the perception and evaluation of any given object, any Image, or "issue" that a group member is asked to "describe" in the data-gathering procedure.

Each concrete part of the real social-interaction system, such as a given person as a participant, as seen and evaluated by the others, can be converted into an evaluated Image by the rating process described earlier. The profile of one Image can be correlated directly with the profile of each other Image over the twenty-six component values of that Image. Or the profile of a given Image as seen by one member can be correlated with the profile of the same Image as seen by another member.

A high positive correlation is construed as indicating a high degree of similarity among the values of two Images, and is expected by social-psychological hypotheses to constitute an attractive element in the relationship of two members as the similarity becomes known. A high negative correlation is similarly construed to contribute to an element of rejection between two members.

It is assumed that as any pair of members have the opportunity to interact with each other, they will tend to move from their initially estimated position in the space either toward a closer location of greater similarity or toward a more separated location of greater difference between them. Polarized clusters may then tend to form and to become more sharply defined as a result of interaction of participants and their growing knowledge of their value similarities and differences.

A cluster of positively correlated images of persons in a particular group may then be seen as constituting a subgroup. A far distant cluster in another part of the space may be seen as potentially, if not actively, an opposed subgroup, polarized or in conflict in relation to the first. A positively correlated cluster of images of philosophical ideas and concepts or a positively correlated set of values may be seen as an ideology. A far distant cluster of images of philosophical ideas or concepts may be seen as an opposing ideology.

The set of all Images can then also be described as an interacting set of value judgments made by the participants. The interaction of values is of course accomplished mainly by communications between participants, and it may be affected by all sorts of interferences with complete communication. But every real element in the real system can be compared in its potential effect to every other real element because all of the elements have been rendered as comparable kinds of entities, that is, value judgments in terms of the same twenty-six value items.

The field of value judgments has a "structure." But the structure is far from rigid. Many or most of the individuals in the system may be confronted with needs to promote changes in the prevailing structure. This means a need for problem solving of some variety, and this means a need to convert new elements of the "situation," both external and internal to the group, into value judgments on which a sufficient number of group members can agree. And this means a certain amount of conflict, both at the individual level and at the group level.

We all have an intuitive understanding from our own experience of the fact that one value judgment can affect another value judgment within our own minds. We feel that all of our value judgments are somehow interdependent and consistent with each other, or should be, if our mind is working right. Most of us are made uncomfortable, even anxious or guilty, to become aware of the fact that one value judgment we have made conflicts with another value judgment that we also have made or cannot help making. If we become aware of acute conflict we may have to retrace our mental steps again and again to make sure that the values really do conflict, or in order to come to the conclusion that one value is more important than the other, so that the one of lesser importance can be discounted or even violated in the particular case. Much discussion in many groups is given over to attempts to untangle and reconcile conflicting value judgments.

Leon Festinger (1957) called one aspect of this discomfort "cognitive dissonance." Perhaps "value conflict" is a broader conception of what is usually involved. William Graham Sumner (1959) spoke of a "strain toward consistency" of the mores of complete societies, although he was not very clear in explaining what was involved, who felt the strain, or how. But in all cases of group problem solving, some choices as to what values should be given what priority are required, whether implicitly or explicitly, in order to achieve a sufficient mobilization of evaluative forces among the members to support collective action. Each thinking individual has these problems of choice, and each intact group has them. A major assumption of the present system is that value judgments always tend to require choices of priority to be given among values.

In an intact group, a change in the evaluation given to any important value likely will involve changes of essentially three different kinds. These kinds are represented by the three most important dimensions of values in the space. The space of value judgments, in its origins and meanings, is an intercorrelation space actually created by the events and experiences over a span of time in the context of a system of social differentiations among members. To propose a change in value judgments always has the potential, including threats to some of the members, of changing the differentiations among them, that is, the social relationships.

The critical differentiations in terms of social positions, as described using the three major dimensions of the intercorrelation space, are as follows:

1. A main array of differentiation typically parallels the U-D dimension, as a continuum of positions of increasingly higher social status, typically associated with greater rewards.
2. Another differentiation, in positions of different degrees of acceptance as a member of a unified group, follows the P-N dimension. This determines the friendliness and liking or unfriendliness and dislike received from other group members.
3. Finally, there appears to be the more complex dimension of F-B. Most

fundamentally perhaps, this is a dimension of different kinds and amounts of contribution to work on group tasks, but in almost all groups these contributions and efforts are coordinated by some kind of leadership or authority. Hence differentiation in the F-B dimension brings with it differential achievement, differential rewards, differential approval by authority, and typically differential degrees of conventionality and obedience in relation to authority and group tradition.

The individual's place in these socially generated dimensions of differentiation among participants, and their consequences within an intact group, can hardly fail to be of some concern to nearly all participants. Social position in each of these scales of difference enhances or degrades the self-picture in relation to each other participant. At the extremes, the consequences of differentiated group position may either promise to improve, or to threaten, an individual's chances for survival.

### Factor-analytic and Circumplex Approaches

To my delight and relief, within the past four years (1994 and 1997) the American Psychological Association has published two very heavy books reviewing two different approaches in psychometric measurement, the factor-analytic approach and the circumplex approach. One of the new books is a multiple-author review of the factor-analytic approach, edited by Paul T. Costa and Thomas A. Widiger (1994). The other new book is a multiple-author review of the circumplex approach edited by Robert Plutchik and Hope R. Conte (1997). These two books more than take the place of any attempt of mine to cover the relevant ground. I will discuss these two approaches, the factor-analytic and the circumplex, and how they relate to my space as I comment on previous specific studies.

For measurement and practical diagnoses in clinical work with patients the two approaches may seem competitive, particularly because they are designed for diagnosis of personality disorders. For theoretical purposes, enhancing understanding of the intercorrelations in the social-interaction space, which I maintain is the source of the generalizations described by both, the two approaches are essentially complementary.

Their complementarity becomes evident, if one recognizes that the intercorrelation space they address is the same, in the most general theoretical sense, as the one I describe—the twenty-six vector intercorrelation space. This space is spherical, essentially three dimensional, each dimension of which is bipolar. The intercorrelations of the variables in both approaches are systematically generated by the participation of individuals in social interaction in intact groups. The factor-analytic approach searches for dimensions and vectors in the three dimensions. The circumplex approach searches for connected circular belts around various circumferences of the sphere.

The circumplex model articulates a belt of descriptive items passing all the way around the circumference of my spherical intercorrelation space, whereas the factor-analytic models are like spokes at ninety-degree intervals (orthogonal to each other) leading out from the center of the spherical space to a particular place on the spherical surface.

## Some Specific Studies in Relation to the Intercorrelation Space

In the early stages of my research and theorizing I had no idea of the magnitude and complications of the problems I was trying to solve, and almost no idea of the implications of my findings for a general model of social-interaction systems, including systems much larger than the small groups I was studying. I know that the present attempt to give a more formal description of the mature theory may have defects. It will not be crystal clear to many readers. It is still not crystal clear in all of its implications to me.

The conception of the three organizing dimensions enabled me to enlarge and transcend, and at the same time to incorporate and summarize much of what I had learned about the more microscopic act-to-act dynamic tendencies of social behavior from the observational studies in the early part of my research using *Interaction Process Analysis* (IPA) (Bales 1950).

The factor analysis of value statements that Couch and I made in the early 1950s and the later very large study I call the "omnibus study" had a very important organizing effect on my underlying theory. The idea of a complete space provided a new key for me. Within this space positively and negatively correlated variables have different locations. The variables (different kinds of values and behaviors) attract and repel each other, and exert force in different directions.

Some of the factor-analytic studies which have been important for me, and important historically in the development of social psychology, will be presented for illustration. In the case of most of these studies, it has not been generally recognized that the many different studies of factor structures roughly match, or fit together and dovetail in important ways, at various rotations. In some cases, a dimension or a vector or two has been completely missing, and there are other irregularities which must be taken into account. The fact that the various factor structures show the similarities they do, and fit together as they do, demonstrates that they are all outcome traces of comparable generating conditions. The relationships of the variables have been generated in the context of social-interaction systems.

The following discussion explores different levels of behaviors, emotions, values, fantasies, and other levels that are involved in a complete intact and operating social-interaction system. Actually the specific studies I have chosen to discuss are only a drop in the bucket. I want to acknowledge some that have been important to me because I early became aware of them.

*Myron Wish and Associates*

Myron Wish arrived at a four-dimensional factor-analytic structure through a series of studies with Deutsch, Kaplan, D'Andrade, and Goodnow, concentrating first on the description of hypothetical social relationships (such as husband and wife, parent and child, lawyer and client) then later concentrating on the observation of individuals in interaction (Wish 1976; Wish, Deutsch, Kaplan 1976; Wish, D'Andrade, and Goodnow 1976).

The first three orthogonal factors of Wish's factor analysis are exactly the same as the three dimensions shown in my cube model, although he gives the dimensions somewhat different names. My U-D dimension, *Dominance versus Submissiveness*, Wish calls "Ascendancy (Plus) versus Ascendancy (Minus)." My P-N dimension, *Positive* or *Friendly versus Negative* or *Unfriendly*, Wish calls "Evaluation (Plus) versus Evaluation (Minus)." My F-B dimension, *Forward* or *Acceptance of the Task Orientation of Established Authority versus Backward* or *Rejection of the Task Orientation of Established Authority,* Wish calls "Task Orientation (Plus) versus Task Orientation (Minus)."

Wish's fourth factor is a dimension he first called "Intensity," later "Arousal." It is minor, and it is not well described by adjectives in Wish's study. This factor may describe the intensity of polarized conflict between persons in any of the opposed vectors in the three-dimensional space. For example, it may be the element of emotional arousal that is often a component of the B-dimension reference vector. Perhaps "Arousal" sometimes splits off as a fourth separate factor. At any rate, Wish finds that there is an opposite end of the Vector F, even if emotional expressiveness is split off. That opposite end is behavior that is counter to task-oriented behavior and is judged by other members or observers in the context of the demands of the task to be "Unproductive" (one of Wish's adjectives).

*Johann Schneider and Peter Orlik*

Schneider and Orlik (1982), using behavior adjectives describing persons, have successfully reproduced the factor space as I describe it. Orlik has constructed a rating form in the German language, with all twenty-six vectors successfully defined. Orlik's (1987) method of grouping the vectors together is new and does not precisely agree with either the factor-analytic or the circumplex approach, but has similarities to both. It is comparable to the location and outlining of areas on the surface of the sphere, like the separate "continents" on a world globe.

*Ralph Stogdill and Associates*

Stimulated by efforts during World War II to improve understanding of leadership, investigators such as Stogdill (1974) made a number of studies of the intercorrelations of ratings of traits they associated with leadership. With the restricted type and number of descriptive adjectives Stogdill and others used, they typically found some version of a two-factor space, probably better conceptualized as a two-*vector* space, since the opposing ends of each vector were not tapped at all. No appropriate adjectives or items were included to represent the opposing ends. The location of these two vectors are apparently the same, or nearly so, as the vectors locating the two types which I recognized and called *task leaders* and *social leaders* (Bales 1956).

One of the vectors that Stogdill called "Initiation of Structure" seems to approximate the values of my Vector 4 UF, *Efficiency, strong impartial management*. The other vector, orthogonal (not opposite) to the first, Stogdill called "consideration." This vector seems to approximate the values of my Vector 2 UP, *Popularity and social success, being liked and admired*. My Vectors 4 UF and 2 UP are orthogonal to each other in the two-dimensional plane of the Field Diagram, although both are correlated with Vector 1 U.

### Arthur S. Couch and Launor F. Carter

Couch and Carter (1952), using factor analysis applied to studies of the interaction of students in initially leaderless groups, systematized the findings of the leadership researches of the Stogdill group into three orthogonal factors. These three factors, with behavioral descriptions, coincide in meaning exactly with the three directions, or vectors, of my cube diagram (figure 1.3) that are labeled U, P, and F. My U vector Couch and Carter called "Individual Prominence." My P vector they called "Group Sociability." My F vector they called "Group Goal Facilitation." My wordings for these vectors in terms of values, rather than behavior, are as follows: Vector 1 U, *Individual financial success, personal prominence and power*; Vector 10 P, *Equality, democratic participation in decision making*; and Vector 12 F, *Conservative, established, "correct" ways of doing things.*

The direct opposite of these three directions—Vectors 26 D, 14 N, and 16 B—were not recognized as part of the general behavior space by the leadership researchers of Stogdill's group, nor by Couch and Carter. Probably nobody doing the leadership research at that time thought that acts in the D, N, and B directions were likely to describe acts of leadership, at least not the kind of leadership they implicitly had in mind, and so they did not provide relevant adjectives on their rating forms. In contrast, in my general framework for describing all social interaction, as in my method for Interaction Process Analysis (IPA), acts with these directions are found. My value wordings for these three vectors are: 26 D, *Giving up personal needs and desires*; 14 N, *Self-protection, self-interest first, self-sufficiency*; and 16 B, *Change to new procedures, different values, creativity.*

*Timothy Leary*

Leary (1957), working with a circumplex of correlations between descriptive items in a clinical setting where diagnosis and treatment of personality problems was the aim, articulated the two dimensions I call U-D and P-N. Leary's terms for my U-D dimension were the same as mine: "Dominance" and "Submission." His terms for my P-N dimension were "Love" and "Hate." Leary did not explicitly recognize the F-B dimension, although his detailed adjective descriptions seem to me to show a "waffling" back and forth in their content along the F-B dimension, some items apparently showing an F component and some of them showing a B component. His failure to recognize the F-B dimension was possibly due to the fact that he was dealing with a population of persons with clinical personality problems, which are probably more evidently connected with emotions than with the F-vector values.

The circumplex method of analysis proceeds by maximizing the correlations of one descriptive item to the next in a circular order. Circumplexes typically show what I call two orthogonal bipolar dimensions, U-D and P-N, as Leary's circumplex does. Circumplexes tend to be less attentive to distinctions in the F-B dimension, as in Leary's case. However, in principle, a circumplex can be defined for *any* complete belt around the three-dimensional intercorrelation globe.

Leary recognized a number of intervening vectors between each of the dimensional ends. His circumplex located in terms of my vectors would earmark the following: proceeding clockwise from 1 U to 2 UP, 10 P, 18 DP, 26 D, 22 DN, 14 N, 6 UN, and back to 1 U. This fine breakdown of intervening vectors is of the essence in circumplex models, of course, since otherwise one could not find connected belts of intercorrelated items.

*Albert Mehrabian*

A different domain, or level, of the total behavioral process, that of feelings and emotions, was explored by Mehrabian and his colleagues (1980). It appears that the three orthogonal factors they describe on the basis of many factor-analytic studies are a direct fit to the three orthogonal dimensions of my model. Each of Mehrabian's factors, as in my model, has an opposite end.

His first factor is called "Dominant." It is meant to apply to the felt emotional quality of the corresponding dominant behavior. His factor seems to be an appropriate emotional aspect of my dominant value Vector 1 U, *Individual financial success, personal prominence and power*. Its opposite end is called "Submissive" in Mehrabian's space, as well as mine.

Mehrabian's orthogonal factor called "Pleasant" refers to the kinds of feelings and emotions that I would expect to correspond to my behavior Vector P, *Friendly*. The behavior that observers will see as friendly will ordinarily be felt as pleasant by either the actor or the other or both. At the opposite end of this factor are the feelings and emotions Mehrabian calls "Unpleasant." This seems to correspond well with my opposite end, Vector N, *Unfriendly*. Behavior seen as unfriendly ordinarily will be accompanied by feelings and emotions felt as unpleasant probably by both the actor and the other.

Interactive behavior that observers see as *Emotionally Expressive* (my behavior Vector B, and perhaps some surrounding vectors, particularly perhaps UNB, UB, and UPB) seem related to the state of feelings and emotions that Mehrabian calls "Arousal." The opposite end of the factor called "Arousal" in Mehrabian's model is a measurable state or trait of the individual that Mehrabian calls "Stimulus Screening." The meaning of this state or trait was determined by various experiments. It means a tendency to hold emotional arousal in check by constriction of attention to a narrow band of stimuli, while screening out other stimuli as distracting. Observers, I suggest, would be expected to see the signs of this state as *Instrumentally Controlled*, my behavior Vector F, or perhaps Vector DF.

Mehrabian's three-dimensional space of feelings and emotions thus appears to be isomorphic with my interpersonal-behavior space, and portrays the congruent subjective feeling and emotional aspect of the overt behavior that observers normally read into the behavior, especially the nonverbal signs of feeling and emotion that the person "gives off."

Mehrabian regarded his factors as "Basic Dimensions for a General Psychological Theory." His concept of generality agrees with the assumption I make that my three dimensions are characteristic of social-interaction systems in general, and of personality differences among participants.

*Wilhelm Wundt*

Very early in the history of psychology, Wundt (1896) used a three-dimensional model to describe feelings. His model appears to be a description of the same space as Mehrabian's. Wundt's model was derived without benefit of factor analysis, but the three dimensions appear to be orthogonal, and each of his dimensions has an opposite end. In Wundt's model the vectors are located, in reference to my vector names in the cube diagram (figure 1.3), as follows: his vector "Lust," meaning approximately "Pleasant feeling," is located corresponding to my Vector P, and the opposite end, called "Unlust," meaning "Unpleasant Feeling," is located corresponding to my Vector N.

My U-D dimension is not recognized as such. Instead two vectors are recognized: one in a forty-five-degree rotation to the Backward side of my cube, corresponding to my Vector UB, and one in a forty-five-degree rotation to the Forward side of my cube, corresponding to my Vector UF. These two are orthogonal to each other, but presumably each of them would be correlated with Vector U. The feeling state corresponding to my Vector UB is called

"Erregung," roughly translated as "Excitement" or "Arousal." The orthogonal feeling state corresponding to my Vector UF is called "Spannung," roughly translated as "Strain" or "Tension."

These two orthogonal vectors are apparently the more *Dominant* ends of two orthogonal dimensions. Each of them has an opposite end, plausibly more *Submissive*. The opposite (more submissive) end of the UB vector, in my vector space is DF. The opposite (more submissive) end of Wundt's vector is "Behruhigung" (Calming of Emotion). The behavioral and value meanings of my Vector DF are consistent with Wundt's concept, and I think are consistent with Mehrabian's concept of "Stimulus Screening" as well.

The opposite (more submissive) end of Wundt's vector Spannung he calls "Lösung" (Releasing of Tension). In interaction itself, the releasing of tension is typically laughing. If the tension is actually lowered, the result presumably would be movement downward, perhaps toward D, but hardly DB, as I have conceptualized DB, my opposite to UF. The fit is problematic.

Wundt's space, the first we have looked at which seems to require a rotation to make a match, illustrates a most important point: in making these kinds of comparisons, it is essential to conceptualize the nature of the total space and its orthogonal dimensions implied by the factors in all rotations, and not simply to look for similarity of the dimensions at a particular rotation. A rotation different from the rotation as I picture and name it in the cube diagram (figure 1.3), can be recognized in a particular factor analysis, but very possibly one or more of my dimensions will be only implicit, and not explicitly named, or perhaps only dimly recognized, if at all. Wundt's rotation does not explicitly recognize my dimension U-D, but it seems to be plausible in the connotations of the others.

The critical feature of similarity to discern when making comparisons is the *isomorphism* of the space. A researcher can easily become distracted from this pursuit when seeking exact matchings of meaning of the names of the dimensions at a given rotation. These less-essential differences may prevent recognition of the basic isomorphism of two or more spaces. Possibly this has been an important barrier to integration of theory in the past.

### Charles Osgood

Osgood's "semantic differential" is possibly the most widely known of the various factor-analytic models relevant to the theory discussed here. It is, as originally conceived, a space of the semantic connotations of concepts (Osgood, Suci, and Tannenbaum 1957). However, it has been widely used to measure characteristics of interpersonal behavior, as for example, by Fred Fiedler (1967) in his work on situational leadership.

The adjectives used by Osgood in his measuring instruments (called "semantic differentials") and the things (or Images, in my terms) that he has measured with them are extremely varied. Some of his adjectives seem to apply to interpersonal behavior and emotions, but many apply in the first instance to impersonal objects, like clouds and feathers, states of affairs, and high-order cognitive abstractions. Osgood has shown that the three-dimensional semantic space is ubiquitous. It is found over many populations of concepts (rated objects) and is cross-culturally robust so far as he could test it.

Osgood's orientation of the three dimensions of the space seems to me to require the same rotation as Wundt's space. My comparisons of rotations are more artistically rigorous than they are statistical. In time they can be checked by comparative factor analyses. Nevertheless I think the intuitive and artistic comparisons are essential. If the artistic fit does not satisfy, it is doubtful that actual statistics will help very much.

The polar terms of Osgood's three factors are simple concepts expressed in basic English: "Good" and "Bad" for what he calls the Evaluation Factor; "Strong" and "Weak" for what he calls the Potency Factor; and "Fast" and "Slow" for what he calls the Activity Factor.

Mehrabian believes that his factors coincide with those of Osgood without rotation, but it seems probable to me that when Osgood's semantic differential is used to characterize concepts of interpersonal behavior, there will be some rotational difference. Osgood's vectors "Fast" and "Strong" will probably both be related to observers' judgments of "Dominance" in interpersonal behavior, and his vectors of "Slow" and "Weak" will both be related to "Submissive" interpersonal behavior. This fit would imply that "Strong" is likely to be close to my Vector UF, and "Fast" is likely to be close to my Vector UB.

Osgood's vectors of "Good" and "Bad" may be quite close to my Vector P, *Friendly*, and Vector N, *Unfriendly*, in the interpersonal-behavior domain, although when actual studies are made, they may be found close to my Vectors PF and NB. If the latter is true, it would imply that there may be some positive correlation between Osgood's vectors "Strong" and "Good," at least when the Images being rated are persons or interpersonal behavior. This is plausible in content associations, but it is not strictly consistent with orthogonality of the vectors. The equivalent in my terms would be "Strong" equals UF, and "Good" equals PF. The common content would be the F vector involvement of each.

According to a hypothetical mapping of the one space on the other, interpersonal behavior that is seen by observers as *Instrumentally Controlled* or *Task Oriented* (F-vector content) will be described on Osgood's semantic differential as "Slow" (my Vector DF), while some interpersonal behavior that is seen by observers as *Emotionally Expressive* (in this case DB) will be seen as "Weak."

Although the fit is not so convincing as one might like, the important point is that even the most abstract cognitive concepts and impersonal objects have a connotative-semantic dimensional structure which appears to be isomorphic with the behavior, emotional, and value domains. The general hypothesis suggested is that the objects and concepts that are used in the course of behavior, or are associated with it, acquire through learning, and through the structure of language itself, a connotative dimensional structure which is isomorphic with those of the social-interaction domains.

### Hans Eysenck and D. Melvin

Eysenck (1954) and Melvin (1953) have presented a two-factor structure of political attitudes and ideology based on Eysenck's earlier factor-analytic analyses of personality factors in the context of clinical work. Melvin has made studies of political attitudes and ideology in a number of different English-speaking countries, and Eysenck has written the published work. The items Melvin used were value statements, or statements of general attitudes on social issues. They were presented in surveys of items to which respondents were asked to agree or disagree. The two factors extracted by factor analysis are orthogonal to each other, and each one is bipolar. In Eysenck's published wording, the first bipolar factor is called "Tough-Minded versus Tender-Minded," and the second is called "Conservative versus Radical." Eysenck concludes that there are four major groupings of political parties or ideologies, which can be distinguished by their position on the two factors, considered jointly.

The items which measure the "Tough-Minded" vector in Eysenck's space are value statements which endorse, recommend, and rationalize behavior that would be called *Dominant* and *Unfriendly* in my interpersonal-behavior space, that is, behavior on and around the UN vector. His "Tough-Minded" vector would fall on my UN vector, and the opposite, his Tender-Minded, would fall on the DP vector, corresponding to behavior that might be described as *Submissive* and *Friendly*. In the same sense, Eysenck's "Conservative" vector is cognate to the F vector of the interpersonal-behavior space, in that the value statements on that vector place a high value on authority or established group norms which endorse, recommend, and rationalize interpersonal behavior that is *Task Oriented* and *Instrumentally Controlled*. Eysenck's "Radical" vector appears to correspond to my B vector.

Thus, according to Eysenck's interpretation, the Fascist ideology recommends behavior that is simultaneously "Tough-Minded" and "Conservative." It appears on the UNF vector of my space, which corresponds to behavior that is *Dominant*, *Unfriendly*, and *Task Oriented*. In a parallel sense, the "Tender-minded Conservatives," the Christian Democratic parties, recommend behavior that is *Task Oriented*, but *Friendly*, and *Submissive* (DPF in my space). What Eysenck calls the "Tender-minded Radicals," or "Liberals," recommend behavior that is *Friendly*, *Submissive*, and *Emotionally Expressive* (DPB in my space). The "Tough-minded Radicals," are the Communists. They recommend behavior that is *Dominant, Unfriendly*, and *Emotionally Expressive* (UNB in my space).

The fit of Eysenck's value space to the interpersonal-behavior space seems very good, in spite of the gap between the social-institutional level, to which the items are mostly directed, and the interpersonal-behavior level to which I have been referring. This has an important theoretical implication: values, which as I believe have their developmental origins in small-scale social interaction, continue to be important motivationally in large-scale social movements, ideologies, and institutions. The one book that occurs to me of having gone some distance in making these connections is *Psychoanalytic Study of the Family* by J. C. Flugel (1921).

From Eysenck's analysis it is also evident that the linkage between task-oriented interpersonal behavior and existing conservative norms and institutions is one which may often be broken and reversed in alienated portions of the population. The general point this illustrates is very important: although the various levels of the total process are of cognate dimensionality, any given level in a given case may show reversals, distortions, and departures from congruence with other levels for dynamic or motivational reasons. This point will be illustrated again with reference to the departures of fantasies and fantasy needs from congruence with either values or interpersonal behavior.

It is worth noting that one dimension of my model is missing in the Eysenck-Melvin analysis. The missing dimension is UP-DN. It is a little difficult to visualize this dimension of polarization as a focus of differences in political-economic attitudes, although one of the vectors of types of leadership according to Stogdill's and others results seems to be UP. It may be that the two polarizations indicated on the two diagonals of Eysenck's space—UNB versus DPF and UNF versus DPB—soak up, or attract, most of the variability of actual societal members because of the actual clustering of contending political parties.

Also notable is the absence from Eysenck's analysis of a position corresponding to my Vector UPF. This position in the space is shown by the analyses of SCG data to be highly valued as "effective," and is most attractive to members of business organizations (see chapter 6). It is highly associated with "effective leadership."

*Robert F. Bales and Arthur S. Couch*

In the early 1950s, as I have described in chapter 4, Couch and I undertook a huge dragnet approach to the problem of the factor structure of value statements and came up with four factors, which at the time we named: "Acceptance of Authority," "Need-determined Expression versus Value-determined Restraint," "Equalitarianism," and "Individualism" (Bales and Couch 1969).

Couch and I, with the help of Gene Kassebaum (1958), also observed and classified the value statements that our group members made in arguments with each other in small interacting groups. We discovered that although the four factors were appropriate for classification of the written value statements, the factors are differently oriented in relation to the behavior space when one is observing actual polarized arguments between people.

The most important difference perhaps was that people who were observed to initiate statements in favor of autocratic authority in an actual argument showed no particular tendency to agree with similar items on a paper survey. And, conversely, people who tended to agree with written items recommending autocratic authority, showed no particular tendency to make such statements to others in actual arguments. Our results indicated that people who initiate statements in actual group arguments recommending autocratic authority are seen by observers to show behavior that is *Dominant, Unfriendly,* and *Task Oriented,* while people who agree with such statements on paper typically show behavior that is *Friendly* and *Task Oriented.*

### David McClelland and the Level of Fantasy

The domain of fantasy or fantasy needs has been developed and studied extensively by McClelland (McClelland et al. 1953; McClelland 1961, 1975). He has not developed his measures by factor analysis, but nevertheless, over the course of time, has developed measures for three vectors of fantasy needs: "Need Power," "Need Affiliation," and "Need Achievement." In general, these appear to be isomorphic with the first three orthogonal vectors of the space of the present system, although the latter presents special problems, as discussed below.

"Need Power" is the fantasy desire to enact *Dominant* behavior (U). "Need Affiliation" is the fantasy desire to enact *Friendly* behavior (P). "Need Achievement" is the fantasy desire to enact *Task-oriented* or *Instrumentally Controlled* behavior of some kind, but as it appears from McClelland's research, not necessarily in conventional or traditional directions.

The opposite ends of these vectors are not articulated by McClelland. According to my expectation that different content domains will tend to show isomorphic similarities, the level of fantasy should tend to show an isomorphic dimensional structure with the main factors of the global social-interaction process. Thus we should be able to find fantasy needs for behavior that is *Submissive (D), Unfriendly* (N), and *Emotionally Expressive* (B). Because these behaviors are all on the "socially undesirable" side in most real systems, the number of persons showing such fantasies would be expected to be low. There can be no doubt that these directions of fantasy do exist in some persons. Such fantasies are seen most often, probably, by forensic psychologists, clinicians, and therapists.

McClelland's concept of "Need Achievement" presents an unusual problem for the hypothesis of isomorphism. "Need Achievement" might seem to be associated with values similar to those of Vector 12 F, *Conservative, established "correct" ways of doing things.* However, when individuals are taught to analyze fantasy protocols for Need-Achievement content, as in McClelland's method of Achievement Training, the effect may be to steer them toward values of individual freedom from the constraints of conventional work-oriented behavior. McClelland intended his Achievement-Training procedure to have this effect, and tried it, with this apparent result in India. He also produced content-analysis survey data, from a variety of societies, which seemed to indicate that changes toward content high in "Need Achievement" are associated with rapid social change toward modernization, and away from traditionalism (McClelland 1961).

In these cases of training of individuals to analyze fantasy protocols, measures of their own fantasies of "Need Achievement" seem to depart from the conservatism of Vector 12 F in ways associated with individual freedom. In one of my groups, the members also took McClelland's tests. "Need Achievement" was highest for members who were rated by other members as near the UNB vector. "Need Achievement" is not dependably correlated with Vector 12 F, and indeed may tend to be negatively associated with it, according to context.

## The Isomorphism and Resonance of Multiple Levels

There are many other models either based on factor analysis or on circumplex analysis which ought to be considered for their special contribution to the emerging picture based on social-interaction systems theory. But it already appears evident that roughly isomorphic, if not completely intercorrelated, models exist over a broad band of levels and aspects of the global intercorrelated processes which arise when persons interact with each other.

The four domains—interpersonal behavior, feelings and emotions, values, and the semantic connotations of concepts—are all, in a methodological sense, accessible through ratings or some type of subjective judgment. I suggest that they are actually different but interdependent aspects of one global social-interaction process. One way of expressing this is to say that they represent different levels of the global process, but that is not an entirely satisfactory description of their relationships. The word "level" is ambiguous and overworked.

It is reasonable to suppose that particular levels may emphasize particular directions or dimensions. The basic dimensions of emotion and feeling appear to emphasize the U-D and P-N dimensions. Very possibly the more complex intellectualization involved in the F-B dimension may give it special characteristics. Rationality and elaboration of controls may be more characteristic of the F vector, for example.

Social interaction occurs simultaneously at multiple levels. When one individual acts, with perceptions of his or her own actions, thoughts, feelings, and values, and others react in a similar multiple-level way to what they perceive and infer about the acting individual, an interactive loop of interdependent processes is closed in upon itself. The processes within the heads and bodies of the individuals, shown in their nonverbal, overt, and verbal behavior, feed rapidly back and forth upon each other through communication, often with amplification and special features of the individual mental processes.

The communication takes place between the various levels or aspects of mental behavior within each individual, as well as between individuals. The total feedback loop of interactive processes now constitutes one resonant and reverberating system, a global totality of social and psychological processes, each part of which potentially affects each and all of the other parts. It is because each of the levels responds to and affects all of the other levels that the global total process and the specific level processes tend to acquire the same dimensionality. It seems appropriate to call such a resonant and reverberating process a social-psychological field, or a dynamic system field.

It is the essential isomorphism of individual fields with the inclusive social-interaction field that furnishes the key to a new approach to field theory in social psychology. The total global process includes the dynamics of the individual subjective fields, each one somewhat different from each other one, according to personality differences. It also includes the group dynamics which arise out of the communicative interaction of the individual fields with each other. It is the isomorphic dimensional structure of individual and social-interaction fields, and the *practicality* of concentrating on about three bipolar dimensions as principally important, that offers the possibility of a workable comprehension and measurement of the unthinkable complication of the real global process. My summary impression is that the various levels do have recognizable similarities in factor structure to each other.

## A Systems Theory of Social Psychology

A theoretical system which allows us to treat in parallel terms with one measurement system both the individual perceptual-evaluative fields and the inclusive social-interaction field of the same individuals may be called a field theory of social psychology, or a *systems theory of social psychology*. An extensive integrated development of such a theory is now within our grasp because we can now see the principal dimensions of these fields. We can see that the intercorrelation spaces are cognate and isomorphic in essential ways, and we have the means to measure and study the interacting variables within them.

The isomorphism of dimensions of the individual and social-interaction fields does not at all mean that, in a particular activated field, the self-pictures and behavior of all of the individuals involved are drawn toward similar locations in the space. But sometimes most of them are. In particular, the Positive or Positive-Forward part of the space seems to be a region of special attraction. Various images and sub-processes are drawn toward unification in this area described by values on Vector 3 UPF, *Active teamwork toward common goals, organizational unity.* When this region is activated in an idealized field only a few individuals may be additionally propelled in the Negative and Backward directions.

More often, the activated field is polarized or otherwise structured in a complex dynamic way. It is easy to visualize, for example, a line of polarization between *conservatives* who are drawn toward Vector 5 UNF, *Active reinforcement of authority, rules and regulations*, and *liberals*, who may be drawn toward Vector 9 UPB, *Protecting less able members, providing help when needed.* The polarization of UNF versus UPB appears in different kinds of groups: in a family between parents and children, in a legislative body between the right and the left with regard to a controversy over social welfare, in a business organization with regard to the conflicting values of management and workers.

The intercorrelation space is a space of polarities and approximate polarities—each of the major dimensions is bipolar, and each of the component directions or vectors is opposed by one or more others which can be expected to be active to some extent. In the real process, values and sub-processes associated with one pole of a dimension tend toward behavior that competes with, or aims to prevent, the realization of values or development of the kinds of behavior and sub-processes associated with values on the opposite pole.

Very often, individuals and the images and values they communicate about are involved in a dynamic struggle: a struggle of polarization between subgroups, each of which tends toward internally oriented unification and an externally oriented polarization toward other subgroups. An actual cluster of persons and values tends to form in one part of the intercorrelation space, or subgroups form in two or more conflicting polarized parts of the space, with unstable fluctuating coalitions of pairs of subgroups, now one pair, and now another, in triangular opposition to the third. ("Triangulation" is a term with a similar meaning from family therapy.)

After a period of stress and hard work in a small-group problem-solving session we often find a period of joking, laughing, and other friendly behavior that tends to restore the unification of the persons and their perceptions of each other tending toward the Positive side of the space. Pleasant feelings tend to activate friendly behavior, which activates concepts and talk of good features of the situation and arouses values and norms of equalitarian sharing. The content of the talk and the friendly behavior tends to arouse feelings of liking, and needs of affiliation. Continued friendly behavior intensifies liking and arouses more active emotion of a congruent pleasant and friendly sort. The persons interacting in this way develop perceptions and images of themselves and others that are in the Positive part of the intercorrelation space, and perhaps they develop images of themselves as members of a continuing group. They try to become more like each other. They imitate and reinforce one another toward successful modification of their behavior in the desired direction.

Janis (1982) called this syndrome "group think." Bion (1961) called it "pairing." Toennies (1957), with regard to the values of complete societies, called it a "Gemeinschaft." Durkheim (1960), pointing to the predominance of similarity in the values around a traditional minimal division of labor, called it a condition of "mechanical solidarity." Parsons called it a condition of solidarity between socially structured roles based on "particularism," "functional diffuseness," and "affectivity."

But, of course one should not forget that there are limits to the extent and duration of movement always in the same direction or set of directions. There are always competing values which can operate as brakes, and usually do, to some extent, although sometimes they fail until a damaging non-optimum extreme has been reached. The recognition of this danger is a feature of major importance in prediction and attempted intervention.

The development of a unified field pattern in one part of the space, for instance around Vector 11 PF, *Responsible idealism, collaborative work*, tends to compete with and preclude the expression of Images and processes in other parts of the space, such as those around Vector 15 NB, *Rejection of established procedures, rejection of conformity*. Conflicting ideas and values are present to some extent in nearly all personalities, and they do not cease to exist just because they are not currently being expressed. They are held in suppression.

The suppression tends to become more oppressive to certain individuals as the majority movement in the PF direction intensifies and continues in time. The feeling of oppression may even grow to the point of alienation for certain individuals who are marginally attached to the majority movement. Hence there are breaking points and instabilities in all types of actual fields. This may be an advantage if the field is undesirable to some of the members—the breaking points and instabilities offer strategic points for introducing change.

A coalition formation of two or more members on the Positive side of the space with regnant values near Vector 10 P, *Equality, democratic participation in decision making*, is quite different from a coalition in which both are on the Negative side of the space near Vector 14 N, *Self-protection, self-interest first, self-sufficiency*. In the latter case, solidarity of the Negative coalition itself would seem to be always under threat.

Quite different again would be the emphasis if the interaction is in a polarization between two subgroups, one centered on values around Vector 4 UF, *Efficiency, strong impartial management*, and the other subgroup centered on values of emotional expression on the Negative and Backward side of the space, near Vector 7 UNB, *Rugged self-oriented individualism, resistance to authority*.

Requirements for successful leadership, teaching, and therapy are quite similar to each other in some ways. All of them may deal with individuals or subgroups who offer serious resistance. If a leader, a teacher, or a therapist is attempting to bring about attitude change in a subgroup centered around Vector 24 DB, *Passive non-cooperation with authority*, the approach might better lean in the direction of more friendly and equalitarian values than in a direction further Forward in the space toward values near Vector 12 F, *Conservative, established, "correct" ways of doing things*. The reason for this is that group solidarity, or interpersonal solidarity between the leader, teacher, or therapist and the resistant individuals, in most cases, needs to be present and activated before attempts to induce more task-oriented behavior are likely to be optimally successful. If friendly relationships with the leader, teacher, or therapist already exist, quite different opportunities are offered for movement in the task-oriented direction.

Boot-camp authoritarianism on the part of a leader, a teacher, or a "brain washer" in the dominant role can extract obedience from recruits, but this kind of process tends to begin and end with hazing and abuse, in order to weaken the self-picture and self-confidence of the victim. It takes hours of repetitive training to instill mindless obedience; it tends to produce brutality in the victim as well as in the perpetrator, and in actual combat it carries the hazard that the senior officer will be shot in the back, whether or not he was the actual drill sergeant.

Learning, memory, and recall probably have a rather different character when they take place under conditions on the Negative side of the space. For example when the intended learner's highest priority values are located near Vector 22 DN, *Passive rejection of popularity, going it alone*, the situation is quite different from one in which the learner's priority values are located on the Positive side, say near Vector 18 DP, *Trust in the goodness of others*. Efforts at behavior modification would not be expected to have dependable long-term favorable results if the rewards appear to the learner to be poison pills, and the teacher is regarded as an untrustworthy authoritarian threat.

Tendencies of participants in a pair relationship to seek "equity" (the subject of a considerable amount of social-psychological research) will surely differ greatly in character and magnitude depending upon whether both persons are involved in work together with regnant values near Vector 11, *Responsible idealism, cooperative work*, or whether the dominant one of the pair, whose value emphasis, consistent with his position in the organization, may be near Vector 5 UNF, *Active reinforcement of authority, rules, and regulations*, and the submissive other, whose value location, as a personality, is near Vector 21 DNF, *Self-sacrifice if necessary to reach organizational goals*. In an organizational setting, or almost any other, the latter kind of relationship is a "bad scene," a sadomasochistic relationship, and the problem of "equity" may be already submerged, or at any rate, transformed.

A mother in interaction with an infant, suffused, as she acts, with values on the *Friendly* and *Emotionally Expressive* side of the space near Vector 9 UPB,

*Protecting less able members, providing help when needed,* is not likely to be much concerned about "equity" in the relationship, and may not try to drive a hard bargain with the infant. On the other hand, if the infant will not be managed in spite of extreme efforts, the mother may redefine the situation into something quite different. She may revert to a more primitive kind of behavior which is also a part of her personality, ordinarily submerged, with tragic results.

It is hard to think of a detailed specialized process studied experimentally in social psychology which most of us would not expect to be affected significantly by the context of the global process, the actual role relationships and values of the persons involved, and the active values of the part of the space in which the global process is developing and amplifying, holding steady, or breaking up.

As social psychologists we are now in a position to study and compare the dynamics of different types of social-psychological fields and the way in which sub-phases of behavior and personality differences in values play a part in them. It appears to me that many, if not most, of the established empirical generalizations and theories of social psychology can readily be located within the framework of the dimensional model and, when so placed, begin to yield additional insights and hypotheses about interrelationships and qualifications. Social-interaction systems theory is the needed framework, I believe, for the long-desired integration of social psychology.

# Part 3

# Overt Interaction

# 6

# Observational Beginnings

*The unassisted hand, and the understanding*
*left to itself, possess but little power. Effects are*
*produced by the use of instruments and helps,*
*which the understanding requires no less than*
*the hand; and as instruments either promote*
*or regulate the motion of the hand, so those*
*that are applied to the mind prompt or*
*protect the understanding.*

—Francis Bacon
*Novum Organum,* 1620

Theorists in the early period of social psychology had no detailed or dynamically organized *systemic* theory of the nature of either the "self" or the "situation." In the language of the time, meanings and values existed as parts of the society prior to the existence and development of any particular self. They are "taken into" the particular self in the course of socialization. Values and meanings within the developing self thus become structured in essentially the same way that society is structured. The person then "ejects" or "projects" those same values and meanings out onto social objects and gives them their meanings at a particular time in "defining the situation" for the act.

No doubt this summary is incomplete, and a little unfair. It could be improved, but it expresses approximately my level of understanding of the theorists of the time (Bales 1941). Mead (1934) was a partial and crucial exception, in that he saw the generative character of concrete interaction itself, but he did not go far in articulating the value content of social-interaction systems.

In retrospect, it seems clear to me what was missing in the theory of the day. With only minor exceptions, there was essentially no empirically based theory that gave any actual schedule or proposed list of values for covering the necessary variety of content. Hardly anybody even raised the following sorts of questions: What are the most critically important values necessary to an adequate definition of the situation? Where do they come from? Why these and not others? How do these critically important values relate to each other?

155

Without a theory that recognizes and tries to give answers to these questions, theories of the "self" (or more exactly, personality) and its dynamics must remain essentially empty of value content. The same must be said of the "situation." Without a theory of the content and variety of values and their dynamics, there is not a chance of adequately understanding what an individual does when he "defines the situation."

There was another huge gap in theory that was hardly noticed, given the ethos of the time. With the exception of the evolutionary interactive behaviorism of Mead, essentially all the schemas for describing self and situation visualized most clearly the motivation and point of view of only a single individual and the time span of a single act of that same individual. Edward Tolman described the act as the behavior that took place "from start to end phase." He was describing the world from the single rat's point of view. But Tolman was not alone. Most of the schemas concerned with acts or action covered only about as much ground as necessary to theorize about the behavior of a single rat in the maze, traversing the maze from one end to the other.

Thinking about behavior in this way, the situation is the setting in which instrumental goal-oriented behavior takes place. Action in the situation proceeds by utilizing available means to achieve ends or goals. Ends are defined by values which determine what is desirable. Means are defined by meanings given to aspects of the situation that can be utilized in action to achieve ends. The aspects of the situation that stand in the way of action, as conditions that cannot be changed or that are difficult to change, can be called barriers. There is nothing essentially wrong about this way of thinking except that it is seriously lacking in content and scope.

Almost none of the psychologists or social psychologists I read in the late 1930s asked how a theorist might think about the mental processes of multiple individuals in interaction, with multiple and partially conflicting values, multiple meanings, multiple means, multiple ends, multiple goals, multiple barriers, multiple acts, all interacting in one large mess over long time spans with lots of repetitive cycles and slowly changing conditions. This multiplicity is the condition when real individuals are in real social interaction.

Hardly anybody in the early days had actually studied social interaction *observationally* in real time, so these problems did not even begin to come into concrete focus for social psychologists. Sociologists, political theorists, and philosophers had been worrying about these problems from a less concrete point of view however, for some long time. Some of these problems, at least, go under the label of the "problem of order in society." How does order, at least such order as does exist, come into being?

I finally decided that in order to get a better grip on how to describe the "self," the "situation," "values," "meanings," and the rest of the "floating universe," I needed to study "social interaction." It was not very clear to me just how that might help, but I had the feeling that what I visualized as the "study of small groups" was practically manageable, and that if I could just observe social interaction in small groups long enough I might get myself straightened out.

I kept trying throughout my graduate training, and well beyond, to work my way out of persistent uncomfortable feelings. It was not only the "situation," "meanings," "values," and "social interaction" that gave me trouble, but almost all other abstract terms. Because of the semantic and syntactic interconnections of words and concepts already furnished by the magnificent English language, I was able to produce what sounded like theoretical sense and real substance in talking about behavior and social systems, but all too often I felt that in terms of empirical facts I really did not know what I was talking about.

I was pretty sure that I did not know what I was talking about since I had been well exposed to the problems and thought traps of semantics by way of Korzybsky, Ogden and Richards, William James, and several other pragmatic philosophers. I knew, as Korzybsky was so fond of saying, that "the map is not the territory." It seemed to me that what I had in my mind was a bundle of not very good maps, and I could not get them properly sorted out and matched up to each other. I knew, as Korzybsky said, that the "word is not the thing." My persistent trouble was that I could not figure out what the "thing" was.

I remember, for example, that it sounded convincing enough to say that "frustration tends to produce aggression." But I realized that there were so many things that might be regarded as frustration, and so many things that might be regarded as aggression, that the generalization seemed to lack meaning. I had the same trouble with "self-interest," "utility," "reinforcement," "reward" and "punishment;" "means" and "ends," "conditions," "structure" and "function," and with "equilibrium."

Unfortunately the same semantic vagueness infested the set of concepts that I myself chose in order to describe "functional problems" of "social-interaction systems." These were: "instrumental," "adaptive," "integrative," and "expressive" functional problems (see Bales 1950). These four concepts seemed to help a little, since they seemed to be appropriate for describing problems of systems of multiple individuals (rather than just the mental processes of one individual) but I found them also to be too slippery in their meaning as I tried to use them. I still felt I did not know what I was talking about. I could not figure out quite why, or what to do about it.

I later realized that one of the major problems grew out of the fact that in reality it is always necessary to deal with systems within systems, within systems, and so on, *ad infinitum*. Any system, which is the focus of scrutiny, is composed of similar systems which are smaller, and similar systems which are larger. Each system seems to be constructed on essentially the same model as the ones which are larger and the ones which are smaller, but with emergent differences at each level. Thus, the scrutinizer must constantly question on which level a functional problem is enacted: Just whose integration? Just whose instrumental problems? Just when does this take place? Adaptation to what? Expressive of what?

## The Setting for My Observations: The Department of Social Relations

Finally I had the opportunity to begin real research as a junior member of the new Department of Social Relations at Harvard. The new department was dedicated to the integration of sociology, social psychology, personality psychology, and social anthropology—quite an order! According to the aspirations of its chairman, Talcott Parsons (and my own aspirations as well), the new department was also informally dedicated to the development of what he called the "general theory of action" (Parsons and Shils 1954). I often thought that the general theory of action must actually be social psychology, and that pleased me, but it did not solve my problems. Unfortunately almost everything I knew was already so much "general" theory that I could not tell what it meant.

I decided to start trying to untangle my theoretical perplexities by the study of social interaction in small groups, through direct observation and recording, act by act. "Social interaction" was the grand integrative concept of the University of Chicago school of sociology. My major professor at the University of Oregon, Samuel Jameson, had been well soaked in it, by way of a channel which ran through the University of Minnesota. He passed the conviction of its importance on to me.

I had to take a little disapproval from one of my senior professors, Professor Pitirim Sorokin, for my decision to study small groups. He was the founder and chairman of the Department of Sociology at Harvard, from which I had received my Ph.D. in Sociology in 1945. The Department of Sociology had been ingested whole in 1945 by the new Department of Social Relations. Sorokin felt no enthusiasm about having his department swallowed, and thereafter stayed home in Winchester as much as he could and tended his azalea garden.

Professor Sorokin's happy hunting ground for studying what he called "social and cultural dynamics" was the entire history of Western Civilization (Sorokin 1937). In fact I derived my beginning concepts of the dynamics of small groups from sociological theories on the grand scale (Bales 1950), including his own theories, but he either did not know this, or ignored it for polemic purposes. Small groups looked like pretty small potatoes to him.

According to Professor Sorokin my decision to study small groups was nonsense. It was one more fad among the other *Fads and Follies in Modern Sociology* (Sorokin 1956). He said my decision was comparable to that of a botanist who decided to define and study the class of "small plants from two to twenty-five inches high as a distinct species," or of a biologist who decided to define and study a "nosey species" as the class of "all organisms which have a nose."

Professor Sorokin did not share my conviction that the dynamics of small social systems and large social systems must be parallel in important ways, and that one might learn something from concentrating on a system small and accessible enough to provide the kind of detailed data needed.

My colleague George Homans, six years my senior, was the other small-group researcher in the new department, and so, in a way, he was also my competitor. However, his rationale for studying small groups was not very different from mine. He said he wanted to study something "small enough to get his mind around."

## The Flavor of Social Interaction in Real Time

For about five years from 1945 to 1950, I observed students in small groups trying to solve problems and make decisions. My present conceptions of *social-interaction systems* and what I now call *dynamic system fields* go back very directly to the experiences of that time.

I wanted to see what happened when small groups of persons who did not know each other were put together with a common task, but with no designated leader and no specified organization. I wanted to see developments from scratch of what sociologists called "group structure," "role differentiation," "leadership," and the like. I was trying to understand the motivations and functions of different kinds of acts, the sequences of acts, their relative frequencies, the ways in which the action switched back and forth among the participants, and so on.

In a typical sample of what I observed, somebody might introduce an opinion. Somebody else would disagree. Somebody else would call attention to the facts that would have to be true if the opinion were justified, and then begin to reel off presumably relevant facts. Somebody else would disagree and start an alternative recitation. Suddenly somebody else, without any prelude, would just jump in and suggest a solution. The suggestion might be followed, not by an actual agreement or a disagreement, as one might logically expect, but by a general laugh, then a joke, then another laugh, another joke, another laugh, and then a general grinning pause all around. After this, the members might sigh, shift positions in their chairs and appear to try again to tackle the task I had given them.

The traditional classification of progressive phases in problem solving in individual mental processes, which I had learned to expect from my earlier psychology courses (processes of cognition, affection, conation, activated in more or less that time order), did not help me much in understanding what was going on in my groups. Neither did John Dewey's account of steps in individual problem solving help much, although it was one of the sets of ideas that inspired me.

I could observe the giving of *information, opinion,* and *suggestion* (roughly similar to what the textbooks called cognition, affection, and conation), but usually these behaviors seemed to occur in no very dependable order, nor to make much progress toward an acceptable solution. The simple categories of phases in mental process and their presumed logically progressive order did not seem to capture effectively the complex nature of the interdependence among persons and the sense of the dynamic process I was observing. In particular, the categories failed to explain why the process was so disorderly. If I had known then what I know today, I might have recognized that these small groups were "complex self-organizing systems" operating on the "edge of chaos" (R. Lewin 1992). Would that have helped? I doubt it.

*Equilibrium or Chaos?*

One of the first things my colleague Chris Heinicke and I discovered was that in the groups we studied, the second session was more "chaotic" than the first (Heinicke and Bales 1953). In our experiment on "developmental trends" the results showed that members' worst trouble in getting organized, their most disturbing conflicts, were likely to break out in the second session, not the first. Some groups seemed to level out and improve for the third and fourth sessions, as if a crisis had passed, but some did not.

While I was observing turmoil in these small initially leaderless groups, my mentor, Talcott Parsons, was working on his book, *The Social System* (1951). Talcott was my main intellectual companion, and from him I received well-developed ideas on the nature of "social systems." The equilibrium theories of Pareto, Walter Cannon, and L. J. Henderson were prominent in Parsons's mind, and were passed on to me. I received them at first with eager belief. I expected to see some kind of tendencies toward "equilibrium" in my groups, to counter the prevailing turmoil. I was looking for order of some kind, almost any kind.

But these ideas, at least as I understood them, did not seem to fit too well in describing what went on in my groups. Gradually clouds of perplexity appeared in my mind. The ideas about "equilibrium" turned into ideas about the "problems of reaching equilibrium." I rationalized to myself: When sociologists speak of a "social system" they usually have in mind a complete society, something much larger, slower moving, and probably more stably organized than the disorderly process I am observing.

In place of Parsons's term "social system," which effused connotations of organization and order, I used the term "social-interaction system," in an effort to capture the idea of an "energy system" of some kind without much discernible order.

In my miniature social-interaction systems, at least part of the time, there seemed to be some kind of ragged emerging order that might be described as "some coordination in spite of considerable opposition." I could see the same sorts of things happening again and again. The thoughts and acts that individuals addressed to each other were not simply the disorganized expressions of unrelated individual personality differences, although a good deal of the time they seemed to be "off the wall" with regard to solving the problem I had given them.

*Problems in Problem Solving: Balance versus Precariousness*

Problem solving in the traditional accounts was described as "instrumentally guided," the process of a single "goal-directed act," or series of such acts, utilizing what "means" were available in the "situation," overcoming or going around "barriers" and leading to a single "goal." These were essentially the main elements included, along with the "meanings" and "values" which defined them, in the various theoretical descriptions of the time as to what constituted the "definition of the situation" by the actor. In psychology lectures, a typical illustration of this type of problem solving was a hungry rat in a maze, exploring blind alleys and dealing with obstructions, finally making it to the other end of the maze, where he received a reward.

Lewin's conceptual scheme of the "life space" was essentially the same scheme, with a few more refinements and complications, such as "level of reality." His famous bathtub-shaped diagram illustrates a problem-solving agent poised to move from one end of the tub-shaped field toward a specific goal at the other end. Along the way are "means regions" and "barriers," representing the particular features of the situation. In pursuit of the goal, the individual, or the group, must utilize the means and circumvent or push through the barriers. In this schema, a group was treated as a point, rather than as a differentiated system.

The group problem-solving process, which I was observing, was constantly interrupted, back-tracked and side-tracked, with signs of growing emotional tensions in and between persons. The moving state of the process seemed sometimes vaguely purposeful, as if at least some members of the group were trying to solve the problem I had given them, and yet the process seemed precariously balanced and unpredictable. Much of the time the specific behaviors of individuals seemed to be either "crisis-driven" or "deficit-driven," rather than "instrumentally guided" over a longer time span toward a goal that all members visualized. Often the behavior of a given participant seemed to be emotionally provoked "because of" something noxious that had just been said to him. Or, although he had not been personally attacked intentionally, he still felt a strong oppositional reaction to some value pronouncement by some other participant.

I thought of these kinds of behavior as "reactive" and "expressive" rather than as simply "instrumental." In other words, the behaving individual seemed to be looking "backward" in time, paying primary attention to something noxious that had just happened to him, rather than looking "forward" in time and paying primary attention to a visualized goal achievement in the future. "Expressive" crises of this kind seemed to break out every so often without warning, like little spontaneous fires. Sometimes the little fires were put out, sometimes they got bigger.

Only occasionally, did somebody say something that was sufficiently thoughtful to be called an explicit "instrumental" attempt, presented to other group members "in order to" solve the problem I had given them and reach the pre-visualized goal I had set for them. I finally had to admit to myself that the group members were really not much interested in the "goal" I had tried to set for them.

A good deal of behavior seemed to be deficit driven, neither particularly emotional, nor directly instrumental, but in the nature of patch-up work that seemed to be necessary to maintain the communication process. Deficits in the logic or continuity of the general argument constantly appeared: in the need to repeat because somebody failed to understand, in the need to discover who might have facts that were thought to be missing, in the need for reasonable or new inferences, in the need for ideas and suggestions, in the need for sufficient value consensus to support a decision.

The participants in my groups did not know each other to begin with. Opinions, beliefs, values, and ideas often appeared which did not seem very relevant to anybody except to the speaker. Overall, the process seemed to be performing many functions, but different ones for different participants, and in different ways—seldom for all of the participants in the same way at the same time. The direction of the process seemed to be oscillating, cycling, and wavering. Sometimes it seemed to take off in a chaotic departure far from the apparent current direction.

Still there seemed to be some kind of diffuse and fragmentary coordination, among some of the members at least, but in the midst of the opposition of some others. I could imagine a social and psychological dynamic *field* of influences, pushing and pulling the members and their motivations this way and that. I came to feel that the observable events were best understood to be only the surface layer, or the overt process *indicators*, of a much larger underlying *field* of interacting events and influences, partly cooperative, partly conflicting, partly irrelevant, but still interdependent and dynamically reactive, a complex system in which almost everything affected almost everything else.

The dynamic *field*, as a semi-organized but changing pattern of simultaneously active elements, seemed to be sensitive to disturbances that occurred anywhere within the observer's field of attention, almost like a kind of reactive living "entity." But if it were an "entity," it was certainly a "complex entity," almost never completely integrated. One set of parts was usually, if not chronically, in conflict with another set of parts. Only once in a while, at the last moment, did the "group" seem to "locomote" hastily from the far end of Lewin's bathtub field to the end with the specified goal. Only once in a while did my "experimental rat," the group, seem to get hold of the cheese.

### Interaction Process Analysis, a Method for Direct Observation

The solution to the persistent itch of semantic vagueness was to get as concrete and operational as possible in my definitions of variables. In my groups I recorded single act after single act, at a rate of about twenty acts per minute in precise time order. I categorized each act as best I could at the time it occurred, recording who performed the act, and to whom it was directed, whether directed to another individual or seemingly to the group as a whole. This was the beginning of the observation method called *Interaction Process Analysis* (IPA) (Bales 1950).

I wanted to develop a workably small set of categories for observation of interactive behavior. The category set needed to be sufficiently specific to include a category for each kind of behavioral act and sufficiently general to be used to study all kinds of social-interaction systems. I started with a long list of eighty-seven categories of types of *acts*, gleaned from the literature and my imagination.

I used this list to code observations in real time as I watched groups in action. The mechanics of my activity were cumbersome compared with today's standards. The original list in typed form was nearly two feet long. I sandwiched the list between two plates of glass in order to perch it atop my "interaction recorder." This was a machine devised of a box frame and a mechanism (an old phonograph motor) for pulling at a steady pace a wide paper tape from one roller to another. As the paper tape (nearly two feet in width) passed under my list of categories, I wrote my recordings on it.

Prior to recording, I assigned a code number to each member of the group. As I observed the group discussion, I struggled to find on my list the appropriate category for each act as it occurred. When I found what seemed like the best category, I wrote down the number of the speaker and the number of the person spoken to on the moving tape. I wrote the two numbers just beside the category in which I chose to classify the act. I tried to remain aware of the up-and-down movement of the time track of acts beside the vertical list of eighty-seven categories.

After the meeting I would unroll the long paper tape (usually about forty feet long) on top of a series of tables placed end to end in the large third-floor hallway of Emerson Hall and start to connect the numbers with pencil lines, up and down. Passers-by seemed nonplused.

On the paper I connected each act with the next one by a pencil line, to trace the time track. The time spans required for overt verbal communication are, roughly, two or three seconds for each intentional act of *giving information*, or *opinion*, or *suggestion*, on the average. I looked for characteristic patterns in the way the time track went up and down on the tape. Sometimes the time track continued at one level for a series of acts of the same kind, sometimes it switched up and down between two or three categories, occasionally it made large sudden movements up or down to a new location and then hung there fluctuating for a while in the new location.

In retrospect it is clear that from the first, I was a believer in some kind of theory of "dynamic nonlinear systems," and was making the kind of time-ordered observations necessary to build a theory about fluctuations of rates in time.

Looking back a little further still, I recall that the first such dynamic problem that I had puzzled about as an undergraduate at the University of Oregon was brought to my attention by recruiters trying to persuade me to join their fraternity. They said that the membership of certain other fraternities on the campus (but not their own) tended to go up and down in size, over periods of several years, in rather mysterious ways. The reasons for these fluctuations in other fraternities, they hinted, might be sinister (something was wrong with the organization). But their own fraternity, they made clear, had no such trouble.

I tried, but was not able to get enough data to test this dark hint of cyclical fluctuations. However, I stumbled onto Durkheim's work on suicide rates. These rates show a yearly cycle, and they also show cycles that are roughly correlated to economic conditions. That caught my imagination, and for a while I studied suicide rates. Later, I studied cycles of prejudice and conflict in race relations between the resident population of California and early Chinese immigrants, who worked on the construction of the cross-continental railroads. Still later, at Harvard as a graduate student, I wrote course papers on Oscar Lewis's account of the daily and weekly cycles of work and home life in Tepotztlan, a Mexican village, and a similar study by Oscar Junek, of a village in the far North. For some reason, I was fascinated by the cyclical aspects of group activity.

As I endeavored to interpret my observation recordings, on the third floor of Emerson Hall, I was finding something fascinating in what appeared to be cycles in the up-and-down movements of the pencil tracks on my long paper tapes. I revised the category system after each meeting, attempting to redefine the scope and contents of each of the categories and to adjust their locations on the list so that the repeated up-and-down patterns would become more regular and more clear.

With my original list of eighty-seven categories, and even with later shorter sets of categories, there were many categories that I never used. I worked to make the number of categories small enough so that the observed frequency in each of the categories would be large enough to count and treat as a rate per period of time. I consolidated and reordered until eventually I arrived at twelve categories of acts.

The final set of twelve categories is shown in figure 6.1. This number had advantages for subdivision into two halves, smaller symmetrical subsections,

**FIGURE 6.1**

**Set of Categories Used for Direct Observation of the Interaction Process**

**Problem Areas**                    **Observation Categories**

| Problem Areas | | Observation Categories |
|---|---|---|
| Expressive-Integrative Social-Emotional Area<br><br>Positive Reactions | A | 1  *Shows solidarity*, raises other's status, gives help, reward |
| | | 2  *Shows tension release*, jokes, laughs, shows satisfaction |
| | | 3  *Agrees*, shows passive acceptance, understands, concurs, complies |
| Instrumental-Adaptive Task Area<br><br>Attempted Answers | B | 4  *Gives suggestion*, direction, implying autonomy for other |
| | | 5  *Gives opinion*, evaluation, analysis, expresses feeling, wish |
| | | 6  *Gives orientation*, information, repeats, clarifies, confirms |
| Instrumental-Adaptive Task Area<br><br>Questions | C | 7  *Asks for orientation*, information, repetition, confirmation |
| | | 8  *Asks for opinion*, evaluation, analysis, expression of feeling |
| | | 9  *Asks for suggestion*, direction, possible ways of action |
| Expressive-Integrative Social Emotional Area<br><br>Negative Reactions | D | 10  *Disagrees*, shows passive rejection, formality, withholds help |
| | | 11  *Shows tension*, asks for help, withdraws out of field |
| | | 12  *Shows antagonism*, deflates other's status, defends or asserts self |

a b c d e f

A sub-classification of system problems to which each pair of categories is most relevant:

    a.  Problems of orientation
    b.  Problems of evaluation
    c.  Problems of control
    d.  Problems of decision
    e.  Problems of tension-management
    f.  Problems of integration

of three each, and so on. Not the least of the advantages of just twelve categories was its suitability to the technological limitations of the time. The maximum number of vertical punches on an IBM card was twelve. I took a certain amount of ribbing from my fellow researcher, Fred Strodtbeck, for arriving and stopping at this magical number.

I punched an IBM card for every act, in sequential time order, showing the category of the act, and who addressed the act to whom. The IBM sorter counter, the technological marvel of the time, then enabled me to consolidate frequencies over any time period and construct a frequency profile of the twelve types of acts. I could divide up a pack of cards into smaller packs selected according to any criterion I desired, so that I could explore different aspects of the process.

I sorted and counted cards in many ways, for example by time periods to study how the rates of different kinds of acts changed by subperiods over the course of a meeting. Other card sorts were made to see how the quality of acts differed according to whether they were a continued series of acts by the same individual or were "reactions" of another individual in response. Yet other card sorts were made to see what kinds of acts were initiated and what kinds were received by specific persons or classes of persons.

Many acts were recorded as addressed to the group as a whole. Still other sorts were made to study how these kinds of acts differed from the kind of acts addressed to specific individuals. Before long I began to study members who received high leadership ratings to see how their profile of acts differed from those who received high ratings on being liked. From this I discovered that in the small groups I was studying there was often a "task leader," who talked a lot but was unaccountably low on being liked, and a "social leader," who did not talk so much but was better liked, and less disliked (Bales 1953b; Bales and Slater 1955; Slater 1955).

On my paper tapes created with the IPA method, I repeatedly saw a long jiggling track of interchange between *giving information* and *giving opinion* seeming to inch its way upward on the paper tape toward a higher level where I had listed *giving suggestion*. Often the line showing this seesaw struggle upward would break suddenly downward to the low level on the tape where I had listed "showing disagreement" and "showing tension." At this point I would see a major alternation between *showing disagreement* and *giving opinion*, sometimes veering still lower into the category of *showing antagonism*. (*Showing antagonism* was at the bottom of the list).

Then at some point I was likely to see a sudden break in the pencil timeline upward into a period of continued "joking and laughing." In turn, the laughing and joking would give way to a brief period of friendly remarks, called "showing solidarity." When the group members reached such a period at the end of a series of phases of increasing conflict, it felt to me like some kind of triumph. That was a good-enough reason for putting jokes and laughs, and the ensuing friendly remarks at the top of the list of twelve categories.

I did not suspect at that time how important this repetitive phase movement would be. Increasing conflict, argument and tension, eventually interrupted by jokes and laughter, and then followed by signs of relaxation and friendly remarks, later proved to be a major point of entry to understanding the dynamics of what was happening underneath in the system as a whole. In retrospect, what I was seeing was a display in miniature of some of the most fundamental dynamic conflicts of values which I now believe are inherent in all social-interaction systems. Over the years, the recognition and better understanding of values and value conflicts has played an increasingly important role in my thinking about social-interaction systems.

In those early observations, a pattern of the ups and downs of overt interactions reflecting value conflicts and their changes was stretched out in a *time series* on a long paper tape. In the rating data on business teams and organizations I later studied, the value conflicts appear as differences in the *patterns of scatterplots* on the Field Diagram which is the principal *window* into the dynamics of social-interaction systems.

### Independence and Interdependence in Traits: Talking, Listening, and the Effect on Liking

In the early days of the IPA studies I called the three factors I later found in the factor-analytic literature by the names: "activity," "task ability," and "likeability." In various ways ratings on these three factors seemed to be more or less orthogonal, or independently variable over measurements of individuals. Individuals tended to maintain their particular combination of the measures over different groups, as if they had almost a "trait-like" character. The three "traits" apparently had a strong influence on the post-meeting ratings received by individual members in new groups.

In one large study (Bales 1956) the following measurements of these traits were made. *Activity* was measured by the gross amount of interaction of an individual observed using Interaction Process Analysis. *Task ability* was measured by post-meeting ratings by all members as to who had the best ideas for solving the problem set for group decision. *Likeability* was measured by post-meeting ratings by all members as to the degree to which they felt liking for each of the participants. *Disliking* was measured separately by a similarly worded question on feeling disliking.

A "Great Man" was defined as one who was high on all three factors. A "Task Specialist" was defined as a person who was high on activity and task ability, but somewhat lower on likeability. A "Social Specialist" was defined as a person who was high on likeability, but somewhat lower on activity and task ability.

One part of the study used group composition as the independent variable. Individuals (all males) were first randomly assembled into five-person groups.

The above measurements on the above three traits were made. The same persons were then assigned to two sets of new groups as similar to each other as possible. One set of groups was provided with the best all-round "Great Man" leader we could find among the persons originally assessed. The alternative matched set of groups was provided with the best potential pair of leaders we could find who might be expected to act as a "Task Specialist" and a "Social Specialist."

As a research team (Bales, Couch, and Slater) we were divided and ambivalent about which one of these group compositions (types of leadership) might do better. Our findings did not show significant differences between the two sets of groups. However, we found that *both* types of composed groups tended to show significantly more post-meeting satisfaction with the quality of task performance than did the *randomly assembled* groups. But, neither type of composed group differed from the randomly assembled groups with respect to satisfaction with interpersonal relations.

In retrospect, I would say that our composition for *both* types of leadership tended to make for convergence and cooperation within the top leadership of the group. Both modes of composition probably tended to make the three factors on the high ends of activity, task ability, and likeability converge together within both sets of groups, that is, away from orthogonality.

Social interaction consists of initial actions and subsequent reactions. In a very approximate way in most intact groups there is a tendency toward what might be called a "reasonable interactive continuation" between these two elements. Task-oriented initial attempts to solve a problem of the group by one member are typically followed by a reaction from some other member or members. The reaction may be an agreement, a disagreement, or a question, but it is feedback of some kind. However, persons with higher ranks on activity may differ greatly in how much of a reaction they permit or encourage.

In another part of the large trait study, we computed a ratio representing the amount of feedback received by a member compared to his total amount given out (see figure 6.2). As figure 6.2 shows, high participators who received (or perhaps only permitted) a low amount of feedback compared to the amount of interaction they gave out were markedly likely to be low on liking received from others, and also likely to be high on dislikes received. Their ratings received on ideas were also likely to be depressed. However, high participators who received (or encouraged) high amounts of feedback compared to the amounts they gave out were likely to receive high ratings on likeability and on the quality of their ideas.

The top participators who apparently increased their amount of interaction above what was considered optimum, were departing from the convergence of the three factors I described earlier as most conducive to effectiveness. As a result, I conclude, their likeability and task ability were reduced in the eyes of other members. They were more likely to be disliked,

FIGURE 6.2

**Average Ratings Received on Liking, Disliking, and Ideas, by Men
of Each Basic Initiating Rank (BIR), According to Their Feedback Ratio**

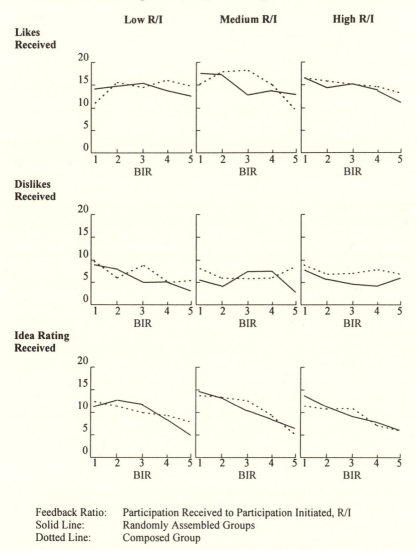

Feedback Ratio:    Participation Received to Participation Initiated, R/I
Solid Line:        Randomly Assembled Groups
Dotted Line:       Composed Group

and their effectiveness was probably reduced. To improve effectiveness it
may be necessary for over-dominant high participators to reduce their activity, and to encourage other members to contribute their ideas in order to
avoid excessive dislike.

### The Communication Network: Visible and Invisible, with No Beginning and No End

In my groups, the "communication network" was "fully interconnected," at least in the physical space of the meeting room. That is, the members sat around a table. Everybody could see everybody else. Everything that was said could be heard by everybody. The groups were small, ranging from two to eight persons.

It was obvious, however, that if I used the notion of "dynamic psychological field" as a context within which the group members communicated with each other, the field had to include much that was not visible. The nonvisible elements, inside different heads, were evidently not "fully interconnected" over all participants.

The visible *field* of the *dynamic system* seemed to include some attempts of members to get along with each other, some attempts to beat each other out, some attempts to take and exercise leadership, some signs of individual purposes which might or might not fit in, as well as facts and logical operations, value judgments, inferences, and constructions of meaning addressed to solving the task problems. Occasionally interpersonal arguments developed into "run-away emotional processes," which seemed more like a spreading disturbance, or even an explosion, than anything intentional and controlled. The visible dynamic interpersonal field, in many instances, included evidences of the division of the total group into two or more contending subgroups, several contending leaders of very different kinds, some indomitable over-talkers as well as some stubbornly inactive and withdrawn isolates.

No social-interaction system really starts from scratch. In research on group process, the start is merely the point of observational entry into the ongoing system. The ongoing system occupies tangible space and time. However, it is important to realize that an adequate concept of a social-interaction system requires the observer to keep in mind somehow a large "extended envelope" both of physical space and of physical time. All of the persons involved, members and observers, have extensive "outside connections" within the large envelope. The total contents of the envelope, outside the immediately visible context and the countless connections, are never consciously known to any of the participants, nor to observers, who are also parts of the system.

The physical spaces occupied by persons are more extensive than the spaces inside their heads and include the space required to convey the communications between persons. In some systems, such as many military and commercial "communication and control" systems, the persons are physically separated. Physical separation in space or time of any kind slows down the processes taking place between participants and makes the communication more vulnerable.

The social organization and culture of the group is built cumulatively as communication goes on. But a tremendously complex set of relations between the elements of culture that participants bring with them exists and interacts simultaneously in the heads of each of the participants. Nobody has conscious access to the complete contents or to the relationships of similarity, opposition, and implication that exist *potentially* between the elements within the envelope. Some of these will be revealed in time, and will have their visible impact. But prior to that, they have existed and interacted within the minds of the participants.

In short, any actual social-interaction system is mostly invisible, unconscious, unknowable, and spread out in physical spaces and physical time spans in complex and interconnected ways. For the rest of my research and teaching career, as it has turned out, I have struggled to untangle the problems implicit in these early observations and experiences.

## Developmental Trends Are Not Very Predictable

Assuming a start from a condition of almost no organization, more regularized structural features of the system tend to emerge and become crystallized, such as the formation of a regularized status order, the establishment of one or more recognized leaders, the development of a division of labor, characteristic splits between more conservative versus more liberal subgroups, the appearance of isolated individuals, and perhaps openly oppositional subgroups. These recognizable features emerge from very tiny beginnings, intermingled in time in the developmental history of a particular group, in no very regular developmental order.

There have been many attempts (including my own, in Bales and Cohen 1979) to describe group dynamics in terms of developmental trends that might be true of all groups, or at least of some kinds of groups. In my opinion, there are far too many variables and differing conditions and situations in which real-life groups are involved to support very strong generalizations.

Most of the generalizations concerning group development, which are described in the literature on small groups, have actually been obtained in a very special context. The context of almost all the relevant studies has been a small leaderless group in some kind of experimental or problem-solving situation, usually one in which leadership is expected by the members, but denied by the person who is formally expected to lead. My own experimental groups in the 1940s, which ran for four meetings, and my self-analytical groups later in the 1960s, some of which ran for a full nine-month school year, are examples.

In any actual group in a real-life setting, from an initial period onward, particular structural features, such as a dominance order, a division of labor among types of leaders, and others, will have developed at least in primitive form. As time goes on, all of these tendencies develop and change in ways affected by the fact that they are interdependent parts of a complex system, acting and reacting to each other in circular and recursive patterns. A particularly difficult dominant personality, with oppositional values, for example, may greatly affect the establishment of a stabilized status order, may in fact prevent a sufficient degree of status consensus to permit a stabilization of leadership and effective production of work.

Each part of a total social-interaction system is potentially relevant to each of the other parts, but the degrees of relevance differ, and the relevance is interdependent with the variability of time lags. Among other things, this implies that almost none of the regularities, or the results of actual practical measurements of them, can stand alone. No part is completely understandable in terms of itself alone.

A multiplicity of measures is necessary for a degree of understanding that will support deliberate efforts for planned change. Not only are many measurements necessary, but in order to understand adequately any kind of regularity detected by any given kind of measurement, it is necessary to understand other parts of the system. In principle, all other parts may be involved.

This certainly has implications for all of the generalizations I obtained in my early work. Consider, for example, the generalization I obtained about the tendency for a division of labor to develop between task and social leaders. This surely depends upon the size of the group, the skill of the leadership, the steepness of the gradient in amounts of participation, the composition of the group in terms of personalities, the amounts of feedback possible, and so on.

My long experience in the observation of newly constituted groups, and many more formal studies later, have led to certain expectations as to what group processes and features are likely to emerge as regularities in a social-interaction system. What are the regularities in overt interaction? In brief description, they are regularities one can understand as "a system of problem-directed attempts" by "first-person" members, and feedback control attempts by "second- and third-person" members. The set of categories shown as figure 6.1 can easily be seen as a set of problem-solving attempts of a member in the *first-person* role and feedbacks from other members in *second- and third-person* roles. The set of categories includes various kinds of communicative acts which, when they take place among group members in sequences constitute a *communication and control feedback system*.

It is obvious that attempts to solve a problem of whatever sort in groups of members who are almost always significantly diverse in values are only effective part of the time. Attempts to solve problems include all types of problems, notably the three types I shall outline below, as a first look at value diversity. It is important to recognize that all attempts of whatever kind are likely to have secondary consequences, often unforeseen, which then also become *problems* and elicit attempts to control. The same categories then serve recursively in the same way as a communication and control feedback system on these *second- and third-order* problems.

What, more concretely, is it about the behavior of some members in social relationships that other members regard as *problems* and try to control? The most elementary features of these *problems* of control, I suggest, may be seen as they appear prior to the human level, by observing the problems that animals of a given species encounter in their interaction and somehow solve, long before the development of the kind of abstract value controls embodied in language at the adult human level.

My sense of the most elementary relationship problems of greatest generality at the primate level is based mostly on reports of ethnologists, such as Jane Goodall. A great deal of my first-hand experience of course, has been in the observation of newly formed, initially leaderless groups in a laboratory setting. What occurs in this setting is no doubt highly specialized and probably not entirely representative of all human kind. Certainly the circumstances in my academic self-analytic groups were more "civilized" than the circumstances of Jane Goodall's chimps, and in many respects were greatly simplified.

There are three very general types of system problems, which I have noted repeatedly whether in my comparatively civilized observation-room laboratory setting or elsewhere. These are the most obtrusive and urgent of human-relationship problems.

1. *Control of dominance, status, and power.* This kind of behavior is a *problem* to most group members, dominant and submissive alike.

2. *Control of unfriendliness.* There are nearly always some members who apparently want to be friendly, but others who apparently want to avoid being drawn in. Efforts may be made to prevent potentially active hostility of some others.

3. *Control of problem-solving efforts toward effective solutions.* On the pre-human level and in the wild, these are problems of finding food, and other problems of adaptation and survival in relation to the physical environment. On the human level, the kinds of *task-like* problems are too numerous to name and too complex to describe, but they are always there, except for very temporary periods of surcease.

Certain individuals tend to be more active than others in the attempt to command attention. Although very early contacts may be somewhat cautious and restrained, a struggle for status, establishment of a dominance order, is likely to set in before long. The onset, and outcome of such status struggles depends in part on whether preexisting arrangements, such as social status in the larger system, and so on, are visible and very relevant to the developing internal status order. An accepted, more or less consensual dominance order may or may not emerge. A lack of sufficient acceptance of a current status order tends to present great problems to the group, and affects almost everything else. Lack of consensus on a dominance order may prevent much success in problem solving indefinitely, and may be fatal to the continued existence of the group as presently constituted.

Competition between incipient leaders and other potential conflicts undermine cordial relationships of acceptance and friendship. Additionally, there may be tendencies to fasten onto present persons' feelings, both of acceptance and rejection, that actually originated in relation to emotionally important persons in previous situations ("transference" and "countertransference"). Negative reactions and feelings tend to increase, whether or not they become overtly apparent. The increase of negative feeling tends to affect problem solving. It tends to decrease the probabilities of agreement and to increase the probabilities of disagreement on task efforts, probably partly independent of the *objective* merit of the disagreement.

In many groups there are differences of great importance between individuals in knowledge, and special intellectual or other abilities relevant to the task problems the group faces. In many teams, particular individuals are selected and brought into the group because of their presumed special knowledge or abilities. As the success or failure of group members in problem solving and other tasks becomes apparent, the differences in apparent abilities between individuals influence the way they react to each other, particularly in the granting or withholding of status. In the struggle for status, however, individuals of actual ability often have to compete against others who tend to exercise sheer dominance based on sources of power other than competence.

Precursors of the three basic types of problems in the simplest and most general form and efforts at control may easily be seen at the primate animal level. But even at that level I believe the social-psychological theorist must pay as much attention to the *reactions* of third-order additional participants in any episode as to the initiating behavior of the first, and the immediate reaction of the second. Among monkeys, not only the "Alpha Male" (king of the troop) but also the "Beta Male" play critical parts in what goes on, and quite often third-order companions of the second are part of the drama.

In any specific human case the initiating behavior of any individual in the *first-person* position in the raising of an issue is directed not only toward some individual in the *second-person* position who is expected to respond, but also in effect, if not intentionally, toward individuals in *third-person* positions. Any first-person initial action may impact strongly, but quite differently on each other member according to their individual differences in values. It makes a difference whether third persons are present, and of course, how they react. The second- and third-person participants, I assume, always do *something* about the behavior of the first, even if they only appear at the moment to evaluate it silently, and approve or disapprove it. What second and third persons do about a first person's initial act varies greatly by persons and other circumstances.

**FIGURE 6.3**
**Mean Profile of N Individuals, by Group Size**

| Group Size | 2 | 3 | 4 | 5 | 6 | 7 |
|---|---|---|---|---|---|---|
| N | 8 | 12 | 16 | 20 | 18 | 28 |
| **Category** | | | | | | |
| 1  Shows Solidarity | 9.2 | 9.1 | 10.3 | 9.7 | 11.2 | 10.5 |
| 2  Shows Tension Release | 11.2 | 11.4 | 12.8 | 14.2 | 18.2 | 16.6 |
| 3  Agrees | 27.2 | 27.0 | 22.3 | 23.1 | 21.6 | 21.3 |
| 4  Gives Suggestion | 14.3 | 13.5 | 13.7 | 15.9 | 18.4 | 19.2 |
| 5  Gives Opinion | 31.7 | 34.0 | 35.0 | 32.0 | 32.1 | 31.2 |
| 6  Gives Orientation | 25.3 | 23.3 | 23.7 | 26.6 | 24.1 | 25.7 |
| 7  Asks for Orientation | 12.0 | 10.2 | 10.5 | 10.2 | 10.2 | 10.1 |
| 8  Asks for Opinion | 9.8 | 8.5 | 8.2 | 8.5 | 7.4 | 7.1 |
| 9  Asks for Suggestion | 5.2 | 5.9 | 5.0 | 6.4 | 4.6 | 5.9 |
| 10  Disagrees | 10.2 | 15.6 | 19.9 | 14.5 | 17.7 | 16.4 |
| 11  Shows Tension | 12.4 | 8.6 | 10.0 | 9.1 | 6.3 | 6.6 |
| 12  Shows Antagonism | 1.0 | 3.5 | 5.2 | 3.3 | 3.9 | 3.8 |

Note:    The profile of each individual is the sum over four sessions of his raw profile in each session, converted to a percentage profile and transformed to arcsine equivalents.

In early explorations of group size (Bales and Borgatta 1955), one of the clearest findings was that two-person groups were uniquely cautious and restrained, with high rates of showing tension, IPA Category 11 (figure 6.1). This was probably because in the two-person case, no third person was present for either of the pair to combine with in case of disagreement. Rates of disagreement, IPA Category 10, were also uniquely low for two-person groups among all sizes studied, as can be seen in figure 6.3.

Theodore M. Mills (Mills 1954) showed that in a three-person group there is a strong tendency for the two more dominant members to combine in a coalition against the less dominant member. Such a coalition is very hard for the third person to deal with, and in such a three-person group, the coalition of the more dominant pair tends to persist. Coalitions in most any size of group have a definite advantage for members who can form one.

In a two-person group there is no possibility of forming a coalition of two or more against one. This appears to be a reason for caution. A third person can be like a "court of appeal." Such a third person may function as the "invisible hand" and open the way retrospectively to a greater role for "reason," or for giving more weight to an opposing value. On the other hand, the support of a third person may reinforce a developing status order of dominance and strengthen a given value position.

This is a good example of what I call a "systemic emergent." Facts like these may help one to realize that the tendency of individuals, randomly brought together, to begin to form *clusters* is not simply a matter of "liking." The advantages of coalitions and clusters appear "out of nowhere" as it were, simply as a result of the *system*, and begin to exert a kind of impersonal organizing influence on the social-interaction system even in an initially random assembly.

### The *Independence* versus the *Interdependence* of System Problems

The twelve IPA categories (figure 6.1) were conceived originally to be overt acts dealing with *system problems*. I gave a number of instances in chapter 5 of factor analyses in the literature which tend to show three factors. These are the factors of behavior and values called U-D, P-N, and F-B. Early on, I considered these three factors as orthogonal to each other, that is, as independent of each other, in the sense that they may be statistically zero correlated with each other over the population studied.

What I want to emphasize now as strongly as possible, is that in intact groups that are "most effective," the behaviors and values which make up and exemplify them are *not* independent. The three types of system problems are potentially independent. They arise from different sources in motivational and situational senses and each one can stand alone in a logical sense. But, in the case of a given intact group, *if* it is to be "most effective," the behavioral solutions that are addressed to the problems and the values concerning them must nevertheless be factually and systemically *inter*dependent.

The body of interaction-process studies of the early period all demonstrate, in different ways, that departures from this identifiable pattern of interdependence are departures toward independent variability of variables that make up the three major factors, and that all such departures detract from optimum effectiveness. The empirical evidence from SCG research, reported in other chapters, supports the same conclusion. SCG research has found, even in groups that are far from "most effective," when participants are asked what values they believe are "most effective," their opinions show marked convergence. Their perceptions overall indicate a certain balanced pattern of interconnection and mutual support in the meanings and frequency emphasis given to the three types of problems. (The evidence is the convergence on the Field Diagram in the PF reference circle for the concept of "most effective" values. See figure 2.10.) I try to elucidate the reasons for the remarkable degree of convergence in chapter 9, on "The Mystery of *Most Effective* Values."

One of the compelling and easily understandable reasons for the actual and factual interdependence of the solutions to the three problems is that resources of attention, time, and effort, are limited. In a given intact group, attention, time, and effort, addressed especially to any one of the three types of problems, particularly at extremes of high intensity of attempts at solution, is likely to lead to the neglect or suppression of activity addressed to at least one of the other two types of problems, at least for the time being. In real time, in an intact group, any one of the three types of problems may become urgent or relatively acute, and require or receive especially concerted attention, special leadership efforts and response, the activation of special values, the development of special meanings in the "definition of the situation," the pursuit of specialized activity, and the expenditure of resources. The optimum balances of activity and value emphasis over all three types of problems at once are disturbed or distorted in one direction or another.

If extended attention and interactive effort is given to the solution of task-like problems, attention and effort is likely to be drawn away from maintaining friendly relations. In fact, interaction is likely to become more unfriendly, more suffused with dominance and attempts to maintain status. As this becomes more marked, attention of members tends to be drawn away from the task and toward objectionable features of other members and their values. Proposals counter to the initial task proposal begin to appear and the deficit of friendliness grows more marked. As this deficit is perceived by some members to grow more marked, a counteraction of the negativism and unfriendliness may appear in the onset of joking and laughing and absorb time and attention for a period. This concentration decreases effective task-oriented behavior, but tends, if successful, to increase the friendliness. Maximum attention to increasing friendliness however, does not, as such, increase task effort, and in some cases, offends the members who prefer more negative relations and resistance to the task. Maximum cultivation of friendliness tends to break down status differences and deprive more dominant members of their control. After a period then, attention and effort may be addressed to the task.

This is a typical and general picture of a *system-process cycle* as it may be spread out in time. A more detailed inspection reveals many short interchanges, diversions from one kind of problem to another, and so on. In principle, all the three types of problems and opposed reactions to them are present in some form (at least as partially activated values) in the minds of different members in different strengths, essentially all the time, almost no matter what is going on at the center of attention. And in principle, every initial act, every second-person response, and every third-person reevaluation takes place in a resonant context of the whole system of meanings and values interacting with each other.

What I hope to have conveyed is a sense of the potentially *competing* relationship of the system problems and their attempted solutions. Within a given intact group, the solutions to the three types of problems may appear to an observer to be *independently variable*, in a partial and temporary sense. This appearance is sustained for short periods of time only if the demands and the attempted solutions to them are within low-to-moderate ranges of urgency. Over a sufficient time span of further interaction, a cycling or phasing of attention and interaction appear. Demand on time and other scarce resources, including threats of change in the order of differential status of members, create imbalance.

### Status Struggle, in the Second Session

There is some apparent tendency in most intact groups to engage in attempts to repair the damages or make up for the costs inflicted during one phase in a subsequent phase, to maintain steady state, or semi-equilibrium. Given the basic initial existence of an interacting group, there is no guarantee that subsequent reduction of strains and repair must, will, or even can happen, given all the conditions. Facts suggesting this were observed in my studies and others of what happened over a series of four sessions of experimental initially leaderless groups (Heinicke and Bales 1953). These studies were separately conducted, first by Heinicke at Northwestern, and then again replicated in essentials by the two of us at Harvard.

We discovered two things that I consider most important. One was that a status struggle in such groups seemed sure to occur, but typically, not in the first session. Interaction in the first sessions tended to be muted, as if the members were testing each other cautiously. But in the second sessions conflict increased significantly, as if this session were the real status struggle (see figure 6.4).

In the subsequent two sessions—sessions three and four—differences between two sets of groups appeared. For one set of groups the conflict abated. For the third and fourth sessions, agreement on who was the leader and what was the status order of the others seemed to be accepted. We discovered that in this set of groups our measure of "status consensus" had been high in the first session, that is, from the beginning (high status consensus).

For the second set of groups, we discovered, the measure of status consensus had been low in the first session, that is, from the beginning. In this set of groups the status struggle in the second session seemed to result in some increase in consensus by the end of the session, but it did not last. Status consensus slumped and did not recover. Over all four sessions the measure of status consensus was low, compared to the first set of groups (high status consensus).

In retrospect, it appears that the original composition made the difference between the two sets of groups. Although we did not have the measures to test it, there probably were too many value differences between individuals in the original assembly of the low status-consensus groups.

## Figure 6.4
### Trends in Status-Consensus for High and Low Groups, with Two Measures of Status-Consensus *Rho* and *W*

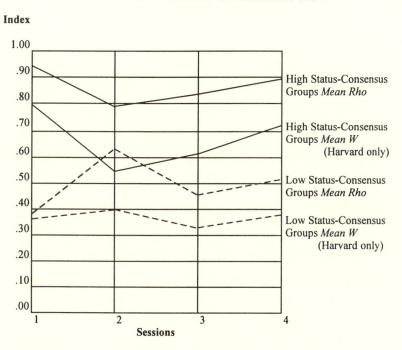

**Index**

High Status-Consensus Groups *Mean Rho*

High Status-Consensus Groups *Mean W* (Harvard only)

Low Status-Consensus Groups *Mean Rho*

Low Status-Consensus Groups *Mean W* (Harvard only)

**Sessions**

## Values Originate in the Effects of Social Interaction

At the time I began observing groups, the prevailing theories hypothesized that social groups and social processes tended to reach and maintain an "equilibrium" of some kind. Try as I might to find support for this hypothesis, my actual results seemed to show that maintenance of equilibrium, while it might or might not be characteristic of some social systems, was a constant *problem* or whole set of problems in the particular groups I could observe. My summary of many of my early studies was a paper entitled "The Equilibrium Problem in Small Groups" (Bales 1953b).

Now, some fifty years later, I speak of variable degrees of "effectiveness," and attempt to measure opinions concerning "effectiveness" for specific intact groups. The overall perspective I find most enlightening in trying to understand the overt interaction process is to regard it as a system of relative *regularities* that has the characteristics of a feedback process. It consists mainly of problem-solving attempts by the communicating members of the group and the feedback of reactions to these attempts by others. It varies within many different types of constraints and conditions. Sometimes it is relatively "effective" and sometimes not.

The content of the *problems* with which the directed attempts and reactive feedback deals include the development of values as to how the process should and should not go, who should or should not do what with regard to whom, when, and how much. Differences between members develop with regard to dominance and submission, friendliness and unfriendliness, task effort and task opposition. The values originating at a microscopic level as the results of specific encounters in concrete interaction (that is, the values and lessons learned by individuals) may be generalized by them in interaction with many others over time as social values considered appropriate in many of the factual and institutional features of the larger society.

The reactions, taken as a whole over time, in their effects as feedback attempts to control active initiators, constitute the "invisible hand" Adam Smith described. But there is no guarantee that the guidance of the invisible hand in a given group will be beneficent or wise and will result in long-time effectiveness and longer time survival of either the individual or the group. Values and the groups which maintain a particular system of values and regularly struggle over them are subject to evolutionary selection. Many of the values, the ideas, meanings, and beliefs with which they are associated, must be reproduced and regenerated over the generation turnover, or else the intact social-interaction system of which they are a part changes or fails to survive.

The empirical evidence indicates that the central conditions of adequate "effectiveness" are, essentially, that the solutions to the three types of problems and value positions pointed out above are regarded and formulated in a way, by at least a majority of the members, so that they are mostly mutually and multiply *convergent and consistent* with each other.

The value solutions with regard to the degrees of social differentiations between the members must be *interdependent* and mutually positively correlated if the group is to be viable and not go downhill, in any number of ways. To the degree that the solutions to the problems are not mutually convergent, the effectiveness of the system is threatened. The threat may be so severe that the system fails to survive as the same system. Such a group becomes a *population*, not a viable intact group. In such a case, a factor analysis of the values of individuals across the total population will tend toward *independence* or orthogonality of the three dimensions, U-D, P-N, and F-B. Orthogonality of solutions to the three interaction problems in the form of three truly independent factors in a factor analysis is fatal to effective operation as an intact group.

The total population of values potentially concerned with social interaction in any system is huge. But I have suggested that the key generative factors are concrete events at the behavioral level, often repeated to the extent that they can be seen as regularities. On the surface, most of these regularities of behavior are very ordinary recognizable characteristics of behavioral *interchanges* or episodes involving two or more persons that go on all the time in the midst of commonplace social interaction.

However, perceptions, concepts, memories, and evaluations of these episodes subsequently grow and change in the minds of members in ways we do not see. Memories and feelings apparently are generalized to some extent and codified in the minds of the individual participants, including their roles as *third-person* witnesses, in the form of values about the way the interaction process "should have gone" and "should go" in the future. These values develop with many differences among individual members. But in particular groups, along with individual differences in the values derived from the memories, there is the development of some, maybe many, *sufficiently similar values* among some one or more subgroups of members (values that are sufficiently compatible to support cooperation among them even though the values are not identical).

The whole dynamic (restless) mix of cooperative and conflicting values develops and tends to persist in the given social-interaction system or group. In spite of its internal conflicts the mix may be called a "value system" because it is built on regularities in the overt social interaction of participants. These regularities include regular conflicts as well as regular cooperation.

I have tried to make the case that the *values concerned with social interaction* originate constantly and currently, moment by moment as attempts to control the behavior of others. Members often do not treat each other well, and inadvertently, even in their most innocent problem-solving attempts and reactions to the attempts of others they increase their diversity in ways they then find damaging. Feelings about the way particular kinds of behavior "ought" to be controlled are then by degrees generalized in the minds of members. In the process of discussion and further interaction among members they are developed intellectually and cognitively into more articulate *values*.

The most *critical* values to sample in the attempt to gain preliminary understanding of the social-interaction system may then be understood to be the values which formulate feelings of "ought" about the most critical differentiations among the members, which unavoidably appear in the operation of the *communication and control feedback system*.

Social psychologists are trying persistently to answer the questions which have been present from the time when the word "situation" was introduced so innocently into the literature by Albion W. Small, but never satisfactorily answered. Some questions are: What is meant by the "situation"? What does it include? How should we describe it?

This is my contemporary answer: The "situation," in principle, consists of the whole activated social-interaction system, including the values of the members that are involved in the context of each act. The "definition of the situation," in the phrase introduced by W. I. Thomas, in principle, really assumes a definition of all aspects of the social-interaction system. One can hardly even begin to describe or understand the "definition of the situation" without systemic concepts.

# 7

# Interaction and Systemic Emergents

In the early period, much of social-psychological theory was centered in a frame of reference containing concepts to describe the "self" and "situation" from the perspective of the single individual as a problem solver.

When I first encountered social psychology I saw things, mostly, from the perspective afforded by the ordinary kind of psychological identification one feels in trying to think about another individual "self" in a "situation." I now realize that I was practically able to keep in mind only a little more than a single self in a fairly simple problem-solving situation through a time span of a closely connected series of a few instrumental acts leading to a single pre-visualized goal.

I was not able to visualize successfully a number of such selves in social interaction with each other over a long span of time. In such a case, each person defines the situation with different values and different goals, each conscious "self" is only a part of an internally complex personality, each person, and indeed, each aspect of a differentiated self is inevitably in some degree of conflict with each other one, as well as in some degree of potential cooperation.

Each time I tried to visualize in concrete detail an actual complex process of social interaction among a group of participants as it might move and develop over longer time spans and what the outcomes might be, the effort seemed more hopeless. The best I was able to do was painfully feeble. Indeed in looking back over my career of research, I conclude that my failure was traumatic, and ever since I have been trying to solve these same problems.

### The Problems Were Not New

In due time I found out, of course, that these puzzles had been around a long time. Hobbes, Locke, Rousseau, Adam Smith, and a great many other philosophers had struggled with them. Some sociologists call this set of problems the "problems of social order." Hobbes's intellectual solution to what he visualized as a "war of all against all" was to conclude that what was needed was a "Leviathan" state, essentially a totalitarian dictator. Locke's solution was to assume there was a "natural law" under the freedom granted to individuals by God which permitted individuals to employ a "law of reason" by which they were able to reach a social consensus and then go on to enact a structure of practical laws. Rousseau posited the possibility of a "social contract" by which individuals surrendered all their freedom and independent powers to a supreme collectivity, the "people."

Adam Smith struggled with the problems of order both with regard to the origin and operation of the "moral sentiments" in the individual and society and with regard to the economic processes involved in building and increasing the "wealth of nations." His various attempts at solution seem to revert at times to the assumption that the order is part of a divine plan, but many modern critics believe that his argument does not necessarily rest on the assumption of a divine plan, and that he was in part simply employing the conventional religious rhetoric of the time.

Adam Smith's solution is of particular interest in the present context since in a number of respects his line of argument seems to be based on what might now be called a "systems" or a "cybernetic" approach, which I am recommending. He gave examples of various kinds of feedbacks stemming from the acts of remotely connected sorts of individuals as part of the process of indirect systemic regulation which he unforgettably named the "invisible hand."

Adam Smith seemed to take the pragmatic point of view that there were too many interacting elements for any single individual or group to understand and manage, but he proposed that fortunately there was a kind of "invisible hand" which by degrees tended to guide the process toward an uneasy solution. The solution he visualized did not demand an impossibly high degree of consensus in advance among members of the society but could be the result of a series of groping approximations. An imperfect consensus could be sufficiently effective, he felt, in spite of a good deal of variability, and could be sufficient even without much benevolence and good will. The consensus he visualized was not an ideologically consistent set of deductions from agreed-upon major premises or a pre-visualized grand design. It was a pragmatic moving result of many trials and many errors. This was the case not only with regard to economic processes but moral sentiments as well.

The invisible hand, in substance and in detail, for Smith was the operation of an ongoing retrospective process of evaluation of past events from the point of view of what Smith called the "Impartial Spectator," or Spectators. The Impartial Spectators, as I translate the idea now, consisted of the social observers to any social-interactional event, but they also continued to exist subsequently as an internalized conscience in the individual. However, they are hardly impartial, either as social third persons or individual consciences.

### Has Anybody Seen the Invisible Hand?

My own solution to the problems of social order is rather similar, but I think

I have seen the invisible hand operating at the microscopic level of social interaction in small groups. I think there was a "smoking gun" which the social-psychological detectives working in the confines of the early conceptual framework of "self" and "situation" did not clearly discover. The critical missing element of the solution to the theoretical puzzle was what might be called the "third-person perspective," that is, the perceptions and possible reactions of third and additional persons who are present as witnesses and subsequent reactors to all dyadic interchanges in groups of more than two in size.

Georg Simmel, it is true, had written much earlier about the ways in which "triads" are different from "dyads." But the crucial facts about triads he pointed out appear to have been too fragmentary or too isolated to have had much effect. In any case Simmel's work did not trip off the development of any new spiral of theory able to detail and explain the development and maintenance of whole "systems" of social interaction.

The early period of theory was centered on the individual "self" and the "situation." But an adequate body of integrated theory in social psychology could not then, nor can it now, be built from that inadequate, essentially dyadic, infrastructure. Too many parts of social-interaction systems and personalities as they actually develop and exist depend upon multiple individuals and complex symbolic representations in the minds of participants. These elements had no effective conceptual representation in the minds of the social-psychological theorists of the time.

There were no technical ways of measuring and taking into account the perceptions and evaluations of other persons and their relationships, which are inevitably present in the mind of the self at the time of interaction, and at the same time, the perceptions and evaluations of those other persons to each other and to the "self."

Freud's metaphorical systems theory of the parts of the individual psyche (Id, Ego, Superego, etc.)—the drives, their sources, their topology, their interaction, and their energy economics in relation to each other as interdependent parts of a system—was about as close as anybody concerned with personality and social psychology had been able to come to a systems theory in the early period.

But in many respects, his theory now seems to be inadequate, especially in the almost undifferentiated concept of values, distributed, we might say, between the Superego, built largely on the father image, the dream censor, and the Ego Ideal. The later "object relations" developments of Melanie Klein and others of the English school began a process of recognizing additional objects, but that body of theory was still not based on any rounded conception of multiple persons and their relations of the kind and scope that are recognized and differentiated in social-interaction systems theory. Freud's theory was "drive based." But, drives are not enough. A theory of objects of the drives is also necessary.

## The Third-Party Perspective

As a social psychologist, one must be able to think beyond the dyadic level of "self" and "other" to third and additional persons in order to have any adequate conception of a "system" of interaction. One must be able to recognize that participants have cognitive and evaluative representations in their minds that go beyond the present to the past, and to the future. One must have ways to take into account the fact that participants represent these relationships to themselves conceptually and use them in interpreting the present. Social psychologists must have available "instruments and helps," as Bacon put it, that make measurement of these cognitive and evaluative perspectives possible.

In the early period, measurements of "attitude" had made a bare beginning, especially in the work of Thurstone and Chave (1937). But attitudes were measured only one at a time. "Values" were mentioned fairly regularly in the literature, but the critically important values and clusters of values were not conceptualized as systemic in origin and operation, and were not measured. Social interaction was regarded as crucial by many, but there were no adequate ways of measuring it. At that time I was sent by my teacher, Sam Jameson, to find what was available in the literature and write a paper on the "measurement of social interaction." I searched everywhere, but I came up almost empty-handed, and with no very good ideas of my own.

At the microscopic level of social interaction, I believe, third-person reactions, perhaps especially during and just after crucial dyadic interactions, are critical in the origins of values. Reactions from this perspective at this time are experienced in the full context of the aroused motivations and existing values of all the persons involved. Reactions to the present interchanges motivate an expansion of cognitive and evaluative representations in the mind of each of the persons, who in effect represent the various aspects of the situation as an interdependent whole or system.

These other parts and aspects of the more extended system, activated by persons reacting from third-person perspectives, are critical, I surmise, in providing the motivational, cognitive, and evaluative leverage to evolve solutions, bit by bit, to the "problems of order." Third-party reactions to single dyadic episodes can change small parts of the evaluative conceptions of some of the participants as to how things "ought to go" in social relationships of that kind. Participants probably have the best opportunity from the third-person perspective to conceptualize and reevaluate dyadic occurrences, to modify their own values of the "ideal."

The same may be said about the witnessing of dyadic interchanges as an opportunity for third-party witnesses to develop more complex representations of the diverse personalities of the multiple persons involved. Personality diversities are emphatically critical parts of the total system. But one must add that in the early period there was hardly any adequate way to conceptualize individual personality differences, and for many psychologists and social psychologists there appeared to be little incentive to recognize how important they are.

The third-person perspective is probably only effectively represented at the level of human intelligence. Only a few kinds of the large monkeys can do more than recognize that the image in the mirror is their own reflection. Children have to learn to exercise a third-party perspective by degrees. But whether or not monkeys or small children can do it, the third-person perspective at the adult human level depends upon much more than the ability to represent in the third-person mind the interaction of two dyadic interactors.

The third-person *perspective*, in principle, includes a retrospective review and revision of the unique characteristics of each of the personalities of the members of the dyad. However, for third persons as well as for dyadic participants, bias arising from various directions of self-interest is a formidable obstacle to the effective exercise of rational leverage and revision. Perfect consensus among any set of third persons is definitely not to be expected. Does this not put the solution of the problems of social order back to square one?

Perfect consensus is an "ideal," a psychologically motivated artificial construction. Probably at best any actual state of consensus in a group is a statistical range of evaluations spread over a more or less normal distribution. However, the actual presence and interaction of members other than those in the dyad surely provides greater leverage in exposing more aspects of the present context, more adequate cognitive representation of the past, and greater recognition of the consequences of the dyadic behavior for other parts of the system than members of the dyad themselves are likely to realize.

At least for some of the members, cognitive awareness and concern may extend even to the point of bringing into focus anxiety-provoking questions as to what difficult choices and changes may be necessary for the survival of the larger system. The ability of enough individuals in the system to represent symbolically in their minds the conflicting and cooperating elements of essentially the whole interdependent social-interaction system and its relation to its environment may be necessary in some cases. For improvement, and perhaps even for survival, the "invisible hand" as it actually operates in the system needs to be made more "visible" and more answerable to the changing implications of a larger rationality, a rationality oriented to system survival and environmental change over longer time spans.

From an evolutionary perspective, the human possession of abilities of this kind, a comprehensive cognitive and evaluative representation by a sufficient number of members, is surely the critical key to leading, improving, and managing cooperative efforts in social-interaction systems of greater complexity, successful adaptation to the demands of the environment, and ultimately, to the survival of the system. Improved concepts and measurements of "effectiveness," as I shall suggest later, can be made to serve as more immediate and accessible surrogates of the concepts of "survival."

It is sad (or perhaps fortunate as a source of variation) that "survival" appears to mean very different things to different individuals. In whatever private way the "self" is visualized by the individual, the survival of the self must surely be the ultimate nucleus of motivation. It is also true, I think, that the individual's cognitive and evaluative version of the best way, or necessary means, to insure survival of the self is always implicitly present in his or her motivation in interaction with others. It appears that in many cases, these convictions can be changed, if at all, only bit by bit, and I suspect, mostly in the context of the microscopic level of dyadic interchanges. Concepts of the meaning of survival, and the necessary means of survival, are stubborn, often socially structured and desperately held to. They are usually embedded in some nucleus of "belief," and they represent the conviction that life depends on the preservation of the visualized means of survival.

In the longer run, every actual social-interaction system is caught in an evolutionary process in the development of its own culture. Eventually each of the elements of the culture, and of the system as a whole, is vulnerable to a kind of natural selection (which also implies elimination) among the values and meanings represented internally in the system. The problems of internal order, as well as the problems of successful adaptation to the demands of the external environment, must be solved, or partially solved, over and over again so long as the system lasts. There are no permanent or complete solutions.

### From Square One and the Unit Act, Forward to Values

I now understand, I think, that my theoretical puzzles about how social order becomes possible could not be solved within the thought model of the early framework. Social psychologists of the early period, by and large, were caught and confined in a "unit act" and a dyadic "self and other" or "self and situation" theoretical framework, as I was. There was a lack of empirical experience, methods, and concepts for dealing first hand with the real concrete nature of natural social-interaction in the immediate time span in the context of a number of interacting persons greater than two.

In the beginning of my efforts to integrate the great number of abstractions that were current, I could not define the "something" of which the parts defined by the abstractions were all aspects. To say that they were all aspects of "behavior" helped very little. Nor did it help enough, although it helped some, to say that they were all aspects of "social interaction."

Most distressing was that I could not see how to deal with the many aspects of "multiplicity" of the objects and concepts considered: the multiplicity of actors, the multiplicity of their goals, the many implicitly conflicting as well as cooperative relationships, the multiplicity of elements of specific acts (goals, means, etc.), the multiplicity of time perspectives, the multiplicity of dynamic changes over time, and others. When and how did all these multiple elements get organized? To what extent did they? What were the most general, or most nearly always relevant, dimensions, or ways, in which they got organized, or even partially organized?

One cannot deal effectively in an intellectual sense with a "multiplicity" without names for observable parts and means of describing them in such a way that the description of any one of the parts will tend to locate it in relation to the other parts, preferably all of them, but if not all of them, at any rate, the most important of them. What is required is a specific and definite descriptive system, based on real measurement that can be applied to each of the most relevant parts. It turns out, I suggest, that the mental and social descriptive system that human beings naturally tend to evolve over time in real social interaction is a system of "values."

To achieve the kind of understanding I was looking for, one needs more than the idea that values are involved in all behavior, or even that values hang together as a "system" of conflicts and cooperations between values. Much more is necessary, of course, than the idea that a "multiplicity" of values is involved. Otherwise, we are essentially back at square one, where we started. How is one to understand the genesis and development of values? As a researcher, how is one to introduce some kind of useful order into the investigation and understanding of a "multiplicity" of values?

In the literature of the early period, human actors other than the self, for the most part, were brought in only occasionally and unsystematically. The main concepts usually had their principal meaning and implications within the frame of reference of the single act or a series of acts of some hypothetical general-purpose individual addressed to some particular goal of that individual. Some of the concepts easily understood in such a simplified context were the concepts of drive, motive, goal, end, means, conditions, barriers, detours, signs, symbols, values, and meanings.

One could say that, almost by default, due to lack of appropriate observation and concepts, human behavior was often understood to be a more or less straightforward matter of utilizing means to a predefined end. "Norms" and values were often regarded as variables, but mostly as individualized, nonsystematized kinds of constraint. The origins and horrendous complications of conflicting values that are introduced into human motivation by social interaction and its emergent regularities and differentiations between persons tended to be unseen or put out of sight.

The experimental demonstration by Sherif of the formation of a single simple social norm in a situation of minimal social interaction prescribed by the experimenter (Sherif, 1936) was regarded as a great triumph—as indeed it was, but it was such a bare beginning, and fitted so well within the existing context of the "unit act" that it did little to bring about theoretical changes toward a systems point of view.

The concepts for describing the "situation" and the "unit act" were usually not much more complicated than the concepts Köhler used for describing his experimental ape, Sultan, confined to his cage, trying to solve the problem of how to get the banana Köhler had hung just out of his reach. In fact, of course, animal studies like those of Köhler and Tolman provided the actual concrete models for many of the important concepts.

In the early period, the concepts for describing the "self" typically included "values" in some vague general sense as an important kind of variable. But there was no empirically based *classification* of what might be called a "minimal-but-necessary-to-be-accounted-for fundamental array of values" in the literature. If one wanted to describe a "value system" there was little help to be had.

These problems were not really approached in any very detailed way until the 1950s, when social anthropologists, particularly Clyde Kluckhohn and his colleagues, began to address them. In the early period, so far as I can tell, there was no notion that there could be what I now try to describe as an empirically based fundamental array of values which inevitably over time constitute themselves, as it were, into an interlocked and partly contradictory system. There was no inventory of identifiable values and their conflicts which a social psychologist always needed to take into account, and measure if possible.

There was no working model of the problems introduced by the interactive relationships of values with each other. There was no generalized model that could be used to measure and describe an actually existing "value system" of a society and to discover its internal problems, conflicts, and capabilities. At the level of the small group or "social situation," there was no empirically established way to conceptualize a rounded fundamental array or system of values, or to visualize the process by which *conflicting* sets of values as parts of that systemic array came into being, or to anticipate either the shorter-term dynamics or the changes over longer times that most likely might result from the relationships of sets of values and conflicting sets of values in particular personalities or in particular groups.

In the early days, as well as now, I was a rather conventional, optimistic, and idealistic searcher for "understanding" of some kind. I wanted social relationships to be harmonious and effective, as most social psychologists and sociologists do. It took me a long time to see clearly that there are certain identifiable and measurable value conflicts that are *inevitably* present in essentially all individual personalities and in essentially all particular groups of individuals in social interaction.

Eventually, however, on the basis of research and experience I reluctantly came to realize that there are certain sets of values and value conflicts, as well as certain sets of value congruences, which are essentially *always* involved to some degree, both within individual mental processes and within any inter-acting group of selves. In real social interaction there is no escaping choices at both individual and social levels. People must and do make them, willy-nilly, knowingly or not. The choices often have value consequences which are not anticipated and in many cases cannot be. But in some cases they probably can be, and knowledgeable understanding might reduce the number of bad decisions.

I believe that social psychologists now have a way to identify an essentially rounded "fundamental array" of the particular sets of conflicting and cooperating values that are always involved in social interaction. These fundamental values in moving patterns or dynamic constellations are a part of every "social-interaction system," as well as every "personality." If I have poorly identified or described the fundamental array, at least it is more clear, I hope, how one may go about improving it. My practical solution is based on empirical research, and no doubt it can be improved by the same method.

Why should the fundamental array of values and choices in social interaction always involve conflict to some degree? The reasons go deeper than the fact that adult individuals always differ to some degree in their values prior to any particular interaction encounter. The generic seeds of the fundamental values most critical to social relationships arise in the first place at a very microscopic minimal level. They arise out of inescapable differentiating features and social implications in every pairing of an initial act of one individual with every reply or reaction of one or more others, and again with every evaluation from the retrospective third-person perspective of one or more individuals in the system.

### There Were a Few Pioneers

The short time perspective of the "single act" of the "single individual," the perspective so central to the minimal frame of reference in the early period of personality and social psychology, is important and always necessary in understanding behavior. But, emphatically, it is not enough. The expansion of problems faced by multiple individuals in interaction changes everything about the "situation," and immensely complicates it.

The customary literary way of recognizing these changes in the early days was simply to add the term "social" to the term "situation." But the simple addition of the word "social" to the word "situation" conveys hardly any intimation of the nature of the complications which actually set in and begin to develop when a number of individuals are involved in real social interaction.

There could not have been any full recognition of the "systemic" contents of the "social situation" in the early days. Social interaction at the actual concrete back-and-forth level and its social complications over time had hardly been studied empirically. I believe this kind of observation and conceptualization is critically important for theoretical understanding. The most critical features of the "social" situation as moment by moment it becomes more complex have their very beginning in the regularization of "systemically interconnected" features of social interaction in the concrete, microscopic, detailed, back-and-forth process, and in the multiple participants' retrospective evaluations of the outcomes. These features are not easily imagined in vivid detail. The unaided imagination alone does not go far enough to produce a fully fledged and useful picture of a social-interaction system.

In retrospect, I believe, one can see in the early accounts of the self and situation, and even of social interaction, that when this kind of analysis was needed, theorists tended to regress in their description back to the unit act of an individual and the problem-solving perspective of a very short isolated time span.

How could this be, one may ask, since sociology and social anthropology (not to mention economics and political science) were well under way in the early period? Societal and cultural features of the large scale of description were of course recognized in the literature, and were familiar to most social psychologists. Concepts such as the division of labor, status and role, stratification, class, authority, power, property, various types of solidarity, and many other structural features of the larger society were of course well recognized.

It was also recognized that in some sense the large-scale features of society had counterpart representations or even evolutionary origins at the microscopic social-psychological level, but the large-scale features had not successfully been brought down to the small interpersonal scale, with methods for measurement, and for the most part, it was not at all clear how to do so.

Small-scale social-interaction systems which might yield usable answers had not been studied in the requisite degree of concrete detail. Personality psychologists in later parts of the century often asked for help in describing what features of social structure and social institutions they should take into account in describing small-scale social situations or the conditions within which personality developed. But the answers they received, so far as I know, were murky and unmanageable. To tell the truth, nobody knew how to answer these questions.

In much social-psychological theorizing of the early period, whenever the theorist needed to think and talk about another participant in the situation, an additional actor was brought in from off-stage to play the required bit-part without much further social context, with hardly any accompanying baggage. Other human beings were mentioned in describing particular situations, for example, others such as "alter," "father figure," or "fireman" in childhood role-playing scenarios, but they were typically treated as mere lay figures. Data about them, which might bear on individual personalities or differences, was neither provided nor considered critical.

These bit-part actors were seldom if ever treated as real interacting participants, themselves caught in a "system" of articulate social relationships, replete with feedbacks, retrospective evaluations and third- and fourth-order system dynamics. The "self" was seldom treated as one of a number of participants, each of whom also had a "self," all interlocked in a complex process of group dynamics which involved inevitable value conflicts, and some probable unpleasant consequences for some of the persons involved.

"Social interaction" was certainly a part of the language of the time. It was made theoretically central by George Herbert Mead (1934). Mead is still one of my great heroes, and in the early days his writings, thanks to Charles Morris and others who assembled notes on his lectures, provided major enlightenment and inspiration to me. His model for the context of interacting persons, usually cooperating with each other, was the "social act." But in fact, almost nobody in the early period, including Mead, had spent much time actually observing and recording social interaction at the microscopic level, act by act, and putting the actual data all together. Even Mead, as I remember, depended heavily on the imaginary confrontation of two angry dogs who showed their teeth a lot, but never quite got around to the threatened fight. I cannot recall whether there was ever a "third dog." Even in illustrations involving "games" and the development of the "generalized other" I cannot remember anybody who did not play by the rules. "Cooperation" in the context of the rules was the expected outcome.

In truth, it is impossible to extract much theoretical insight about social interaction as it develops among many group participants simply by trying to imagine act-by-act sequences through a long series of "back-and-forth" moves. Even if one is pretty good at chess one can hardly get through more than a few imagined moves of social interaction. As in chess, from any point in the play or position of the pieces on the board there are far too many branching continuations leading in different directions. One tends to give up.

Kurt Lewin bravely tried to follow the branching of social interaction by an awkward "back-and-forth" approach with the example of a married couple trying to reach a common goal in their respective "life spaces." But Lewin got bogged down at about the third move, and quietly abandoned the attempt.

Although their study was not an observational study, W. I. Thomas and Florian Znaniecki ([1918–20]1958) deserve my appreciation for their theoretical treatment of the "situation," "attitudes," and "values" and for the immense back-and-forth detail of their documentary study of the letters of family members of Polish peasants in urban America. I regret to say, however, that Thomas and Znaniecki seem to me to have badly misconceptualized the nature of "values." They treated "values" as completely external to the make up of the present individual personality. Thus, a coin was "a value." Their equivalent term for "values" was "attitudes."

When I put out my graduate-student dragnet for studies that would throw light on what was currently meant by the concept "social situation," J. L. Moreno (1934) had just published his studies of networks of liking (based on his sociometric questionnaire asking for interpersonal choices). I was impressed by the technique of measurement and the diagrams, but neither the theory nor the diagrams seemed to "unroll" much further for me into any series of theoretical insights. The networks of liking seemed to float in the air, with no clear relation to the more complex social context.

Kurt Lewin's (1936) topological "field" theory and his study of "group atmospheres" with Lippitt and White (1939), based on detailed real-time behavioral observation, made it plain that fruitful and theoretically interesting studies could be done using experimental small groups. But I could not make Lewin's topological theory of the life space do any real theoretical work. One critical defect was that there was no systematic way to gather or use observable data to make the diagrams. In Lewin's language, the "constructs" of the theory were simply intuitively "ordered" to common-sense features of the concrete situation.

Emory Bogardus (1925) and his social-distance questionnaire provided an interesting measurement technique which looked as if it might help, but varying degrees of "social distance," like Moreno's diagrams of the networks of interpersonal choices, seemed to me to float more or less isolated from any systemic context that might give them theoretical antecedents or consequences for other aspects of a larger system of relationships. One might ask, What is the "territory" within which "distance" is being measured? To Moreno one might ask, What other "choices" are inevitably linked with liking or disliking because of their inclusion in some larger system?

Dorothy Swain Thomas (1929) and some other researchers had made actual real-time observations and recordings of children's behavior in play groups, and their observational categories were of some later help to me. But their categories were couched in concrete forms of child-like behavior, hardly suitable for general theoretical purposes, and of course, had no "systemic" setting.

Frederick Thrasher (1927) devoted close study at first hand to urban gangs, and his work helped me a great deal. It convinced me that I needed to go ahead with the study of small groups and the "roles" that developed. But Thrasher's descriptions did not deal with the process of social interaction itself in a measurable way, and most of the roles were concretely tied to the gang context: the clown, the fat boy, and the like. Are there generalized roles which one may expect to find in any kind of interacting group? If so, what are they?

Talcott Parsons, my later mentor in graduate school, had begun his magnum opus, *The Structure of Social Action* (1937), with a complex conceptual analysis of the "unit act," in order to show the different assumptions various earlier theorists (Durkheim, Weber, Pareto, Marshall) had made about the elements always involved in their concepts of the unit act. But as Parsons insisted (see also Parsons 1968a), the analysis of social action, one unit at a time, from the actor's point of view, does not give the major theoretical leverage one needs for representing the emergent features of a "system" of interaction, particularly the emergence of norms and values.

At the time Parsons wrote his early work (1937), nobody seemed to really know any very good way to describe in detail, or to think about, the systemic consequences of multiple individuals in the very microscopic processes of interaction, with multiple goals, multiple means, multiple meanings, multiple values, and so on. There was almost no base of actual observation of the processes of social interaction, no articulate and rounded theory of how "systems" of relationships among individuals in interaction formed, what regularities and structures nearly always emerged, and why. In brief, there was no global theory of what I now think of as a "social-interaction system," which at the same time suggested practical methods of measurement.

Direct observation of human interactive behavior was not popular in those days. In fact it never has been, and it is not now. Unfortunately the direct-observational approach of more or less free social interaction is contrary to the methodological ethos of experimental control that has dominated social psychology for most of the past century. If, as an experimenter, one controls all the variables one can, the tendencies of those same variables to form an interdependent and often unruly system of behavior and values will be kept mostly out of sight.

### How Can One Get Out of the Cage of the Unit Act?

In my case it took a long period of observation of groups trying to solve problems which I had given them to propel me out of the doomed expectation that a linear individualistic or dyadic framework based essentially on the internal means-to-end stages of the "unit act" would allow me to understand what was going on in group problem solving.

The determination to learn from observation (rather than by verbal recombinations of the already very abstract concepts of the time) led me to invent what Francis Bacon long ago called "instruments and helps." In my case, these were instruments for classifying and recording what I could observe, as close to the visible concrete and immediate present as I could get. The development and use of these instruments was accompanied and followed by much pondering on the data.

Probably the most important instruments and helps I developed consisted of two parallel methods for the first-hand observation and real-time recording of acts of social interaction. The classifying categories and observation procedures for the first method were called *Interaction Process Analysis*. The classifying categories and observation procedures for the second method were called *Value Content Analysis*. The two methods were later combined into one method, called SYMLOG. The term "multiple level," a constituent of the SYMLOG acronym, originally meant that the method required the observer to pay attention not only to interactive behavior and to values, but also to nonverbal behavior, fantasies, and some other aspects of content.

I finally became unavoidably aware of the significance of certain obvious emergent regularities of behavior. They were obvious on the face of it, and recognizable at the time. But they came out more impressively in statistical compilations. By degrees, I realized more clearly the momentary interdependence of the parts of the process on each other. In my increasingly sophisticated mind's eye I could see that their cumulative effects were implicitly present in the mental processes of participants themselves during the time of interaction.

I sensed the generalized theoretical importance of cumulative regularities and the disturbances they created as well as the order they introduced. I saw them not only as variables within the particular small systems I had under observation, but as actual early stages and embryonic prototypes of the comparable variables and parallel relationships in large social systems. Alternatively, looking toward the individual personality, I saw their mental counterparts as embryonic prototypes for the simultaneous development of the value systems and dynamics. The old Freudian concept of the Superego, as the organization of values in the individual personality, became a complex value system of twenty-six contending value vectors (see chapter 5).

By long observation, my innocence was gradually impaired. When I developed the IPA categories (a long and thoughtful period of observation in itself) I intentionally omitted in the final set of twelve any category called "shows dominance." I took it for granted, in my innocent optimism, that "status" in the social-interaction systems I was observing would be an emergent "achieved status" growing naturally out of the fact that members would naturally recognize that the problem-solving contributions of certain members were of more help and value than those of others. I wanted to see "dominance" emerge inductively out of excellence and to coincide with merit in dealing with the problems I had given the group. I did not want to prejudge differential status to be shown at the time the acts occurred.

I was disillusioned. In time I had to recognize that the exercise of brute dominance often began at once in the form of overtalking on the part of some individual members. In a broader sense, the exercise of the "power" of these members was an unavoidable part of the "problem" for other group members. Merit in solving the problem I had given the participants might play some part later in the granting of status, but dominance was an initial condition of difference in personality between members. To deal with it was, in most cases, a more important and urgent "problem" for other participants than solving "my problem."

Dominance existed in its own right in the comparative personality traits of the assembled participants, although no doubt its importance was exacerbated in my groups, where there was no appointed leader and I myself did not act to manage the process. It became pretty clear that the possession and exercise of power through sheer dominance was not due to particular problems inherent in the group task, nor to excellence in task performance. The fact was that from the beginning in my groups of individuals there were lions and there were lambs, as well as a few goats. In order to achieve problem-solving effectiveness, the lions and the lambs somehow had to induce each other to lie down peaceably with each other. And, the problem-solving intellectuals needed to have at least some cooperation from the lions, as well as from a few other personality types who were not at all interested in solving the task problems I had assigned.

Is it true that power is essentially different from merit in larger social systems? I now think that it is true in some form in all social-interaction systems, but I suspect that in some ideological frames of mind, for example, in the ideology of the lions, unpleasant facts like these tend to be ignored and forgotten so far as possible. Perhaps some lambs ignore it too.

In the case of newly assembled, initially leaderless groups, *differentiations* in the types and quantities of behavior that different individuals show tend to emerge quite rapidly. Some of the acts in my groups were addressed to the particular case problems that I had asked the group members to discuss. But many of the acts and interchanges seemed to relate more directly to personality differences, particularly value differences, that individuals had brought into the group initially, as well as to obtrusive dominance and emergent leadership attempts and status concerns.

In most cases, at least within the frame of a given meeting, the quality and quantity of acts of specific individuals tended to become progressively more different from each other, and more in conflict, until some apparent breaking point, which was usually signaled by a period of joking and laughing tripped off by some clown among the members. In most groups this cycling of growing conflict interrupted by joking and laughing occurred a number of times in a given meeting.

The seemingly inevitably developing differences between individuals, perhaps particularly the inexorable development of differences among them in their amounts of participation, appeared to bring advantages and satisfaction to the more frequent participators, and, at the same time, disadvantages and dissatisfaction to at least some of the less frequent. If one watched closely for the expressions on faces, one could read the nonverbal signs.

The less frequent participators, some of whom seemed to feel wronged and disadvantaged, tended in time to react more and more negatively to what was happening to them. What was happening to them, in many cases, was that a pair or a few of the members who first seized the opportunity seemed to have formed a closed circle of back-and-forth remarks and agreements, or had mounted a quarrel that would not settle down. In either case, the amount of participation of the few involved in the overt interaction was mounting busily.

Some of the less advantaged members seemed to look around the group for still other members who might join them in a coalition to control the way things were going. They would begin to object, though not always directly. Often the objections took the form of very broad "value statements" as to how social interaction in general, or in some unspecified situation, "ought" to go. The thrust of the argument, if made specific, was that it ought to go in some way more or less the opposite of the way it was going in the present group. Often these generalizations were pronounced with some heat, with the beginning signs of "moral indignation."

The members in the more advantaged positions were likely to maintain their previously formed coalition, for example, a coalition between a talkative leader-candidate and a supporting "yes"-saying member. Such a pair usually tended to oppose the emerging proposed values of the disadvantaged coalition.

A stubborn polarization between two opposed coalitions all too often set in. Effective and accepted leadership apparently could not be established, even after a second meeting. None of the participants apparently could provide a new emphasis in a direction that elicited enough support to break the deadlock. An observer might doubt that the group with its present composition could survive under real conditions outside the laboratory.

I became convinced that I needed to have a better idea of the range of values and probable value conflicts. A critical element in the development of a workable systems point of view for me was the development of what I called *Value Content Analysis*.

## Value Content Analysis Is More Than *Attitude Measurement*

"Values," in current psychological language, are sometimes thought of as very general attitudes that apply to many situations, rather than just one or a few. Attitude measurement (which had begun in the early period) usually involves measuring the degree of favorableness or unfavorableness of a respondent toward some socially visible object or issue of social conflict or uncertainty.

A characterization of a statement as having a particular "value content" in the procedure I called *Value Content Analysis* gives much more information to the observer than the information that the speaker is "for" or "against" the object talked about. This is because a particular value statement in VCA is judged and rated as having a specific place in a specified larger "system" or rounded, inclusive, and closed array of values. Its "place" in the larger system will involve more than its placement in just the one dimension of "for" or "against" because the larger system has more than that one dimension.

VCA assumes that an actual value "system" in the group observed is a part of the real system of social interaction, which itself is also made up of many kinds of behavior in relation to each other and to the values. The "system" of values is assumed to be made up of many interdependent values which support and oppose each other in various ways (or in various dimensions). If the researcher has somehow discovered or invented a theoretically exhaustive or closed classification of a limited number of value variables which he maintains are bound to be found in any social-interaction system, and if the researcher's invention provides a specific identification and description of each of the values included in the closed system, then the observer can classify in one and only one place the "value content" of any particular value statement that a speaker in the group makes about an issue under discussion.

To identify the "value content" of an act in VCA is simply to identify which one of the value variables in the theoretically complete system the statement most closely resembles, and to write down who made the statement, to whom, and when. All value statements have a value content that can be classified somewhere in the system. But where does such a system come from? This is the place in the theory where one almost has to know the answer before one can find the answer. Chapters 4 and 5 have suggested how one can approach the problem inductively. The answer in the briefest possible description is "factor analysis." The theoretically closed and complete array of value classes is the twenty-six-item set, used in the rating process called IOVAL.

## Images in the Mind

People in interaction can be said to talk about, and make value statements about "images" (such as, "authority," "John," "equality," "our leader," etc.), although they usually do not talk as if they are talking about "images" as such. One gathers that, except in quite unusual cases, they assume that they are talking about an "object" ("out there"). In most cases the mental images the speaker has in mind at the time he or she talks about them seem to the observer to have been already cognitively formed and already evaluated, in the mind of the speaker, although at the same time they appear to be related in some way to what is going on in the group.

The observer is likely to conclude that the participant who makes a value statement about an image usually already has very generalized attitudes about the object, or image. The image somehow has a flavor of "good" or "bad" in the mind of the person who talks about it. The person usually gives some indications in the tone of voice or in the language used or the accompanying nonverbal behavior that he or she is either "for" or "against" whatever it is that the image stands for. Very often he or she is trying to persuade one or more other members that such and such a general way of acting is good or bad, and implicitly an observer can guess that it is felt to be good or bad for the speaker's self-image.

Images, of course, include the mental pictures that interacting persons have of each other as complete individual persons or personalities. The mental pictures we have of other persons also tend to have a flavor of good or bad, depending in part upon our perception and evaluation of the other person's behavior, the values he or she has professed, how that person has treated one's self or one's friends, and so on.

Anything that can be represented as a concept or an image is a mental "object." It is associated with an extensive network of "meanings" or further extensions in the mind of a participant. The image and its network of meanings is typically the focus of a kind of summary attitude in the person's mind, depending on the present situational context. Values are so general, however, and often so ambiguous, that if the context changes, the meaning of the value, or its import as it is actually applied to the more concrete situation, can also change. The meanings attached to a value may even completely shift under the pressure of a particular context. An object, or a means to a given end, that formerly was bad, if the context shifts, may become an instrument of good. Deception, for example, is normally bad if practiced on your friends, but in wartime it becomes not only good, but necessary, to be practiced on your enemies.

### Values in Themselves Can Be Further Evaluated

The attitude toward the object of the image and the network of meanings as well, or any part of the network, can be reevaluated in the mind in terms of whether or not it is consistent with still more general attitudes or other values of the evaluator. In turn, values, the most generalized attitudes, can be, and are, themselves reevaluated by the self and by other participants in comparison with still other values. It is often not clear to any of the participants in a group, or at least not to a majority, which values are more important than other values, and what to do in case of conflicts between two competing values.

Thus the participants use certain of their values, by persuasion, rhetoric, or any number of psychological "mechanisms of defense" or modes of attack, to call into question and modify or change the meaning of other values, both in their own mind or the minds of others. One might almost believe that for every participant, the whole complicated network of attitudes, meanings, and the most abstract values to which they are associated may be "cranked around" like the huge telescope on Mt. Wilson, and adjusted bit by bit to some acceptable fit to whatever objects need to be brought into focus.

As interaction and communication go on, the logical and evaluative aspects of the argument build up in complication and also in their potential power to persuade individual participants. Clusters of the values that are brought to the general attention and memory of the interacting participants are gradually assembled and mobilized around one or a set of images that are held in the attention of the participants by repeated mention. The clusters are built on the basis of the value contents and selected meanings brought to attention in the present context.

Whether such clusters of values are mobilized in support of each other as somewhat similar, or whether they are mobilized as clusters in opposition, they tend to acquire a clearer and more compact and compelling form as a total activated constellation. The individual values are "mobilized" into larger contending clusters as individuals learn how other individuals feel, and how they themselves feel about aspects of the problem they had not thought about before.

There may be several clusters. If one could actually see the values in motion, one might imagine that the constellation of the whole pattern of clusters is almost "self-organizing," in the sense that the authorship of particular values, and the initial positions on the issues of some of the members, may fall out of sight in the overall process of mobilization. If the total fitting of the activated value and meaning network to the concrete situation is like the ponderous cranking around of the Mt. Wilson telescope, the observer, as well as the members, may lose sight of just who or what combination of people is turning the crank.

Important parts of the total field or pattern of values are typically invisible of course to an observer, or to the other participants, because they exist in more remote parts of the "free association" processes internal to the minds of particular members. The moving value constellation that the observer becomes aware of can be treated, in abstraction from the specific authorship of particular values, as a changing "dynamic system" or "field" of value clusters. With some qualifications that are not completely clear, it seems to be true that initial value similarity between any two individuals tends to increase their similarity, while initial value differences tend to make them still more different.

It may even appear to an observer as if the values and feelings themselves are loosed from their initial moorings in the minds of individual members. It may appear as if the values and feelings themselves were engaged in a kind of milling struggle, a kind of chaotic mating dance. Individual values desert their usual mates and search for new ones.

By its very nature the value system of a social-interaction system is always unsettled, partly unresolved, in some degree of conflict with itself, at least implicitly. In reality, of course, the values are always the values of particular persons. Each of these particular persons has a social position and a self-picture to protect and is busy doing so. Ultimately, of course, it is the evaluative urges of the individual members themselves that make the value and meaning system run, move, and change shape.

## The Factor Analysis of Values

The values involved in any actually interacting group of individuals must be numerous beyond all accounting. How can one construct an observational procedure like VCA to deal with overwhelming multiplicity? Once I was thoroughly impressed with the fact that many of the conflicts in the groups I was observing seemed to be centered on values, I faced up to the problem of trying to understand the variety of values. My approach was optimistic and simple minded as usual: I listened carefully to many sessions of interaction, copied down each instance of what seemed to me at the time to be a "value statement" and accumulated examples of value statements, as many as I could. Most statements that seemed to qualify as values were classified in the IPA category of *Gives Opinion*.

Chapter 4 is an account of how that inductive approach was extended by an omnivorous raid on the literature, and theft of all the "value statements" that my colleagues and I could locate in a broad range of the literature that seemed relevant: psychological, philosophical, religious or otherwise. That chapter tells how the huge pile of more than 800 candidate "value statements" that we brought back home from the raid was boiled down and simplified by factor analysis.

The problem of determining what range of value content to sample and in what degree of detail to go for actual diagnostic measurement in a typical given social-interaction system was solved to a workable approximation by the inductive simplification that can be achieved through factor analysis and further intellectual elaboration (see chapter 5 and Appendix A).

## Factor Analyses in the Literature

To face the practical problems of measurement squarely, one has to admit that there are possibly millions of values and value differences which one might be able to identify in any actual situation of social interaction. How can a researcher deal with this overwhelming complexity? I have just indicated that factor analysis can play a crucial role, as it did in my case.

It is my contention that a variety of factor analyses made in the past by different investigators have providentially provided a theoretical key as to how to simplify the number and nature of the variables needed to probe the value system of any social-interaction system in a representative and practical way.

The theoretical key is the discovery that the dimensions of the factors as they have actually been found in a number of different studies reported in the literature can be "rotated" and "fitted to each other" in such a way as to enable the researcher to see and understand the essential theoretical similarities in the "dimensions" of the factor space they have probed. It appears to me that at a more abstract theoretical level, at what might be called a "meta level," many different factor analyses by different researchers dealing with different aspects of behavior (not just "values" as such) have probed the "same" space. Moreover, I think it can be seen "why." The "space" is the "same" in that it is a generic intercorrelation space that is naturally created and recreated in any real live social-interaction system.

Since the development of factor analysis early in the century by Thurstone (1947) and others, quite a large number of studies have been made of the factor structure of very disparate kinds of content, such as connotations of words, types of behavior, personality traits, social, economic, and political attitudes, philosophical and religious beliefs, explicit value statements, and many other aspects of social behavior and culture.

I believe that the results of many of these studies converge, at a somewhat higher level of abstraction, in showing that the orthogonal factors discovered are practically quite limited in number, and that they exist and relate to each other, to put it metaphorically, as if they had been discovered in the same factor space of many measures in the same large population. This imaginary "same" space, or meta-space, its factors, their various rotations and combinations in some of the most familiar studies, has been described in chapter 5.

Recognition of the general similarity of these factors, and their average correlational relationships, when studied over many different populations and over different content domains, is a critical element in the solution of the problem as to how one can deal with the overwhelming number and complexity of values in fully fledged value systems. The similarities between values on and close to the main factors provide clues as to how the millions of values presumably involved in human social interaction are actually intercorrelated and so can be reduced and consolidated into a smaller number of measurable variables, both for theoretical understanding, and for the design of practical sampling and measurement.

The underlying reason for the "convergence," or theoretical similarities at the abstract level, I believe, lies in the fact that the different kinds of content of values, if one studies their intercorrelations in the same intact group or population of real interacting persons, are all part-processes of the same kind of entity or organization, namely, a "social-interaction system." The values, as well as all of the overt acts, all affect each other, in a circular and recursive way, in closer and more simultaneous interconnection than we tend to imagine.

It gradually became clear to me that for sampling and measurement purposes a practical classification of the most important values needed for an approximate understanding of a particular social-interaction system could be formulated in terms of a limited number of variables, located and described by their relation to the still more limited skeleton of the orthogonal (independent) factors that tend to be found in a broadly based population of factor analyses. These variables, which can be made into "items" for use in describing Images of socially important "objects" were later called the twenty-six vectors of the intercorrelation space (see chapter 5 and Appendix A).

Can only twenty-six vectors for sampling and measurement possibly be enough? Only recently I have learned about the variety of evolutionary developments that have produced the forty or so differently constructed kinds of eyes possessed by different biological species. I am indebted to Richard Dawkins (1996) for his wonderful book *Climbing Mt. Improbable*, explaining for a disbelieving lay audience how the seeming miracle of the design and construction of the eye could possibly have come about by evolutionary processes.

There are only twenty-six measurement probes in my diagnostic procedure for value systems. There is at least a metaphorical similarity between the employment of only twenty-six systematically spread-out vectors or measurement probes in my diagnostic procedure for obtaining an assembled picture of a value system of a group and the kind of biological eye called a compound or supercompound eye—the rounded convex kind of eye possessed by the fly.

In all eyes, even the best and most complex, the number of light receptors is limited. They have to be arranged and pointed precisely, and paradoxically, in such a way that most of the available light that might come to each one is blocked out, so that it is selective. In a compound eye each receptor gives a neural report of only a small parcel of photons, the rays of light from only a single point on the object to be seen. These receptors, however, are arranged in a systematically spread-out way over a rounded global surface, or within the rounded interior of a cup that makes up the eye.

The particular cunning way in which the receptors are spread out, and the way in which the nerves coming from the receptors are hooked up with each other accomplishes a re-sorting and rearrangement of the partial bits. The brain, because it has somehow learned by experience or "knows how" by genetic inheritance, assembles a meaningful "picture" or ordered and interconnected arrangement of the parts. In its configuration the arrangement as a whole reflects what is important for the survival of the organism about the objects in the environment.

Chapter 1 has described the Field Diagram of the social-interaction "system field" and how it gets constructed as a visual graphic picture by the mathematical model that serves as the brain that unscrambles and assembles in an orderly way the data that raters in the group provide. The Field Diagram picture in effect provides a leader and group participants with something like a compound eye that yields a picture of assembled information about what is going on in the group, a picture the group members have not previously had for their conscious awareness and analysis, a picture that in some cases may have survival value.

## What is a Social Interaction System?

A social-interaction system may be thought of as a manifold of contrary and convergent variables of values and behavior of different individuals acting upon each other, the different part-processes of which, nevertheless, all hang together as repetitive and persistent, and so need to be studied and understood as an interdependent "whole."

The idea of such a system has been around a long time in one form or another (such as in the form of the much disputed metaphorical idea of a "group mind," or a "process gestalt"), but it has been very difficult to give such a complex organization an effective substance, workable limits, or a definitive structure at the social-psychological level. A major part of the difficulty is that most of the important part-processes are not directly visible, but exist mentally in the minds of the individually different participants. Nevertheless, they can be made "visible" by methods of measurement which now exist, and function as a "compound eye."

The idea of the real substantive existence of a "social-interaction system" is not yet familiar. The idea that such systems are indeed the proper subject matter of social-psychological research and theorizing is still not understood, or it is discredited or quietly rejected by some. The leading alternative idea is that the proper subject matter of social psychology is the psychology of the generalized individual as affected on particular occasions by particular features of a social context. But I think a systems approach is an idea whose time has come. Primary to its effective recognition and visualization, I believe, is the ability to identify key part-processes, to measure their varying states and levels, and to demonstrate empirically their correlations and interdependencies in intact groups under varying conditions. These things have been accomplished, at least to a limited extent.

Social-interaction systems, I believe, at their most embryonic or beginning level, tend to have certain similar problems for individual members, and interdependencies in the way the behaviors and values of the multiple members fit together or fail to do so. The problems are initially present or emerge relatively soon after interaction begins. Certain measurable regularities of behavior tend to emerge, and many of them consist of widening differences between individual participants. The different kinds of behavior become distributed among different members. The behaviors are differentiated in their frequencies, in the times of their occurrences, the ways in which the frequencies of given kinds of behavior and value emphases follow each other, provoke each other, and rise and fall in cycles over time.

The interdependence of variables in social-interaction systems is given in the first place by the brute fact that the participants are all interacting within the same place and time, that they can help and hurt each other in so many ways, and that the solutions they choose to the problems they inevitably face with regard to each other can determine the survival or demise of the particular group as a working system or set of relationships.

The various interdependencies are regularized and codified over time by the members themselves in the form of "values," although the members themselves may not call them by that name. I have come to believe that the study of values by essentially the kinds of methods I have described is the shortest, most economical, and most comprehensive approach to the beginning understanding of a social-interaction system.

This can be the case, I believe, basically because values tend to mirror and codify everything else about the system. Or to put it the other way around, everything behavioral in the system, especially the interaction between participants, tends to be evaluated by the members most immediately involved, and those in third-party positions. Bit by bit the evaluations and attitudes of the members tend to evolve in a developmental or "evolutionary" process through repetitive encounters toward more generalized and more generally accepted "values." There are always conflicts and variant positions in the evaluation, because people are always socially differentiated and are affected in different ways by almost any particular value solution to their most important social problems.

In many cases, the surviving values, in their partially conflicting and partly supporting entirety, have the interdependent and unstable, but persistent, properties of a "value system." They exert a kind of partial control over the more overt behavioral parts of the system, but the control is never completely successful. Nor is the set of definitions of preferred behavior ever completely consistent, either logically or evaluatively. It is not possible to derive all parts of the value system deductively from any single identifiable set of premises or beliefs, although attempts to do so by the development of particular "ideologies" nearly always tend to develop.

The set of ideals that does evolve for a working majority is never a monolithic consensus. It is always, even at its nearest approach to consensus, a distribution of concepts and feelings as to what would be "ideal" and what is reprehensible. Even with its normally distributed set of variations, the set of ideals is constantly compromised and undermined in all possible directions by persons and subgroups, in part responding to the pressures of their real circumstances, and in part in response to their personality differences and the strains created by their social relationships.

## A Common-Sense Description of Some System Problems

The particular problems or solutions confronting individuals in social-interaction systems do not seem to me to start or proceed in any very dependable order. It is rather as if the problems were all incipient in principle from the first, at least in groups of adults or near adults, and any of the various potentials is likely to become overt and develop further at any time. Because attention to any specific one of them seems to be tripped off by so many small differences in urgency and by any number of kinds of accidents, I think that it is better for observers and researchers to have the whole roster of major potentials in mind, so far as they can, and to be prepared for any of them to surface and command attention. For convenience only, then, I mention them in a particular order below, as first, second, and so on.

A first set of problems, as I have described them briefly above, are members' problems of controlling over-dominance at the interpersonal level. Interpersonal "dominance" as a personality trait implies the ability and the tendency to use raw power. By "raw power," I mean the raw factual ability of whatever kind in the immediate present to control the way others behave, apart from any "legitimacy" which may have been conferred by others.

"Authority" is a typical organizational solution addressed to the problems posed by the existence of raw power. Authority is different from raw power (although some members tend not to recognize the difference). Possession of "authority" depends upon a number of prior settlements in the group concerning "rights," "property," "agency," "representation," and the like, as to whether or not authority is properly possessed, by a person or persons attempting to appeal to it for justification of their behavior.

The admitted possession of authority by an agent ordinarily depends upon some previous social process of conferring legitimacy to that agent, a "right" that the majority of the group may have the "prior right" to confer, such as by election, or appointment, or some acknowledgment by a sufficient number of members that the designated agent has the "right" to exercise power in certain ways. Persons who have been given the rights to exercise authority are often given access to some kinds and degrees of the use of raw power, but the use of it is typically limited and defined. (It is no longer "raw.") However it is typically the case that there are other persons in the group, or in subgroups, without authority who nevertheless possess the means to exercise raw power.

The non-legitimized ability to exercise raw power in the face of opposition can derive from many sources, including personality traits associated with "dominance," physical size and strength, speed of action and reaction, possession or access to resources, money in particular, and typically in larger groups, to the possession of weapons, the occupation of physical territory and the possession of communication facilities. From almost any initial starting point of social interaction that one can think of, power is differentially distributed among participants, and this differential distribution is a source of problems to other participants. Observable variables correlated with a positive value placed on the possession of raw power in the small groups studied are listed under Vector 1 U in the Intercorrelation Space (see Appendix A).

A second set of problems that can be counted on to arise is the continuing need for effective problem solving of any kind that requires the mobilization of effort and task abilities among the participants in the performance of some set of tasks, or more broadly, mobilization of the task abilities that are needed in adapting successfully to the changing external situation of the group as a whole.

The solutions of these kinds of problems, as they will be found over a large population of groups of various kinds and sizes and kinds of environments, do not appear to me on the face of it to be related in any automatically or logically consistent way to the possession of raw dominance or power. The participants with the required abilities, or in a position of advantage with regard to the solution of these task problems, may factually be helped or hindered, or ignored, by the participants in positions of power.

Some of the variables correlated with a positive value placed on a position of advantage in respect to these "task-like" problems are listed under Vector 12 F in the Intercorrelation Space. Values on conservative group beliefs and in particular the religious nature of these beliefs are probably not always present in every small group. But in larger institutional settings such values are presumably associated with the legitimization of authority and obedience.

A third source of problems can be located and described as a group of needs or problems in the maintenance of sufficient group solidarity to permit and support cooperation and coordination. Again, there is no necessary correlation of the values of individuals as to the timing and urgency, or mode of solution of these problems with either the possession of raw power, or the possession of the ability to solve the problems of adaptation to the external environment. This source of problems is represented by Vector 10 P in the Intercorrelation Space.

As in the case of the two previously discussed problems—the distribution of raw power among the members, and the distribution of actual abilities to solve task problems among the members—this third variety of problems, problems of group solidarity, is independently variable from the other two, in principle. Individuals who have existing feelings of solidarity with each other by any fact of nature do not necessarily coincide in their distribution in any dependable way with the other two distributions. Yet, it turns out in research that in groups that are "ideal" or "most effective" in the eyes of participants, the values approving the P vector tend to be positively correlated with those of the F vector and those of the U vector. In other words, for effectiveness, the values pertaining to all three Vectors—U, P, and F—need to diverge from independence toward positive correlations with each other.

Now one has to expect the appearance sooner or later of *negative reactions* to problem solutions in each of the three areas in which problem solutions are typically posed, Vectors U, P, and F.

The differentiation of individuals according to possession of power, both raw and legitimate, leaves or virtually forces some persons to be at the low, or negative end of the scale. Whether they protest, or, whether, as more typically is the case, they remain passive and silent, they pose problems in that they appear to be alienated and are not available to support the U, P, and F solutions that may be proposed or implemented. The opposing end of the U vector is represented as Vector 26 D. Some of the correlates of values approving the D vector are found in Appendix A.

The solutions to the task problems facing the group (values on the F vector) presuppose abilities as well as values that are not possessed by all members of the group. As development of the group proceeds, the acceptance of some degree of authority, obedience, beliefs justifying these, and a number of kinds of correct performance come to be approved and justified as conventional and required, by the individuals who support them. A differentiated scale emerges with some proportion of the members potentially or actually at the negative end. They tend to oppose, by whatever means they have, the whole set of F solutions and values. Some correlates of their reactions in the Bales and Couch studies are described under the Vector 16 B in Appendix A.

Not all individuals either want to maintain their solidarity with other individuals who favor group solidarity, or some may not be able to do so. Solidarity implies certain responsibilities and duties in most cases which may interfere with individual freedom. There is then a negative end of the P vector, a set of values opposed to solidarity and in favor of individual freedom, called Vector 14 N. Correlates of this vector can be found in Appendix A.

### Scarce Resources and the Likelihood of Conflict

Attempts to solve or to deal even somewhat ineffectively with any of these six types of problems require time, effort, and the expenditure of resources, time, and effort at least, if not other resources. Resources available to the group as a whole are always limited and constantly have to be allocated and reallocated in some way from one time to another, to some combination of the six areas of problems. The expenditures actually devoted to solutions of any one of the six problem areas may become preemptive of resources available for the other five. Even under the most optimum balance or priority in the division of resources among the six major problem areas, there are still residual conflicts in the allocation of resources. The conflicts are due not only to the constant shortage of resources, but usually even more to the irreducible conflicts among members according to their conflicting interests, values, and beliefs.

Effective problem-solving behavior in relation to any of the six problem areas requires a fairly complicated *series* of logical steps in the mental and social operations of at least some, perhaps a majority, of the group members. Resources are required, even at the most preliminary stage: time to define the problem, to communicate the necessary information, opinion, and suggestions, time to deal with various types of feedback that result—agreements, disagreements, further questions, alternative and conflicting proposals. Members require the abilities to tolerate rising tensions while resources of time and effort are being spent on a particular set of problems and a much larger set remains unsolved.

Even at the very beginning of problem-solving efforts, almost inescapable conflicting demands come into effect. If the problem-solving efforts are to be actually effective when later put into operation, the communication and coordination involved in arriving at a group decision tends strongly to force several kinds of *differentiation* in the types and quantities of interactive behavior among the members. Attempts at leadership in a given value direction always imply differential emphasis to be given to the realization of certain values over others. For this reason alone, agreement and disagreement are both likely to appear, and opposition leadership is likely to appear overtly before long, perhaps immediately, at least with some degree of strength.

Differences in the quality and quantities of these kinds of problem-solving behavior carry with them advantages and disadvantages to the specific persons who find themselves affected by favorable or unfavorable positions in the developing scales of differentiation. Some talk to excess; others are crowded out; some are addressed frequently and are drawn in; others are ignored and can get in only by extreme effort, or by attaching their efforts to a coalition which only partly satisfies their values, and the like.

One may expect that values disapproving certain kinds of the differentiations in behavior that have developed in the course of problem solving are almost certain to develop among the persons who are disadvantaged. Potentially, the disadvantaged members may have sufficient value agreement among themselves to form a coalition and attack the persons who are in positions of advantage. If such an attack becomes overt, the persons who have acquired positions of advantage will probably tend to draw closer into a more effective coalition, suppress their internal disagreements for the time being, and fight back.

Sooner or later it will become evident that the solidarity of the total group is being damaged—cooperation and coordination are being affected. A sufficiently supported group decision appears to be impossible to achieve. In some cases problem-solving activity of a different kind tends to set in, expressed and signaled by joking and laughing in many cases, mending fences, celebrating solidarity, and showing belated attention to neglected members.

But even if an "optimum" balance, or order of priority of time and resources devoted to the six areas of problems can be restored and held approximately for any extended period of time (not likely in fact), not all individuals will be satisfied, in groups of average composition of disparate personalities. Even with an "optimum" balance leading to "effectiveness" at an "ideal" level, some members are likely to be left out who are opposed both to the values of problem solving in relation to the external situation, and to successful maintenance of solidarity over a sufficient portion of the group.

These residual members still left in opposition are likely to be those inclined to values of passive or active resistance, of extreme individual independence or of anarchy, mild or extreme. A coalition of individuals with D, N, and B values, like the coalition of individuals who favor U, P, and F values, will likely be a combination of convenience, actually still full of potentially damaging conflicts.

Why is conflict to some degree so likely? I believe a good and plausible answer may be given in terms of the dynamics of social-interaction systems in the family, schools, and other groups that Cooley called "primary groups," in which earlier personality formation and socialization takes place. In these groups, a variety of individual personality constellations, with all kinds of the conflicting values to be expected in social-interaction systems, is always created because so many families and primary groups are far from ideal, and all too frequently are actually pathological in their impact on their individual members, parents as well as children.

An analysis, or set of assumptions and deductions of this sort, will give additional insight as to why and how a range of cooperating and opposing values originates in the personality and characterizes to some degree the dynamics of all systems of social interaction.

From the empirical side, in my case, factor analysis of the intercorrelations of value statements, the means and distributions of different value contents and different aspects of behavior provided a more advantageous and balanced set of vectors for actual measurement than a less formally guided kind of analysis would have. But I have taken the informal tack, and the observational tack, as well as the formal tack, in my efforts to reach a point of view that seems somewhat adequate to me, although of course it is still very abstract and preliminary.

But at an introductory level, one needs to have some concrete pictures of persons in interaction in order to see how values may originate out of problem-solving behavior. In my experience, these concrete pictures typically came out of long intuitive familiarity based on observation with appropriate "instruments and helps" as Bacon called them. If one is only familiar with data that has been gathered by somebody else and treated only quantitatively, and then one is told that the whole set of relations is somehow comprehended in "three dimensions," it is hard to overcome the feeling that some kind of excessive formality is taking over, and that some kind of obsessive "nut" is at work! I implore your patience!

## The Early Studies of Interaction Using IPA

I hope to make it evident that the framework of the current theory throws additional light on the main import and findings of my earlier studies of overt interaction in laboratory problem-solving groups.

The three dynamically interdependent dimensions of "system fields" (U-D, P-N, and F-B) as portrayed on a Field Diagram were in fact foreshadowed and well represented in the logical relations of the categories of *Interaction Process Analysis* and in the nature of the early major findings using that observation system. But the three dimensions of the system fields that typically form in social interaction (though not likely completely orthogonal) and the correlational content of the space of dynamically interdependent variables, including especially, strategic system-relevant "values," become much clearer when the behavioral variables of IPA and its findings are placed, as we can now place and understand them, in the larger intercorrelation space of the many additional variables and relationships that now find their place in social-interaction systems theory. This placement can be traced in the descriptions of the locations of the IPA variables in the Intercorrelation Space (Appendix A) .

### The Well-Developed Value Instrumentation

The identification of a manageable set of value variables that it will always be relevant to measure for diagnostic purposes is the key to measurement by a third method: the use of well-designed questionnaires in well-designed sampling survey methods, including if possible, complete enumeration of all members. It is assumed that whatever can be evaluated in the mind of a participant can be measured by a researcher who forms an appropriate rating question defining an Image for the rater's concentrated attention, and asks the rater to apply a specific rating procedure designed to apply a predetermined set of twenty-six carefully worded values as proposed descriptions, or reactions to, the Image, or "object" to be evaluated.

The rating procedure actually employed in the contemporary method asks the rater to apply each of twenty-six "values descriptions" that are part of the researcher's theoretical system (see figure 1.2). The twenty-six-item set of values has been carefully developed according to theoretical criteria in such a way that the evaluation of the object by the application of *all* twenty-six values yields a single resulting focused location of the Image in a three-dimensional bipolar evaluative space. The location of the Image reflects the evaluative location of the Image with regard to all six vectors or value areas outlined above.

The single location of the Image in the evaluative space as rated by a single participant, for example his or her perception of the *self*, gives the necessary starting point for what seems to me to be a truly spectacular gain in knowledge about the dynamics of the system of values, with regard to the specific Image, at least, and then secondarily about the dynamics of the various kinds of behavior that exemplify and are associated with the Image and the values it represents.

## A Systems Approach

My early problems with social-psychological theory stemmed mainly from my inability to organize, measure, and put into the same larger frame of reference the *more abstract* concepts used in talking about the partial aspects of interaction. The abstractions were drawn from concrete processes, but they were drawn in all kinds of different and unspecified directions, and their relations to each other were often not clear.

I now believe, and propose, that the most relevant larger frame of reference or array of directions from which the abstractions are drawn may be conceptualized most effectively for theoretical and measurement purposes as a "social-interaction system." The system is described by the present method in most relevant detail by the relative locations of all variables in the complete set of twenty-six directions or vectors in the Intercorrelation Space (Appendix A). The sample set of almost evenly spaced twenty-six vectors or directions is a most important part of the present "theoretical system." The actual concrete process from which the abstractions are drawn may be called the actual social-interaction system.

When I mention the actual social-interaction system, I mean to refer to a system or network of interdependencies and feedbacks in the real-time-ordered behavior of multiple individuals in a specific small group, or, by extension, to an actual larger group or organization where members are closely interconnected by interactive communication. Larger groups, even complete societies are also properly called "social-interaction systems," and are parallel in many ways, particularly with regard to their value systems, although they are much harder to study in microscopic detail, for obvious reasons. The communicative connections are generally much more incomplete than in small "intact" groups.

The most critically important values having to do with human relationships arise, I suggest, out of certain kinds of measurable "differentiations" that tend to develop in the interaction process itself. The empirical studies reviewed in the next chapter tend to show, I suggest, "differences" between members, that is, "differentiations" of various critical sorts: in the qualitative kinds of overt communicative behavior, in the relative amounts of communicative behavior, in the persons who are addressed and to whom attention is paid, and in the timing of communicative behavior that members address to each other.

It appears to me that certain of these differentiations almost inevitably affect the social positions and self-concepts of certain persons in adverse as well as favorable ways and to a degree that can hardly be avoided if effective progress toward solution is to be made in the discussion of any kind of problem. These differences have partly unwelcome consequences for certain of the individuals who differ in their needs and values. To exaggerate only slightly, one may say that in ordinary social interaction somebody is likely to be disadvantaged to some degree. Winning and losing social status and other valued aspects of social position goes on all the time. However, there are great individual differences in what particular persons want and need.

Values originate in the individual mind at the microscopic level, I suggest, as mental controls that are evolved in the midst of interaction, in efforts to control the interaction process itself, regardless of the particular content or source of the problems the members in interaction are attempting to solve. Values often have their most primitive "seed" in emergent feelings of "moral indignation," or in more simple anger, fear, or anxiety, or erotic attraction, in direct reaction to behavior that has just occurred, or is presently occurring.

In some cases the individual is part of the most directly engaged dyad. In other cases, much more numerous, the individual is observing from a "third-person perspective" and reacting empathetically. The more complicated cognitive development of values in larger groups, and society itself, begins in many cases, I believe, in the attempts of a "victim" of the behavior of some other participant to redress a felt "injustice," and to find one or more coalition partners ("third persons") who will at least agree that the victim has been wronged, and help persuade still others.

In this "systems" point of view, in which a researcher always systematically looks for more indirect reactions and consequences of intended problem-solving behavior, "injustice" is imposed upon victims not only from intentionally motivated ill treatment of some persons by some others. It is also, in part, an indirect result of the kinds of differentiation that almost inevitably occur in the very process of interaction addressed to problem solving, even when participants take great care to avoid adverse consequences.

Thus it occurs, I suggest, that the "*dimensions* of differentiation" among *values* are essentially the same, in their microscopic genesis and in their essential content, as the "*dimensions* of differentiation" in social relationships among persons in ordinary social interaction. Differentiations among persons, and differentiations among values, arise out of essentially unavoidable "*dimensions* of differentiation" in the problem-solving process as it takes place in any social-interaction system. I suggest that the value system of a social-interaction system is the most critical and generalized means of controlling and stabilizing the participants' own processes of overt interaction with each other, and their more global social relationships with each other.

## Factor Analysis Helped Me More Than Psychoanalysis

Most important, probably, in the development of my understanding of social-interaction systems was the gradually unfolding discovery in my own research, and in the social-psychological literature as well, that *factor analyses* of different aspects of behavior, including values, personality traits, kinds of interpersonal behavior, feelings, connotations of concepts, and others, showed a limited number of "factors" and that the content of the different factors and the relationship of the factors to each other as they appeared in one factor analysis after another seemed to be similar to each other.

These discoveries in turn suggested that measurement of a limited number of factors could constitute a representative sample of many other vectors which might be distinguished in terms of content. Sampling the vectors under the guidance of factor analysis, which shows a minimal number of major dimensions and their intercorrelations, may be a part of the practical solution to the problem that the multiplicity of values in real social-interaction systems is potentially overwhelming.

In the context of groups I was regularly observing, I began to develop rating systems that group members used for describing the personalities and behavior of each other. Rating item sets were built on the three-dimensional factor structure that kept turning up in research. I used the three dimensions, the six vectors (which are simply a more detailed way of looking at the three bipolar dimensions), and the half-way intermediate vectors between the six vectors, which yields a complete set of twenty-six vectors, as the basis for exploring the ways in which group participants perceived and evaluated each other as persons, personalities, and group members. This is the basis (the geometric rationale) of the limited set of twenty-six vectors used in the present system of measurement.

Research using factor analysis suggests that if a very large number of items are used, certain "families" of values tend to "cluster" together, or to be positively correlated with each other in many minds in more or less the same ways. Moreover, for each of the main clusters of positively correlated values, one can locate directly contrary or conflicting values, and these values also tend to cluster together with each other. A given family of values and its conflicting opposite can then be thought of as a "dimension" of bipolarity.

The number of such conflicting families of values can be reduced once a particular dimension of polarity can be identified, by continued research and common experience to find other families or clusters of values that seem to be "unrelated" to the identified bipolar dimension. That is, the values of the one cluster are not positively correlated with the values of the other cluster in the minds of most raters, nor are they negatively related on the average. They are simply uncorrelated, or "zero correlated" to the identified dimension. (In the language of factor analysis these are called "orthogonal" factors.)

As an example, one may think first about the dimension of "dominant" versus "submissive" as personality traits, or kinds of interpersonal behavior. Now consider the dimension of "friendly" versus "unfriendly." So far as most raters are concerned, some of the people they know are both friendly and dominant, and others are both friendly and submissive. Still other people they know are both unfriendly and dominant, while still other people are both unfriendly and submissive. If a person tells you that a stranger he has just met is dominant, you do not yet know whether that stranger is friendly or unfriendly, or perhaps both or neither.

This kind of unpredictability gives one the leverage for treating the newly identified cluster as an independent or "orthogonal" "bipolar dimension." When one continues this kind of examination of correlations, at least one more bipolar dimension can typically be found. It seems to have something to do with several interrelated kinds of values—some values having to do with task orientation versus opposition to task or work demands, other values having to do with acceptance of authority of some kind, versus opposition to it, and still other values having to do with acceptance of conventional beliefs and attitudes, versus opposition. Religious conservatism of some variety, or rejection of it, is often a part of this family of values.

In some analyses of some domains having to do with various aspects of social interaction, one or two additional dimensions may be found, but for most practical purposes, in terms of factor analyses that I know about, the three dimensions mentioned and considered to be orthogonal to each other seem to cover most of the ground.

But what I have just called "clusters" of values, in fact, are not sharply defined. After repeated work and the addition of more items in the population of items one may conclude that it is best to suppose that the whole three-dimensional space is more or less completely filled, or can be filled, by values one can define by imagining particular combinations of characteristics in the three-dimensional space.

## Social Interaction and Value Systems

Values are only part of an actual social-interaction system, of course. They are less obvious than the overt interaction. They are not directly visible, as overt interpersonal interaction is. But they can be measured and are absolutely real in the operating mental processes of participants in real social interaction.

Social interaction always involves the ever-present need of participants to control among themselves the present mode of their social interaction itself, regardless of the more specific content of the problems dealt with. Certain predictable problems of social and personal relationships inevitably emerge in some form out of these necessities in newly formed groups. They receive at least an emergent factual temporary solution.

The factual solution at the point of origin may be a very poor one, from the point of view of its immediate effects on particular group members, and in terms of its longer term implications for "effectiveness." The inevitable review of the solution from "third-person reevaluative perspectives" may result in changing the values of some of the participants and observers. These changed values in turn will be given more specific meaning later in new situations.

Over the longer term, they will tend to be offered, selected, or rejected "differentially" in the process of cultural evolution of the group.

These emergent solutions consist at first of mere "buds" of elementary kinds of differences in behavior. These metaphorical buds apparently tend to "mature" into more fully developed values and meanings in the minds of members as interaction continues. These mental concepts do in fact partially control behavior, but in part, they fail. Other and more complex or expanded values and meanings then develop as reactions to success and failure.

The key insight to this theoretical approach, it seems to me, is that an interdependent "system" of values and meanings grows up, the embryonic elements of which correspond to the ever present need of participants to control among themselves the present mode of their own social-interaction processes. These attempts at the immediate concrete level to control the present emerging process by the formation of sufficiently consensual values, referring in their content to the desirable and undesirable forms of members' behavior toward each other, is the very embryo of the "fractal structure" of values and meanings in both small and large dynamic systems.

The term "fractal" is part of more recent mathematical theory. It refers to the observable fact of "self-similarity" in the patterns of elements and their relationships in more molecular and more macroscopic forms of a dynamic system. It is my belief and assumption that social-interaction systems of all sizes have "self-similar" patterns of inter-member behavior, values, and relationships. Value systems are fractal in nature.

If the factor structure of interactive social behaviors and the factor structure of values can be matched, as they appear to me to be in the series of vector listings called the Intercorrelation Space (see Appendix A), one begins to see that it may be possible to identify a strategically sampled set of values which do indeed constitute the strategically different elements of an interdependent "dynamic system," and to measure them. I believe that the essential fractal pattern of meanings and values can be measured within individual personalities. The same values may be distributed in a fractally similar pattern among the individuals in interaction in small groups. And the same "self-similar" pattern may be detected as the symbolic root of the expanding systems of metaphorical similarities of the behavior and value systems of larger groups, the society, social institutions, and cultures.

Social-psychological understanding of the self and situation at the level of subjective reality of the individual actor needs to include understanding the effects of one or more larger "systems" of influential variables, specifically those which are perceived dimly as structural features of the larger social system, such as occupational roles, social classes, solidary groups; political parties, and the like. The individual person may or may not be aware of all of these systemic variables as they appear in the large scale of organization, and the social psychologist in many cases may also still be unprepared to take much complication into account. But in fact, involvement in these larger-scale systems is essentially always powerfully at work in human social and interpersonal relations, even at the most microscopic levels, influencing the conception of the self, one's values, and the motivational orientation of all of the individuals involved.

Even today, it seems to me, after nearly a century of development, mainstream personality and social psychology, and sociology as well, lack some of the most important concepts and methods of measurement necessary to conceptualize and better understand interlocked systems of behavior, values, meanings, and their dynamics at the microscopic level. From my present perspective, I think the lack of adequate theory and systematic understanding of values, as circular and interlocked sets with their internal conflicting and cooperating relationships, may be the most important deficiency. Values are the more permanent repository of the dynamically important relationships.

Present personality tests seem to me to be deficient in their ability to measure values as personality traits with the necessary degree of coverage required. One needs to have measurements that enable one to anticipate to an adequate extent the individual's probable reaction to, and involvement in, the systemic features that essentially always emerge in social interaction, at least at the microscopic, small-group scale. Until measures of values are considerably improved and treated as systemic variables, individual personality measurements are not likely to be very good predictors of adjustment of normal individuals in normal groups, nor very good predictors of group performance. Values are not complete or explicit enough in descriptions derived from present personality measurement instruments to allow us to take into account the dependence of the individual's situation in a particular group on the actual presence of others of similar and conflicting values.

In actual cases of detailed consultation in groups one needs to know as much as can be found out or inferred about the overall distribution of individuals of given personality and value types. One needs to know the likely dynamics of polarization and unification of values under the most common conditions, and thus something about the particular situation in which each different individual is likely to find him or herself. One would like to know with which other person each of the individuals in the group is likely to cooperate and conflict, and on what kinds of values and issues. One needs to know how the particular values and behavior of each individual are likely to affect the situations of the others, and how these variables may affect, perhaps strategically, the general overall field pattern.

## What Goes on in the Mind?

For each member of the group the mental representations of acts stand in relation to each other as aspects or parts of the "self" and the "situation." To the extent that a situation requires some kind of problem solving, each actor tries in his or her own way to "define" and "evaluate" each part in relation to each other. Possible acts stand in relation to other possible acts as goals, means, more ultimate ends, as conditions to each other, in opposition to each other, in support of each other. Overall, these parts are greatly different from each other in importance or value. And most of these parts involve the attitudes, values, acts, and even the "free associations" in the minds of others.

As I think of it now, after having spent many years of observation and participation in self-analytic groups, each mental representation, potentially, is associated also in a mental network of associated meanings particular to the individual personality, with innumerable other precursors, consequences, and normative representations or evaluative controls. Each act as it emerges into overt form, in fact, is pregnant with the mental awareness, to some extent, in the mind of the acting person and to some extent in the minds of other members, of its implications, its meanings for the self and for the social relations of the interacting persons and expectations of its possible consequences. An effective observer has to have a mind prepared to sense and read the minimal indications given in a process which has many of the characteristics of a process of "free association."

In my limited experience, the most helpful framework for careful listening in order to spot hidden currents in ordinary interaction is definitely not a framework of the possible contents of the original or elaborated drives of the biological "Id" in Freudian terms, nor the class interests of the participants in Marxian terms, nor the "stages in group development" in social-psychological terms, nor indications of particular personality traits of particular members, nor traits of optimal leadership, nor any of a number of other frameworks.

The most helpful framework is a framework of the features that may be expected to emerge as characteristics of a good general model of social-interaction systems and a clear concept of what is necessary to its optimal effectiveness, in terms of the model. This framework is essentially a set of values, on the part of the investigator, probably not greatly different from that of most members, but highly educated, relativistic, tolerant, bent on the broadest possible understanding of what is going on.

I am inclined to think that our best clues as to the nature of the mental system, its content and mode of operation, can be gathered by observation and close accounting of what happens when individuals interact with each other for extended periods. As interaction continues, from its microscopic and embryonic beginnings, regularities and sequential relations between acts and types of acts begin to appear, or "emerge" as natural characteristics of action and reaction of different individuals in the social-interaction system. Later on we may think of the differentiations among individuals that appear as "structural features" or "core variables," or the values of the twenty-six vectors of the intercorrelation space of the system, and undertake always to measure or estimate them as well as we can.

As these "systemic emergents" develop further we begin to see at least some of them more clearly as problem-solving efforts, although perhaps they are efforts to solve problems we have not clearly recognized, as sequences of acts addressed to the solution of problems, both external and internal to the interacting group itself. It may not be so clear as to just what the problem is. Most groups have many problems, both large and small. Unfortunately, many, if not most, "solutions" have unforeseen consequences, which also provoke more problems.

Acts may be seen to occur in sequences which seem logically required in order to solve problems: sequences of information, opinions, and suggestions. These sequences are sometimes quite long. They take time and energy. They require, employ, and use up resources. Resources such as information, problem-solving abilities, general intelligence, even good will, are not initially evenly divided among the participants, nor are they later evenly distributed.

Acts are communications addressed to the group as a whole or to particular persons. Acts provoke, and logically require, in the minds of most participants, answering acts as feedback. Acts that are specifically addressed to particular other participants tend to require an answer from the person addressed. These expectations of logical continuation of the process tend to start and then multiply the differences between persons, and these differences affect social position and feelings of comfort or injury. The natural reactions of individuals in the course of time gives information on the success, costs, and results of problem-solving efforts in the eyes of others. Others add their own contributions, and these provoke additional answering feedback in turn.

Even among participants of good will, the desire of individuals to be "right," a desire to have the group realize their particular and different values and move in the right direction, as they see it, tends to result in a "status struggle" of some sort. It becomes clear very soon in most cases where there is real interaction that there may be individual differences so great in values, desires, and interests (even if there are only two persons in the group, and they do their best to avoid a quarrel) that the differences cannot be overcome. Not all participants can be equally satisfied, nor can all values be equally realized.

It appears that the status struggle sometimes results in a more or less stable resolution, a relative "status consensus," an accepted "status order" among most of the participants. But sometimes it does not. Some groups appear to be unfortunate in their assembly from the first. They cannot solve their status problems; they cannot come to sufficient consensus on their leadership; they cannot hold dissident leadership and dissident values sufficiently in check. They continue in conflict without end until at some point it becomes evident that they are unable to survive without external compulsion or rescue.

From my own observations and experience, I am almost ready to admit that some groups are bound to fail. The initial selection of members and the composition of the group, with regard to certain variables (particularly differences of values and their meanings in the given situation) may doom it to failure. The combinations of these elements are so important that for a great many real groups, their ability to get along effectively, to solve their problems, and to "survive" in the longer run, is seriously at risk from the first.

What are the variables that may differ fatally from the first? It is discouraging to recognize them for a researcher who has spent his life in attempts to improve groups already composed and in process. Only certain variables seem to me to be amenable to change in the normal operation of a given group. Certain others tend to be relatively fixed, or changeable only by long-term efforts: personality differences (especially differences in particular central "values" that have survival significance for the person), as well as differences in intelligence, problem-solving know how, problem-relevant skills, and "real creativity" (as distinguished from a "value on creativity"). These are among the variables that are probably best optimized by selection, if at all possible, in the original assessments of individuals, that is, in the original composition of the group. On the optimistic side, however, it may well be that the relative emphasis that may be given to different values, and the more specific meanings that may be given to values, are among the variables most accessible to change.

### The Theory in Application

Presently the most highly developed part of the theory in practice is centered around the measurement of values in a particular business group, team, or organization. The method is based on a serious attempt to select a limited but systematically rounded set of those values which one hopes will give the most strategic information about the state and dynamics of the particular group. But the theory, the instruments and the method are general in their design for broad application to many kinds of groups, teams, and organizations.

Information is gathered by well-designed surveys, followed by group discussion based on feedback of the survey data to the members who have produced it. The aim is to help individual members and designated leaders to improve the operation of the group, its productivity, and the satisfaction of leaders, members, clients, and other organizational members who receive and evaluate the work or products of the specific group.

It is the working assumption that this combination of survey measurement and feedback of information on the relative strength and distribution of strategically selected and sampled system-oriented values is the most essential and economical approach to understanding the nature and dynamics of the particular group, and its particular problems.

The fundamental theoretical perspective is to regard the particular group as a case or example of a "social-interaction system." The underlying assumption is that the particular group will have many characteristics in common with the general theoretical model, and that comparison of its variables with the norms of the more general empirical normative model will generate information useful in better understanding the particular group, and in helping its members plan changes they hope will help. The empirical normative models are based on very large samples from populations of members of business organizations.

The classification of what are believed to be the most strategic system values into the twenty-six descriptive items used in gathering the ratings is regarded as a set of measurable value variables which constitute a "rounded comprehensive system," an interconnected and intercorrelated minimal set, which substantially covers and strategically samples the most essential value variables from among the whole system of values actually operative in the system.

## Then and Now

What the early frame of reference fails to provide is any systematic or sufficiently useful way to represent the core features of the social-interaction system in which the individual in any social situation is a part, particularly the "always to be expected" system of values and their relationships to each other, and the principal features of the social-interaction process by which change is brought about.

The simplified concept of the "social situation" in the early period filled important theoretical gaps, but it filled them almost invisibly with the magic word "social." I believe one may easily see now that even the main features of any real social situation cannot be described or understood in any systematic way without some kind of more complex theory of social-interaction systems to help guide either the naked eye, or more formal research.

And of course, involvement of any given member of the system in more than one real system of social interaction is to be expected. These "external" involvements are always part of the substantive content, although mostly at the invisible mental level, of the individual's immediate "social situation." These other external real systems involve each member with other important individuals in those external systems. And at the same time the relations between outside groups, as groups or large organizations, may be an influence. The participant we presently observe may be only partially aware of these outside influences. Although this range of influences, since they are outside the observed group, inevitably leaves blind spots in the observer's understanding, nevertheless an awareness that these are in fact parts of the field for each particular individual may increase the observer's sensitivity to whatever slight cues may come into view.

I believe that analysis of the Field Diagrams and other displays of the present theory for a given group enable one truly to "get above" the "individual actor and situation" and the isolated "unit act" as the frame of reference—they enable one to describe the many probable current situations and possible sources of interactive influences tracing to many complex personality features of the many actors, and their simultaneous inclusion in outside systems. Perhaps the sensitive study of the various Field Diagrams that one may obtain in a given case will help one to approximate what Adam Smith tried to express in his metaphor of the "invisible hand" and the perspective of the "Impartial Spectator."

It is from that perspective perhaps, in feedback of the results of data gathered on the social-interaction system in which the individual is involved, that the application of reason by many individuals in purposeful interaction has the best chance of making a difference in the way things go. This can happen, although the self and each of the others in the social situation, each in his or her own partial situation, may be too much in ignorance of relevant facts, too weak in the ability to affect change, too biased regarding perceptions and values, and too uncoordinated with others to effectively guide the whole complex process.

One can see majority and minority subgroups in the clusterings of images on the Field Diagram, and surmise what conflicts of values and meanings are actually at issue between individual persons and subgroups of persons. One can see the relations between subgroups, and between the group as a whole and the external situation, with its problems and value conflicts. One can see just where in this complex set of influences one's *self* is located, since it too is shown in a particular location in the Field Diagram.

Fortunately, in feedback sessions in actual practice, the group members, from their different perspectives, are typically able to see more in many particular respects than the prepared consultant can see, and they often provide crucial concrete details. They can, and do, enlighten each other, and they enlighten the consultant as well, as to the reasons for their ratings.

The probable main features of the situation of any one actor, including one's own self, can be analyzed in detail in terms of that member's relations to each of the other persons in the situation. There is a huge backlog of information about the typical personality features of individuals who are located by their fellow members in particular locations on the Field Diagram. The measurement procedure and the Field Diagram, supplemented by feedback of rating data in interviews, give actual robust meaning to the more abstract concept of the "social situation."

In any real social situation, where choices make a difference, as in teaching, therapy, or leadership, it helps to know what to look for. All of these forms of helping, and other similar forms, take place in systems of social interaction, and the same kinds of knowledge about individual personality differences and the patterns of cooperation and conflicts shown in the Field Diagrams are relevant cues as to what to look for. The main expectable features of the "social-interaction system" are the things to look for, whether or not they may be shown in a single Field Diagram. These expectable features are foreshadowed in outline form in the general relationships of variables in the Intercorrelation Space (Appendix A).

# 8

# Systemic Emergents and *Effectiveness*

The early studies using Interaction Process Analysis are summarized in a report called "The Equilibrium Problem in Small Groups" (1953b). Here I shall look at a number of these studies in retrospect and attempt to point out the ways in which they constituted steps toward the present theory, and are still a part of the contemporary groundwork.

In the earliest period I was trying to reduce what I could observe, act by act, into some more regular concept of the process consistent with a serial order of acts. In figure 6.1 I have shown the set of twelve categories of types of acts with which I emerged, and called Interaction Process Analysis (IPA).

### Review of IPA Categories

The set of IPA categories (figure 6.1), as a whole, illustrates a concept of the general nature of the process as a feedback system of communication and control among a set of participants. Types of *initial problem-solving attempts* (*giving orientation, opinion,* and *suggestion*), may be followed by *positive reactions* (*agrees, shows tension release,* or *shows solidarity*). This is one direction of outcome. The opposite direction of outcome is a set of *negative reactions* (*disagrees, shows tension,* or *shows antagonism*). *Questions* (*asking for orientation, opinion,* or *suggestion*) may have begun the cycle, or may follow at any point.

Each separate act is the act of a single identified participant at a specific place in the serial order. Quantification is thus possible, according to many different breakdowns. Some of these tabulations seem to illustrate further the concept of the process as a feedback system. One of the most interesting, I think, is a comparison of the frequencies of the four large sections: *Attempted Answers, Positive Reactions, Negative Reactions,* and *Questions.*

Although there are many differences according to conditions, figure 8.1 illustrates a fairly typical set of relationships between these sections. It shows the frequency profiles of a *highly satisfied* group (the highest of a set of sixteen groups) and a *dissatisfied* group (the lowest) working on a standard group-decision problem we used for many studies.

**FIGURE 8.1**

Profile of a *Satisfied* and *Dissatisfied* Group on Case Discussion Task

**Meeting Profiles in Percentage Rates**

| Type of Act | Satisfied* | Dissatisfied** | Average of the two | Average rates by section |
|---|---|---|---|---|
| 1  Shows Solidarity | .7 | .8 | .7 | |
| 2  Shows Tension Release | 7.9 | 6.8 | 7.3 | 25.0 |
| 3  Agrees | 24.9 | 9.6 | 17.0 | |
| 4  Gives Suggestion | 8.2 | 3.6 | 5.9 | |
| 5  Gives Opinion | 26.7 | 30.5 | 28.7 | 56.7 |
| 6  Gives Orientation | 22.4 | 21.9 | 22.1 | |
| 7  Asks for Orientation | 1.7 | 5.7 | 3.8 | |
| 8  Asks for Opinion | 1.7 | 2.2 | 2.0 | 6.9 |
| 9  Asks for Suggestion | .5 | 1.6 | 1.1 | |
| 10  Disagrees | 4.0 | 12.4 | 8.3 | |
| 11  Shows Tension | 1.0 | 2.6 | 1.8 | 11.4 |
| 12  Shows Antagonism | .3 | 2.2 | 1.3 | |
| **Percentage Total** | 100.0 | 100.0 | 100.0 | 100.0 |
| **Raw Score Total** | 719 | 767 | 1486 | |

\*    The highest of sixteen groups. The members rated their own satisfaction
     with their solution after the meeting at an average of 10.4 on a scale
     running from 0 to a highest possible rating of 12.

\*\*   The lowest of sixteen groups. Comparable satisfaction rating in this group
     was 2.6.

For the two profiles added together, the *Average rates by section* associated with *attempted answers* (Section B, composed of Categories 4, 5, and 6)
constituted a little over half (56.7 percent). About half of the Attempts elicited *positive reactions* (25.0 percent, for Section A, composed of Categories
1, 2, and 3). A smaller portion of the Attempts (11.4 percent of the total acts),
elicited *negative reactions* (Section D, composed of Categories 10, 11, and
12). Finally, a still smaller portion (6.9 percent of the total acts) were *questions* (Section C, composed of Categories 7, 8, and 9).

These relationships are consistent with the general idea that the relationships between the four types are the final result of a repetitive series of cycles,
each of which consists of (1) a disturbance of the system state, precipitated by
the introduction of a new idea, opinion, or suggestion (a proaction), followed
by (2) a *dwindling series of feedbacks* as the disturbance is terminated, equili-
brated, or assimilated by other participants in the system. In this way of look-

ing at the total process of interaction, *proactions* constitute about half, and *reactions* constitute roughly the other half. This is consistent with the approximate characterization that *social interaction* consists of *proactions* by particular individuals followed by *reactions* of the rest.

But this approximate balance, as shown in figure 8.1, is the average of two very different component profiles: one of a *highly satisfied* group, the other a *dissatisfied* one. If one regards the process of interaction as showing tendencies toward equilibrium, it is still very evident that sometimes it succeeds, or perhaps more than succeeds, but other times it results in relative failure.

I propose to reinterpret these results in terms of their effects on the correlations of the three factor-analytic dimensions: U-D, P-N, and F-B. In the *satisfied* groups, the high rates of *giving suggestion* followed by high rates of *agreement* and low rates of *disagreement* would tend toward convergence in the correlations of the solutions of the three bipolar dimensions. I now suggest that we take this profile as a tentative model of an "effective" Interaction Process Profile.

In contrast, in the *dissatisfied* groups, the lower rates of *suggestion* followed by low rates of *agreement* and high rates of *disagreement* would tend to produce divergence toward *orthogonality*, or even negative correlations between the Vectors U, P, and F. Although there are many ways of being ineffective, we may take this profile as a tentative model of an *ineffective* Interaction Process Profile.

In the set of sixteen groups which produced these results, the members were assembled randomly. The convergence and divergence of the Vectors U, P, and F may reasonably be attributed to fortunate and unfortunate combinations or compositions of values of the members. But in the broad variety of groups and environmental situations in real life, one would expect that the requirements and demands of tasks and external environmental situations might also result in quite different profiles, especially perhaps in the relative frequencies of *information*, *opinion*, and *suggestion*.

In the studies of the period 1945 to 1950, which formed the basis of the method *Interaction Process Analysis* (Bales 1950, 1953a), a standard task and standard conditions were used, all aimed toward the development of empirical norms for later study of experimental variation of conditions. (Chapter 6 gives a brief description of the same studies.) Each group met for four meetings. The subjects were all males, Harvard undergraduates, who were obtained through the Harvard employment service. They were randomly assembled. Typically none of the members in a group knew each other prior to the first meeting.

In each of its four meetings, the group examined and discussed a "human-relations case." A different case was used for each of the four meetings, but the cases were all formally quite similar. Each case was a summary of facts, five pages in length, about a person in an administrative setting who was having some kind of difficulty with the men under him, and had some superior putting pressure on him to get some technically important job done.

The summaries for a given case discussion were distributed separately to the subjects. After each member had read his summary, the actual typed copy of the case was collected from each by the experimenter. The manner of presentation was such that the subjects were made specifically uncertain as to whether or not they possessed exactly the same facts, but they were assured that each possessed an accurate, though perhaps incomplete, factual summary. In fact, each group member received the identical five pages.

The subjects were asked to consider themselves to be members of the administrative staff of the central administrator in the case. He has asked them to meet and consider the case. He wants an answer to two questions: (1) Why are the persons in the case behaving as they do? and (2) What should he do about it? The members of the discussion group were asked to come to their decision in forty minutes. No leader was appointed.

The host experimenter then left the room. The discussion was observed through a one-way mirror and sound recorded. The interaction was observed and recorded using the twelve IPA categories. After the meeting the members filled out a questionnaire asking about their reactions, their satisfaction, their relations to each other, liking, disliking, and opinions about their discussion group.

This particular task was designed to contain what we supposed were the typical kinds of problems of communication and interaction that groups usually encounter to some extent in all kinds of problem-solving and group-decision tasks. The key problems of *orientation, evaluation,* and *control* (identified as a, b, and c in figure 6.1) were each, to a major degree, unsolved at the beginning of observation and required by the task.

1.  Problems of *orientation*. Members of the group had some degree of ignorance and uncertainty about the relevant facts, but individually possessed facts relevant to decision. Their problem of arriving at a common cognitive orientation or definition of the situation had to be solved, if at all, through interaction.

2.  Problems of *evaluation*. Members of the group ordinarily possessed somewhat different values or interests and the task was such that it involved several different values and interests as criteria by which the facts of the situation and the proposed course of action were to be judged. The problem of arriving at common value judgments necessary to a concrete plan had to be solved, if at all, through interaction.

3.  Problems of *control*. Such problems are manifested in attempts of the members to influence directly the action of each other and arrive at a concrete plan by substantive suggestions. The task was expected to set up a moderately strong pressure for group decision, with the expectation that the excellence of the decision could and would be evaluated by each of

them as well as by the experimenter. Thus, the decision could be expected to affect member status.

These abstract conditions, with emphasis varying according to circumstances, are met in very much this form in a great many group conferences, work groups, committees, and the like. Nevertheless, tasks vary, not only in these features but in others which may be of great importance.

Once a baseline on the standard task had been established, we expected other sets of conditions could be partly described, at least, as modifications or accentuations or reversals of the laboratory conditions. We hoped to be able to use discrepancies from our typical baseline patterns of observed interaction as diagnostic indicators of the *personalities, culture,* and *role organization* of the participants, since these are all sets of conditions which we expected would influence the way interaction actually goes.

### Illustration of Steps in a Group Decision: An Air Defense Network

Over the study of a great many case discussions under the standard conditions in the student groups, I had gradually formed the impression that there was a more or less predictable ratio of *giving orientation, giving opinion,* and *giving suggestion.* To reach the stage of making a single suggestion it seemed to be usual in our group-decision discussions that there would previously have been about two acts of *giving information,* and about four acts of *giving opinion.* It was the ratio of doubling that caught my interest: one to two to four. Could there be any non-magical reason for this?

In 1954 or thereabouts, the RAND Corporation, which had been supporting some of my research, invited me to observe the operation of a simulated air defense network in the laboratory. The simulation consisted of operators, behind a large plotting pane of glass, keeping track of the flights of planes as reported in by remote radar sites scattered over a very large geographic territory, officers in charge of sending out intercepting fighter planes, and so on. The setting, sending, and tracking were all simulated, but the officers and crew were real Air Force personnel. John Kennedy, a psychologist colleague, and I were among the observers of the whole scene. Allen Newell had done the computer programming which kept the simulated planes on the simulated scopes. Herbert Simon was also on the scene, and we were all in close touch.

In the course of musing with John Kennedy on the interaction process among the operating crew, I suggested that the necessary logical steps of the process reminded me of those represented by my method Interaction Process Analysis. Figure 8.2 is the diagram I eventually produced to illustrate the parallels. Kennedy agreed that the diagram seemed to him to make pretty good sense. When Allen Newell heard me say that the seven steps could be sorted into a series of two steps of *giving information,* four steps of *giving*

## FIGURE 8.2
## Elementary Steps in Building a Group Decision

### Interaction Form of Message Sent to Other System Members

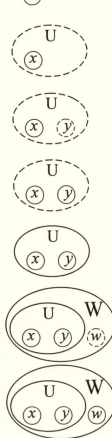

1  States primary observation:

"I observe a particular event, x." (I see a new track on the radar.)

*Gives Information*

2  Makes tentative induction:

"This particular event, x, may belong to a general class of objects, U." (This radar track may be Unknown.)

*Gives Opinion*

3  Deduces conditional prediction:

"If this particular event, x, does belong to the general class, U, then it should be found associated with another particular event, y." (If this track is Unknown, then we should have no flight plan for a plane in this location.)

*Gives Opinion*

4  States observation of check fact:

"I observe the predicted particular event, y." (I have checked, and we have no flight plan for this radar track.)

*Gives Information*

5  Identifies object as a member of a class:

"I therefore identify x-y as an object which is a member of the predicted general class of objects, U." (The absence of a flight plan for this radar track indicates that the object is Unknown.)

*Gives Opinion*

6  States major premise relating classes of objects:

"All members of the general class of objects, U, should be treated by ways of the general class, W." (All Unknown objects should be intercepted and identified.)

*Gives Opinion*

7  Proposes specific action:

"This particular object, x-y, should therefore be treated in a particular way, w." (Fighter pilots, take off immediately, intercept, and identify this Unknown object.)

*Gives Suggestion*

*opinion*, and a final step of *giving suggestion* (see figure 8.2), he immediately suggested that we take a verbatim recording of the communications of the crew, classify the acts and count them. We did, and the ratio came out sufficiently close to convince him that it was promising to try to simulate problem-solving processes on the computer. He and Herbert Simon later did, with notable success (Newell and Simon 1972).

What is to be learned from the comparison of the communications in the air defense network and the communications in my problem-solving groups? For one thing, my diagram reads as if one individual, with access to all the information and thinking alone, could go through all the steps. No interaction between separate members seems to be logically required. In this way, the required process seems to be similar to the rat-in-the-maze model, except that in this case the problem-solving rat would need to be exceptionally smart and well informed.

The real point, however, is that in my diagram of the problem-solving steps, the members of the crew are treated as if they had no differences of personality, no differences of values, and no problems of differences in status or social organization in any other respect. In fact, the members of the crew and the officers had gone through extensive training (the regulation Air Force training) to minimize what might result from differences in personality, to minimize any relations of interpersonal liking or disliking, to inculcate the necessary similarities in values, and to establish the habitual attitudes consistent with maintenance of the prescribed leadership and command structure. All members had been specifically trained to perform their explicit parts of a defined division of labor, in the technical sense. They were paid to perform all of these technical functions and knew they faced sanctions of some kind if they failed persistently.

In these respects the differences from my initially leaderless self-analytic groups were about as great as we can imagine. My groups were faced with a great array of problems in all of these respects. This can hardly be overemphasized. Problem solving in real groups, in fact, always involves the solution of problems of the internal organization of the group. These may be largely solved for the time being by previous interaction and the development of values and norms. If they are not, then a problem-solving group, like my self-analytic initially leaderless group, faces all the problems of internal organization. Moreover, none of the problems, whether previously solved or not, whether internal or external, remains solved.

By its nature, problem solving, either of internal or external problems, disturbs any existing state of the system. Without belaboring the obvious further, I want to emphasize the following point. When all of the *social-interaction* elements are removed, the *logical* (or even logistic) elements of solving the problem are still there. A number of differentiated logical steps have to be strung together in a given order, without fail and without errors, in order to reach the desired end result. By implication, the logical job requires a certain kind of order and continuity. It requires several different kinds of elements, put together "just so."

The logical requirements of problem solving make it likely that one, or more, of the participants will want and need to keep talking for an asymmetrically long time. To the extent that they do, the members who do so tend to preempt time, dominance, and potential status for themselves, and for the values they promote, from the members who are left to react later.

Figure 8.3 demonstrates the tendency to keep on talking, once started. The number of consecutive acts, once a given participant starts talking, may be called a "run" of a given length. Real interaction is hardly a matter of a single act by one participant followed by a single act by another, and so on. In such a case, all "runs" would be just one act in length. Fred Strodtbeck and I estimated the quantitative impact of the tendency to keep on talking by counting the length of "runs" over a large body of our observations. Figure 8.3 shows that the probability of a given run being longer than one act is about 55 percent. This may be compared to a chance model, which assumes a fifty-fifty chance that the speaker will yield to another at the conclusion of each act. From there on, the preponderance of the observed tendency to keep on talking over the chance model gets more and more striking. This tendency to keep on talking, related to the necessary steps to make a logical argument, thus tends to change the status order.

To put the dilemma (and paradox) in an even broader light: the process of problem solving, even when successful in its more ultimate sense, is very likely to disturb, for the time being, the existing state of the social-interaction system. Problem solving, in its immediate requirements and effects, tends to introduce further divergence in the intercorrelation of the three major vectors—U, P, and F—which I have taken as the critical elements in overall long-term "effectiveness" of system operation. The *process*, at least, of problem solving tends to produce *divergence*, rather than *convergence*. To make things

**FIGURE 8.3**

**Number of Instances in which Runs Longer than a Given
Length Occur, Compared to a Chance Model**

| Runs Longer Than: | Raw Numbers | | Percentage (Probability) | |
|:---:|:---:|:---:|:---:|:---:|
| | Observed | Model | Observed | Model |
| 0 | 23778 | 23778 | 100.00 | 100.00 |
| 1 | 13039 | 11889 | 54.84 | 50.00 |
| 2 | 7372 | 5945 | 31.01 | 25.00 |
| 3 | 4427 | 2972 | 18.62 | 12.50 |
| 4 | 2734 | 1486 | 11.50 | 6.25 |
| 5 | 1866 | 743 | 7.85 | 3.12 |
| 6 | 1304 | 372 | 5.49 | 1.56 |
| 7 | 927 | 186 | 3.90 | .78 |
| 8 | 647 | 93 | 2.72 | .39 |

worse, there is no guarantee that the solution proposed or accepted will be "effective" in the longer run.

## Phases in Group Problem Solving

I have described my early development of the twelve categories of acts distinguished in IPA. Almost my first observational triumph was the recognition of regularities in the movement of the time track up and down on my long paper tapes (described briefly in chapter 6). The up-and-down movement appeared because I kept arranging and rearranging the vertical order of the categories at the same time that I consolidated types of acts into fewer categories. I was trying to clarify and simplify the up-and-down movements. These were act-to-act jiggles, with occasional long jumps and hang-ups and hang-downs. My feeling was that there were also long-time changes in the overall balance of the different kinds of acts by sub-periods of time, changes that made sense as *phases in group problem solving*.

When I had settled on the number and order of listing of the categories, I began to examine earlier records. I struck gold in the old record of Allport's meeting of the "Group Mind" (a thesis-prospectus conference among a student candidate and faculty members). Briefly described, the finding was that there was indeed (at least for that group) a time of most frequent occurrence for each of the pairs of categories I had distinguished as dealing, in a hypothetical time sequential order, with problems of orientation, of evaluation, of control, of decision, tension-management, and integration.

A series of figures (8.4a, 8.4b, 8.4c, 8.4d, 8.4e, 8.4f) showing an analysis of Allport's "Group Mind" group will demonstrate what I mean. The first time track (figure 8.4a) shows the aggregated frequencies, by successive time periods, of acts associated with Categories 7, *asking for orientation*, and 6, *giving orientation* (figure 6.1 shows these two categories paired and labeled "a"). It is clear that acts of this pair were highest in frequency, against their own mean, in the earliest part of the meeting, and declined to a low point almost at the end. It is true that there appears to be a minor "hiccup" toward the middle, but the general tendency seems clear. Incidentally, the two categories, 7 and 6, are placed in the very middle of the Observation Set of twelve, and their interchange tended to produce only a minor "jiggle" of the time track on the *interaction-recorder* tape (described in chapter 6).

The second time track (figure 8.4b) shows the successive frequency rates of the next two categories out from the middle of the twelve on the vertical list—Category 8, *asking for opinion*, and Category 5, *giving opinion*. The highest rate of this pair of categories occurred in the period after a considerable decline in the pair concerned with orienting information. This track also shows a "hiccup" in its general course, but the average tendency after its highest point is toward a lower point at the end. The up and down of the track

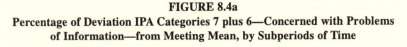

FIGURE 8.4a

Percentage of Deviation IPA Categories 7 plus 6—Concerned with Problems of Information—from Meeting Mean, by Subperiods of Time

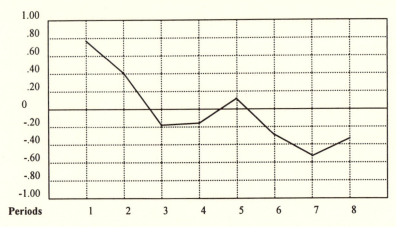

The combined rate of the first pair of Categories, 7 and 6, shows its greatest preponderance in the first period of the meeting and thereafter shows a declining trend.

FIGURE 8.4b

Percentage of Deviation of IPA Categories 8 plus 5—Concerned with Problems of Evaluation—from Meeting Mean, by Subperiods of Time

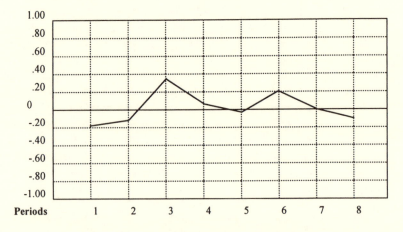

The combined rate of the second pair of Categories, 8 and 5, shows its greatest preponderance in the third period of the meeting. (No pair was at its peak during the second period, but the first pair was still high.)

**FIGURE 8.4c**

**Percentage Deviation of IPA Categories 9 plus 4—Concerned with Problems of Control—from Meeting Mean, by Subperiods of Time**

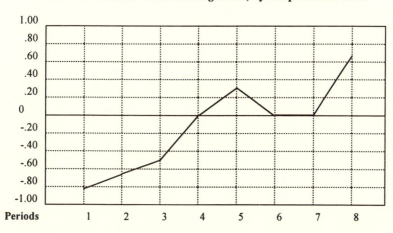

The combined rate of the third pair of Categories, 9 and 4, shows a prominent peak, but not its highest, in Period Five. (No pair was at its peak during Period Four, but the second pair was at its mean.)

**FIGURE 8.4d**

**Percentage Deviation of IPA Categories 10 and 3—Concerned with Problems of Decision—from Meeting Mean, by Subperiods of Time**

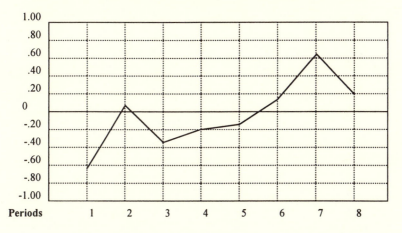

The combined rate of the fourth pair of Categories, 10 and 3, shows its highest peak in the seventh period of the meeting. (No pair was at its peak during Period Six, but a secondary peak of Evaluation was prominent during this period.)

**FIGURE 8.4e**

**Percentage Deviation of IPA Categories 11 and 2—Concerned with Problems of Tension Reduction—from Meeting Mean, by Subperiods of Time**

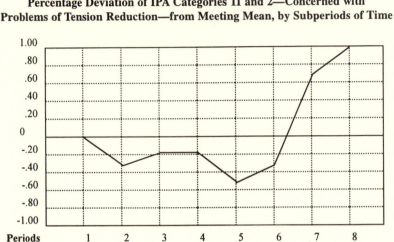

The combined rate of the fifth pair of Categories, 11 and 2, shows its highest peak in the last period of the meeting. In the previous period also this rate was high.

on the tape between this pair of categories was wider than a jiggle. It was more of a "waggle," since the members of the pair were more widely separated on the vertical list.

The third time track (figure 8.4c) shows the movement of the pair of Categories 9, *asking for suggestion*, and 4, *giving suggestion*. This pair is at its lowest point in the beginning, and rises to its highest point at the end. It shows a high point in Period 5. After another build up of *information* in Period 5 followed by a hump of *opinion* in Period 6, *suggestion* resumes its climb toward its high point at the end.

In sum, the movement for the three pairs of categories most clearly concerned with the external task is consistent with the idea that each pair is at least partly contingent, or logically dependent, upon the build up of the preceding steps. (Note the order of the steps in the air defense communication and control system, figure 8.2.)

The next three time tracks (figures 8.4d, 8.4e, and 8.4f) are of categories of acts which I have characterized as types of feedback in *reaction* to the previous categories of problem-solving *attempts*. There are two types, *positive* and *negative*. The *positive reactions* consist of *agreement, showing tension release*, and *showing solidarity* (Categories 1, 2, and 3). The *negative reactions*

**FIGURE 8.4f**
Percentage Deviation of IPA Categories 12 and 1—Concerned with
Problems of Reintegration—from Meeting Mean, by Subperiods of Time

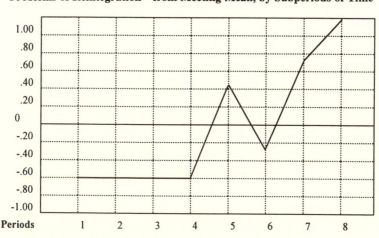

The combined rate of the sixth pair of Categories, 12 and 1, shows its highest
peak also in the last period of the meeting. It also had a preliminary rise during
Period Five, when Problems of Control were at their peak. This rise was
primarily on the antagonistic side, while the final peak was primarily on the
solidary side.

consist of *disagreement, showing tension,* and *showing antagonism* (Categories 10, 11, and 12). I have called these types of feedback *social-emotional
reactions* which have *expressive-integrative* significance. They express the
feelings of individual members, usually about what has been said or is going
on. But they also subsequently affect the overall solidarity of the group, its
degree of friendliness or unfriendliness, and subsequently its ability to recover from the strains of previous problem-solving efforts and proceed toward problem solving again.

In figure 8.4d, Category 3, *agreement,* and Category 10, *disagreement,* are
treated as a pair, although they are opposites in vector direction in the
Intercorrelation Space (see Appendix A). They are similar in that they are still
oriented to the immediately preceding problem-solving attempts in a relatively unemotional way, and may be relatively impersonal in their motivation. But they are also alike in that they tend to arouse emotion in some others,
and may in fact be partly motivated by emotion in the person who acts. In
either case, they begin to turn the decision more definitely toward acceptance
or rejection, of the preceding problem-solving attempt. Their time track, taken
together, starts at a low point in Period 1, and reaches its climax in Period 7,

just before the final period of most extreme emotional reactions, which appear to take over in Period 8.

In figure 8.4e, the time track of the pair of Category 11, *shows tension*, and Category 2, *shows tension release*, reaches its high point in the final Period, 8. At that point, acts in Category 2 usually predominate and consist in repeated jokes and laughs. At the very beginning of the meeting, however, the pair appear to be elevated over their later low point in Period 5.

The time track (figure 8.4f) of the most extremely positive and negative pair—Category 1, *showing solidarity*, and Category 12, *showing antagonism*—was at its lowest point all through the first four periods. Something happened in Period 5 to send the rate suddenly up. I cannot remember what it was, but it appears to be associated with the "hiccup" I mentioned earlier. It apparently passed, and the rate of this pair of categories reaches its high point in Period 8, at the very end, no doubt on the side of *showing solidarity*.

I have no doubt that this *golden* illustration of time tendencies and interdependencies, and my possibly biased description, give a clearer impression than the countless problem-solving sessions that might be observed a million times over, worldwide. I am also fairly sure that the leadership skills and shaped-up logical mind of Professor Allport, as well as his urbane manner, helped to give the session an order conforming to my theoretical expectations. His mind was a part of the "Group Mind" in this case after all, even though he poked some fun at the old controversial concept. Nonetheless, for purposes of helping our theoretical understanding as to what order of phases in time are likely to be associated with "most effective" outcomes, the picture these time tracks give is probably pretty close.

One may rightly wonder if this single golden illustration of time trends in the various categories of the interaction process is truly characteristic or representative. Figure 8.5 shows time trends based on a large sample of more varied and irregular problem-solving group sessions on many kinds of tasks in leaderless groups (see Bales and Strodtbeck 1951). When a problem of *orientation, evaluation,* or *control* shows marked evidence of difficulty, we call the problem "full-fledged." Otherwise, we speak of it as being "truncated." In figure 8.5, the picture is not quite so clear as in the golden illustration, but it still holds up in situations where the problem is "full fledged." The real observed order in a given group is certainly not always "most effective." Figure 8.5 gives a general picture of the phase movement over three successive time periods. Perhaps surprisingly, it is still quite similar to the picture given in figures 8.4a through 8.4f.

### The Group-Average Interaction Profile for a Meeting

The Interaction Process Profile in figure 8.6 gives a characteristic picture for our standard full-fledged task of the summary profile of frequencies of the

**FIGURE 8.5**
**Relative Frequency of Acts by Type in Each of the**
**Three Time Periods Based upon Twenty-two Sessions**

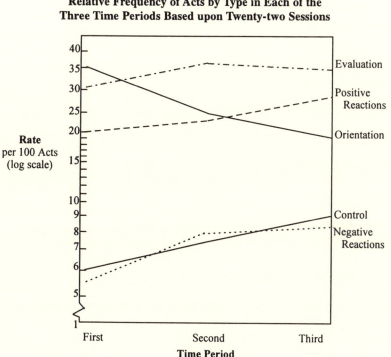

twelve different kinds of acts, over all kinds of individual differences by participants, and over all time phases within complete meetings. The ratios of *giving information, opinion,* and *suggestion* are not quite so regular as I suggested for my diagram of the logical steps in the air defense crew operation (figure 8.2), but they are an approximation. *Agreement* is about twice as likely as *disagreement, showing tension release* is about twice as likely as *showing tension,* and *showing solidarity* is more than twice as likely as *showing antagonism.* All of these average tendencies give a useful base of comparison.

But a comparison of this profile with the profiles of the *satisfied* and *dissatisfied* groups in figure 8.1 indicates that the profile of figure 8.6 is not likely to indicate the "most effective" outcomes that one might hope for. There are indications that better orientation to the problem and more information about the facts at the beginning of meetings, if not all the way through, might improve problem solutions with regard to the task. Members often fail to utilize effectively the information available to them.

I assume that the composition of these groups—randomly assembled and initially leaderless—introduced a whole array of problems of leadership

FIGURE 8.6
Interaction Profile for the Average of All Interactions
for Large Numbers of Small Discussion Groups

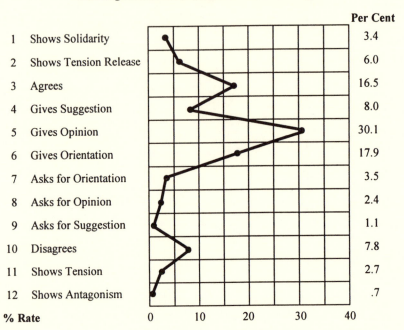

|    |                      | Per Cent |
|----|----------------------|----------|
| 1  | Shows Solidarity     | 3.4      |
| 2  | Shows Tension Release| 6.0      |
| 3  | Agrees               | 16.5     |
| 4  | Gives Suggestion     | 8.0      |
| 5  | Gives Opinion        | 30.1     |
| 6  | Gives Orientation    | 17.9     |
| 7  | Asks for Orientation | 3.5      |
| 8  | Asks for Opinion     | 2.4      |
| 9  | Asks for Suggestion  | 1.1      |
| 10 | Disagrees            | 7.8      |
| 11 | Shows Tension        | 2.7      |
| 12 | Shows Antagonism     | .7       |

% Rate        0    10    20    30    40

and other social relationships that were more urgent than one would ordinarily find in established groups. For a new randomly assembled group to be required to find solutions to these problems is definitely not optimum for their effectiveness at solving task problems, or perhaps the social problems either. (Of course I did not expect it to be. The experimental purpose was to throw the problems of leadership and social relationships into bold relief, for observation.)

### First Acts and Following Acts

From the point of view of most participants most of the time, the immediate pressure is to give some reasonable response to what has just been said or done. One's job in part, in today's political language, is "spin control." Most of the time, a problem-solving attempt has just been made. Hence the first act in an individual's own sequence of participation is performed under the expectation that it will be a *reaction* in reference to the prior act. Only after this reaction can the individual continue with further attempts to influence the process. What are called here "first acts" occur whenever a participant enters

**FIGURE 8.7**
**A Comparison of a Speaker's First Act with His Next Act**

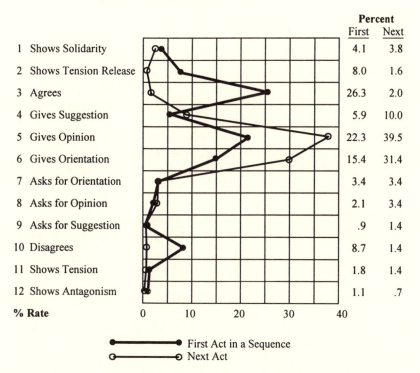

|  |  | Percent | |
|---|---|---|---|
|  |  | First | Next |
| 1 | Shows Solidarity | 4.1 | 3.8 |
| 2 | Shows Tension Release | 8.0 | 1.6 |
| 3 | Agrees | 26.3 | 2.0 |
| 4 | Gives Suggestion | 5.9 | 10.0 |
| 5 | Gives Opinion | 22.3 | 39.5 |
| 6 | Gives Orientation | 15.4 | 31.4 |
| 7 | Asks for Orientation | 3.4 | 3.4 |
| 8 | Asks for Opinion | 2.1 | 3.4 |
| 9 | Asks for Suggestion | .9 | 1.4 |
| 10 | Disagrees | 8.7 | 1.4 |
| 11 | Shows Tension | 1.8 | 1.4 |
| 12 | Shows Antagonism | 1.1 | .7 |

**% Rate**  0   10   20   30   40

●————————● First Act in a Sequence
○————————○ Next Act

the overt process after having been silent while another person is speaking. Thus, first acts occur all the way through the whole process, and each person may have many.

Figure 8.7 compares the profile of *First Acts* (all participants added together) with following acts of the same participant, if he or she continues *Next Acts*. The profile in the heavy line shows the distribution of kinds of first acts. That the rates of *showing agreement* and *disagreement* should be relatively high seems reasonable, as does evidence of some problem-solving attempts and some tension release.

A striking difference can be seen between the interaction profiles of first and next acts. The emphasis changes markedly, if the participant chooses to continue with a next act (shown by the light line in figure 8.7). The average participant who chooses to continue does so either to say why he reacted as he did or to pursue his own tack. The rates of *giving orientation, opinion*, and *suggestion* each tend to approximately double over their prominence in the first act, as we see from the profile in the light line. But we know from study of the tendency to keep on talking (figure 8.3) that only a little over half of the time a participant makes the choice to continue.

## The Critical Moments of Choice

I suggest that the moments just prior to the first act and after the first act are critical *moments of choice* for the individual participant. If an individual chooses to agree, he publicly appears to join the preceding participant as a supporter of the other's apparent attempt at leadership. If he chooses to disagree, he makes the first move to become an opposition leader. The choice, one way or the other, even if quite impersonal in motivation and possibly made only with an eye on the external problem of the group as a whole, nevertheless begins or continues to define an individual's social role and that of the preceding actor as potential focal persons with regard to a focal issue. The choice, critical to an individual's social role in the group, is whether to be a protagonist, a supporter, or an antagonist. To be a supporter is to make the first move toward a coalition. To be an antagonist is to make the first move toward an opposition coalition.

If the individual then chooses to go on for a second act, and a third, he begins an implicit bid for a higher rank in the order of dominance. If the individual does not go on, he begins an implicit lowering of rank. Thus, the choices at the first and second act of the person's sequence fatefully determine the social definition of his or her social role in all of the three major dimensions of social differentiation: friendly versus unfriendly, task oriented versus non-task oriented, and dominant versus submissive.

This is the very juncture, in time, place, and specific person, where personality traits—particularly values, intelligence, knowledge, special skills, rationality, memories, previous attempts to solve the problems—come to a fateful focus in two successive particular concrete acts. The two choices, each time a person makes them, influence more ultimate outcomes, not only with regard to the external problems of the system, but within the social-emotional arena and the social-interaction system dynamic field. The reactions of others thereupon begin to define further the constraints and possibilities for the individual actor.

The pregnancy of these critical moments cannot really be sensed without understanding that the whole value system of the person is possibly activated and brought to the point of decision and action in these fateful moments. In the present system of theory and measurement it is assumed that at least twenty-six measurable values, with multiple meanings in relation to the "self" and the "situation," have been roiling around in the mind of the person about to act, in search of a resolution before the overt act can emerge. Moreover, the same thing is happening in the minds of all the other participants. The person at the point of decision is aware of at least some of what is happening in the minds of others, and how they view him. This is the "situation."

At these critical moments it all comes together for the actor, or it comes apart. No wonder that some individuals, as actors of the moment, are paralyzed by "stage fright." In the language of complexity theorists, this is the "edge of chaos." Let us pray for a compound eye! Let us pray for a "higher computing power"! May the "invisible hand" rest kindly over us, may the "power" be with us! This may also be the moment of a possible mutation, a moment of emerging creativity. No wonder social psychologists have not been able to specify what they need to know to describe the "situation."

The implications for leaders, teachers, trainers, educators, and therapists are also daunting. If real change is to be brought about, the choices made by the individual at these critical moments must be brought into a clearer focus for the individual and for the group, and must result in the emergence of overt behavior that is different from before. All attempts to elicit change are preliminary and subsidiary to those critical moments of choice.

### System Effects of Actions and Reactions, Both Positive and Negative

For the observer of face-to-face interaction at the overt level it appears, as we know from the preceding figure 8.7, that the first act of a person following the last act of some other is *provoked* by the last act of the other as the *stimulus* and thus has a *reactive* quality. The activity of the preceding participant likely has tended to build up mental activity in the present participant (including tensions) to some point where he or she enters the process and changes to activity of an expressive-integrative relevance, which tends to reduce or increase the tension. But then there is the fateful choice point at which the reacting person may or may not change the focus and continue again with instrumental-adaptive activity.

The problem of maintaining a steady state in the interaction process itself as a regularly cycling system (apart from its value and meaning content and its more ultimate outcomes) is essentially a problem of establishing an *orbit of activity* whereby the action and reaction sequences go through a repetitive cycle. In this cycle, the disturbances created in one phase may or may not be reduced in a subsequent phase. It is a persistent dilemma that apparently no one disturbance can be reduced without creating another.

Figure 8.7 indicates that when the prior act of another member has been an *attempted answer*, the probability is that the present act will be a *positive reaction*, specifically an *agreement*, rather than a continuation in the task area. Nonetheless, there are appreciable tendencies for the reacting person to continue directly with further *opinion* or information. Probabilities of *positive reactions* (for these groups) far outweigh probabilities of *negative reactions*. This is probably quite generally true, though occasionally we observe groups where it is not the case. When *positive reactions* do not considerably outweigh *negative reactions*, everybody knows there is trouble.

Theoretically, I tend to assume that a preponderance of *positive reactions* over negative is a *condition* of maintenance of the steady state of the overt interaction system itself. My reasoning is as follows: I assume that the instrumental-adaptive goals of the system as a whole in relation to its external situation involve the maintenance of a certain level of accomplishment output in the direction of effectiveness. I further assume that this level *tends to fall* without the constant application of effort, energy, and activity applied successfully to the realities of the external situation. The level of *accomplishment* cannot be maintained for long without also maintaining the level of diffuse *satisfaction*, among the individual members, and this depends upon the achievement of expressive-integrative goals of different sorts among the different individuals.

Thus a full stable *orbit* will presumably have to include tension release, gratification, and a feedback of positive sanctions to the person(s) performing the instrumental activities in such a way as to *reinforce* the continuation of what they are doing.

*Negative reactions* tend to inhibit the behavior which preceded (except perhaps for opposition members) but do not provide the basis for establishing a stable, positively defined orbit. Nor does generalization from *negative reactions* help appreciably in finding a positively defined orbit. Knowledge that something has failed tends to cancel out or inhibit possible untried orbits, while the unstable "seeking" or "trial and error" fluctuation of the system continues.

Furthermore, each failure and each negative reaction tends to result *in its own right* in further disturbance (although the opposition may be gratified), and thus reduces the satisfaction levels directly (of the protagonist and his or her coalition). Assuming a quantitative equivalence of units of action observed (a shaky, but not inconceivable assumption), at least one *positive reaction* would be required for each *negative reaction*, simply to counteract the disturbances introduced by the *negative reactions*. If *positive reactions* are only equal to *negative reactions*, the system fails to counteract the disturbances introduced by the *friction* of its own controlling apparatus. The accomplishment and satisfaction levels will tend to sink because of lack of effort and instrumental activity applied constructively and successfully to the problems posed in the external situation of the system.

The conclusion from this argument is that only if an orbit is found in which *positive reactions* preponderate over *negative*, can the accomplishment and satisfaction levels be maintained in a steady state. The degree to which *positive reactions* must outweigh *negative reactions* in order to maintain steady levels will then depend upon such factors as levels of expectation or aspiration as related to values, the stringency of situational demands, the abilities or resources of the actors in relation to aspirations and situational demands, the degree of unification of their efforts, and so on.

One obvious inference from this theoretical formulation is that the levels of satisfaction of members at the end of a session of problem-solving attempts will be a function of the degree to which *positive reactions* have outweighed *negative reactions* during the process. The two illustrative profiles given earlier as figure 8.1 show this relationship.

Another possible inference is that the satisfaction ratings of individual members (as distinct from that of the group as a whole) will tend to be a function of the preponderance of *positive reactions* they have received over the *negative reactions* they have received. This hypothesis was not thoroughly explored, but there were some indications that higher-rank members tended to receive higher relative proportions of *positive reactions*, and, in general, tended to have higher satisfaction ratings. The degree of satisfaction, on the average, seems to be highest with the members of highest status, and to grade down as status grades down.

Despite indications of satisfaction being linked with other variables, there are no perfect correlations. There are many reasons. A primary reason is that *satisfaction* is not a simple variable. (Neither is *utility*, the *greatest good*, or other value-relative variables of economic fame.) Value differences among members and the possible formation of opposing coalitions would tend to set the stage for differences in satisfaction. Outcomes that bring satisfaction to some members might tend to bring dissatisfaction to those of opposite values.

## Questions in the Interaction Process

The probabilities that a *question* from the other will provoke a complementary or cognate *attempted answer* are very high. There is nothing very remarkable about this, but it does provide evidence of a kind of *reasonable continuity* in the process—the persistence of the system in an instrumental-adaptive direction of movement, once started, in spite of the fact that the action changes hands from one member to another. *Questions* provide a means of turning the process toward the instrumental-adaptive direction, with a low probability of provoking an affective or a negative reaction. *Questions* are an extremely effective way of turning the initiative over to the other.

In our groups the number of *questions* which appeared to be self-conscious anticipatory attempts to guide the process in this way was quite small. They probably appeared more often after strains arising from earlier failures, as a result of disagreement, argument, and *backtracking* from premature attempts to proceed more *directively*.

*Questions* provide a "neutral way out," a "patch-up" procedure of last recourse when *negative reactions* are anticipated. This way of looking at the process gives a reasonable explanation as to why the rates of *questions* were so low in our groups (about half that of *negative reactions*). *Questions* constitute the last of the *dwindling series of feedbacks*, mentioned earlier, and tend to be called into play only after more direct and obvious feedback controls have failed to equilibrate the system.

Because *questions* usually prevent the asking individual from going ahead to give his own ideas, they provide little opportunity to change the individual's status, or to redefine his role. Opportunities for status bids and role redefinition are handed over to the other. Thus, where competition is high (as it was generally in our initially leaderless groups) there will be a tendency to avoid *questions*, except as a last resort. Those who have a fixed high status, and those who have essentially accepted a low status, can afford to ask *questions*, but not those who are in the thick of competition.

### Active Participation: Who speaks to Whom, and How Much?

Figure 8.8 shows how the distribution of total amounts of participation among the members of the group tended to vary according to rank in our initially leaderless experimental groups. Distributions are shown for groups of sizes three through eight.

At the time of our studies of group size there was interest in the work of George Kingsley Zipf (1949), who maintained that with regard to a great many quite different phenomena, the differential distribution of frequencies in rank order tended to be a "harmonic" distribution. In such a distribution, the Rank 2 frequency tends to be half the frequency of Rank 1. The Rank 3 frequency tends to be one third the frequency of Rank 1, and so on, down through a dwindling series of fractions.

My fellow researchers and I (Bales, Strodtbeck, Mills, and Roseborough 1951) decided to try the fit of this harmonic distribution for our groups of different sizes. In figure 8.8, the harmonic distribution is shown by the curved solid line. The observed percentages of acts initiated by the members of the group are shown in the rank-ordered series of circular dots. Rank 1 is the highest rank, for the member with the highest number of acts.

The relationships shown in figure 8.8 must be taken as only suggestive. Strodtbeck's statistical tests indicated that the variations were significantly different from the model. About that time I also remembered, too late and with chagrin, that I had included a large number of results for size four which had been sent to me by a friend at the University of Michigan. These data were for interaction on a round-robin task that was completely different from our standard task.

The fits of raw data to the curve are not exact, but they are close enough from size five on up to make one wonder if something systemic is going on. For groups of size five through eight, the total initiated by the Rank 1 member is apparently asymmetrically high as compared to all others. Several emergent regularities in the interaction of participants seem to account for some characteristics of the final curves, and have significance as indications of the

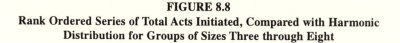

**FIGURE 8.8**
**Rank Ordered Series of Total Acts Initiated, Compared with Harmonic**
**Distribution for Groups of Sizes Three through Eight**

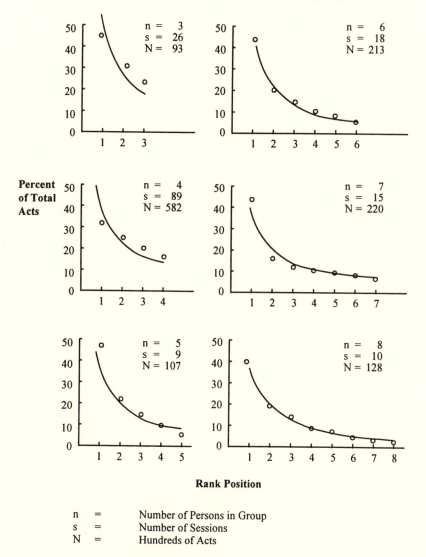

n  =    Number of Persons in Group
s  =    Number of Sessions
N  =    Hundreds of Acts

emergence of leadership and related role characteristics of members. These regularities appear in the matrices of who speaks to whom.

Figure 8.9 shows a series of aggregated *who-to-whom* matrices for groups of sizes two through eight. All cells have been reduced to percentage rates. Each matrix is the result of aggregating the results for a considerable number of sessions for a number of groups of the same size. Each matrix has been separately ordered before the aggregation. Thus when we speak of the Rank 1 member, for example, we are not talking about a single particular member, but an aggregated sum of members who emerged as Rank 1 in a particular session. The acts of each session, taken separately, have been sorted into the cells which describe the different possible combinations of who is speaking and to whom. Sizes of group are of course kept separately. Separate sessions for each size have been aggregated by adding the corresponding cells straight down vertically through the stack of session matrices.

In the generalized form of the matrix for all sizes of groups, the total number of acts initiated (*Total Init*) by the member of each rank, in descending rank order, is shown as the final column at the far right. For that given session, then, the members were assigned an identifying rank, based on the total number of acts they had *initiated* in that session. In other words, the rank achieved by the individual in that session is then treated as his identifying code name throughout the rest of the matrix of cells. These identifying codes are used for the vertical list at the left of the square matrix labeled *Acts From*, and are repeated in the same order across the top of the square matrix labeled *Acts To*, to designate the addressee of the act.

The scoring system recognizes acts addressed to the "group as a whole" as a possible addressee, shown in the column labeled *Sum to O* (meaning to "all"). This column is preceded by a column labeled *Sum to I*, containing the sum of the preceding row, acts that were all addressed to "I" (meaning to specific "individuals," rather than the group as a whole). A row of totals labeled *Sum Received* appears along the bottom of the matrix of acts received by specific rank-named individuals.

It seems quite clear that, for groups of size five and larger, the Rank 1 member is asymmetrically high, although not uniformly twice as high as the Rank 2 member, as Zipf's law would prescribe. The asymmetry, starting with size five even exceeds Zipf's series. Starting with size five, the Rank 1 member seems dependably to be asymmetrically higher than the Rank 2 member on *Sum Received* (as well as on *Total Init*). But something is going on with Rank 2 member also. Even from size three on up, the amount that Rank 2 member addresses to Rank 1 is asymmetrically and markedly higher than the amount Rank 2 addresses to Rank 3 or any lower rank. Apparently Rank 1 and Rank 2 members tend to constitute an especially important pair in the directions and quantity of communication in the groups of sizes greater than two. But from size four on up, Rank 1 receives asymmetrically from Rank 2, but does not address Rank 2 with any great surplus.

What is going on? If one looks at the amounts that Rank 1 member addresses to the group as a whole (his *Sum to O*) beginning with size five, it becomes clear that Rank 1 is specializing heavily in addressing communications to the group as a whole. It appears that a kind of circular flow of com-

## FIGURE 8.9
## Acts Initiated and Received in Groups of Sizes Two through Eight

### Groups of Size Two
Number of groups in sample = 41
Number of acts in sample = 12,765

| Acts From | Acts To 1 | Acts To 2 | Sum to I | Sum to O | Total Init. |
|---|---|---|---|---|---|
| 1 | — | 57.3 | 57.3 | — | 57.3 |
| 2 | 42.7 | — | 42.7 | — | 42.7 |
| Sum Received | 42.7 | 57.3 | 100.00 | — | 100.0 |

### Groups of Size Three
Number of groups in sample = 26
Number of acts in sample = 9,304

| Acts From | Acts To 1 | Acts To 2 | Acts To 3 | Sum to I | Sum to O | Total Init. |
|---|---|---|---|---|---|---|
| 1 | — | 15.3 | 7.1 | 22.4 | 22.0 | 44.4 |
| 2 | 15.6 | — | 5.4 | 21.0 | 11.7 | 32.7 |
| 3 | 7.9 | 5.7 | — | 13.6 | 9.3 | 22.9 |
| Sum Received | 23.5 | 21.0 | 12.5 | 57.0 | 43.0 | 100.0 |

### Groups of Size Four
Number of groups in sample = 89
Number of acts in sample = 58,218

| Acts From | Acts To 1 | Acts To 2 | Acts To 3 | Acts To 4 | Sum to I | Sum to O | Total Init. |
|---|---|---|---|---|---|---|---|
| 1 | — | 8.3 | 6.5 | 3.6 | 18.4 | 13.8 | 32.2 |
| 2 | 10.3 | — | 4.4 | 3.2 | 17.9 | 11.0 | 28.9 |
| 3 | 8.0 | 5.2 | — | 2.2 | 15.4 | 7.4 | 22.8 |
| 4 | 4.2 | 3.5 | 2.8 | — | 10.5 | 5.6 | 16.1 |
| Sum Received | 22.5 | 17.0 | 2.8 | 9.0 | 62.2 | 37.8 | 100.0 |

munication has developed in which Rank 1 addresses the group as a whole (*Sum to O*) about twice as often as he addresses specific individuals (*Sum to I*). Rank 2 member and all other members of the group, although in descending rank order, tend to address (or "react to") Rank 1 in asymmetrically large amounts, compared to the amounts they address to the other members. Rank 1 appears to initiate acts to other members in decreasing amounts that agree

**FIGURE 8.9** (continued)

**Groups of Size Five**
        Number of groups in sample = 9
        Number of acts in sample = 10,714

| Acts From | Acts To 1 | 2 | 3 | 4 | 5 | Sum to I | Sum to O | Total Init. |
|---|---|---|---|---|---|---|---|---|
| 1 | — | 5.0 | 4.0 | 3.9 | 1.9 | 14.8 | 32.1 | 46.9 |
| 2 | 11.6 | — | 2.3 | 2.1 | .5 | 16.5 | 5.4 | 21.9 |
| 3 | 8.4 | 1.8 | — | .7 | .5 | 11.4 | 4.0 | 15.4 |
| 4 | 5.7 | 1.3 | .4 | — | .3 | 7.7 | 2.6 | 10.3 |
| 5 | 2.7 | .6 | .5 | .4 | — | 4.2 | 1.3 | 5.5 |
| Sum Received | 28.4 | 8.7 | 7.2 | 7.1 | 3.2 | 54.6 | 45.4 | 100.0 |

**Groups of Size Six**
        Number of groups in sample = 18
        Number of acts in sample = 21,311

| Acts From | Acts To 1 | 2 | 3 | 4 | 5 | 6 | Sum to I | Sum to O | Total Init. |
|---|---|---|---|---|---|---|---|---|---|
| 1 | — | 5.8 | 4.5 | 2.6 | 2.1 | 1.5 | 16.5 | 26.6 | 43.1 |
| 2 | 8.2 | — | 2.1 | 1.5 | .9 | .5 | 13.2 | 5.6 | 18.8 |
| 3 | 6.4 | 2.0 | — | 1.3 | .6 | .3 | 10.6 | 3.6 | 14.2 |
| 4 | 4.5 | 1.5 | 1.2 | — | .4 | .2 | 7.8 | 3.2 | 11.0 |
| 5 | 3.1 | 1.1 | .7 | .4 | — | .1 | 5.4 | 2.1 | 7.5 |
| 6 | 2.2 | .6 | .5 | .3 | .1 | — | 3.7 | 1.7 | 5.4 |
| Sum Received | 24.4 | 11.0 | 9.0 | 6.1 | 4.1 | 2.6 | 57.2 | 42.8 | 100.0 |

**Groups of Size Seven**
        Number of groups in sample = 15
        Number of acts in sample = 22,044

| Acts From | Acts To 1 | 2 | 3 | 4 | 5 | 6 | 7 | Sum to I | Sum to O | Total Init. |
|---|---|---|---|---|---|---|---|---|---|---|
| 1 | — | 4.2 | 2.8 | 2.5 | 1.8 | 1.0 | .8 | 13.1 | 30.0 | 43.1 |
| 2 | 6.4 | — | 1.8 | 1.0 | 1.0 | .5 | .4 | 11.1 | 4.1 | 15.2 |
| 3 | 4.6 | 1.6 | — | .9 | .6 | .5 | .2 | 8.4 | 3.5 | 11.9 |
| 4 | 3.6 | 1.0 | .9 | — | .7 | .4 | .2 | 6.8 | 3.1 | 9.9 |
| 5 | 3.0 | 1.2 | .7 | .6 | — | .4 | .2 | 6.1 | 2.5 | 8.6 |
| 6 | 2.0 | .6 | .5 | .3 | .5 | — | .2 | .4.1 | 2.2 | 6.3 |
| 7 | 1.6 | .6 | .4 | .3 | .3 | .2 | — | 3.4 | 1.6 | 5.0 |
| Sum Received | 21.2 | 9.2 | 7.1 | 5.6 | 4.9 | 3.0 | 2.0 | 53.0 | 47.0 | 100.0 |

**FIGURE 8.9** (continued)

**Groups of Size Eight**
    Number of groups in sample = 10
    Number of acts in sample = 12,830

| From | \multicolumn{8}{c}{Acts To} | Sum to I | Sum to O | Total Init. |
|------|---|---|---|---|---|---|---|---|---|---|---|
| | 1 | 2 | 3 | 4 | 5 | 6 | 7 | 8 | | | |
| 1 | — | 3.6 | 3.5 | 2.3 | 1.7 | 1.0 | .8 | .7 | 13.6 | 26.2 | 39.8 |
| 2 | 8.1 | — | 1.2 | 1.3 | .8 | .4 | .3 | .4 | 12.5 | 4.1 | 16.6 |
| 3 | 5.9 | .8 | — | .5 | .6 | .5 | .2 | .1 | 8.6 | 4.1 | 12.7 |
| 4 | 4.1 | 1.0 | .8 | — | .4 | .3 | .2 | .0 | 6.8 | 3.0 | 9.8 |
| 5 | 3.8 | .9 | .5 | .5 | — | .5 | .2 | .0 | 6.4 | 2.2 | 8.6 |
| 6 | 1.8 | .3 | .6 | .1 | .4 | — | .1 | .0 | 3.3 | 2.2 | 5.5 |
| 7 | 1.1 | .3 | .3 | .2 | .2 | .2 | — | .0 | 2.3 | 2.0 | 4.3 |
| 8 | .8 | .2 | .1 | .0 | .0 | .0 | .0 | — | 1.1 | 1.6 | 2.7 |
| Sum Received | 25.6 | 7.1 | 7.0 | 4.9 | 4.1 | 2.9 | 1.8 | 1.2 | 54.6 | 45.4 | 100.0 |

with their respective ranks, but are lower than the amounts they have addressed to him, and which in total (*Sum to I*) amount to something less than half of the amount Rank 1 addresses to the group as a whole (*Sum to O*).

It appears that Rank 1 member has taken over, has acquired or has been forced into, a specialized role, in which he is not only the central link in the circular chain of communication, but also the main initiator of problem-solving attempts. Rank 2 member appears to have become the principal reactor, and all others appear to have become mainly reactors in a rank order of descending rank. The amounts the members of rank lower than Rank 2 address to other members near their own rank appear to be about equal to the amounts they receive from the other members of ranks adjacent to their own.

The general tendency is for the member with Rank 1 on interaction to also be rated as Rank 1 for other measures. Thus, the member rated Rank 1 for participation, the most dominant (U), is rated often in the post-meeting ratings as having had the Best Ideas (Rank 1 on quality of F behavior). However, the Rank 2 member, who has specialized in giving reactions to the initiations of the Rank 1 member, tends to receive the most votes on being Best Liked (Rank 2 on P received). These characteristics are consistent with "effective," defined as positive correlations between U, P, and F vectors. But the role of Best Liked is still ambiguous.

### Task and Affiliation: Initiating Ideas and Receiving Likes

Philip Slater was my principle collaborator in exploring the relationships between characteristics of interaction and ratings received from all members after the session (Slater 1955; Bales and Slater 1955). I had earlier discovered a curious anomaly in the ratings of Best Liked. It appeared that the Rank 1 member on interaction initiated was highest, as expected, on receiving ratings as having the Best Ideas, but was unaccountably low on receiving Likes (see figure 6.4). The Rank 2 member instead was at the high point of receiving Liking (Bales 1953b). The study reported as figure 6.4 contained the same evidence, and the possible evidence that it was due to "overtalking" and not allowing sufficient feedback, on the part of the Rank 1 member, based on a large sample of data.

Further analysis of these data compiled by Slater (1955) is illustrated in figure 8.10, which shows the average interaction profiles, both *initiated* and *received*, of the members who were rated as having had the Best Ideas (I) and those who were Best Liked (L) after the same session. They are not markedly different, but there are indications of a division of labor. The Idea specialist appears to be asymmetrically high in *giving opinion* and *suggestion*, and low on *showing solidarity*, *tension release*, and *agreement*. But he is also asymmetrically high on receiving *agreement*, and possibly low on receiving *disagreement*.

The Best Liked member, apparently in a complementary way, appears to be asymmetrically high on *showing solidarity*, *tension release*, and *agreement*, low on *giving opinion* and *suggestion*, but also high on *showing disagreement*, *tension increase*, and *showing antagonism*. He is also asymmetrically high on receiving *solidarity* and *tension release*, and, although the differences are not statistically significant, he nevertheless appears to be somewhat high on receiving *disagreement* and *antagonism*.

I think the indications are that the Best Liked member is not simply a "yes man," in response to the top initiator, but, in a more general sense, is a leader in giving "Social Emotional Reactions," both Positive and Negative, in contrast to the top participator who specializes in "Problem-solving Attempts." It may be that the Best Liked member tends to be better liked than the Best Idea member because the Best Liked member better represents, on the average, the reactions of all the rest of the lower rank members. It is also quite likely that some leaders of the opposition may show up in the Rank 2 position.

Other data indicate that there is a strong tendency for the two roles associated with Best Ideas and Best Liked ratings received from other members to separate over time, not only in their modes of interaction, and places in the rank order, but also in the minds of other group members. Slater found that in first sessions of a series of four, the same person might receive the highest ranking on both roles about 52 percent of the time. By the end of the second meeting the percentage of coincidence of the two roles held by the same person had fallen to about 9 percent. After the third meeting, the coincidence had increased to about 16 percent, but then again after the fourth meeting the coincidence was down again to about 9 percent.

I conclude that the emergence of this kind of specialization is more or less "in the cards," and although it is very likely dependent on personality differ-

**FIGURE 8.10**

Composite Profiles of Twenty-three Top Men on *Idea* Ranking
and Twenty-three Top Men on *Liked* Ranking for the Same Sessions

| | Interaction Category | Initiated | | Received | |
|---|---|---|---|---|---|
| | | Idea Men | Liked Men | Idea Men | Liked Men |
| 1 | Shows Solidarity | 4.19 | 4.79 | 2.90 | 3.68 |
| 2 | Shows Tension Release | 5.97 | 7.71 | 8.40 | 10.38 |
| 3 | Agrees | 14.60 | 14.97 | 22.92 | 17.88 |
| 4 | Gives Suggestion | 8.66 | 5.68 | 6.14 | 6.36 |
| 5 | Gives Opinion | 31.30 | 27.20 | 26.28 | 28.86 |
| 6 | Gives Orientation | 17.90 | 17.91 | 15.24 | 13.73 |
| 7 | Asks for Orientation | 3.66 | 3.43 | 2.78 | 3.01 |
| 8 | Asks for Opinion | 2.39 | 2.73 | 2.00 | 1.98 |
| 9 | Asks for Suggestion | .98 | 1.58 | .72 | .33 |
| 10 | Disagrees | 7.31 | 8.43 | 9.50 | 10.21 |
| 11 | Shows Tension | 1.97 | 3.67 | 1.30 | 1.37 |
| 12 | Shows Antagonism | 1.07 | 1.90 | 1.74 | 2.21 |

\* Differences between the two men were tested on the following sets of categories. Levels of significance are shown in parentheses:

| | | |
|---|---|---|
| Initiated: | 1 + 2 | (.05 level) |
| | 4 + 5 | (.01 level) |
| | 10+ 11 + 12 | (.05 level) |
| Received: | 1 + 2 | (.05 level) |
| | 4 + 5 | (not significant) |
| | 10 + 11 + 12 | (not significant) |

ences, it is not necessarily a result of very conscious decisions and intentions on the part of any of the participants. Since it tends to centralize and focus the problem-solving efforts of the group as a whole on two specific individuals, it may have a very strong effect for good or ill on the more ultimate effectiveness of the group. Failure or ineffective performance in either role may be among the leading determinants of the relative success or failure, lack of effectiveness, of the group as a whole.

## Shared Leadership: Is There a Coalition between the Two Top-Ranking Members?

Figure 8.11 shows Slater's analysis of the special character of the relationship between the member rated as having the Best Ideas (I) and the member rated as Best Liked (L). It also shows the differences in this relationship be-

**FIGURE 8.11**
**Characteristics of Interaction between Top-Ranking Men**
**on Ideas (I) and Top-Ranking Men on Being *Liked* (L)**

| Characteristics of Interaction Observed | Percentage of cases in which characteristic occurred | | Significance level for High and Low groups combined |
|---|---|---|---|
| | High Groups | Low Groups | |
| I *interacted* with L more than he did with any other members | 57.1 | 52.9 | ** |
| I *interacted* with L more than any other member interacted with L | 64.3* | 50.0 | ** |
| I *agreed* with L more than he did with any other member | 57.1 | 44.1 | * |
| I *agreed* with L more than any other member agreed with L | 75.0** | 44.1 | ** |
| L *interacted* with I more than he did with any other member | 92.9*** | 47.1 | *** |
| L *interacted* with I more than any other member interacted with I | 71.4** | 32.4 | * |
| L *agreed* with I more than he did with any other member | 85.7*** | 44.1 | *** |
| L *agreed* with I more than any other member agreed with I | 46.4 | 29.4 | — |
| Percentage expected by chance | 32.1 | 28.8 | |

Level of significance:   No asterisk for not significant;
* for .05; ** for .01; *** for .001.

tween groups in which the members were in relatively high consensus (*High Groups*) with each other on their rankings compared with groups in which the members show low consensus, or much disagreement in their ratings (*Low Groups*). (For developmental differences between groups of high and low status consensus, see figure 6.3.)

Slater's comparison of the interchanges between the two roles strongly suggests a de facto coalition, if not a knowing and intended one. The relationship appears to be predominantly positive in the high-consensus groups. Each of the two agreed with the other more than they did with any other member, at a high level of significance. Moreover they seem to rather specialize in agreement with each other, compared to the agreement members of lower rank give to them. This pattern is consistent with the assumption that positive correlations between vectors U, P, and F are characteristic of "most effective" groups.

In the low-consensus groups all of these indicators of a positive coalition tend to slump, some of them essentially cut in half. I suspect that what we are seeing here is a Best Liked member who does not like the Best Idea man, who may be an opposition leader. Thus, there is no guarantee that the top two participators may not be the principal focus of conflict in the group, and yet hold a virtual monopoly on the participation time. If so, the prospects for a "most effective" ultimate outcome, either for solution of externally posed problems of the group or for solution of its internal problems, are poor indeed. My guess is that the most likely prior "cause" of an unfortunate impasse like this is that the values the top participants (or others as well) have initially brought into the group are in conflict.

My detailed studies of the necessities of group problem solving, the emergent characteristic regularities of overt interaction, and the differentially uncomfortable situations into which individuals were placed helped me understand the kinds of values that seem constantly to originate anew in interaction. The realization that the values of individuals were typically well established and already internally conflicting before group members even came into contact eventually led me to the conclusion that I had to understand more about values, especially "most effective" values.

# Part 4

# Effectiveness

# 9

# The Mystery of *Most Effective* Values

A series of potentially important questions arise from the compact symmetry and precise placement of the cluster of value locations in answer to the following rating question:

> In general, what kinds of values would be ideal for you to show in order to be *most effective*?

Figure 9.1 is a Field Diagram showing 1000 responses to this question concerning personal "effectiveness" (EFF). What is remarkable about this pattern? The center of the whole empirical cluster is in fact remarkably close to the center of the three theoretically posited Areas which form the PF circle on the Overlay: the Most Effective Teamwork Core, the Liberal Teamwork Side, and the Conservative Teamwork Side, all taken together. These three Areas contain 90.3 percent of the image locations on this Field Diagram for "most effective." This is a very high degree of relative consensus.

It is true that there are a few scattered images outside the "charmed" PF circle of the Overlay. There are a few images in the Group-centered Wing (1.6 percent) and in the Authority-centered Wing (2.5 percent), but the degree of unification (the compactness of the circular cluster) is still remarkably high, and at the same time symmetrically balanced between the Liberal Side and the Conservative Side. This balance is not an artifact of the method or the mathematical model. It is a notable empirical fact that, for our very large data set at least, the member locations in terms of their overall identification with liberal and conservative values are almost exactly evenly balanced for the images of "most effective." Why should this be?

The density pattern of the cluster itself shown in figure 9.1 is nearly circular. That is, changes in density intervals look almost like a contour map of a bell-shaped mountain. The density gradient up from any beginning point at the bottom periphery of the mountain rises in a very smooth and regular S-shaped curve of ascent up the mountain to a single center area of highest density. In fact, tests for conformity to a bivariate normal distribution (a bell-shaped curve) along both dimensions, P-N and F-B, at the point where they

**FIGURE 9.1**
**Scatterplot Field Diagram of 1000 Ratings on *Values that Would***
***Be Ideal for You to Show in Order to Be Most Effective* (EFF)**

VALUES ON ACCEPTING TASK-ORIENTATION OF ESTABLISHED AUTHORITY

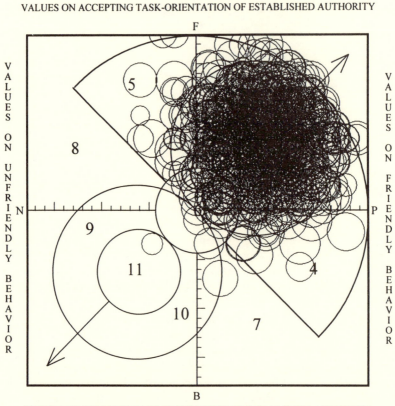

VALUES ON OPPOSING TASK-ORIENTATION OF ESTABLISHED AUTHORITY

*Source*: © 1997 SYMLOG Consulting Group, San Diego, CA. Reprinted by permission.

cut through the center of the cluster show that it is very close to a bivariate normal distribution along the plane of the Field Diagram.

The smooth increase in density as we move in converging paths toward the "top of the mountain" tends to imply a *unification* toward consensus among the raters. Starting at the top as we move down the mountain, no matter on which two opposite sides, toward the periphery, however, the increasing distance between points on opposite sides of the mountain indicate a tendency toward separation of raters' concepts of "most effective" values.

The value profiles of individuals whose value locations are at opposite points anywhere around the lower periphery of the mountain (ignoring scattered images outside the charmed circle) are sufficiently different from each other to tend toward zero correlation with each other.

The emergent pattern toward unification at the top of the density mountain appears to me to imply something like an "emergent wisdom" of the aggregate. However, given the many different starting points of individual value profiles represented by points around the circular periphery at the bottom of the mountain, one must recognize that the emergent pattern is *not* the result of widespread logical similarity of the beginning value premises among all raters at the starting points. The regularity and symmetry we see is surely not the result of a deliberately enacted "social contract" of the kind hypothesized by Rousseau, for example, as the logical way to solve the problems of conflict in social systems.

Is it possible that the pattern we see can be regarded as an empirical evolutionary approximate solution to the "problem of social order"? Is a rounded bell-shaped cluster of value locations the best that can be achieved, rather than a consistent and uniform set of premises, leading to a socially deliberated and enacted complete solution (a real social contract)? Is the best solution that real people in interaction can achieve to their problems of ethical conduct simply an approximately normal bell-shaped distribution of value positions, *ideal* for "most effective," around a particular average point, of a very complex set of values that tend to emerge from social interaction itself?

## Are We Dealing with an Artifact?

Is it possible that our method of measurement, which measures thirteen value items on each side, contributes to the liberal-conservative balance across the midpoint of the PF vector? No doubt the equal number of items measuring values on each side contributes ultimately to making this exactness of the balance possible, but the balance of items does not determine the unique outcome of the equal distribution that we see. How can we be sure of this?

There is only one other rating question on any other of the nineteen Images for which we have comparable data that shows the same almost exact symmetry (see IDL). This is the following rating question, also about "most effective" values:

> In general, what kinds of values would be *ideal* for this person to show in behavior in order to be *most effective*?

Responses to the question came from coworkers of a team leader or member, who was about to depart for a leadership workshop.

Figure 9.2 shows the Field Diagram for answers to this rating question on *ideal* (IDL). Its circular form and balance is remarkably similar to that of figure 9.1. Answers to all of the seventeen other Image rating questions show

**FIGURE 9.2**

**Scatterplot Field Diagram of 1000 Ratings on** *Values that Would Be Ideal for this Person to Show in Order to Be Most Effective* **(IDL)**

VALUES ON ACCEPTING TASK-ORIENTATION OF ESTABLISHED AUTHORITY

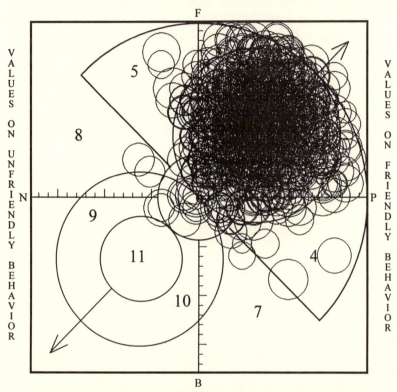

VALUES ON OPPOSING TASK-ORIENTATION OF ESTABLISHED AUTHORITY

*Source*: © 1997 SYMLOG Consulting Group, San Diego, CA. Reprinted by permission.

significant imbalance either to one side or the other (mostly to the Negative side) or show a wide scatter to other parts of the field, Negative and Backward.

It will be remembered that the twenty-six values of the complete value profile are arranged in a regular circular order all the way around the field. They wind three times in a counterclockwise circular order around the flat plane of the Field Diagram. When a rater assigns a high frequency rating for a specific value as a description of a given Image, the effect (implemented by the vector engine) is to move the location of that final image a small distance in the direction on the field designated by the code name of the value item. The location of the compact circular cluster in the PF quadrant of the field, in both of the two Field Diagrams shown in figures 9.1 and 9.2, thus implies that the raters generally gave high frequency ratings to the value items carrying code names containing both the code elements P and F.

The location of the compact circular cluster in the PF quadrant also implies that the values carrying code names containing the elements N and B have been given relatively low frequency ratings, as compared to the ratings on the P and F values. If this were not so, on the average, the complete cluster could not be contained in the PF quadrant of the Field Diagram. But the subtractive effects of the N- and B-coded values (the subtractions implemented by the vector engine) do not necessarily work toward a close balance of the liberal and conservative directions on each side of the PF vector. They may do so in fact, but not necessarily. They do not do so, for example, even for the ratings on *wish* (which are considerably overbalanced toward the Positive side), and *reject* (which are overbalanced toward the Negative side).

Another possible contributor to the compact circular form is the uniformly constricted rating scale that is required for the ratings of all twenty-six vectors. The lowest possible rating is zero, and the highest possible rating is two, no matter what the value item. This constriction of range might be thought to tend to mute the effects of any very prominent or high-frequency values. But this constriction, so far as it may be relevant, only tends to make the circular form *possible*. It does not artificially determine the circular form, nor the balance between liberal and conservative sides.

It is true that two other Images seem to approximate the feature of the compact circular form about equally well. They both focus attention on what values ought to be realized in the future. These two Images both contain the words "most effective" but their Field Diagram patterns do not maintain the liberal-conservative balance. The Field Diagrams for these two Images are shown as figures 9.3 and 9.4. Figure 9.3 shows answers to the question below concerning the future of the team (FTM):

In general, what kinds of values need to be shown by your team in the *future* in order to be most effective?

Figure 9.4 shows answers to the question below concerning the future of the organization (FUT):

In general, what kinds of values need to be shown in the culture of your organization in the *future* in order to be most effective?

Both of these Image patterns are overbalanced and heavy on the liberal side. In this sense one may suppose that they may contain some of the same ten-

**FIGURE 9.3**
**Scatterplot Field Diagram of 1000 Ratings on *Values that Need to Be Shown***
***by Your Team in the Future in Order to Be Most Effective* (FTM)**

VALUES ON ACCEPTING TASK-ORIENTATION OF ESTABLISHED AUTHORITY

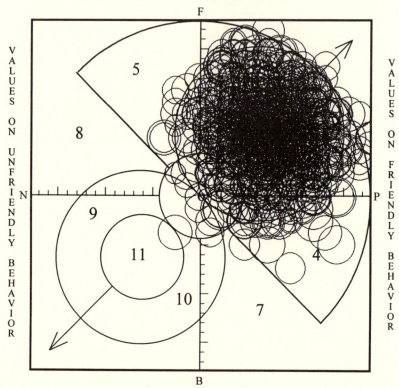

VALUES ON OPPOSING TASK-ORIENTATION OF ESTABLISHED AUTHORITY

*Source*: © 1997 SYMLOG Consulting Group, San Diego, CA. Reprinted by permission.

dencies to compensate for the negative features of the *current culture* that seem to characterize the *wish* pattern.

The value profiles for figures 9.3 and 9.4, FTM and FUT, are shown in Appendix C. The high and low endorsement of particular values on these particular profiles reveal what might be interpreted as a pattern of "regrets for the present and good intentions for the future." The following value items for both of these future-oriented profiles tend to be *low* compared to the SCG

**FIGURE 9.4**

**Scatterplot Field Diagram of 1000 Ratings on *Values that Need to Be Shown in the Culture of Your Organization in the Future in Order to Be Most Effective* (FUT)**

VALUES ON ACCEPTING TASK-ORIENTATION OF ESTABLISHED AUTHORITY

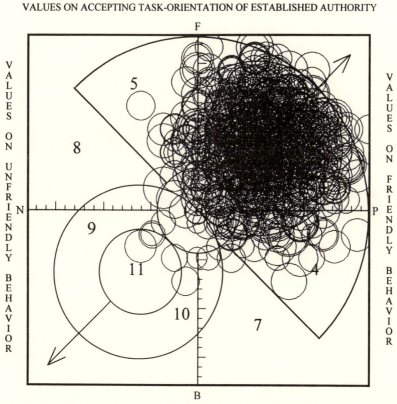

VALUES ON OPPOSING TASK-ORIENTATION OF ESTABLISHED AUTHORITY

*Source:* © 1997 SYMLOG Consulting Group, San Diego, CA. Reprinted by permission.

Optimum value profile, implying, probably, that the raters feel that emphasis on these values currently is too great and should be *decreased* in the future:

1   U       *Individual financial success, personal prominence and power*
             (-6 X-units for FTM, and -4 for FUT)

2   UP      *Popularity and social success, being liked and admired*
             (-6 X-units for FTM, and -4 for FUT)

6    UN    *Tough minded, self-oriented assertiveness*
            (-5 X-units for FTM, and -4 for FUT)

7    UNB   *Rugged, self-oriented individualism, resistance to authority*
            (-3 X-units for FTM, and -3 for FUT)

Both profiles, on the other hand, tend to show the following values as somewhat *high*, compared with the SCG Optimum value profile, implying that the raters feel that emphasis on these values is currently too low and should be *increased* in the future:

3    UPF   *Active teamwork toward common goals, organizational unity*
            (+2 X-units for FTM, and +2 for FUT)

4    UF    *Efficiency, strong impartial management*
            (+3 X-units for FTM, and +3 for FUT)

10   P     *Equality, democratic participation in decision making*
            (+4 X-units for FTM, and +3 for FUT)

11   PF    *Responsible idealism, collaborative work*
            (+4 X-units for FTM, and +4 for FUT)

16   B     *Change to new procedures, different values, creativity*
            (+4 X-units for FTM, and +4 for FUT)

18   DP    *Trust in the goodness of others*
            (+3 X-units for FTM, and +3 for FUT)

In summary, one may conclude that only the Field Diagrams for ratings on *ideal* for "most effective" values show the most puzzling and mysterious balance and compact unification of images.

One "fitting" operation should be noted as possibly making some contribution to the *mystery* of the unusual compactness, circularity, and centering of the patterns of rated Images containing the words "most effective."

The design of the Overlay (figure 2.9) is a *theory* of the consequences for "effectiveness" of the *total pattern* of distribution of individual value locations over all the eleven possible different value Areas. The Overlay, accompanied by the Value Area Density Chart (see figure 2.12), is a theory applied to the empirical pattern of the total plot of a given rated Image in order to draw further theoretical inferences concerning probable effectiveness of the total distribution, according to the percentage of the number of images found to be finally located in each Area.

As a "fitting operation," the empirical pattern of small individual graphic circles for any rated Image is slightly expanded to adjust its size to the overall design of the Overlay. A constant of 1.2 called the *Expansion Multiplier* is applied to each of the final-location scores, generated by the vector engine, for the P-N and F-B dimensions. The size of the multiplier has been empirically determined. It is just about enough, on the average, to bring the center-point location of the empirical cluster of the ratings in the PF quadrant about halfway out on the PF vector (nine units from the center of the Field Diagram), in the middle of the Reference Circle (Areas 1, 2, and 3).

The overall shape of the cluster has not been changed at all by this operation—the cluster is simply a little more expansive in all vector directions than it would otherwise be. None of the angles of separation between small graphic images has been changed. The relation of the vectors to the *center of the field* has not been changed. The application of the expansion multiplier has not changed in any way the balance between the liberal and conservative sides of the PF vector. Thus the expansion multiplier does nothing to account for the compact overall circular form of the "most effective" pattern, and it does nothing to account for the almost exact balance between the liberal and conservative sides of the distribution.

### Back to the *Mystery*: What Then Is Responsible?

None of the mathematical operations or features described above is responsible for the "mysterious" or unique features of the two plots (figures 9.1 and 9.2) for the Image of *ideal* for "most effective." These unique features are the almost exact balance between the liberal and conservative sides, the compact circular form of the clusters, and the unusually high concentration of the images in the three Value Overlay Areas, with the peak of density in the Most Effective Teamwork Core Area.

Earlier I have suggested that the center of the Most Effective Teamwork Core may possibly be cognitively represented in the minds of raters as a psychologically real image common to the large population of raters, and that such an image may possibly act as a psychologically visualized "goal" of some kind (a "group goal"). Two factors argue somewhat against the plausibility of this idea for our random samples of 1000.

First, the PF circle of the Overlay (Areas 1, 2, and 3, combined) actually contains a considerable variety of locations of members, as represented by their image circles, with different values. The members on the two opposite sides from the middle point are expected to be prone to some conflict with each other, as well as cooperation.

Second, our random samples of 1000 are not drawn from any single intact group. Hence, real social interaction and psychologically felt *attraction* between the actual members of the rating population cannot be assumed to exist, for our samples.

Neither of these considerations is clinching, however, since the samples, although randomly drawn from a large population of intact groups, may still be representing, indirectly, the kinds of conditions of attraction between members placed similarly in actual intact groups.

Nevertheless, to me, the implications are strong that one should look to the possibility that the unique features of the "most effective" plot are a systemically formed aggregate result (what I have typically called a systemic *emergent*) of the particular pattern of ratings received over the whole profile of twenty-six different values, taken one by one. Each of the twenty-six values must be involved. The mean of each of the value item frequencies needs to be explained separately, each in its own right.

The profile of twenty-six value frequencies shown as the SCG Optimum value profile for the Bargraph is called by the code name MEP, meaning *most effective profile*. This particular profile of frequencies for the twenty-six vectors, when transformed by the vector engine into a score and plotted, after application of the expansion multiplier, produces a single final location for a little graphic image on the Field Diagram that is almost the exact center of the PF circle of the Value Area Overlay—the center of the Most Effective Teamwork Core. On the Field Diagram, shown as figure 9.5, the location of MEP, though not shown, coincides with IDL. The shape of the *most effective profile* (MEP) on the Bargraph and the image circle at center point of the PF cluster represent the identical set of numbers. They are alternative mathematical representations derived from the profile of twenty-six average ratings of an Image.

It is true that many other frequency profiles can be artificially composed that will give the final result of the center point of the PF circle on the Overlay. But the SCG Optimum value profile is not artificially composed. It is empirically derived from real data. It is based on the addition of several quite similar large aggregations of real ratings as I shall explain further in the next chapter.

### The Problem of Social Order All Over Again: A Long Train of Necessary Elements

The "mystery of most effective values" may be recognized as a more detailed version of the "problem of social order." The solution to the problem of social order I postulate involves a combination of elements in a developmental process, operating on each other over time, from the microscopic level of act-to-act interaction up through longer spans of time of evolutionary selection of values themselves over the complete system.

A relatively tolerable social order does not in fact emerge in all social-interaction systems. But it appears to do so to a tolerable approximation in some cases, given time. In all systems there may be a limit to the degree of order that can be achieved. The order in even the best cases may be somewhat imperfect and unstable. A sound theoretical explanation of the problem of social order must take into account the emergence of essential elements to the solution even without a high degree of rationality, without much information, without extensive foresight as to undesirable emergent consequences, and in spite of persistent probability of error and persistent behavioral and value conflicts.

This is the nub of the "problem." Something like the following elements seem to me to be the probable components of the "solution," such as it comes out.

## FIGURE 9.5
### Group Average Field Diagram of Locations of
### Nineteen Important Reference Images

VALUES ON ACCEPTING TASK-ORIENTATION OF ESTABLISHED AUTHORITY

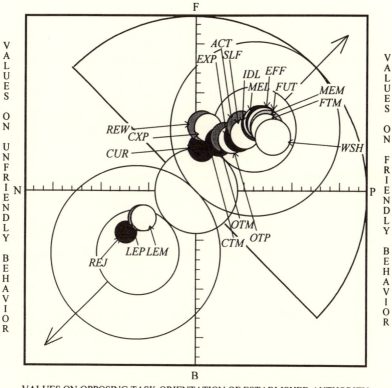

VALUES ON OPPOSING TASK-ORIENTATION OF ESTABLISHED AUTHORITY

*Source:* © 1997 SYMLOG Consulting Group, San Diego, CA. Reprinted by permission.

## A Psychological Need to Survive

I posit that there is a collection of "needs to survive," in the given physical constitution of the individual, based on a large number of more detailed evolutionary mechanisms which have been acquired in the process of selection and survival of the species. For adult individuals, at least some of these postulated "needs" may have a deep psychological reality of some kind (that is, some primitive cognitive structuring cues which orient the drive).

Although these primitive needs or tendencies have more specific intentional aims at the level of single persons, and are relevant in various ways—such as needs for food, warmth, sex, aggression, defense from attack, and the like—the solution to the problem of how order can develop in a system of social interaction does not depend upon a precise identification and enumeration of needs like this. The postulation of specific instincts, sentiments, and the like, explored in the early part of the century, for example by William McDougall (1908), will not explain how social order becomes possible.

Whatever the deep psychological motivations, mechanisms, and tendencies are, they come to be channeled, articulated, and restrained in various ways through the unique developmental processes and experiences of the individual. But it is most important to realize, I believe, that the deeper energizing mechanisms of the postulated needs to "survive" may and do assume *any number of psychologically unique, paradoxical, and contradictory meanings* for different individuals in the courses of their development, including homicide, suicide, and self-sacrifice, as means of "survival" of some aspect of the self, such as the soul in an afterlife as conceived by some individuals.

These extreme paradoxical forms of "survival" are probably more often found in the context of particular religious beliefs and a strong religious group or subgroup formation. But they are quite possible, as we all know, and have fundamental implications for the nature of motivation. They imply that the psychological connections between the ultimate sources of energy (needs to survive) and the cognitively specific explicit meanings that define for the individual what he or she must do to survive are mostly given by learning and unique experience, though partly by explicit instruction and group structured belief. And the meanings for the individual may be paradoxical indeed.

In some cases strong drives may become cognitively and affectively "fixated" on the realization of certain particular values (rather than others) as the most important and demanding values of the personality. In the most strongly fixated cases, reason and strong deterrents may become impotent to prevent the realization of the fixated drive. (On "fixation" in relation to alcohol addiction, see Bales 1945a.)

*Patterns of Social Interaction Are Imbedded in Individual Experience*

Interpersonal values have ever-renewing generative sources in the detailed, concrete processes of interpersonal-behavioral interaction. Aggregate behavioral and value differentiations between individuals emerge more or less unavoidably and automatically out of the factual features and necessities of communicative interaction, problem solving, and group decision making. These differences have emotionally significant results for each individual.

The social differences become socially recognized and evaluated by other group members. The ways the person conceptualizes the self and social roles in this framework become parts of the personality. Any fixated needs to survive tend to become core features of the self and self-concept. More fully generalized values that support and oppose current large-scale social, political, economic, and religious features of the larger society develop from this more concrete and personal experiential base.

*Values Differentiate and Coalesce*

All twenty-six value vectors (a measurable representative sample of the more complex and extensive value system), as generalized "trait"-like structures of the personality, have inherent conflicts with each other, variable strengths and variable meanings. Differing complex personal and interpersonal systems of values are operative in the minds of all participants (according to their maturity) at the time they enter into any particular interaction and these differences act as ever-present determinants of their initiated behavior and reactions. The differing personal value systems of participants should be expected to have different effects on the character and value direction of initiated behavior and reactive feedbacks, the aggregations of behavior, the systemic emergents from the aggregations, and dynamic changes in the system.

The "third-person perspective" is embodied in the presence and participation of other group members in the interaction between any two members. Third persons who witness dyadic encounters begin to define what they consider just or unjust in the behavior of each member of the dyad. This retrospective perspective plays a critical shaping and moderating role in the formation of the feedback the third persons give, at the time or later. It also shapes the emergence and generalization of values in the growing "culture" of the group or system as a whole. Members form value judgments about the present and more remote effects of dyadic behavior encounters that they have just witnessed. These judgments may be verbalized and codified for further transmission.

Logical and communication necessities, which operate in even short-term problem solving, tend to give rise to a three-fold differentiation among the value directions taken by leaders: differences between task leaders, social leaders, and opposition leaders, with regard to given issues and salient images that arise. Particular members tend to be drawn toward particular leaders or are repelled from them according to the different value appeals of the different leaders. The total group begins to divide into subgroups.

Over longer runs of interaction there are likely to be typical tendencies toward the development and differentiation of the value system as a whole into approximately three ideologically based clusters, or possibly more: an authority-centered cluster, a group-centered cluster, and an opposition-centered cluster. These value clusters tend to be separated from each other in the global intercorrelation space, and to be at least partially polarized in relation to each other. The value conflicts between members of the clusters tend to result in chronic competition between the members of the three, or more, clusters.

### Ideological Clusters

Figure 9.6 shows a Field Diagram different from any that have been shown so far. The sole purpose for including this diagram, which is a little difficult to understand, is to demonstrate that the twenty-six values tend to cluster into various groups which may be called "ideological clusters." The diagram shows the analysis of the set of responses for the following rating question:

> In general, what kinds of values would be ideal for you to show in order to be *most effective*?

This same question was the basis for the data displayed in the Scatterplot Field Diagram on personally effective (EFF) in figure 9.1. The display in figure 9.6 is called the *Value Disagreement Field Diagram*.

The Value Disagreement Field Diagram is like a Scatterplot Field Diagram in the following respects: (1) the planar field is described by the P-N and F-B dimensions, which intersect at its center; (2) the image circle size represents the U-D dimension; and, (3) the theoretical space is bounded by a circle on the Field Diagram with a radius of eighteen units.

Yet the Value Disagreement Field Diagram differs markedly with respect to content and the mathematical basis for plotting image circles. The crucial differences from the ordinary Field Diagram are these: (1) There are always and only twenty-six image circles on the Disagreement Field Diagram. Each represents one of the twenty-six value vectors and is labeled with its code name; (2) The *center of the field* is the location of *maximum consensus among all raters* on any given value item; (3) The bull's-eye-target bands outlined by the dotted lines are included to make it possible to specify *how far out* from the center of the field a given value item is located. This distance *out* toward the boundary of the field indicates the degree of *disagreement among the total group of raters* on the meaning they give to the value item in describing the Image asked about in the rating question.

The *greater the distance out* toward the boundary of the field the image of the given value item is located, the *more disagreement* has been shown in the ratings themselves over the total group of raters. The plot is designed to highlight specific values and subgroups of values on which the ratings show disagreement of certain of the raters from the usual meaning of the values.

For statistically interested readers, it may be stated that the mathematical model for the Value Disagreement Field Diagram is an *item-to-scale* correlation model for each of the three dimensions (or bipolar scales) of the intercorrelation space. See Bales, Koenigs, and Roman (1987). Due to the

**FIGURE 9.6**
**Value Disagreement Field Diagram for the Rating Question EFF:**
*Values that Would Be Ideal for You to Show in Order to Be Most Effective*

VALUES ON ACCEPTING TASK-ORIENTATION OF ESTABLISHED AUTHORITY

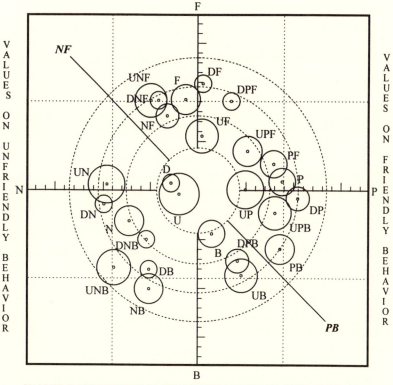

VALUES ON OPPOSING TASK-ORIENTATION OF ESTABLISHED AUTHORITY

*Source:* © 1997 SYMLOG Consulting Group, San Diego, CA. Reprinted by permission.

constrained rating scale of the present system, high agreement among all raters, *either for or against* a given value, tends to result in *low variability* of
ratings among the raters, and *thus low correlation of the item to the scale.*
Zero correlations, indicating the highest agreement or consensus among all
raters, are plotted at the center point of the field. Higher correlations, indicating disagreement, are plotted out toward the periphery of the field.

Considerable disagreement of a number of raters from the average of the rest of the group on a specific value or set of values may or may not indicate the existence of an intact and communicating dissident subgroup of members, but it indicates the latent possibility of such an intact subgroup. A latent possibility may develop into a reality through interaction and communication. The latent possibility may not be specifically recognized at the time of the original rating, but may become clear in feedback.

The same plot is also designed to show which values are correlated with which others concerning the issues raised by the Image presented in the rating question. It is a paradoxical fact that a psychologically real value, as it actually persists over time as a very generalized trait in a real personality, may have many meanings, and change meaning according to the situation, according to the Image it is used to describe. Thus a particular issue may produce a different clustering of the generalized value items than their clustering in reaction to another issue.

A standard weighting has been built into the scoring model (the vector engine) which tends to make the location of the image of the given value item on the Value Disagreement Field Diagram identical with the vector location shown on the large cube model, shown as figure 1.3. In the cube model, the vector for Item UNF, for example (*Active reinforcement of authority, rules, and regulations*) is separated from the vector for Item UF (*Efficiency, strong impartial management*) by 45 degrees. In the vector-engine weighting system, these two vectors are correlated. But in the process of rating the specific Image presented by the rating question, each raters tends to make each value item mean what he or she wants it to mean.

Hence, raters may tend to group the items into clusters partly because they seem to the raters to be ideologically or evaluatively consistent in relation to the particular issues raised by the Image. Particular items or groups of items are drawn closer together on the plot than expected according to the vector separations built into the vector engine. In other cases, clusters of items are further separated from each other. For startling evidence of how marked this clustering may be, see Bales, Koenigs, and Roman (1987).

When a significant number of raters give a special similar meaning to a group of items for ideological reasons, they tend to make that group of items correlate *with each other* more closely than they are expected to be by the scoring model. This results in the visual grouping of these items closer together on the Field Diagram. The item or group of items with a special meaning to some number of raters tends to show on the plot as a *stick-out*, located some distance out on the bull's-eye-target bands from the center of the field toward the outer boundary. On figure 9.6, the Value Disagreement Field Diagram for the Image *ideal* for "most effective," there are really no prominent stick-outs. The images for UNB and NB, however, are the furthest out.

The Value Disagreement Field Diagram tends to show two things, then, related but not identical to each other. First, the stick-out in the location of a value item toward the boundary of the field indicates the disagreement of some number of raters of that item with the meaning given to the item on the average by other group members. Second, the shift in the expected vector location of the item toward the vector location of other items, so that several items tend to appear to be clustered together, indicates that the dissident raters have given the several items in an apparent cluster a greater similarity of meaning than expected by the scoring model in the vector engine.

The Value Disagreement Field Diagram in figure 9.6 is presented primarily to show that *even* for the Image of *ideal* for "most effective" there are apparent tendencies toward clustering of items and separations of the clusters from each other.

Perhaps the most compact cluster of items is the one that may be identified as *authority-centered*. It is composed of Items UNF, NF, DNF, UF, F, DF, and DPF. It may be noted that the three items containing the Negative N component—UNF, NF, and DNF—appear to have been moved by the raters into closer association with those which have a straight F orientation. Probably some of the raters who prefer the values in the authority-centered cluster have tended not to notice that the Items UNF, NF, and DNF have a more Negative element than Items UF, F, and DF. And they may not have noticed that Item DPF (*Dedication, faithfulness, loyalty to the organization*) has a more generally *friendly* element of meaning, to most raters in the group-centered subgroup, than the authority-centered raters themselves attribute to it.

The largest angular separation between approximate clusters is between the *authority-centered* cluster and the *radical-opposition* cluster. This latter cluster consists of items with N and B components: UN, N, DN, UNB, NB, DNB, and DB. It is apparent that the Item DB has been moved a considerable distance in the Negative direction from its hypothetical position of being equally correlated with both the NB and PB vectors.

There is also a substantial angular separation between the Radical-Opposition cluster and what may be considered a minor transitional cluster corresponding to Value Area 7, the *Libertarian Fringe*. The cluster is small, consisting of UB, B, and DPB. The Items UB and B appear to have been given a more positive significance than expected by the weighting direction built into the vector engine (simply straight in the B direction). The angular separation between these three images and what may be called the *group-centered* cluster is very small, and perhaps one might decide to ignore it.

The items which appear to be most closely identified with the group-centered cluster all contain a P component: UPF, PF, UP, P, DP, UPB, and PB. The separation between this group-centered cluster and the authority-centered cluster around the F vector is also small.

The small separation between the group-centered cluster and the authority-centered cluster is consistent with the possibility of movement toward relative unification of the two clusters of members implied by the compact circular density plot of final member locations shown earlier in figure 9.1. (Remember that figure 9.6 shows the relationships of the twenty-six specific value items to each other, whereas figure 9.1 shows the relationships of 1000 complete member images, each image of which is made up of the directional tendencies of all twenty-six of the values attributed to the Image by a given member.)

It may be noted that all the value items in both the group-centered and the authority-centered clusters are on the P and F side of the great dividing line between the PF and the NB halves of the field. This is consistent with the fact that the images of persons, as the final results of the differential frequencies of their twenty-six value profiles, are able to reach a symmetrical aggregation in the PF circle, as shown by the person position plot in figure 9.1.

It is notable that the greatest angular separations between clusters of values are those which tend to isolate the radical-opposition cluster of values in the NB quadrant of the field from either of the two other major clusters of values, which are both in the PF half of the total field.

It is also relevant to report that this Value Disagreement plot, among all those for the eighteen other Images rated (not shown), is essentially the most compact, and shows the greatest degree of consensus over all. That is, it shows the least evidence of disagreement of dissident minorities of raters. Even among the raters who tended to be closest to the NB quadrant, favorable ratings of NB values are not extreme enough (or characteristic of enough raters) to destroy the circular symmetry in the opposed PF area of the ratings of "most effective" in figure 9.1.

## Coalitions Are Probably Critical Determinants

*Particular* coalitions between specific pairs of competitors (whether competing individual leaders or competing subgroups or competing ideologies) probably tend to be critical determinants of who wins in the conflicts between subgroups. Pair coalitions of clusters large enough to form a majority, potentially enable dominance of that majority over the minority third-party competing leaders or subgroups or ideologies. The combined size of two ideological clusters in a pair coalition tends to increase the extent of their power in relation to a remaining third cluster. (The importance of other factors in the power differences between subgroups will be pointed out below.)

Subgroups, even though they may be parts of a pair coalition of ideological clusters, have inescapable internal differences between the value profiles of their members. These differences in values affect their relative attractiveness to new adherents, hence their changing size, hence their degree of internal effectiveness as a subgroup, hence their staying power as a part of a dominant majority coalition.

Particular coalitions of any two ideological clusters of members who do not succeed in maintaining a dominant majority of the total membership of the system probably tend to give way to another coalition between two ideological clusters. This changes the power balance and the value direction of the system.

*Cooperation Is Generally More Effective Than Conflict*

If cooperation between any particular pair of ideological subgroups is possible in spite of differences, cooperation between them has natural advantages over conflict between them, both in promoting "effective" goal achievement of the coalition partners vis-à-vis the external environment, and in enhancing the staying power of that particular coalition in relation to other subgroups. Hence, a coalition of the particular pair or grouping of the subgroups which is best able to cooperate is likely to be more able to gain and keep majority domination. Cooperation at the human level may not absolutely require a specific altruistic genetic basis, although how altruism might have gotten a genetic start is a long standing problem. My guess is that at the human level, applied intelligence and subsequent effectiveness vis-à-vis the environment may be enough to supply a critical evolutionary bias in the survival of cooperative values.

*Risk of Domination by a Minority*

Power is hardly ever simply only a matter of the number of persons involved in an ideological cluster. The possession of resources in relation to the environment, the ownership of property, and the command of force, to mention only three factors, typically become increasingly critical as one considers larger systems. Power in these and other senses may overcome raw numbers of persons and majority coalitions. Domination of the total system by a minority, or several conflicting minorities, is not rare. Historically, if one could take into account all the relevant cases, it is surely the most common case. What does that do to the solution to the problem of how order becomes possible? Does domination solve the problem, perforce?

My sense is that this kind of domination may establish a factual order of compliance, but it does not solve the problems of "justice." The moral sentiments, the moral indignation, and the sense of how human relations "ought" to be, so far as I can tell, have their ever-renewing sources very far down in the concrete processes of interpersonal interaction. They are not extinguished by a factual order of compliance to a powerful minority domination backed by force. They remain active in a more abstract form, as compensatory wishes, fantasies, convictions of what is right, hopes for a better future, beliefs·in the coming of a more invisible champion of justice and mercy, and the like. Religion, in brief, is one of the homes of these hopes for survival and improvement. Revolutionary sentiments and preparations for revolution are the principal other resorts.

### A Clue to the Mystery: Different Meanings at Different Reality Levels

The value system, in short, becomes separated into more than one order or layer of reality, concreteness, time of realization. I suppose that the concept of *ideal* for "most effective" tends to tap into the more abstract and future-oriented layer. Chris Argyris (1964), a well-known organizational theorist, has a term for the more abstract layer. He describes these beliefs and values as *espoused*. I suppose that ideal values are endorsed, they may be held dear, but they are not expected to be wholly and literally currently binding.

I would guess that the concept of "effective" in the phrase "ideal in order to be most effective" probably has its primary psychological meaning for most raters in terms of visualized effectiveness of the self and internal aspects of one's own subgroup. There is probably also a psychological link in the minds of most raters between the concepts of "most effective" and the expectation of "actual fitness to survive in the external environment," although the link may be illusory in longer-term actuality. The test of fitness to survive in the external environment is necessarily vague and infinitely postponable. The term *ideal* probably also tends to forestall realistic consideration of some of the actual difficulties stemming from both the internal social aspects of the system and from the environment.

The concept of "most effective" is probably linked by associative psychological ties to many different meanings of *survival*, for different individuals and subgroups. The term "effective" is ambiguous enough to be interpreted in many ways.

But even at the ideal level, there is no guarantee that the values thought to be "most effective" in any given social-interaction system will assume the compact circular form shown in the member location Field Diagram of figure 9.1, with the density of member locations so evenly divided between the more liberal and the more conservative sides. Are there other factors that may help explain these features?

### *An Omniscient Perspective: Effectiveness vis-à-vis the Larger Environment*

Evolutionary processes over time presumably tend to select particular values and meanings, and eliminate or minimize the felt effectiveness of others. There is probably a bias in the longer run that operates to select values which are "most effective" in relation to the external environment. If a minority coalition does not oppose the majority coalition, the values most effective in relation to the external environment will likely be values which permit, and to some extent promote, cooperation within the majority coalition. If there is an actual preponderance of cooperative and effectively ordered processes among the dominant majority of members of the population it is probably primarily due to evolutionary processes at the cultural level over longer time spans. But even in this case there tends to be an irreducible conflict to some extent between the values of individuals, as individual persons, and the values of others also in the majority coalition.

Not all subgroups or pair coalitions are equally successful or effective vis-à-vis the larger environment. In the longer run, coalitions between *particular pairs* of subgroups, rather than alternative coalitions, might be expected to yield greater effectiveness for the group as a whole in coping with and adapting to the demands and opportunities of the external environment.

In the Field Diagram of figure 9.1, the particular pair of value clusters, and supporting subgroups, which clearly constitute the dominant coalition, is the coalition of the authority-centered cluster and the group-centered cluster. They are about equal in number of members. There are many reasons for supposing that this pair combination, rather than a coalition of either one with the radical-opposition, is the most stable and probably effective in both the internal and external senses of all the possible pair combinations. Many social-interaction systems which endure for long times with comparative stability and minimal internal conflict and minimal internal domination might be found to approximate this combination.

### Real-World Pessimism

There are many possible departures from a coalition of the authority-centered and group-centered clusters. A dominant minority with essential monopoly of power over all three clusters is one that characterizes many societies in the current world. A one-sided preponderance of an authority-centered cluster in coalition with a powerful ownership minority is another. (The Field Diagram for *current culture* of American business organizations, figure 2.8, appears to be an example.) One could easily continue with an exploration of the possible combinations and find many illuminating examples. But this would lead too far afield for the present book, and most of the cases would probably not be very gratifying examples of successful solutions of the problem of "social order."

To blurt out the truth with brutal brevity: in the real world, the problem of social order is not well solved. And we still do not have a theoretical grasp of a way in which it may be solved very completely or for long. The answer to the problem as to how social order may be more widely achieved is still "blowing in the wind."

In fact, as we know very well by now, the compact, centralized, and balanced pattern of *ideal* for "most effective" (figure 9.1) we are trying to explain is not a pattern that appears to be shown very often in the behavior of literal reality. It appears to be, as the word "ideal" implies, a pattern of "less realistic aspirations," in which many important impediments of particular situations and the member composition of particular systems may be more or less ignored.

This may be granted, but some *mystery* still remains. How does it happen that the pattern of "less realistic aspirations" itself is so compact, so nearly circular, so uniformly graded toward its most dense center, and so nearly equally balanced between the more liberal and the more conservative sides?

## Minimization of Hurt across All Situations

Our method of research has certain features that are unusual. For one thing, the twenty-six value vectors have been chosen and carefully worded with the aim of sampling a complete three-dimensional space of intercorrelated values and behavioral variables in intervals as equally spaced as possible over the complete global surface of the intercorrelation space. The items on the rating form describe values that apply to relationships between people in social interaction. They apply to the *microscopic* level of dyadic interchanges between individuals and third-person reactors. And, in more general form, they apply as well to the level of large groups, complete societies, and even international relations.

This generality of application is no accident, of course. The three-dimensional factor space from which the specific value items were articulated, I feel sure, is not an artifact. It is an abstract average description of the most probable internal correlational relationships between kinds of actions and kinds of reactions of real differentiated individuals, as they tend to develop, with some variations, in essentially all intact systems of human social interaction, large or small.

There is an observable microscopic process by which the correlations develop. The process which shapes the relationships, I would say, is a microevolutionary process. *Variation* and *selection* are the mechanisms by which an evolutionary process shapes the probability of a result that appears later in time. In first-hand interaction, specific acts, both initiated and received, tend to be evaluated by those who receive and judge them. The value judgments themselves are evaluated by still other persons, over time, and are approved or disapproved. They develop in individual minds as more generalized *values*. The values are then shaped by evolutionary processes.

The key insight (assumption, hypothesis) for me is that any interpersonal behavior or kind of action in any value direction that goes beyond a certain frequency and intensity tends to hurt somebody. There is a *victim*. When it is below that frequency and intensity, there are also likely to be hurtful effects, but these are not likely to be so immediately forthcoming and perceptible to members immediately present. In many cases it takes time for the effects to propagate through other parts of the system.

When a group member gets hurt by the actions of some other member, moral indignation tends to be felt by the victim, and often by some third-person participants. Moral indignation tends to give rise to more explicit cognitive definition in the formulation of the values in the minds of participants. There is a cognitive and logical need to identify more precisely what it is that is objectionable, wrong, unjust, so as to detect it if it appears again, or prevent it.

In the rating system of the present theory and method, the tabulation of the ratings for and against a particular value item, continued over a very large sample of respondents, kept track of one by one, can be viewed as having a *shaping* and *selective* effect on the emerging total analogous in an important sense to a time process of evolution. Each rater has a different backlog of experience with many situations, and has developed an internal value profile of tendencies to act and feel in given ways in reaction to the huge variety of situations that have been encountered.

The rating of a particular value item as a description of a particular Image is like a third-party value judgment. It involves two judgments, one of the Image and one of the value described by the item itself. We are interested in both, but at the moment we are more interested in the value judgment of the value item itself. The Image of "most effective" for the given rater is held constant over twenty-six ratings. We want to know why each *value item*, as standing for a *value* of the rater, ends up at a particular average frequency, high or low, when it is used to describe the concept or Image of *ideal* in order to be "most effective."

In the case of this Image, "most effective," each endorsement or condemnation of a given item as appropriately descriptive tends to *shape* or contribute to the emerging frequency distribution of endorsement of the item as a description of the Image of the item, or the value, itself. Typically, as the ratings of each individual rater are added to the array, a bulge of highest frequency of endorsement on the X-bar of the Bargraph for the given value item develops, and, both above and below it, a tail of diminishing frequency trails off.

But a key fact is that the larger the population, the more varied the raters are likely to be (that is, more representative of the total variety and different proportionate numbers of persons in the system as a whole). This in turn implies that the larger the population of raters, the larger the variety of situations the raters may have encountered or witnessed in the past. Perhaps it is likely to be true that, within a given interdependent intact system, by increasing the total number of raters and the situations they have encountered we approach an *average* member's reaction to having been hurt, or helped, by a particular kind of action by another group member.

It appears then that, unless our sampling is defective, by increasing the proportion of all members of the system who are included among our raters, our estimate of the average endorsement of a given value item description on the value frequency Bargraph tends to "home in" on a characteristic absolute frequency for the large population as a whole. If our population is made up of a great many intact groups, the peculiarities of particular intact groups tend to get "washed out," and the similarities tend to emerge.

### Disapprovals Are More Widespread Than Endorsements

But it is still not clear why the twenty-six average frequencies of the SCG Optimum profile over a whole large sample of member raters tend to result in a single multiply-impelled and multiply-compromised final location of the Image of *ideal* for "most effective" (EFF) so precisely in the middle, between the more liberal and more conservative sides, of the PF "charmed" circle.

According to SCG research, in general, if a rater tends to endorse the values found at one end of a vector, that rater tends to reject the values of the vector directly opposite. (See the Field Diagrams for *wish* and *reject*, figures 2.3 and 2.4, and the two corresponding Bargraphs, figures 2.5 and 2.6.)

For example, suppose a rater *endorses* a given value, say 10 P, *Equality, democratic participation in decision making*, as a good description of the concept *ideal* in order to be "most effective" and gives that value a rating of two (*Often*). That same rater is likely to *reject* the value on the opposite end, in this case, 14 N, *Self-protection, self-interest first, self-sufficiency*, as a description of the same concept *ideal* in order to be "most effective." The rater will likely give a rating of zero (*Rarely*) on value Item 14 N. Since the vector engine will subtract the rating on the N item from the rating on the P item, the result will be "two minus zero equals two." The vector engine will then (in effect) move the prospective final image location for EFF two units in the P direction. It will make the same comparison for each of the two opposite vectors for that rater all the way around the space, and so arrive at a final location on the Field Diagram for the image EFF as seen by the particular rater.

Now, a critical question pops into my mind: does the rater only tend to disapprove the *precise opposite* of the value he most favors? Suddenly it becomes intuitively clear: of course not! The most telling set of facts to the contrary is what we have learned earlier about the tendency of values to form into clusters that oppose each other. As a first approximation we have recognized an authority-centered cluster, a group-centered cluster, and an opposition-centered cluster as a common kind of clustering. We have recognized that subgroups of individuals often tend to form around each value cluster, and to oppose, as a rule, *both* other clusters of values and members in *both* other subgroups. So far as this is true, we conclude that of the twenty-six values recognized in our rounded system, more values are likely to be disapproved, at least to some extent, than are likely to be approved. If true, this is a key fact.

Why? Because it is probably an important part of the explanation of the rounded shape and general location of the density plot we are trying to understand. The group-centered member, who in the example above, prefers P above all other values, is likely to disapprove N, and mark it as *rarely* applicable to *ideal* in order to be "most effective." But F may also be disapproved to some extent, because it tends to be a part of the authority-centered cluster, or at any rate, the NF values. The same rater who prefers P is likely also to disapprove NB, since it is correlated with N, and also because it tends to be a part of the opposition-centered cluster.

Along with the probable wide arc of values likely to be rejected, the member who most favors P is likely to favor most highly the values with a P element. The values in the wide arc of negative vectors stretching from F to NB are likely to be disapproved to some extent, and to receive ratings close to zero. This may leave only the narrower sector of values stretching perhaps from PF to PB with ratings close to two.

The same tendencies to reject values in a wider arc than those that are accepted are also hypothetically present in raters in each of the two remaining value clusters. The raters who prefer the authority-centered cluster probably will tend to reject the values in the wide arc from NB to P. And the raters who prefer the opposition-centered cluster will possibly tend to reject the values in a still wider arc, including the whole PF half of the space, perhaps even from PB to NF.

The actual tendencies to reject particular arc sets of values are empirical questions, of course, and the relevant research by value clusters has not yet been done. However, it appears that for our groups there are relatively high probabilities of rejection of wide arcs of values over approximately three quadrants of the field from adherents of one, two, or three of the value clusters. The emergent implication is that only the values in the PF quadrant of the field are left relatively strong. It is true that the PF values will probably be disapproved by members of a radical-opposition subgroup, but in most intact systems most of the time this subgroup is likely to be quite small.

To draw an analogy to an evolutionary process we might say that the PF ideal values appear to be most likely to survive because they are generally less likely to be disapproved and weakened over time by the opposition of one or more of the three value-centered subgroups. This is one side of the probable set of determinants. The other side is the probable value of cooperation in relation to the demands of survival from the external environment, and the effectiveness of cooperative values in promoting internal integration and mitigation of internal conflict.

Of course one must keep in mind that we are talking about ideal ("espoused" or "wished for") values, and have supposed that values at this less literal level of reality are importantly shaped and motivated by widespread and repeated mental attempts to compensate for inadequacies and dissatisfactions at the more literal concrete level. This compensatory quality, in my opinion, does not automatically imply that ideal values are unrealizable, and therefore should be depreciated. On the contrary, they are likely to be accumulations of genuine wisdom. In my philosophy, at least, value decisions should take them seriously into account, but also bring to bear, without fail, the most extensive information that can be acquired about all aspects of the system as they currently exist, and the most intense application that can be mustered of reason and prediction of probable effects.

Members adhering to one or more of each of the ideological subgroups will likely tend to disapprove a fairly wide arc of the complete circle of values as descriptions of *ideal* for "most effective." For each of these subgroups the disapproved arc of values is likely to be on the opposite side of the space from their preferred values. Since the locations of the three subgroups are separated from each other, the three arcs of values they disapprove will tend to be different and overlapping, and in fact will tend to extend roughly three-quarters of the way around the complete circle, including values of the NF quadrant, the PB quadrant, and the NB quadrant of the complete field.

The values of the PF quadrant, however, will tend to be spared, except for the disapproval of the members in the NB quadrant, who ordinarily are not numerous. This minimization of disapproval seems to be a plausible explanation of the general location of the density plot, centered in the PF circle. On every side of the center point of the PF vector the number of members disapproving probably will increase as the separation increases, and the number approving will decrease. This will tend to make the residual of most highly approved values roughly circular in form, as we repeatedly find it to be.

There will actually be many overlapping arcs around the complete globe of values. Each arc tends to identify disapproval of certain values, by certain members and subgroups, as *not* "ideal for effective." Those which are "not ideal" will tend to be marked as *Rarely* descriptive of the Image of "most effective." Hence the opposite end of the vector that is disapproved will tend to be left relatively high, with ratings toward *Often* for each of the preferred values. The arcs of disapproval in every direction from the center of the PF area will tend to make the approved residue circular, and at the same time will tend to account for the pile up of greatest density in the center.

This will tend to take place, so long as the values in the residual PF direction are left with less disapproval than those in the other directions. We can see from the Bargraph of the Image *reject*, figure 2.6, that in fact the values UPF, UF, PF, and DPF, are, for our large sample, the least rejected values among the twenty-six. Conversely, UPF, UF, PF, and DPF are the very same values that are most highly approved on the EFF Bargraph (see Appendix C). So these four values are the most highly approved and the least disapproved, over the total population of raters.

## A Critical Balance

These values, exactly in between the F vector and the P vector (except for UF), have the highest endorsement as *ideal* in order to be "most effective." It appears then, that these two directions of value—direction F and direction P—are both regarded as important to survival and about equally important, *despite* their qualitative differences, conflicts in their requirements, and their tendencies to give rise to conflicting ideologically based subgroups. A majority of the population appears to believe that it would be *ideal* in order to be "most effective" for survival if energy and resources could be divided about equally between these two vectors: P and F.

A coalition between the more liberal group-centered subgroup and the more conservative authority-centered subgroup is often large enough to include a majority of the membership of the system as a whole and can make decisions that approximately divide resources evenly between the two on specific issues at specific times. Probably a fifty-fifty compromise on specific issues of conflict is the division point most likely to produce agreement.

But it is difficult to hold an evenly balanced compromise over time on many value conflicts. We have seen many instances in which the behavior and devotion of resources tends to fluctuate from one side to the other over time, even at the microscopic level of act-to-act interaction in the process of problem solving and decision making. And often, in reality, in given intact groups, a balance that is restored back and forth over time is not accomplished, but one side or the other is chronically favored. Perhaps it is true that groups devoted to the performance of work tend to be overbalanced to some degree toward the F side, while groups devoted to learning, therapy, and recovery from stress tend to be overbalanced to some degree toward the P side.

This explanation of the converging density toward the center and the rounded periphery of the locations of the "most effective" Image does not require the hypothesis that there is a cognitive image of the center point that is explicitly visualized by a wide variety of members as the most desirable and attractive point. The effects can well be *emergent* effects of competitive cooperation.

It seems to me that this is the residual part of the *mystery* that is hardest to explain. In fact, we typically find it only when the Image rated is some version of the idealized Image of "most effective." If *ideal* ratings do in fact tend to be compensatory for felt deficiencies at the reality level, the ideal level would seem to give an opportunity for more liberal raters to grudgingly admit the legitimacy of some more conservative values at the ideal level, while the more conservative raters in turn may be able to admit the legitimacy at the ideal level of some more liberal values.

The large size of our samples, representing as many points of view as possible, all the way around the circle of the twenty-six vectors, may be likely to fill in otherwise neglected areas of the value space due to sampling. The constricted uniform rating scale which limits the intensity and frequency that can be expressed would also seem to play some part, since neither the liberal nor the conservative side can be given extreme weighting by single raters or subgroups of raters. But all of these possibilities taken together seem to leave out a systemic origin of the equal balance.

Is it possible that the elementary nature of social interaction at the most concrete level, over many varying kinds of encounters, when viewed by enough persons from the third-person perspective over a long enough time, tends to show up most graphically the real needs that are addressed by the values of each of the three general directions of behavior—the U direction, the P direction, and the F direction—as well as the problems they generate when shown in excessive or deficient frequencies and intensities? It seems possible to me that interaction at this most elementary level demonstrates to participants most clearly and vividly the real costs at the interpersonal level of overemphasizing or underemphasizing any one of the three to the detriment of either of the other two.

These costs could be estimated by separate measures of satisfaction and dissatisfaction using the six items that directly sample the three key vectors. Dissatisfaction presumably tends to give rise over time to disapproved values. Different ideological subgroups tend to have different characteristic arcs of approved and disapproved values. But as I have suggested, the arcs of disapproval probably tend to overlap in most intact groups of sufficient size and leave only a smaller residuum of values that can be approved as "effective," at least at the idealized level, and even then only insofar as they approach a specific average profile of frequencies.

In an intact group, orthogonality of the three dimensions (zero correlations, rather than mutually positive correlations between the U, P, and F values) tends to be produced by departures of behavior and values from the small residual area on the Field Diagram called the Most Effective Teamwork Core. The departures may take place in any or all six of the vectors of the space, by frequencies which overemphasize or underemphasize an average "optimum" of any of the twenty-six values. All departures from an average "optimum" probably tend to be damaging, if long continued, and not compensated. Damaging effects, if detected, tend to produce disapproval from some individuals or subgroups.

Most groups have to deal with realities, external or internal, that some members, and maybe many members, do not like. Most groups in fact do depart in various ways from what many members believe is "most effective." Dissatisfied members apparently tend to compensate for dissatisfactions by the development of rationalizations, hopes, wishes, beliefs, and idealized values at less than a concrete level of reality. If this kind of compensation does not suffice, behavioral resistance and oppositional values are likely to increase, and to appeal to a growing number of members.

I believe that change may be quite possible in many cases if the problems can be more clearly defined, and if the specific steps that might help become more evident. But can there actually be an Optimum value profile which can detect the most important problems and give cues as to what is most likely to help?

# 10

# Can There Be an *Optimum* Value Profile?

In the present measurement system, a single value profile, the same set of twenty-six different frequencies, is used as a criterion for comparing the profiles of all rated Images with each other. Deviations of four X-units on the Bargraph, either over, or under the SCG Optimum profile are used as predictors or indicators of probable or potential "problems" in the operation of the system, whether that of an individual, a team, or an organization. The observed Bargraph frequencies compared to the Optimum profile frequencies are used by the consultant in feedback sessions with the group of raters as a basis for discussion as to whether the indicated problems really exist, and if so, whether identification of the problems may help in possible planning for change.

Can there actually be an "optimum" profile in a meaningful substantive sense for a whole profile of twenty-six values, whether of an individual, a group, an organization, or a complete society? Could there possibly be a single profile, that would be optimum even across different societies and cultures? Even if that could be possible in theory, how could it be the exact one that is here called the Most Effective Profile? How would one know that it is actually "right"? Is it possible to determine empirically that the same normative profile that is shown on all Bargraphs as the "E line" is "most effective" in some specific sense or senses? Most effective for what?

Raters in other cultures, even those using the English rating form, quite properly ask these questions. At first they want to know whether the norm was derived in their culture, as they think it should be. In fact, the norms and Report texts can be adjusted for particular cultures and situations, given enough data and an accurate analysis of reasons why it should be done. But the need is not yet apparent. On the contrary, members in business organizations in all cultures where the method has actually been used comment on the accuracy of the Reports derived from the SCG Optimum value profile in recognizing and throwing light on their problems.

Perhaps the apparently accurate fit of the normative Profile is more credible when it becomes clear that the accuracy of the fit is obtained by very careful initial adjustment of the item wordings so that they have the meaning in the culture that is required by the theory.

The twenty-six rating categories function as the "data entry points" by which entry is made from the actual interacting group into the generalizations that form the body of the theory. In adapting the method to a new cultural context, the body of the theory regarding the intercorrelation space is permitted to "stand still," as it were, and the item wordings are adjusted, if need be, till they make an organic meaningful fit to the intended theoretical meaning for native raters in the specific culture. (See Bales, Koenigs, and Roman 1987.)

As a result of this fitting strategy, the normative profile can also temporarily be allowed to stand still, because it is, in its major shape, a derivative of the major features of a large amount of previous data, the body of theory, and the assumed nature of the value systems to which the theory refers.

In the longer run, the body of theory itself can only be permitted to stand still because it is (or, in fact, *only if it is*) founded on an accurate analysis and embodiment of features of value systems which remain essentially the same at a level of abstraction and generality above most cultural differences. Practically speaking this means "at the level of the intercorrelation space," although the correlations in the space are not assumed to be perfectly stable and best adjusted to system similarities over the broadest range possible. All aspects of the system are open to both empirical and logical tests.

## The Practical Meaning of *Optimum*

The SCG Optimum profile is designed for use in consulting, in feedback sessions, to make comparisons of various profiles possible and easy. Prior to the feedback session, computer analysis of the ratings has been used to produce customized reports. A separate Report has been prepared for each person describing the ways in which his or her total profile, received from all the other raters, differs from the Optimum profile.

The Report contains some tentative interpretations as to what the deviations may mean in terms of the behavior the individual may have shown, from the point of view of others, and how this behavior may relate to the "most effective" criterion. The MEP is thus a means of relating the perceptions of individuals to each other on a simplified summary basis. Instead of the ultimate detail as to just how each member has seen each other member in terms of each of the twenty-six evaluative categories, the summary profile received by the individual from all the other raters, on the average, is compared to the single evaluative profile, MEP, the *most effective profile.*

The data and interpretations of chapters 8 and 9 suggest that the *most effective profile* means a pattern of interactive behavior that, on the average over time, is most likely to minimize disagreement and to maximize agreement on social-relations values typically involved in group problem solving and decision making, over a wide range of issues. This generalization, however, probably applies primarily to the quality of human relations likely to be experienced in the process of solving problems, not to the subsequent actual effectiveness of decisions or solutions in relation to the external environment, although it may have some implications in this latter respect also.

The enumeration of the above qualifications of the words "optimum" and "most effective," I hope, will have a calming effect on sentiments of outrage that may be felt by some members of a group of clients. But developing a method and theory that will actually realize the predictions proposed is still a tall order. The Optimum profile is very far from a prescription to "do nothing" or to "agree to everything."

### How the Normative Profile Is Computed

The actual frequencies of the normative profile at this writing (1997) were obtained from a careful selection and averaging of several sizable sets of empirical data available at the time of last revision (1990). Ratings of several strategically varied Images, gathered as a part of regularly repeated leadership training programs, provided what seemed to be an unusually relevant selection of data sources. Enough data, including data from some other cultures, are now available for another revision, but inspection of many relevant recent samples indicate that differences would be very minor.

In view of the stability we have found in the past, we do not expect additional data from the United States and Canada to change the Optimum profile more than one or two X-units here or there, if that. Preliminary data from English-speaking raters in business organizations in Western Europe, South Africa, and the Pacific Rim give preliminary indications that the same profile will continue to be a satisfactory basis for comparing observed profiles and generating feedback reports among English-speaking raters.

Validation and trials in application of translations of the rating items into some twelve different languages are presently in progress. Successful translations of the rating items into other languages require careful adjustment of the exact wording to make sure that the intended theoretical meanings are approximated as well as possible (see Bales, Koenigs, and Roman 1987). The validation process requires original expert translations, back translations from bilinguals, revisions, statistical analysis of sufficient representative data from raters native to the culture and engaged in business organizations to determine that the meanings they give to the rating categories are as close as possible to the meanings intended, and revision again as necessary, based on success in real application.

But from results so far it appears that the criteria of valid translation can be met to a close approximation and that the same Optimum profile, and the same Reports, are in fact appropriate.

## Data Sources for the SCG Optimum Value Profile

The data sources for the 1990 empirical normative profile, and the general reasons why I chose them as relevant, are outlined below.

Data source (1): 253 participants in a standard SCG training program in leadership and teamwork were rated by five to seven coworkers in their intact home team in answer to the rating question:

> In general, what kinds of values would be *ideal* for this person to show in order to be *most effective*? (IDL)

The SCG data bank provided 1,666 profiles of this kind.

Data source (1) represents the perspective of a group member evaluating his or her concept of *ideal* for "most effective," in the context of an intact group, applied to the actual candidate for a training program in leadership. The candidate in most cases was the rater's leader or manager, preparing to go to a leadership training program. The candidate had asked team members to make the ratings. To assure anonymity for the raters, they had been asked to send the completed rating forms directly to the consultant at the program site. If the rater had been dissatisfied with the candidate, he or she might be expected to want the candidate to change in some ways, and to "send the message" by the ratings. In this context the concept of the "ideal" might be exaggerated to some extent in both the endorsed and rejected value directions by the ways the rater desires the candidate (in most cases, his or her own team leader) to change. These ratings probably represent the member's interests and values, which may not coincide with those of the leader.

Data source (2): Each of the participants who attended the leadership training program rated himself or herself in answer to the following parallel rating question:

> In general, what kinds of values would be ideal for you to show in order to be *most effective*? (EFF)

The data bank provided 253 profiles of this kind.

Data source (2) represents the perspective of the participant, involved in a program aimed at improvement of leadership in the specific context of his or her own team, critically evaluating the *self* in comparison with his or her own ideal. Such a rater might soften or modify the meaning of the items used to describe the ideal, in a self-justifying way, in order to come out looking as good as possible. As the leader or manager of a team, the rater might also be acutely aware of some needs of the group or some environmental demands on the group that were not so obvious to the members who were the raters in Data source (1). These ratings probably represent the interests and values of the leader, which may not coincide with those of the members.

Data source (3): In contrast to the rating questions asking about "ideal," each participant in the leadership training program (most of them leaders in their own teams) rated each of their member coworkers in the intact home team on the following rating question:

In general, what kinds of values does this person show in his or her behavior? (OTP)

The data bank provided 1,662 profiles of this kind.

Data source (3) represents the perspective of the participant in a leadership training program who is evaluating or describing the *actual* behavior of others in the group with whom he or she works as the leader of the team. The leader's felt needs to influence the behavior and values of all the various individual other members potentially come to bear. The other members may be very different from each other. Possibly various members are quite far from the leader's ideal. Very likely some of them are in some degree of competition or conflict with each other, and perhaps with the leader. Possibly some needed roles in the group are not taken by any of the members. Factors like these would be expected to influence the ratings of members made by the leader of a group. These ratings probably represent reality problems the leader feels he or she has to deal with stemming from personalities of group members. These views may not agree with members' views of themselves or the importance of their real problems.

Although these ratings are presumably leader-biased, they represent a "dose of reality" for the constructor of any "optimum profile" as to what behavior and values may be expected to be shown in contrast to concepts of "ideal." This adjustment toward "reality" is important since the Optimum profile is the basis for a report to each rater in the group as to how his or her values may compare with a reasonable standard as to what may be actually both effective and attainable. "Optimum," then, is also meant to include criteria as to what is appropriate in a feedback situation for learning, teaching, and change. To present the *wish* profile, for example, as "a reasonable standard as to what may be actually both effective and attainable," does not seem "optimum."

Data source (4): Participants in a quite different series of leadership training courses were asked a rating question that probably taps a broad sample of kinds of work settings and leadership demands:

In general, what kinds of values does the *most effective leader* of a task-oriented team you have known show in his or her behavior? (MEL)

The data bank provided 567 profiles of this kind.

Data source (4) casts the net of possible Images the rater may consider more widely, probably, than any of the previous sources. The rating question asks for ratings of the "most effective leader of a task-oriented group" but adds the qualification that the rater must have actually *known* the person rated sometime in the past or present. This definition appears to make it probable that a wide variety of leaders, in many different groups and situations, possibly including some instances of unexpected effectiveness in particular dramatic and unusual cases, may be represented in the sample of Images that occur to raters.

It seems likely that these ratings may show up cases where effectiveness as actually witnessed is not seen to be so closely associated with behavior and values in the PF vector, as the previous chapter might have suggested. In fact, as we know from later data, the Image of "most effective leader" (MEL) for the large sample of 1000 is *low* in density for the Most Effective Teamwork Core (42.5 percent), *high* in the Liberal Teamwork Side (23.5 percent), and *high* in *both* the Group-centered Wing (3.5 percent) and the Authority-centered Wing (3.6 percent). There is also a whiff of an indication that perceived "most effective leadership" occasionally may be found popping up from the Individualistic Fringe (0.2 percent).

### Different Perspectives

Differences between the four source profiles used in computing the actual Optimum profile represent differences in values between persons in different positions and situations in the total interaction process.

Members rate leaders as to ideal effectiveness, and leaders rate themselves as to the values they feel make for the greatest effectiveness.

Members rate leaders as to ideal effectiveness, leaders rate members as to values actually shown in their behavior. This latter rating is the main correction of the "ideal" ratings to make the Optimum profile estimate more sensitive to "reality."

Members rate leaders in their own intact group as to ideal effectiveness, and members in another set of groups rate the most effective leader they have ever known. Inclusion of this profile (MEL) is an attempt to make the Optimum profile estimate more sensitive to the reality of ideological differences among members.

The MEL profile for the samples of 1000 is in fact *high* in *both* the Group-centered Wing and the Authority-centered Wing. This is also true for the Images MEM, EXP, OTP, and OTM. All of the Area Density Charts (not shown) appear to show and reflect considerable ideological diversity among the members. It may be that the ability of the leader to understand and show diversity in values, perhaps particularly with regard to the Liberal-versus-Conservative diversity of members, is important to "most effective leadership." Or it may be that timely swings of the leader to the right or left are occasionally spectacularly successful and memorable to members who see themselves to the right or the left.

The four data sources and perspectives of the rater samples described above amplify, moderate, modify, and correct each other in various ways. Ratings of both *ideal concepts* and perceptions of *actual persons* are represented. Both ratings of the *self* and ratings of *others* are represented. Both the interests or felt needs of those in the position of *group members*, or coworkers responsible to leadership, and the interests and felt needs of those in a position of *leadership* are represented. Both *present perceptions* and more distant *memories* are represented. A large number of different groups, different kinds of groups, and different group situations in business organizations are represented.

These comparisons do not exhaust all the comparisons that might be useful, of course, but it is clear that there are value differences between the ideal profiles and the actual profiles of group members that pose conflicts of values. The conflicts between persons in different roles and positions may be partially resolvable by additional information and attempts to understand each other, but I suspect that many conflicts are not.

The same SCG Optimum value profile is used to show up differences between all types of Images, such as *wish, self, expect, other, least effective member, current culture, future*, and so on (see the list of nineteen in Appendix B). Any attempt to formulate a single general-purpose "optimum value profile" will have to involve value judgments on the part of the formulator as to what Images to measure, whose values to measure, and how to reconcile the differences.

To cut the Gordian Knot in the present case I computed a separate Bargraph profile for each of the four sources described above. The frequencies shown for each of the twenty-six vectors on the four profiles were then added together and averaged. This procedure thus ignored the differences in the number of raters in each of the four sources, and weighted each type of source equally. The social processes by which such conflicts are dealt with in real life are more or less arbitrary, also: majority rule, mediation, compromise, arbitration, bargaining, splitting the difference, and similar procedures, sometimes including sheer domination.

The actual exercise or performance of "most effective" leadership, or "most effective" group membership, in general, surely involves taking into account a large number of different factors, and many different values and interests, as perceived by persons in many very different positions.

I have assumed that an adequately complete system of values, values that are involved in long-time survival of a group, and even in ordinary social interaction over short runs, are inevitably in conflict with each other to some degree, as well as in some degree of cooperation. If these assumptions are true, then the best that a group of any kind can do by way of realizing an ideal value system with regard to internal affairs is to achieve an estimated overall *balance of emphasis* (and perhaps temporary changes of emphasis for special situations). I have proposed a pragmatic, research-based balance of emphasis that appears to generate the fewest problems of value realization for the so-cial-interaction system as a whole, over some compromise between shorter and longer time effectiveness.

This mealy-mouthed attempt to define a "balance of emphasis" is still vague in spite of all the built-in complications, but it may avoid some of the para-doxes involved in the old formula of the "greatest good for the greatest num-ber" (see Kenneth Arrow 1951). At least it has the virtue that once a "most effective profile" is chosen, it specifies a profile of measurable numbers. Pro-files different from it can be compared with it, and specific differences can be focused on for discussion in particular cases. And since it is operationally based on underlying research operations, it is open to continued improve-ment by further research.

The SCG Optimum value profile is an empirically derived estimate on my part of the best balance of value emphasis that a group can achieve, based on the best evidence available to me at the time, and the most broadly based value judgments I was able to make, taking into account all the factors that I could. In application all observed profiles are compared to this standard, in order to detail their peculiar differences.

The standards specified by the SCG Optimum value profile are not impos-sibly high. Some groups and many individuals can and do achieve a system balance of value emphasis that averages out over time with a profile that matches very closely the rates the Optimum profile specifies. Many groups do not come close, but still manage to exist over considerable periods, al-though presumably at significant cost.

An important example of a non-optimum profile which nevertheless ap-pears to have had survival value in many organizations is the profile of Ameri-can business *current culture*. But it also seems clear that there are many costs imposed by the current culture in many business organizations, as seen by members, and as seen by many leaders, both within the organization and within the community and larger setting.

At best, so far as I can tell, the actual balance of values of the profile in all groups within shorter time spans tends to oscillate, waver, and drift in various ways, dependent upon many conditions, internal as well as external.

Although I am a strong advocate of trying to solve problems by persistent rational attempts based on the most complete information that can be brought to bear, with fervent hopes for creativity, I doubt that creative problem solv-ing, as a way of dealing with value conflicts, can solve all value conflicts, no matter how important or effective real creativity may be in particular short-run cases. Nor can the discovery or development of attractive or compelling "superordinate goals" resolve value conflicts, although this may help, par-ticularly in shorter time runs. Mediation, compromise, conciliation, arbitra-tion, even sometimes domination, are usually involved to some extent, often in a major way.

Thus, the so-called Optimum value profile does not represent a "fundamental solution" to all important value conflicts, nor does it represent an unfailing ethical guide. Rather, it represents what one may hope to have identified as a "most effective *balance*" of perceived value realization under representative average real conditions.

In the attempt to develop the most useful empirical normative profile for consulting use, a number of problems are involved to which there are probably no definitive answers. These include the way in which the sample data sources are chosen, the questions asked, the size of the samples, and the way in which the conflicting interests and values of the different sources are balanced against each other (in the case of the present MEP, simply by equal weighting of each source and averaging over the four data sources). These are all obviously important in the construction and possible revisions of the empirical normative profile, and there are no doubt many more. As the data base continues to grow and improve, and as theoretical insight improves, improvement of all of these components may be possible.

But it should also be recognized that the present profile has been used for six years in all kinds of situations, and it appears to be a remarkably useful set of numbers for detecting problems of members and the group as a whole in practice.

### The Normative Profile for the *Reject* Image

The *reject* rating question, typically used to gather relevant data for feedback in a particular setting, is worded as follows:

In general, what kinds of values do you tend to *reject*, either in yourself or others?

The Bargraph for 1000 observed *reject* Images (REJ) against the SCG normative *reject* value profile was shown earlier as figure 2.6.

When a newly observed *reject* Bargraph is shown against the SCG *reject* normative profile, an observed *high* means "especially rejected," and a *low* means "less rejected that one might expect." None of the observed frequencies of the new sample of 1000, shown as figure 2.6, deviates from the SCG normative *reject* profile enough to trip off a report text.

As a comment on test-retest reliability, it may be reported here that earlier work with samples of 200 of various Images indicates that repeat samples of 200 *reject* (and also *wish*) Images are apparently large enough to conform quite closely to the normative pattern expected. And also, it appears to me from pragmatic experience that the arbitrary trip points (+4 and -4 X-units, not adjusted for different N's) are set far enough out so as not to get tripped off very often by the random variations shown in samples of size 200, or even smaller.

The shape of the *reject* normative profile is essentially the mirror image of the shape of the SCG Optimum profile. It is empirically independently based, however, and not just a graphically produced reversal of the regular Optimum profile.

In figure 2.5 a newly observed sample of 1000 ratings of the *wish* Image are shown against the SCG Optimum value profile. Six of the value vectors have a *high* frequency (at least +4 X-units over the SCG Optimum value profile). It is worth looking up their content (see Appendix C) as an indicator of the kinds of values that are probably frustrated in many business organizations. The differences of the *wish* profile from the SCG Optimum are a sample indication that the SCG Optimum profile is a useful basis of comparison of Images. The *wishes* are different qualitatively from the Optimum in about the same way one might intuitively expect.

A number of special studies have shown that the correlations between the N = 26 profiles of average *wish* frequencies of endorsement and the corresponding N = 26 profiles of average *reject* frequencies are typically in the neighborhood of -.98. The *negative* correlations between the *self* ratings, which closely approximate the regular SCG Optimum value profile, and the *reject* normative profile frequencies are similarly very high.

These high negative correlations speak well for the validity of the meanings that the rating populations typically give to the individual value descriptors. The high correlations also tend to confirm the adequacy of the short three-interval frequency scale (0, 1, 2) used in making the ratings.

The high negative correlations between the profiles of *wish* ratings and the profiles of *reject* ratings are an indication of the strength of the polarizations in the minds of raters between the values which they approve and those which they disapprove. But it is equally important to note that none of the twenty-six values is without some degree of endorsement among some of the raters, as either descriptive of some other person's values or as preferred for the self.

There are rare cases where a value that is *wished for* or favored is also *especially rejected*. This paradox appears to be an important indicator of a value area that arouses "ambivalent" or conflicting feelings. Perhaps the conflict is an internal psychological dilemma that exists for many or most of the individual raters. Alternatively, the conflict may exist as an overt polarization between two cliques or subgroups within the rating population, each of which feels strongly and rates extremely.

There are also paradoxical cases where a given value is *low* on the *wish* profile but is less *rejected* than one might expect. One possibility for this kind of finding is that the value itself, or the wording of the item describing it, does not have much meaning for the rating population. This can be an important discovery for exploration in feedback to the raters.

### Ideology and the Normative Profile

By an "ideology" in this context I mean a concept of an "ideal" value system based on a limited set of values that appear to the rater to be logically consistent with each other and the belief that these values should be maximized at the cost of minimizing or suppressing all values that seem logically inconsistent with that set. Such an ideology tends to suppress the more factually normal frequencies of all logically inconsistent values in the eyes of the rater.

This kind of minimization of all conflicting values may be desirable and acceptable to the persons who hold the ideology, but it tends systematically to frustrate and offend others who do not share the ideology, and so to precipitate polarizations.

If an observed Bargraph is sufficiently influenced by an attempt of some number of members to conform to or enforce a particular ideology, or if the Bargraph frequencies are influenced by a distorting rigidity or narrowness of any kind, even an overconforming perfectionism in the exact PF direction, the final average location of the summary image on the Field Diagram will be drawn away from the center of the Most Effective Teamwork Core in some dissident direction, and very possibly far enough to fall into one of the other Areas.

Even the SCG Optimum profile, derived from many observed rating profiles as described above, implies that disagreement, and various kinds of negative and nonconforming behavior, in appropriate frequencies are desirable, necessary, or inevitable to "most effective" performance as the raters see it, at least for them as individuals, if not for all members of the group.

One may suppose that some of these negative and nonconforming behaviors may be considered to be *indirectly* instrumental in reaching goals individuals consider most effective. For example, perhaps disagreement may lead to the examination of more alternatives and so contribute to the realism of decisions. Irving Janis in his studies of poor group decisions as a result of "group think," recommends including a devil's advocate in the group as a way to help guard against unrealistic conformity (Janis 1972). Various values in the N or B areas may have their uses. Nonconformity to outworn norms may actually lead to an increase in effectiveness. Some behaviors may be unavoidable, given the nature of the characteristics and needs of real people in the circumstances of the real world.

One way of looking at the reasons for endorsement of the values in the N and B directions may be to adopt a resigned acceptance of imperfections that are mostly those of individuals. A second look at the actual content of these values gives more substantial and persuasive reasons. All one needs to do, I think, is to read the descriptions of the values coded UNB, UB, UPB, NB, B, PB, DNB, DB, and DPB with an open mind in order to realize that expression of these values at certain times, in certain circumstances, certain proportions and combinations with other values, may be necessary to the vital metabolism and even survival of groups, organizations, and societies. (Thomas

Jefferson in a famous statement in favor of revolution at the time of the French Revolution made essentially this argument.)

These considerations are important unless one can assume that a number of implausible assumptions are true, such as these: authority is always right; goals are always wisely chosen and should never be changed; one should never pause to recover from work; the situation facing the group never changes; the majority is always right; creativity is never needed; nobody needs friends; and so on. There are certainly conditions in group life that justify some legitimate frequency of showing the values in the N and B portions of the space.

I believe one may go so far as to say that if the values shown in the N and B portions of the space are shown at frequencies significantly *below* the optimum shown on the Optimum profile, these low frequencies may allow, over a longer time in system life, the accumulation and growth of damaging problems that are left unnoticed and uncorrected. Ideological suppression of these values may ultimately be more damaging than the immediate drag of their expression on movement in the PF direction. Surely this must be the rationale for ambivalently regarded norms in favor of free speech and other similar disputed freedoms in the U.S. constitution. But these considerations can hardly settle the problems of "how much is optimum."

*Maximal* movement in the PF direction is presented as a desirable goal by some theories of leadership training, for example, in the theory of Blake and Mouton's Managerial Grid (1964). According to my reasoning and the implications of the present theory, the attempt to achieve *maximal* movement even further in the optimal PF direction than the MEP center point of the vector can have undesirable effects by encouraging the undue and unrealistic suppression of all logically inconsistent values.

I once had an old professor in political science, called "Stiffy" Barnett. He dressed in black and wore a shoestring bow tie. He used to insist that anything carried to an extreme was dangerous. Every morning he would begin by pulling a newspaper clipping out of a shoe box, reading it, and then commenting. One morning the clipping was about an old man who spent all of his time after retirement in a rocking chair on the back porch reading the Bible. He rocked off the porch and broke his neck.

The SCG Optimum profile is not unrealistically "ideological" even in the PF direction. The values that are in the *rejected* direction for most of the raters are represented in low frequencies on the profile, but the values of low frequency are still included as part of the total picture. The Optimum profile allows for the expression of all the twenty-six values on the profile to some degree. If its value averages do represent an "optimum balance" of conflicting values, its optimum character is not based on a literal logical or ideological consistency. If it is consistent, it is consistent at a more abstract level of long-time workability and consistency with survival of the total system.

The MEP average over all twenty-six conflicting and supporting values on the Field Diagram falls almost exactly between the conservative and the liberal sides of the general population in business organizations. This is still a bit of a puzzle. It should be clearly realized, however, that the neat and precise location of the final MEP image circle, directly between the two reference Vectors P and F, is not an indication of perfect consensus in substance among raters as to what is "most effective" for teamwork—it is an average location in a trinomial normal distribution that happens to exactly balance the vector strengths toward the two sides, F and P, of a chronic conflict of values.

### Use of the Normative Profile in Practical Application

The SCG Optimum profile is used as a tentative benchmark of "expectations" against which "observed" profiles of specific persons and groups can be compared. Experience indicates that if the observed profile is from a task-oriented group of the sort found in business organizations, deviations from it may be taken seriously as signs that something non-optimal but possibly avoidable is affecting the process, and the ratings of the members are reflecting the unusual problem.

The discovery of deviations from the Optimum profile in a given group is likely to have different, probably controversial, meanings and implications for persons in different parts of the group. But it is my experience and belief that the rewards of discussion and analysis aimed at determining the sources of the deviations are generally well worth the risk of conflict.

Deviations may be the beginning signs of dynamic processes which may escalate or amplify without warning, or, on the other hand, they may indicate potential escalations that can be damped or neutralized without great difficulty by appropriate action. Deviations should be thoughtfully reevaluated as to their appropriateness given the situation in its totality, their present costs and benefits, their probable longer term amplification or diminution, and their probable side effects.

While the current (1990) SCG Optimum value profile is firmly based empirically, and appears to work extremely well for practical purposes as an indicator of the directions of change from an unbalanced observed profile that will probably improve group operation if they can be made, it should be recognized that it is an average picture. The statement of the average, of course, articulates only part of what should be taken into account in actual use. Circumstances may alter cases. The appropriateness of the value frequencies specified on the Optimum profile should always be recognized as a tentative estimate, a beginning basis for discussion.

Here are some examples of ways in which the normative profile may not quite fit specific cases in which one may want to use it. Some of the items may be worded in a way that is too extreme, too unpopular or too popular, in the particular setting, to measure quite in the way intended. The normal frequencies may not be quite appropriate for extreme or unusual situations. The ratings may underrepresent or overrepresent some common human failings and needs of actual individuals in the actual group. Over-stressed task groups and individuals may be overrepresented (or underrepresented). Short-time emergency situations may be underrepresented, and normal long-time situations may be overrepresented, or vice-versa.

Leaders and groups in a "performance" phase, as compared to a "learning" phase, may be overrepresented. Leaders and groups in a "learning" phase are undoubtedly underrepresented. It may well be that the goals and conditions appropriate to "learning" are different enough from those appropriate to "performance" so that it would be preferable to develop a profile that would be optimum for group processes devoted specifically to learning of various types.

Female raters may be underrepresented for some situations of use, and so may be female leaders. Members who are not leaders may be underrepresented. Members of particular races, or ethnic origin, or region, or particular location in the society, and so on, may not be adequately represented, or may be overrepresented. Raters who have a strong need to excel or achieve may be overrepresented (most of the raters whose data were used as sources for the normative profile were themselves leaders who had chosen to come to the training program; however, possibly others were "sent" for reasons that we have not been able to take into account). Certain levels in the organization may be overrepresented (such as middle-level managers) while other levels are underrepresented.

The Optimum profile should be interpreted in such a way that in practice appropriate allowances may be made, or at least discussed, for these and other sources of differences in ratings. Its central purpose in use is to raise appropriate questions for discussion in feedback.

# 11

# Reprise

The need for field theory as a basic perspective and an integrative frame of reference in social psychology is far from dead. The basic idea of field theory was important in social psychology long before Lewin's version, and it is still important. It is the recognition that any given psychological process or piece of overt behavior always takes place in a larger context of other psychological and behavioral processes (Dewey 1898). I think it may be better in our case to call this larger context the social-interaction system, rather than a field. The field we can specifically measure and construct is only a window into the dynamics of the total system. It is still the case, however, that the constellation of images on a Field Diagram, or in some similar graphic window, is necessary for optimum comprehension.

Psychological and behavioral processes (if they take place within some constraining boundary so that the effects of action at a given time are contained and returned as feedback) tend to constitute a system, or, in alternative language, an interactive gestalt. The parts influence each other systematically and recursively in such a way that some inclusive, relatively simple and often powerful pattern of unification and polarization of elements emerges through a kind of continuing "dynamic organizing and reorganizing process."

There is a pervasive theoretical need to be able to take this contextual interactive gestalt into account. In social psychology, I suggest, the most relevant interactive gestalt is what I call the real, intact, social-interaction system. Measurement of the gestalt of values is probably the most economical means of cognitive access to what is going on in the system as a whole at a given time. And its condition at a given time may be portrayed in the disposition of elements in a Field Diagram.

But the disposition of particular elements in a Field Diagram at any given time is only sufficiently understandable for the support of rational action if it is recognized to be only the temporarily more visible state of a more complex underlying real social-interaction system. The more complex underlying real system needs to be understood and taken into account realistically, so far as one can. Part of the importance of understanding the nature of that system is that actions taken under strong pressures of the presently active and visible field may ignore other aspects of the system and this, in time, may give rise to otherwise unanticipated and undesirable consequences.

It is important to recognize that, in most cases, the problems and values that will later come into prominence when those unanticipated consequences appear are typically already present and dynamically operating in various degrees and various shapes, although in weaker and more uncoordinated ways. They are present in the form of implicit awareness and the conflicted "conscience" and suppressed values of the present participants, sometimes in the ineffective protests of minorities, or in the alienated opinions of silent members, and in the rising and falling rates of other important index variables of system operation.

These unseen or unnoticed elements are in fact parts of the present real dynamic field, even if they are not overt and visible. The probable nature and effects of these elements representing unanticipated consequences are only likely to be anticipated in any degree of detail if one understands the more regular features of the generalized social-interaction system as a whole over time, and if one is able to take into account the effects of individual personality differences.

The reason for serious individual personality and value differences, basically, is that all of the participants have acquired the beginning differentiated shapes of their value systems and their behavioral repertoires of preferred and avoided roles in their earlier socialization and development. This development has taken place in the context of their earlier roles and experiences in social systems, families, and other primary groups that were all variations, though sometimes seriously deviant variations, of the general, more optimum model. For better or for worse, families and play groups are social-interaction systems, and unavoidably they are systemically compelled to become differentiated.

Perhaps the most stunning recent demonstration of this system tendency toward differentiation in real, historically well-documented family contexts is the study entitled *Born to Rebel* by Frank Sulloway (1997), a historian of science. He has discovered that the eldest sons of famous scientists, that is, those who also become scientists, tend overwhelmingly to follow conservatively in their father's footsteps as to their scientific theory, while later-born sons, if they become scientists, tend overwhelmingly to take a rebellious, radical point of view. The implication is that the preferred role, that of the good son, has been preemptively taken by the eldest, and the most attractive remaining role is that of rebellion against the father's and elder brother's conservative position. Unification of a conventional existing subsystem of father and elder son tends to provoke the polarization toward radical resistance on the part of later-born sons.

There have been attempts in the past to define more adequately the elements in the "situation," for example, in the area of research called "person-situation interaction" (Magnussen and Endler 1977; Solomon 1981). These were moves in the right direction. But so far as I can tell, this approach has not made a major difference in the overall integration of social psychology. These attempts were not comprehensive enough in their measurement of the many variables in recursive relationships in the way that is made possible by a more mature systems theory.

At about the same time as the person-interaction emphasis, there was the beginning of a convergence between some anthropological researchers working in the area of human relations in organizations, on the one hand, and researchers in the areas of ethnology and neurophysiology on the other (Richardson 1978). The basic idea underlying this hoped-for convergence was the assumption that, in the long process of evolution, an intimate interactive linkage has been established between overt, nonverbal, social-interactional aspects of behavior (involvement in the situation) and the emotional, neurophysiological processes in the limbic system of the brain. This again, I feel, was a move in the right direction. But mainstream social-psychological theory seems not to have been much affected.

Only very recently (fall of 1996), the recipient of the Cooley-Mead Award of the Social Psychological Section of the American Sociological Society, Melvin Seeman, took as the subject of his address "The Elusive Situation" and suggested that it is time for sociological social psychologists to turn their attention to the "systematic analysis of social situations."

"Micro Social Orders" is a theme of the 1998 meetings of the social-psychology section of the American Sociological Association. Edward Lawler, the chairman, writes:

> This is a broad theme that crosscuts virtually all of the theoretical traditions of sociological social psychology, captured by questions such as: How are "stable" or "persistent" or "recurrent" patterns of interaction created, reproduced, or sustained in or by social relationships and groups? The development and maintenance of "micro social orders" is a central problem of sociological social psychology, and also a problem that relates social psychology to fundamental issues of the larger discipline. (Quoted from Newsletter of the Section, fall 1997)

The need for a systems theory is not new. It is pervasive. It will not go away. But up until now, I suggest, something has been missing, persistently missing. The problem has been not so much one of recognizing the need for a systems theory. For mainstream social psychology as a whole, the problem has always been, and still is, how to get an overall grasp of the many interacting variables involved; how to measure them and put the information together; how to get a set of manageable handles on a very complex globally interactive process; and how to best intervene to bring about changes in real systems.

It is not possible to get out of the atomistic one-thing-at-a-time approach without a more complex higher-order theory of the relationships of the most crucial of the many variables involved and the reasons for their entailment and entrainment that can be comprehensively grasped and tested. We need a theory of the overall dimensions of differentiation and dynamic tendencies of the global social-interactive process in order to place the correlations within an understandable relationship to each other. We need to be able to see how the pieces fit together, how they are likely to reinforce and contravene each other, how they are all parts of a moving dynamic system with built-in conflicts and potentials of resonant reinforcement and amplification.

It has been the inability to approach problems like these comprehensively, and in widely varying real field contexts, I believe, that is primarily responsible for the pervasive complaints that social psychology lacks integration, and that its experimental findings lack ecological validity (Rosnow 1981).

I believe that the most important missing element has been the ability to recognize and sample a strategic representative system of values in the system under study, to measure the values in their system context, and to understand the relationships of values to each other and to the other behavioral processes they most strongly influence.

I submit that we have the beginnings of a new systemic field theory in social psychology. The overall dimensions of the dynamic field define the space of possibilities within which currently active real fields assume specific patterns. Systemically produced kinds of value conflicts and problems in social relationships define the nature of various types of system fields that form in the space under various conditions, and suggest how they are most likely to alter under the influences of most effective attempts at leadership.

# Appendices

# Appendix A

# The Intercorrelation Space

## Vector Description Titles

Main titles of the vectors, **Vector Description Titles**, are from Bales's original analysis in *Personality and Interpersonal Behavior* (Bales 1970, chapters 10–35).

**Behavior Rating Item** is the description rated at the behavioral level (Bales and Cohen 1979, p. 21).

**Values Rating Item** is the vector description from Bales's IOVAL rating form (copyrighted 1983). IOVAL items were copyrighted 1996 by the SYMLOG Consulting Group. Commercial use is not permitted. For research use, apply for permission.

## Correlated Variables

**Highly Correlated Personality Tests, Highly Correlated Observed Behaviors, and Correlated Ratings and Guesses** show items most highly correlated with each of the twenty-six vectors in the three-dimensional scale space. A study by Couch and Bales of sixty males in twelve groups of five members, meeting five times, provided the data. The group members were given personality tests and observed using the categories for *Interaction Process Analysis* (IPA) (Bales 1950) and Value Content Analysis (VCA) (Kassebaum 1958).

**Generalizations from Markers** are estimated or hypothetical, obtained by inferential interpolation from the high correlations with the VCA factors which were found in direct observation.

*Value Profile* **Items** that are highly correlated with the vector were interpolated by Bales into the observed social interaction space of the group study from their location in the Bales and Couch *Value Profile* scale analysis (1969).

Gene Kassebaum, the observer for value statements used an observation form called Value Content Analysis, containing as categories the names of the four scales of Bales and Couch's scale analysis of the preceding Value Profile study. The who-to-whom directions of the value statements were simultaneously scored. Thus the evidence for location of the Initiation and Reception of each type of value statement is *direct* and observationally based for the location in the intercorrelation space of value statements identified specifically with Vectors UNF, UNB, P, and N, both as to acts Initiated and as to acts Received.

From these locations, called **Markers,** Bales then made inferential interpolations of all individual items of the 144-item Value Profile study into the present system-field intercorrelation space. These interpolations were based on careful content analysis and on the locations of individual items between the orthogonal scales of Bales and Couch's scale analysis of 144 items of the Value Profile.

## 1  VECTOR U: *TOWARD MATERIAL SUCCESS AND POWER*

| | |
|---|---|
| **Behavior Rating Item** | Active, dominant, talks a lot |
| **Values Rating Item** | Individual financial success, personal prominence and power |
| **Highly Correlated Personality Tests** | Thurstone's Temperament scale called *Active*<br>Cattell's 16 PF scale called *Adventurous*<br>Thurstone's Temperament scale called *Dominant* |
| **Highly Correlated Observed Behaviors** | IPA Matrix *Total Initiated*<br>IPA Matrix *Sum Received from Others*<br>IPA Matrix *Sum Initiated to Others* |
| **Correlated Ratings and Guesses** | External observers rate him high on *Self-confidence*<br>Rates self high on *Self-confidence*<br>Guesses that others will rate him high on *Self-confidence*<br>Rates self high as *Valuable for a Logical Task*<br>Rates others high on being *Warm and Personal* |
| **Generalizations from Markers** | Initiates value statements advocating *Material Success and Power*<br>Receives value statements advocating *Material Success and Power*<br>Agrees with others who make value statements advocating *Material Success and Power* |
| *Value Profile* **Items** | He has achieved success who has lived well, laughed often, and loved much.<br>Our modern industrial and scientific developments are signs of a greater degree of success than that attained by any previous society.<br>The past is dead, there are new worlds to conquer, the world belongs to the future. |

## 2  VECTOR UP: *TOWARD SOCIAL SUCCESS*

| | |
|---|---|
| **Behavior Rating Item** | Extroverted, outgoing, positive |
| **Values Rating Item** | Popularity and social success, being liked and admired |
| **Highly Correlated Personality Tests** | MMPI scale called *Dominance*<br>Couch's scale called *Emotionality, Extrovertive*<br>MMPI scale called *Leadership*<br>Couch's scale on *Agreement Response Set* (tendency to agree regardless of content) |
| **Highly Correlated Observed Behaviors** | Initiating IPA category *Asks for Information*<br>Receiving IPA category *Gives Suggestion* |
| **Correlated Ratings and Guesses** | External observers rate him high on *Personal Involvement*<br>Group members rate him high on *Personal Involvement*<br>Rates self high on *Personal Involvement*<br>Guesses that other members will rate him high on *Personal Involvement*<br>Rates self high on *Interest in the Task*<br>Guesses that others will rate him high on *Interest in the Task* |

Group members rate him high on being *Valuable for a Logical Task*

Guesses that others will rate him high on *Valuable for a Logical Task*

Rates self as *Warm and Personal*

| | |
|---|---|
| **Generalizations from Markers** | Receives value statements in favor of *Tough-minded Assertiveness* (from others who are probably defending their own opposing values) |
| *Value Profile* **Items** | (none) |

## 3 VECTOR UPF: *TOWARD SOCIAL SOLIDARITY AND PROGRESS*

| | |
|---|---|
| **Behavior Rating Item** | A purposeful, democratic task leader |
| **Values Rating Item** | Active teamwork toward common goals, organizational unity |
| **Highly Correlated Personality Tests** | Cattell's 16 PF scale called *Warm* (possibly better called *Sociable*) |
| **Highly Correlated Observed Behaviors** | (none) |
| **Correlated Ratings and Guesses** | Rates other members high on arousing his feelings of *Liking*<br>External observers rate him high on *Interest in the Task*<br>Group members rate him high on *Interest in the Task*<br>External observers rate him high as *Valuable for a Logical Task* |
| **Generalizations from Markers** | Initiates value statements advocating *Social Solidarity and Progress*<br>Agrees with value statements addressed to him by others advocating *Social Solidarity and Progress*<br>Receives value statements in favor of *Rugged Individualism and Gratification* (from others who are probably defending their own opposing values) (directly observed marker) |
| *Value Profile* **Items** | A good group is democratic—the members should talk things over and decide unanimously what should be done. |

## 4 VECTOR UF: *TOWARD GROUP LOYALTY AND COOPERATION*

| | |
|---|---|
| **Behavior Rating Item** | An assertive, business-like manager |
| **Values Rating Item** | Efficiency, strong impartial management |
| **Highly Correlated Personality Tests** | Cattell's 16 PF scale called *Sophistication* (also called *Polished*) |
| **Highly Correlated Observed Behaviors** | Initiating IPA category *Gives Suggestion* |
| **Correlated Ratings and Guesses** | Makes others feel he rates them high on *Individualism* |
| **Generalizations from Markers** | Initiates value statements advocating *Group Loyalty and Cooperation*<br>Receives value statements in favor of *Value Relativ-* |

*ism and Expression* (from others who are probably defending their own opposing values)

*Value Profile* Items

Good group members should accept criticisms of their points of view without argument, in order to preserve a harmonious group.

Racial discrimination should be made a criminal offense which is punishable by a stiff jail sentence.

An individual finds himself in merging with a social group, joining with others in resolute and determined activity for the realization of social goals.

There is a plan to life, which works to keep all living things moving together, and a man should learn to live his whole life in harmony with that plan.

When we live in the proper way—stay in harmony with the forces of nature and keep all that we have in good condition, then all will go along well in the world.

A group cannot get their job done without voluntary cooperation from everybody.

There is no satisfaction in any good without a companion.

## 5  VECTOR UNF: *TOWARD AUTOCRATIC AUTHORITY*

**Behavior Rating Item**   Authoritarian, controlling, disapproving

**Values Rating Item**   Active reinforcement of authority, rules, and regulations

**Highly Correlated Personality Tests**   Slater's scale on *Inhibitory Demands and Discipline* (subject describes his parents)
MMPI scale called *Prejudice*

**Highly Correlated Observed Behaviors**   Receiving IPA category *Seems Unfriendly*
Receiving IPA category *Disagrees* (receives Disagreement)

**Correlated Ratings and Guesses**   Other members are high on rating him as tending to *Arouse Their Dislike*

**Generalizations from Markers**   Initiates value statements (regardless of particular content) (directly observed marker)

Receives value statements (regardless of particular content) (directly observed marker)

Initiates value statements advocating *Autocratic Authority* (directly observed marker)

Receives value statements in favor of *Emotional Supportiveness and Warmth* (from others who are probably defending their own opposing values)

Receives value statements in favor of *Equalitarianism* (from others who are probably defending their own observed values) (directly observed marker)

Receives value statements in favor of *Individualistic Isolationism* (from others who are probably defending their own opposing values) (directly observed marker)

Receives value statements in favor of *Permissive Liberalism* (from others who are probably defending their own opposing values)

Receives value statements in favor of *Rejection of Social Solidarity* (from others who are probably defending their own opposing values)

**Value Profile** Items    (Many of these items are from the *F Scale* and derivatives.)

An insult to our honor should always be punished.

In most groups it is better to choose somebody to take charge and run things, and then hold him responsible, even if he does some things the members do not like.

In general, full economic security is bad; most men would not work if they did not need the money for eating and living.

Leaders of lynchings should be given the same cruel treatment they give their victims.

The immigration of foreigners should be kept down so that we can provide for our own citizens first.

Familiarity breeds contempt.

A well-raised child is one who does not have to be told twice to do something.

Disobeying an order is one thing you cannot excuse—if one can get away with disobedience, why cannot everybody?

The facts on crime and sexual immorality show that we will have to crack down harder on young people if we are going to save our moral standards.

When you have made a threat you should be prepared to carry it out, and you should not make an exception because it applies to your friends.

No sane, normal, decent person could ever think of hurting a close friend or relative.

No weakness or difficulty can hold us back if we have enough will power.

Character and honesty will tell in the long run; most people get pretty much what they deserve.

A person who has bad manners, bad habits, and bad breeding can hardly expect to get along with decent people.

There is hardly anything lower than a person who does not feel great love, gratitude, and respect for his parents.

Human nature being what it is, there will always be war and conflict.

Friendship should go just so far in working relationships.

What youth needs most is strict discipline, rugged determination, and the will to work and fight for family and country.

There should be a definite hierarchy in an organization, with definite duties for everybody.

In any organization if you lay down a rule, it must be obeyed and enforced.

Depressions are like headaches and stomachaches, it

is natural for even the healthiest society to have them once in a while.

Most people do not realize how much our lives are controlled by plots hatched in secret places.

Patriotism and loyalty are the first and most important requirements of a good citizen.

Art ought to show the world of nature in a natural realistic way, not in some distorted imaginary way.

What this country needs most, more than laws and political programs, is a few courageous, tireless, devoted leaders, in whom the people can put their faith.

A man must make his own decisions, uninfluenced by the opinion of others.

It is only right for a person to feel that his country or religion is better than any other.

Any red-blooded American will fight to defend his property.

Obedience and respect for authority are the most important virtues children should learn.

The higher type of man makes a sense of duty the groundwork of his character.

Young people sometimes get rebellious ideas, but as they grow up, they get over them and settle down.

Every person has a set time to live, and when his time comes to die, there is nothing he can do about it.

You have to respect authority and when you stop respecting authority, your situation is not worth much.

When a person has a problem or a worry, it is best for him not to think about it, but to keep busy with more cheerful things.

Most of our problems would be solved if we could get rid of the immoral, crooked, and feebleminded people.

A good group has to limit the participation of critics who hamper action.

In art, music, and literature there is too much eccentric, exotic, Bohemian stuff being produced at the present time.

A child should not be allowed to talk back to his parents, or else he will lose respect for them.

There is no better guide to success than the lives of the great men of history.

If people would talk less and work more, everybody would be better off.

The worst danger to real Americanism during the past fifty years has come from foreign ideas and agitators.

It is useless to quarrel with destiny.

A person should let himself be molded by the great silent purposes of the universe which silently and irresistibly achieve their goal.

Inherited racial characteristics have more real
importance in shaping the individual and nation
than most people are ready to admit.

## 6    VECTOR UN: *TOWARD TOUGH-MINDED ASSERTIVENESS*

| | |
|---|---|
| **Behavior Rating Item** | Domineering, tough-minded, powerful |
| **Values Rating Item** | Tough-minded, self-oriented assertiveness |
| **Highly Correlated Personality Tests** | Thurstone's temperament scale called *Active* |
| | MMPI scale called *Hypochondriasis* |
| | MMPI scale called *Hysteria* |
| | MMPI scale called *Manic* |
| | MMPI scale called *Psychopathic* |
| | MMPI scale called *Schizophrenic* |
| **Highly Correlated Observed Behaviors** | (none) |
| **Correlated Ratings and Guesses** | Makes others feel he rates them high on *Arousing* (his) *Dislike* |
| | Group members rate him high on *Self-confidence* |
| | External observers rate him high on *Domination* |
| | Group members rate him high on *Domination* |
| | Rates self high on *Domination* |
| | Rates self high on *Resentful* |
| **Generalizations from Markers** | Initiates value statements advocating *Tough-minded Assertiveness* |
| | Agrees with others who advocate *Tough-minded Assertiveness* |
| | Agrees with others who advocate *Individual Isolationism* (directly observed) |
| | Receives value statements in favor of *Social Success* (from others who are probably defending their own opposing values) |
| *Value Profile* **Items** | Man's future depends primarily upon the technical advances made by scientific knowledge. |
| | A rich life requires constant activity, the use of muscles, and openness to adventure. |
| | The most important function of modern leaders is to bring about the accomplishment of practical goals. |
| | The real appeal of love is in its sense of challenge, danger, and adventure. |
| | Not in cautious foresight nor in relaxed ease does life attain completion, but in outward energetic action, the excitement of power in the present moment. |
| | The most important function of education is its preparation for practical achievement and financial reward. |
| | The most important qualities of a real man are determination and driving ambition. |
| | The greatest satisfaction in life is a feeling of the actuality of the present, of tireless activity, movement, and doing. |

7  VECTOR UNB: *TOWARD RUGGED INDIVIDUALISM AND GRATIFICATION*

| | |
|---|---|
| **Behavior Rating Item** | Provocative, egocentric, shows off |
| **Values Rating Item** | Rugged, self-oriented individualism, resistance to authority |
| **Highly Correlated Personality Tests** | Cattell's 16 PF scale called *Eccentric*<br>MMPI scale called *Impulsivity*<br>Cattell's 16 PF scale called *Nervous Tension*<br>MMPI scale called *Paranoid* |
| **Highly Correlated Observed Behaviors** | Receiving IPA category *Shows Tension* |
| **Correlated Ratings and Guesses** | External observers rate him high on favoring *Expression and Gratification*<br>Group members rate him high on favoring *Expression and Gratification*<br>Group members rate him high on *Entertaining*<br>Group members rate him high on *Arousing Their Curiosity*<br>Guesses that others will rate him high on *Domination* |
| **Generalizations from Markers** | Initiates value statements advocating *Rugged Individualism and Gratification* (directly observed marker)<br>Agrees with value statements by others advocating *Rugged Individualism and Gratification* (directly observed)<br>Agrees with value statements of others advocating *Rejection of Conservative Group Beliefs*<br>Receives value statements in favor of *Social Solidarity and Progress* (from others who are probably defending their own opposing values)<br>Receives value statements in favor of *Value-Determined Restraint* (from others who are probably defending their own opposing values)<br>Receives value statements in favor of *Altruistic Love* (from others who are probably defending their own opposing values) |
| *Value Profile* **Items** | Every normal man must be tempted, at times, to spit on his hands, raise the black flag, and begin slitting throats.<br>The past is no more, the future may never be, the present is all that we can be sure of.<br>Love action, and care little that others may think you rash.<br>Let us eat, drink, and be merry, for tomorrow we die.<br>The greatest fortunes are for those who leave the common path and blaze a trail for themselves.<br>Life is something to be enjoyed to the full, sensuously, with relish and enthusiasm.<br>Whoever would be a man, must be a nonconformist.<br>A person should always be master of his own fate. |

A man can learn better by striking out boldly on his own than he can by following the advice of others.

To be superior a man must stand alone.

Since there are no values that can be eternal, the only real values are those which meet the needs of the given moment.

Nothing is static, nothing is everlasting; at any moment one must be ready to meet the change in environment by a necessary change in one's moral views.

## 8  VECTOR UB: *TOWARD VALUE RELATIVISM AND EXPRESSION*

| | |
|---|---|
| **Behavior Rating Item** | Jokes around, expressive, dramatic |
| **Values Rating Item** | Having a good time, releasing tension, relaxing control |
| **Highly Correlated Personality Tests** | Cattell's 16 PF scale called *Dominance*<br>Cattell's 16 PF scale called *Extrovertive* |
| **Highly Correlated Observed Behaviors** | Initiating IPA category *Dramatizes or Jokes* |
| **Correlated Ratings and Guesses** | Makes other group members feel he rates them high on *Equalitarian*<br>Makes other group members feel he rates them high on *Acceptance of Authority*<br>Rates self high on *Entertaining*<br>External observers rate him high on *Extroversion*<br>Group members rate him high on *Extroversion*<br>Rates self high on *Extroversion* |
| **Generalizations from Markers** | Initiates value statements advocating *Value Relativism and Expression*<br>Agrees with others who initiate value statements advocating *Value Relativism and Expression*<br>Receives value statements in favor of *Group Loyalty and Cooperation* (from others who are probably defending their own opposing values) |
| *Value Profile* **Items** | The solution to almost any human problem should be based on the situation at the time, not on some general moral rule.<br>Society should be quicker to adopt new customs and to throw aside mere traditions and old-fashioned habits.<br>No scheme for living proposed by various religions and moralities is entirely suitable for every purpose, yet each scheme can offer something for everyone, one should use all of them, and no one alone.<br>Life is more a festival than a workshop for moral discipline.<br>There is no human desire so mean that it does not deserve expression and gratification.<br>No man ever improved his impulses by refusing to express them. |

**9  VECTOR UPB:** *TOWARD EMOTIONAL SUPPORTIVENESS AND WARMTH*

| | |
|---|---|
| **Behavior Rating Item** | Entertaining, sociable, smiling, warm |
| **Values Rating Item** | Protecting less able members, providing help when needed |
| **Highly Correlated Personality Tests** | Slater's scale of values on *Emotional Supportiveness and Warmth* (subject describes parents) <br> MMPI scale called *Spontaneity* |
| **Highly Correlated Observed Behaviors** | (none) |
| **Correlated Ratings and Guesses** | Group members rate him high on *Entertaining* <br> He rates others high on *Entertaining* <br> External observers rate him high on *Arousing Their Liking* <br> External observers rate him high on being *Warm and Personal* <br> Rates self high on being *Warm and Personal* |
| **Generalizations from Markers** | Initiates value statements advocating *Emotional Supportiveness and Warmth* <br> Agrees with others who initiate value statements in favor of *Emotional Supportiveness and Warmth* <br> Receives value statements in favor of *Autocratic Authority* (from others who are probably defending their own opposing values) (directly observed marker) |
| ***Value Profile* Items** | (none) |

**10 VECTOR P:** *TOWARD EQUALITARIANISM*

| | |
|---|---|
| **Behavior Rating Item** | Friendly, equalitarian |
| **Values Rating Item** | Equality, democratic participation in decision making |
| **Highly Correlated Personality Tests** | MMPI scale called *Ego Strength* <br> MMPI scale called *Intellectual Efficiency* |
| **Highly Correlated Observed Behaviors** | Initiating IPA category *Seems Friendly* <br> Initiating IPA category *Asks for Opinion* <br> Receiving IPA category *Gives Information* |
| **Correlated Ratings and Guesses** | External observers rate him high on *Arousing Their Admiration* <br> Guesses that others will rate him high on *Arousing Their Admiration* <br> Rates others high on *Entertaining* <br> Guesses that others will rate him high on *Arousing Their Liking* <br> Rates others high on *Valuable for a Logical Task* <br> Generalizations from Markers <br> Initiates value statements advocating *Equalitarianism* (directly observed marker) |
| ***Value Profile* Items** | There should be equality for everyone—because we are all human beings. <br> A group of equals will work a lot better than a group with a rigid hierarchy. |

Each one should get what he needs—the things we
have belong to all of us.

There has been too much talk and not enough real
action in doing away with racial discrimination.

It is the duty of every good citizen to correct anti-
minority remarks made in his presence.

In any group it is more important to keep a friendly
atmosphere than to be efficient.

In a small group there should be no real leaders—
everybody should have an equal say.

The only true prosperity of the nation as a whole must
be based on the prosperity of the working class.

Poverty could be almost entirely done away with if
we made certain basic changes in our social and
economic system.

Everybody should have an equal chance and an equal
say.

No matter what the circumstances, one should never
arbitrarily tell people what to do.

## 11 VECTOR PF: *TOWARD ALTRUISTIC LOVE*

**Behavior Rating Item**   Works cooperatively with others

**Values Rating Item**   Responsible idealism, collaborative work

**Highly Correlated**   Couch's scale called *Authoritarian Conformity*
**Personality Tests**   Cattell's 16 PF scale called *Conscientious* (also called
*Persistent*)
Bales's hypothetical orthogonal addition to Slater's
scale *Optimistic Idealism* (subject describes
parents)
MMPI scale called *Role Playing Ability*

**Highly Correlated**   Initiating IPA category *Agrees*
**Observed Behaviors**   Receiving IPA category *Gives Opinion*
Correlated Ratings and Guesses
Rates others high on *Arousing Admiration*

**Generalizations**   Initiates value statements advocating *Altruistic Love*
**from Markers**   Agrees with value statements by others advocating
*Autocratic Authority* (directly observed marker)
Agrees with value statements by others advocating
*Group Loyalty and Cooperation*
Agrees with value statements by others advocating
*Value-Determined Restraint*

*Value Profile* **Items**   We are all born to love—it is the principle of
existence and its only true end.
It is sympathetic love among persons which alone
gives significance to life.

## 12 VECTOR F: *TOWARD CONSERVATIVE GROUP BELIEFS*

**Behavior Rating Item**   Analytical, task-oriented, problem-solving

**Values Rating Item**   Conservative, established, "correct" ways of doing
things

| | |
|---|---|
| **Highly Correlated Personality Tests** | (none) |
| **Highly Correlated Observed Behaviors** | Receiving IPA category from others *Asks for Suggestion* <br> Initiating IPA category *Gives Opinion* <br> Receiving IPA category from others *Agrees* |
| **Correlated Ratings and Guesses** | Rates others high on *Arousing His Curiosity* <br> Group members rate him high as tending to *Arouse Their Curiosity* |
| **Generalizations from Markers** | Initiates value statements to others advocating *Conservative Group Beliefs* <br> Receives value statements in favor of *Rejection of Conservative Group Beliefs* (from others who are probably defending their own opposing values) |
| ***Value Profile* Items** | Many events in human history took place only because a supreme being stepped in to make them happen. <br> Life would hardly be worth living without the promise of immortality and life after death. <br> In addition to faith we need help from God in order to resist temptation. <br> Every person should have help from some supernatural power whose decisions he obeys without question. <br> The chief end of man is nothing other than eternal salvation. <br> Theology will ultimately prove more important for mankind than the sciences. <br> Every explanation of man and the world is incomplete unless it takes into account God's will. |

## 13 VECTOR NF: *TOWARD VALUE-DETERMINED RESTRAINT*

| | |
|---|---|
| **Behavior Rating Item** | Legalistic, has to be right |
| **Values Rating Item** | Restraining individual desires for organizational goals |
| **Highly Correlated Personality Tests** | MMPI scale called *Feminine Masochism* (in males) |
| **Highly Correlated Observed Behaviors** | (none) |
| **Correlated Ratings and Guesses** | High on making others feel he rates them high on favoring *Expression and Gratification* <br> High on observers' rating as *Arousing Their Dislike* |
| **Generalizations from Markers** | Initiates value statements advocating *Value-Determined Restraint* |
| ***Value Profile* Items** | The ultimate and true reality is above the senses, immaterial, spiritual, unchanging, and everlasting. <br> In the ultimate scale, truth only comes from inner experience—from inspiration, mystical union, revelation, or pure meditation. <br> One should hold high ideals, purify himself, and restrain his desires for pleasure. |

Not to attain happiness, but to be worthy of it, is the purpose of our existence.

One should aim to simplify one's external life and to moderate those desires whose satisfaction is dependent on physical or social forces outside of oneself.

Man should control his bodily senses, his emotions, feelings, and wishes.

He that loses his conscience has nothing left that is worth keeping.

Misfortune is to be conquered by bearing it.

## 14 VECTOR N: *TOWARD INDIVIDUALISTIC ISOLATIONISM*

| | |
|---|---|
| **Behavior Rating Item** | Unfriendly, negativistic |
| **Values Rating Item** | Self-protection, self-interest first, self-sufficiency |
| **Highly Correlated Personality Tests** | MMPI scale called *Psychasthenia* |
| | MMPI scale called *Manifest Anxiety* |
| | MMPI scale called *Dependency* |
| | Cattell's 16 PF scale called *Insecure* |
| | Cattell's 16 PF scale called *Suspecting* |
| **Highly Correlated Observed Behaviors** | Initiating IPA category *Disagrees* |
| | Initiating IPA category *Seems Unfriendly* |
| **Correlated Ratings and Guesses** | High on group members' rating of him on *Individualism* |
| | High on rating others as seeming *Anxious* |
| | High on making others feel he rates them high on seeming *Anxious* |
| | High on making others feel he rates them high on *Domination* |
| | High on guessing others will rate him high on *Resentful* |
| | High on rating self as high on undefined variable *Understanding* |
| **Generalizations from Markers** | Initiates value statements advocating *Individualistic Isolationism* (directly observed marker) |
| **Value Profile Items** | It is the man who stands alone who excites our admiration. |
| | In life an individual should for the most part "go it alone," assuring himself of privacy, having much time to himself, attempting to control his own life. |
| | One's life should be directed completely by intelligence and rationality. |
| | One must avoid dependence upon persons and things, the center of life should be found within one's self. |

## 15 VECTOR NB: *TOWARD REJECTION OF SOCIAL CONFORMITY*

| | |
|---|---|
| **Behavior Rating Item** | Irritable, cynical, won't cooperate |
| **Values Rating Item** | Rejection of established procedures, rejection of conformity |
| **Highly Correlated Personality Tests** | Cattell's 16 PF scale called *Emotional Sensitivity* |
| | Cattell's 16 PF scale called *Insecure* |
| | Cattell's 16 PF scale called *Radical* |

| | |
|---|---|
| **Highly Correlated Observed Behaviors** | (none) |
| **Correlated Ratings and Guesses** | Rates others high on *Domination* |
| **Generalizations from Markers** | Initiates value statements advocating *Rejection of Social Conformity* <br> Agrees with others who initiate value statements advocating *Withholding of Cooperation* <br> Agrees with others who initiate value statements advocating *Identification with the Underprivileged* |
| *Value Profile* **Items** | The individualist is the man who is most likely to discover the best road to a new future. |

## 16 VECTOR B: *TOWARD REJECTION OF CONSERVATIVE GROUP BELIEF*

| | |
|---|---|
| **Behavior Rating Item** | Shows feelings and emotions |
| **Values Rating Item** | Change to new procedures, different values, creativity |
| **Highly Correlated Personality Tests** | Couch's new scale called *Ascension, Wish-fulfillment* (for example dreams of flying) |
| **Highly Correlated Observed Behaviors** | (none) |
| **Correlated Ratings and Guesses** | High tendency to rate others high on *Acceptance of Authority* |
| **Generalizations from Markers** | (none) |
| *Value Profile* **Items** | Man can solve all his important problems without help from a Supreme Being. <br> All the evidence that has been impartially accumulated goes to show that the universe has evolved in accordance with natural principles, so there is no necessity to assume a first cause, cosmic purpose, or God behind it. <br> Heaven and hell are products of man's imagination, and do not actually exist. <br> Morals must vary according to circumstances and situations—there are no sacred, unalterable, eternal rules which must always be obeyed. <br> Christianity and all other religions are, at best, only partially true. |

## 17 VECTOR PB: *TOWARD PERMISSIVE LIBERALISM*

| | |
|---|---|
| **Behavior Rating Item** | Affectionate, likeable, fun to be with |
| **Values Rating Item** | Friendship, mutual pleasure, recreation |
| **Highly Correlated Personality Tests** | (none) |
| **Highly Correlated Observed Behaviors** | Receiving IPA category *Dramatizes or Jokes* |
| **Correlated Ratings and Guesses** | High on making others feel he rates them high on *Entertaining* |

High on receiving ratings from other members that he
is high on *Arousing* (their) *Liking*
High on receiving ratings from group members on
*Arousing* (their) *Admiration*
High on rating others high on *Personal Involvement*
High on making others feel he rates them high on
*Warm and Personal*

| | |
|---|---|
| **Generalizations from Markers** | (none) |
| *Value Profile* **Items** | Divorce should be subject to fewer old-fashioned restrictions and become more a matter of mutual consent. |

## 18 VECTOR DP: *TOWARD TRUST IN THE GOODNESS OF OTHERS*

| | |
|---|---|
| **Behavior Rating Item** | Looks up to others, appreciative, trustful |
| **Values Rating Item** | Trust in the goodness of others |
| **Highly Correlated Personality Tests** | Cattell's 16 PF scale called *Mature* <br> MMPI scale called *Achievement* <br> Thurstone's Temperament scale called *Calm* <br> MMPI scale called *Tolerance* |
| **Highly Correlated Observed Behaviors** | (none) |
| **Correlated Ratings and Guesses** | High on rating self as high on *Acceptance of Authority* <br> High on making others feel he rates them high on *Arousing His Admiration* <br> High on observers' rating of him as *Equalitarian* <br> High on rating self as *Equalitarian* <br> High on rating others as *Self-confident* <br> High on making others feel he rates them high on being *Valuable for a Logical Task* <br> High on observers' rating of him as being *Understanding* <br> High on group members' rating of him as being *Understanding* <br> High on making others feel he rates them high on being *Understanding* |
| **Generalizations from Markers** | Agrees with value statements initiated by others advocating *Equalitarianism* <br> Receives value statements in favor of *Rejection of Success* (from others who are probably defending their own opposing values) <br> Initiates value statements advocating *Trust in the Goodness of Others* <br> Agrees with value statements of others advocating *Trust in the Goodness of Others* |
| *Value Profile* **Items** | (none) |

## 19 VECTOR DPF: *TOWARD SALVATION THROUGH LOVE*

| | |
|---|---|
| **Behavior Rating Item** | Gentle, willing to accept responsibility |
| **Values Rating Item** | Dedication, faithfulness, loyalty to the organization |

| Highly Correlated Personality Tests | MMPI scale called *Responsibility* |
|---|---|
| Highly Correlated Observed Behaviors | (none) |
| Correlated Ratings and Guesses | High on guessing others will rate him high on *Equalitarianism* |
| Generalizations from Markers | Initiates value statements advocating *Salvation through Love*<br>Agrees with others who initiate value statements advocating *Altruistic Love*<br>Agrees with others who initiate value statements advocating *Conservative Group Beliefs*<br>Receives value statements in favor of *Failure and Withdrawal* (from others who are probably defending their own opposing values) |
| *Value Profile* Items | Tenderness is more important than passion in love.<br>There are no human problems that love cannot solve. |

## 20 VECTOR DF: *TOWARD SELF-KNOWLEDGE AND SUBJECTIVITY*

| Behavior Rating Item | Obedient, works submissively |
|---|---|
| Values Rating Item | Obedience to the chain of command, complying with authority |
| Highly Correlated Personality Tests | Initiating IPA category *Asks for Suggestion* |
| Highly Correlated Observed Behaviors | (none) |
| Correlated Ratings and Guesses | High on observers' rating of him as *Acceptant of Authority*<br>High on group members' rating of him as *Acceptant of Authority*<br>High on rating other members as high on *Individualism*<br>High on rating self as high on *Psychological Inertia*<br>High on guessing other members will rate him as high on *Psychological Inertia* |
| Generalizations from Markers | Initiates value statements advocating *Self-knowledge and Subjectivity*<br>Receives value statements in favor of *Withholding of Cooperation* (from others who are probably defending their own opposing values) |
| *Value Profile* Items | Contemplation is the highest form of human activity.<br>The most rewarding object of study any man can find is his own inner life.<br>No time is better spent than that devoted to thinking about the ultimate purposes of life.<br>The rich internal world of ideals, of sensitive feelings, of reverie, and of self-knowledge, is man's true home.<br>Excessive desires should be avoided and moderation in all things should be sought. |

**21 VECTOR DNF:** *TOWARD SELF-SACRIFICE FOR VALUES*

| | |
|---|---|
| **Behavior Rating Item** | Self-punishing, works too hard |
| **Values Rating Item** | Self-sacrifice if necessary to reach organizational goals |
| **Highly Correlated Personality Tests** | (none) |
| **Highly Correlated Observed Behaviors** | (none) |
| **Correlated Ratings and Guesses** | High on group members' rating of him as seeming *Anxious*<br>High on rating self as seeming *Anxious*<br>High on guessing that others will rate him as *Arousing Their Curiosity*<br>High on receiving value statements initiated by others advocating *Identification with the Underprivileged*<br>High on group members' rating of him as showing high *Psychological Inertia*<br>High on making other group members feel he rates them high on *Self-confidence* |
| **Generalizations from Markers** | Initiates value statements advocating *Self-sacrifice for Values*<br>Agrees with others who make value statements advocating *Self-sacrifice for Values* |
| ***Value Profile* Items** | There is no worthy purpose but the resolution to do right.<br>To starve is a small matter, to lose one's virtue is a great one.<br>There is nothing the body suffers that the soul may not profit by.<br>To lay down your life for a friend—this is the summit of a good life.<br>A person should let himself be molded by the great objective purposes of the universe, which silently and irresistibly achieve their goal. |

**22 VECTOR DN:** *TOWARD REJECTION OF SOCIAL SUCCESS*

| | |
|---|---|
| **Behavior Rating Item** | Depressed, sad, resentful, rejecting |
| **Values Rating Item** | Passive rejection of popularity, going it alone |
| **Highly Correlated Personality Tests** | MMPI scale called *Social Introversion*<br>MMPI scale called *Depression*<br>MMPI scale called *Repression-Denial* |
| **Highly Correlated Observed Behaviors** | Receiving IPA category *Asks for Opinion* |
| **Correlated Ratings and Guesses** | High on observers' rating of him as seeming *Anxious*<br>High on group members' rating of him as *Arousing Their Curiosity*<br>High on observers' rating of him on *Individualism*<br>High on rating self on *Individualism*<br>High on observers' rating of him as *Resentful*<br>High on group members' rating of him as being *Resentful* |

| | |
|---|---|
| **Generalizations from Markers** | Initiates value statements advocating *Rejection of Social Success* |
| | Receives value statements in favor of *Trust in the Goodness of Others* (from others who are probably defending their own opposing values) |
| *Value Profile* **Items** | (none) |

## 23 VECTOR DNB: *TOWARD FAILURE AND WITHDRAWAL*

| | |
|---|---|
| **Behavior Rating Item** | Alienated, quits, withdraws |
| **Values Rating Item** | Admission of failure, withdrawal of effort |
| **Highly Correlated Personality Tests** | Cattell's 16 PF scale called *Independent Self-sufficiency* |
| | MMPI scale called *Feminine Interests* (in males) (group members were all males) |
| **Highly Correlated Observed Behaviors** | (none) |
| **Correlated Ratings and Guesses** | High on guessing that others will rate him high on *Arousing Their Dislike* |
| | High on rating other members as *Arousing His Dislike* |
| **Generalizations from Markers** | Initiates value statements advocating *Failure and Withdrawal* |
| | Agrees with value statements initiated by others advocating *Failure and Withdrawal* |
| | Receives value statements in favor of *Salvation through Love* (from others who are probably defending their own opposing values) |
| *Value Profile* **Items** | (none) |

## 24 VECTOR DB: *TOWARD WITHHOLDING OF COOPERATION*

| | |
|---|---|
| **Behavior Rating Item** | Afraid to try, doubts own ability |
| **Values Rating Item** | Passive noncooperation with authority |
| **Highly Correlated Personality Tests** | (none) |
| **Highly Correlated Observed Behaviors** | Receiving IPA category *Asks for Information* |
| | Initiating IPA category *Shows Tension* (includes laughing) |
| **Correlated Ratings and Guesses** | High on guessing others will rate him high on *Favoring Expression and Gratification* |
| | High on rating others high on *Favoring Expression and Gratification* |
| | High on receiving value statements initiated by others advocating *Self-knowledge and Subjectivity* |
| **Generalizations from Markers** | Initiates value statements advocating *Withholding of Cooperation* |
| *Value Profile* **Items** | (none) |

**25 VECTOR DPB:** *TOWARD IDENTIFICATION WITH THE UNDERPRIVILEGED*

| | |
|---|---|
| **Behavior Rating Item** | Quietly happy, just to be with others |
| **Values Rating Item** | Quiet contentment, taking it easy |
| **Highly Correlated Personality Tests** | (none) |
| **Highly Correlated Observed Behaviors** | (none) |
| **Correlated Ratings and Guesses** | (none) |
| **Generalizations from Markers** | Initiates value statements advocating *Identification with the Underprivileged*<br>Receives value statements in favor of *Self-sacrifice for Values* (from others who are probably defending their own opposing values) |
| *Value Profile* **Items** | A teenager should be allowed to decide most things for himself.<br>Labor unions in large corporations should be given a major part in deciding company policy.<br>It is up to the government to make sure everyone has a secure job and a good standard of living. |

**26 VECTOR D:** *TOWARD DEVALUATION OF THE SELF*

| | |
|---|---|
| **Behavior Rating Item** | Passive, introverted, says little |
| **Values Rating Item** | Giving up personal needs and desires, passivity |
| **Highly Correlated Personality Tests** | (none) |
| **Highly Correlated Observed Behaviors** | Initiating IPA category *Gives Information*<br>Low IPA Matrix on *Total Initiated* |
| **Correlated Ratings and Guesses** | High on guessing that others will rate him high on *Acceptant of Authority*<br>High on rating others as high on *Extroversion*<br>High on making others feel he rates them high on *Extroversion*<br>High on guessing that others will rate him high on *Individualism* |
| **Generalizations from Markers** | Initiates value statements advocating *Devaluation of the Self*<br>Receives value statements from the others advocating *Devaluation of the Self*<br>Agrees with others who make value statements advocating *Devaluation of the Self* |
| *Value Profile* **Items** | (none) |

# Appendix B

# Wordings of the Rating Questions
# for Nineteen Selected Images

1 **MEM**    In general, what kinds of values does the *most effective member* of a task-oriented team you have known show in his or her behavior?

2 **WSH**    In general, what kinds of values do you *wish* to show in your own behavior, whether or not you are actually able to do so?

3 **IDL**    In general, what kinds of values would be *ideal* for this person to show in order to be *most effective*?

4 **EFF**    In general, what kinds of values would be ideal for you to show in order to be *most effective*?

5 **MEL**    In general, what kinds of values does the *most effective leader* of a task-oriented team you have known show in his or her behavior?

6 **FTM**    In general, what kinds of values need to be shown by your team in the *future* in order to be most effective?

7 **FUT**    In general, what kinds of values need to be shown in the culture of your organization in the *future* in order to be most effective?

8 **ACT**    In general, what kinds of values does this person *actually* show in his or her behavior?

9 **SLF**    In general, what kinds of values do *you* actually show in your behavior?

10 **EXP**    In general, what kinds of values do you *expect* others will rate you as showing in your behavior?

11 **OTP**    In general, what kinds of values does this person show in his or her behavior? (asked of participants in leadership training about their back-home coworkers)

12 **OTM**    In general, what kinds of values does this person show in his or her behavior? (asked of members of intact teams about their team mates)

13 **CXP**    In general, what kinds of values do you *expect* your significant clients or customers would rate your organization as showing toward them?

14 **REW**    In general, what kinds of values are members of your organization actually *rewarded* for showing in behavior now?

15 **CTM**    In general, what kinds of values does your team *currently* show in behavior?

16 **CUR**    In general, what kinds of values are *currently* shown in the culture of your organization?

17 **LEP**    In general, what kinds of values do members of your team show in behavior when the team is *least productive*?

18 **LEM**    In general, what kinds of values does the *least effective member* of a task-oriented team you have known show in his or her behavior?

19 **REJ**    In general, what kinds of values do you tend to *reject*, either in yourself or in others?

# Appendix C

# Average Value Frequency Profiles
# for Nineteen Selected Images

**FIGURE C.1**
**Comparison Table of Mean Endorsements from Bargraph Profiles
on Each of the Twenty-six Value Items for Nineteen Selected Images
and the SCG Optimum**

| Value Items | Selected Images | | | | | | | | | |
|---|---|---|---|---|---|---|---|---|---|---|
| | 1 MEM | 2 WSH | 3 IDL | 4 EFF | 5 MEL | 6 FTM | 7 FUT | 8 ACT | 9 SLF | 10 EXP |
| 1 U | 17 | 19 | 15 | 15 | 17 | 11 | 13 | 17 | 15 | 17 |
| 2 UP | 21 | 24 | 22 | 21 | 21 | 15 | 17 | 21 | 21 | 21 |
| 3 UPF | 31 | 31 | 31 | 32 | 30 | 32 | 32 | 25 | 28 | 26 |
| 4 UF | 29 | 30 | 30 | 30 | 28 | 30 | 30 | 21 | 23 | 21 |
| 5 UNF | 21 | 20 | 24 | 20 | 18 | 17 | 20 | 21 | 20 | 20 |
| 6 UN | 18 | 18 | 18 | 16 | 18 | 13 | 14 | 19 | 18 | 18 |
| 7 UNB | 7 | 9 | 9 | 7 | 9 | 6 | 6 | 7 | 10 | 10 |
| 8 UB | 21 | 23 | 21 | 20 | 19 | 22 | 21 | 17 | 19 | 17 |
| 9 UPB | 25 | 27 | 25 | 24 | 21 | 24 | 23 | 21 | 24 | 23 |
| 10 P | 28 | 28 | 27 | 27 | 24 | 28 | 27 | 22 | 24 | 22 |
| 11 PF | 29 | 29 | 27 | 28 | 23 | 29 | 29 | 22 | 23 | 22 |
| 12 F | 18 | 18 | 20 | 18 | 14 | 15 | 16 | 21 | 19 | 20 |
| 13 NF | 21 | 20 | 20 | 21 | 16 | 20 | 20 | 18 | 20 | 19 |
| 14 N | 8 | 7 | 7 | 5 | 4 | 4 | 7 | 12 | 9 | 10 |
| 15 NB | 10 | 11 | 10 | 11 | 10 | 12 | 12 | 6 | 11 | 11 |
| 16 B | 25 | 27 | 24 | 25 | 22 | 26 | 27 | 20 | 22 | 22 |
| 17 PB | 23 | 25 | 23 | 22 | 22 | 23 | 24 | 22 | 20 | 20 |
| 18 DP | 26 | 28 | 24 | 26 | 26 | 27 | 27 | 21 | 24 | 24 |
| 19 DPF | 29 | 29 | 30 | 29 | 30 | 29 | 29 | 29 | 29 | 27 |
| 20 DF | 25 | 24 | 25 | 24 | 24 | 22 | 24 | 26 | 25 | 24 |
| 21 DNF | 22 | 23 | 23 | 24 | 23 | 23 | 22 | 22 | 23 | 20 |
| 22 DN | 9 | 10 | 11 | 9 | 9 | 9 | 9 | 11 | 12 | 12 |
| 23 DNB | 6 | 7 | 9 | 8 | 6 | 8 | 9 | 7 | 8 | 7 |
| 24 DB | 3 | 3 | 4 | 3 | 3 | 3 | 3 | 4 | 5 | 6 |
| 25 DPB | 11 | 11 | 11 | 8 | 6 | 6 | 8 | 8 | 8 | 9 |
| 26 D | 9 | 9 | 12 | 11 | 10 | 10 | 10 | 11 | 13 | 12 |

\*      Possible endorsement ranges from 0 to 33.

329

**FIGURE C.1** (continued)

| | | | Selected Images | | | | | | | Value Items |
|---|---|---|---|---|---|---|---|---|---|---|
| 11 OTP | 12 OTM | 13 CXP | 14 REW | 15 CTM | 16 CUR | 17 LEP | 18 LEM | 19 REJ | OPT** | |
| 14 | 17 | 17 | 17 | 14 | 17 | 21 | 17 | 17 | 17 | 1 U |
| 19 | 19 | 16 | 17 | 16 | 17 | 17 | 13 | 7 | 21 | 2 UP |
| 24 | 23 | 19 | 17 | 20 | 17 | 17 | 4 | 0 | 30 | 3 UPF |
| 20 | 19 | 18 | 17 | 18 | 15 | 5 | 5 | 3 | 27 | 4 UF |
| 20 | 21 | 22 | 18 | 17 | 20 | 16 | 16 | 13 | 20 | 5 UNF |
| 18 | 18 | 18 | 16 | 16 | 16 | 20 | 19 | 17 | 18 | 6 UN |
| 9 | 10 | 9 | 6 | 9 | 9 | 22 | 21 | 21 | 9 | 7 UNB |
| 17 | 15 | 11 | 7 | 15 | 12 | 9 | 12 | 8 | 19 | 8 UB |
| 20 | 18 | 14 | 10 | 17 | 15 | 7 | 5 | 4 | 23 | 9 UPB |
| 21 | 21 | 15 | 11 | 19 | 13 | 6 | 5 | 4 | 24 | 10 P |
| 21 | 21 | 18 | 15 | 19 | 16 | 4 | 5 | 3 | 25 | 11 PF |
| 21 | 20 | 22 | 20 | 19 | 21 | 18 | 18 | 14 | 18 | 12 F |
| 18 | 18 | 18 | 16 | 15 | 18 | 10 | 8 | 10 | 18 | 13 NF |
| 14 | 14 | 15 | 12 | 14 | 18 | 27 | 27 | 24 | 7 | 14 N |
| 8 | 10 | 8 | 6 | 10 | 10 | 17 | 18 | 18 | 10 | 15 NB |
| 17 | 17 | 16 | 14 | 19 | 15 | 6 | 7 | 6 | 22 | 16 B |
| 22 | 19 | 14 | 11 | 16 | 15 | 6 | 10 | 4 | 22 | 17 PB |
| 21 | 19 | 16 | 10 | 18 | 14 | 5 | 7 | 5 | 24 | 18 DP |
| 25 | 25 | 23 | 18 | 24 | 21 | 7 | 8 | 3 | 29 | 19 DPF |
| 25 | 25 | 24 | 21 | 24 | 24 | 13 | 13 | 9 | 24 | 20 DF |
| 19 | 19 | 19 | 17 | 19 | 17 | 6 | 5 | 8 | 22 | 21 DNF |
| 11 | 12 | 9 | 7 | 11 | 11 | 20 | 20 | 18 | 9 | 22 DN |
| 7 | 7 | 7 | 4 | 6 | 8 | 17 | 16 | 21 | 6 | 23 DNB |
| 6 | 6 | 6 | 4 | 7 | 11 | 22 | 22 | 25 | 3 | 24 DB |
| 11 | 11 | 8 | 5 | 8 | 10 | 20 | 16 | 18 | 8 | 25 DPB |
| 11 | 11 | 10 | 9 | 12 | 12 | 14 | 10 | 19 | 9 | 26 D |

**    OPT is the SCG Optimum Profile.

# Appendix D

# Biographical Background

In 1945, after five years as a graduate student in sociology at Harvard, with Talcott Parsons as my principal mentor, I became an instructor in the new Department of Social Relations. The new department, started in 1945, was founded as an experiment in the integration of sociology, social psychology, personality psychology, and social anthropology.

In the earliest years of my research in the new department, roughly from 1945 to 1955, I studied groups in the attempt to develop an observational method, at first in natural settings, then in the laboratory where I could observe from behind a one-way mirror.

One of the first groups I observed with technical intent, but in a natural setting, was a group convened by Talcott Parsons, the chairman of the new Department of Social Relations. The group was a gathering of the founders and faculty members of the new Department of Social Relations. The gathering was held at Harry Murray's Beacon Hill apartment, perhaps to give it a little extra tone of social status. Harry Murray optimistically called this group "The Levelers," in the hope that some theoretical differences among the faculty might be leveled out. But before long George Homans, a perennial noncooperator among the hopefuls, discovered serious pot holes, and the road did not get leveled, neither at that meeting nor later.

The second group I observed with technical intent, as I remember, was a thesis-planning committee chaired by Gordon Allport. Gordon, as a historian of social psychology, called these committees for thesis planning "The Group Mind." He chose this name, I am sure, as an ironic reminder of the long controversy over this problematic concept in the early history of social psychology (see McDougall 1920).

But no doubt Gordon also intended the reference to twit his competitive older brother, Floyd, who was one of the most prominent and vocal social psychologists in the long controversy in the literature over the reality of "the group mind." Floyd Allport had done his heroic best to wrestle the offending concept of "the group mind" to the ground.

This old controversy, as to whether such a concept is justified, and if so, what it can mean, is still very much alive, now in one form, now another. Nobody dares mention the name now, but the nature of the phenomena to which it referred is still a nest of problems. The problems are centrally relevant to the argument of the present book. I hope I have a better solution as to the nature of the "reality" to which it was meant to point. What was called an instance of "the group mind" in the earliest days (mob action as described by Gustave Le Bon, for example) was essentially what I call a "dynamic system field" today.

My third learning experience in the technical observation of groups was a year-long series of meetings of the "clinical diagnostic council" at Harry Murray's famous Psychological Clinic on Plympton Street. Assessment of individual personalities by a group of clinicians was Harry's chosen integrative procedure—the one he had used previously in his case studies for *Explorations in Personality* (Murray 1938). This time the diagnosticians included Brewster Smith, Jerome S. Bruner, and Robert W. White, in their research for *Opinions and Personality* (Smith, Bruner, and White 1956).

George Homans and I, both interested in the study of small groups (although we did not often consult each other!), observed this diagnostic council from the far end of the long library of the old clinic in which the meetings were held. George made sound recordings with Harry Murray's new "vinyl record cutter," while I wrote down scores on a moving paper tape on the top of a big black box I called the "interaction recorder."

At that time, social psychologists were hyper-conscious of the importance of "nonverbal behavior." My black box made a huge clank and showed a ruby light to mark the end of each minute, so that I would not forget to look for "nonverbal behavior." This periodic clank was disturbing to the group we were observing, but we were all willing to put up with almost anything to get on with research. George and I were both very proud of our new equipment.

That spring (1946), Jack French and Ronald Lippitt appeared at the Clinic and invited me to join them along with Kurt Lewin's students and associates at the National Training Laboratory's first summer session on group development in Bethel, Maine. I studied "T Groups" there (in the argot of Bethel, T Groups were Training Groups). I trained observers of the T Groups, prepared feedback profiles of the scores, and refined the categories for my new method called "interaction process analysis."

Finally, maybe in the fall of 1946, my long-awaited "group observation room" with the one-way mirror was completed. The one-way mirror was made of genuine double-paned glass. It was a great improvement over the old-fashioned burlap screen Harry Murray had rigged up in a tiny attic room in his clinic on Plympton Street for the observation of interviews.

The new group observation room was provided by grants obtained by Samuel Stouffer, the Director and founder of the new Laboratory of Social Relations, to go with the new Department of Social Relaitons. The site was Emerson Hall, in space that had originally belonged to the Department of Philosophy. I was told that it was the same space that had been fitted up at one time as a laboratory for William James. I felt that this was certainly a good omen!

After the time of William James, the suite of rooms had been converted into a set of small darkrooms for the Department of Psychology Laboratory. It was wired with a system of buzzers for Floyd Allport's "alone-and-together" (social facilitation) experiments. I was not so sure this was a good omen, given Floyd Allport's limited concept of the meaning of the "group mind," since I wanted to study groups. But I felt that something was stirring in social psychology that my predecessor Floyd Allport did not quite understand. Maybe I could understand it better? Finally, at the time of the founding of the Department and Laboratory of Social Relations, the suite of rooms passed into the ownership of the new Laboratory, and became the group meeting and observation room.

Thus began a long period of group study. I was occupied for several years in the study of problem-solving and decision-making groups, of sizes two through eight, through four consecutive sessions each. It was during this period that I developed *Interaction Process Analysis* (Bales 1950) and made a number of findings which proved to be crucial to my present perspective. These findings are now substantial parts of the theory of social-interaction systems.

My collaborators during this time and later were mostly graduate students, Postdoctoral Fellows or Research Associates in the Laboratory, with an occasional undergraduate, and an occasional faculty member. They included Fred L. Strodtbeck,

Christophe Heinicke, John T. Evans, Sigmund Gruber, Gibson E. Winter, Edgar F. Borgatta, A. Paul Hare, Philip E. Slater, Elliot G. Mischler, Nancy Waxler, Theodore M. Mills, Mary Roseborough Salisbury, Michael S. Olmstead, Hugh Philp, Richard D. Mann, Gene G. Kassebaum, Joseph Berger, Bernard Cohen, Warren Bachelis, Nathan Altshuler, Robert Avery, Elizabeth Cohen, George A. Talland, Lindsey Churchill, Paul Breer, Philip Bonacich, and Morris Zelditch.

Frederick Mosteller, the principle statistician of the new Department and Laboratory, was a special friend and advisor on the statistical problems of my method of observing and recording interaction. And I was in constant interaction with my mentor, Talcott Parsons, whose office was just next door. He was busy at this time writing his book, *The Social System* (Parsons 1951).

The results of my work during this period have been published in several sources: as a book on the method, *Interaction Process Analysis* (1950); in a number of articles with collaborators which I have reviewed briefly in the present book; and in two collaborative books with Talcott Parsons, *Working Papers in the Theory of Action* (Parsons, Bales, and Shils 1953b) and *Family, Socialization, and Interaction Process* (Parsons and Bales 1955).

### On the Trail of *Values*

The study of "values" in crosscultural perspective was a focus of great research interest among the faculty of the Department of Social Relations in its early period, sparked by the anthropological studies of Clyde Kluckhohn and the ethnic family studies of Florence Kluckhohn, John Spiegel, and others. One visitor, Charles Morris, the editor of the assembled works of George Herbert Mead, was especially important to me. Charles Morris brought to the faculty research group his factor-analytic studies of values. His test instrument, called "Paths of Life" (Morris 1956), was derived from his study of world philosophies and religious orientations, and he had data from crosscultural studies.

Arthur Couch, first my student and later my colleague, arrived on my horizon in the early 1950s. His knowledge of factor analysis, and his studies of authoritarianism and leadership with his mentor Launor Carter, at the University of Rochester, made an absolutely crucial contribution and a lasting impression on me and all of my future work. He taught me most of what I know of factor analysis, and aided and abetted my interest in "values." Foremost amongst the values which preoccupied us were the values of authoritarianism, as explored in *The Authoritarian Personality* (Adorno et al. 1950).

The awakening of interest in values was crucial for my later work, since "values as shown in behavior," as I now phrase the combination for purposes of measurement, seems to me to be the level of analysis (rather than the behavior stripped of content, as formulated in the IPA method that offers the most strategic entry into an understanding of the nature and dynamics of "social-interaction systems."

I still remember with great clarity one crucial event in the midst of my observations of problem-solving groups from behind the one-way mirror. The task of the groups was to analyze a case study and to consider all of the facts that had been distributed among the group members. They were to come up with advice for their hypothetical administrative superior on what he should do about a problem that had arisen among the group of persons working for him.

In this case, the supervisor in a machine shop wanted to know what to do about the workers in the shop who were "snapping towels" at each other. The case was actually the descendant of a Harvard Business School case, which I had rewritten to provide a case for problem-solving discussion in my experimental groups.

The group I was observing had worked themselves up into a heated argument about what should be done. Suddenly one member fairly exploded in rage at another, shouting, "You have to respect authority, and when you don't respect authority, your situation isn't worth...much!" His face was working and he was speechless for lack of anything bad enough to say.

I was in the dark observation room behind the one-way mirror. Nevertheless I was hit between the eyes by the expression of rage and contempt on his face! I remember desperately thinking, "But I wrote the case. It isn't real!" The "case" simply dissolved in my mind into the fiction it really was. I suddenly became aware of what the present reality in the mind of the enraged member must be, and it shocked me. I have been impressed ever since with the real-life importance of "values."

Behind the one-way mirror in the observation room I felt it was obviously time to do something systematic about observing indications of values in these group discussions. Together with the graduate students of the time, Art Couch and I combed a wide range of literature for "value statements" that we could use as items in a test of values. Capitalizing on Couch's knowledge of factor analysis (and free time at night on the new computers of a local insurance company), we constructed a broad test of values we called the "Value Profile" in the mid-1950s (Bales and Couch 1969).

Couch was much impressed by Harry Murray's approach in *Explorations in Personality* (Murray 1938) and was determined to vindicate that approach, carry it further, and give it a stiffer backbone by a large experimental study with the full statistical treatment of the data, particularly by factor analysis. He accomplished what he set out to do, almost unbelievably, given the mountain of data he gathered, and his accomplishment still lives in his monumental two-volume dissertation *Psychological Determinants of Interpersonal Behavior* (1960).

It was the basic statistical data from this study that I took along and puzzled over during my sabbatical year, as I dragged the whole batch of correlations with me over a large part of southern Europe in 1963–64. The groupings of the items which correlated with each other, which Couch and I had discovered earlier in the work on the Value Profile, and the many other variables included in Couch's large study, were critical clues in establishing my first comprehensive intuitive understanding of the factor-analytic dimensions of what can be called the "value space." Hans Eysenck's factor study of social and economic attitudes, called *The Psychology of Politics* (1954), was also critically helpful. I finally accomplished a feeling of understanding of this space to my satisfaction during a period of feverish work and high theoretical excitement in the spring of 1964—on the French Riviera, of all places!

Couch's study was a complex, multi-domain series of factor analyses of an unprecedentedly large number of variables. It included standard personality test batteries; Murray's list of needs; tests Couch himself constructed on concealment defenses, perceived press, and behavioral press; projective tests; a fantasy inventory devised by Murray; and the new Value Profile.

The instruments also included IPA observations of the interaction of the sixty studied participants in a series of five sessions each of five-person groups, value content analysis (the observational method I had devised for scoring the value content of argumentative statements made by participants), comprehensive post-meeting questionnaires, individual interviews, and a number of other variables.

This huge omnibus study produced a number of different factor analyses from which I ultimately derived my beginning conceptual framework of a three-dimensional "value space," which later was to become the framework for what I called the "new field theory in social psychology" (Bales 1985). It has now become the framework for the still more inclusive and generalized "intercorrelation space" of my present theory of "social-interaction systems."

Couch's omnibus study produced a huge population of intercorrelations. Couch did not emerge from his analysis of the data with just three dimensions centered on values, as I did. He emerged with six different factor analyses in his dissertation. I made a long intuitive study of all of the items, their factor loadings, and each of the other variables included in his six different factor analyses. I have since added by interpolation many other items and intercorrelations from a number of other factor-analytic studies available in the literature, and now refer to this cumulative compendium as the body of intercorrelations on which the theory of social-interaction systems is built.

Without Couch's work, and I think without Harry Murray's earlier explorations in the background, the present theory would not have come into existence. I observed all of the groups, made scores using interaction process analysis, made the post-meeting ratings along with Couch and other observers, and toiled over the mountain of intercorrelations and factor loadings for literally ten years. My summary, reordering, and implementation of this period of work is contained in my book *Personality and Interpersonal Behavior* (Bales 1970).

### Self-Analytic Groups

In about 1954, before all this factor-analytic work took place, I came out from behind the one-way mirror to participate in a different kind of venture: the teaching of groups in a course concerned with the analysis of "human relations cases." The course was originated around 1946 by Hugh Cabot for undergraduates in the college at Harvard. It was modeled after the case-discussion course in administrative practices at the Harvard Business School.

I have been told that case analysis was introduced into the Business School by its Dean, Wallace Donham, in the 1920s. He had been impressed by case analysis at the Law School. When Hugh Cabot's appointment came to an end, Clyde Kluckhohn and David Riesman, along with Talcott Parsons, rescued the course from a natural death by nominating me to take it over. Many changes followed.

Several of my collaborators in teaching this course had earlier found their way to it as research and teaching fellow assistants from my own research group: Philip E. Slater, Theodore M. Mills, Richard D. Mann, and Dexter Dunphy. Kio Morimoto and Charles P. Whitlock from the Bureau of Study Council taught in the course, as did William Perry. Later the teachers in this course included David Shapiro, Warren Bennis, Nicky Nichols, Lane Conn, Sara Conn, Jack Sansolo, and Thomas Cottle. Norman Zinberg was also recruited to help us. He was a practicing psychoanalyst, associated with the Medical School, the Massachusetts Mental Health Center, and the Boston Psychoanalytic Society and Institute.

Thus, the teaching staff of the course was well stocked with expertise in personality and clinical psychology, as well as social psychology and sociology. To complete the interdisciplinary character of our orientation, some of our case materials were taken from social anthropological sources. Our weekly seminars were inspiring learning experiences for me.

I was trained as a research candidate at the Boston Psychoanalytic Institute during a four-year period in the mid-1950s, on a Fellowship from the Commonwealth Fund, a venture promoted by Talcott Parsons to familiarize younger faculty of the department with psychoanalysis. I owe a great debt to my training analyst, Grete Bibring, and to Helen Tartakoff at the Institute for her course in psychoanalytic technique. I liked the course so much I took it three times! I applied the respectful and tentative approach to interpretation in psychoanalysis she epitomized so well (little by little, like peeling an onion) to interpretation of events in the teaching of my "academic self-analytic groups."

In my groups there was no "wild analysis," which developed in other places as a harbinger of the revolution of the 1960s. In my groups there was no marathon high pressure, nothing done in the dark or in the swimming pool, none of the excesses of the wild group movement of the 1960s. I resented the black eye I felt this kind of carrying on in the 1960s gave serious academic research with groups.

By degrees, after I took over the case-analysis course from Hugh Cabot, I added sound recording of the sessions, student written reports of events in the group, and increasing "self-analysis" of these events. In time the case analysis gave way entirely to analysis of current conflicts and other events in the group. I called these groups "academic self-analytic groups." These groups continued to meet in the format of a college course under a series of different catalog names. In the latter stages the course was called "Group Psychology." But I always referred to the groups as "self-analytic groups." As soon as I could manage it, the course began to meet under observation in the group observation laboratory.

My methods during this period, as a mostly silent group leader and teacher, were observational and "clinical" rather than experimental. But all the while, I worked in the background to develop and refine systematic methods for describing the group processes and preparing "feedback" to the group members. I hoped that well-constructed feedback would help group members to improve their understanding of their own personalities, their relationships in the groups, and their abilities to work together and solve problems.

### Computer Technology and Feedback to Group Members

All during the long period from about 1954 to about 1970, during the same time I taught in the self-analytic groups, I focused all the resources I could bring to bear from the Laboratory of Social Relations, of which I had meantime become the Director, on the technical problems of making better methods for the study of groups. These included, in particular, taking advantage of the new possibilities offered by the advent of powerful computers.

From the time I became Director of the Laboratory of Social Relations, on the death of Sam Stouffer, about 1960, Arthur Couch served as the Assistant Director of the Laboratory. He performed very valuable services for the Department and Laboratory, particularly in his development of "Data Text." This, so far as I know, was the very first large computer program which made it possible to process numerical data, perform content analysis of textual material, and perform complex statistical analyses on both.

At the same time, my colleague Philip Stone stepped in to help computerize the recording and feedback of content analysis of the sessions of my self-analytic groups. Our collaborators in the first steps of this process included Dexter Dunphy and Zvi Namenwirth. Daniel Ogilvie and Marshall Smith continued with Philip Stone in a separate major project to produce one of the first successful and still active methods of computer-aided content analysis in their program called "The General Inquirer" (Stone, Dunphy, Smith, and Ogilvie 1966). A dissertation by Dexter Dunphy demonstrated the utility of this system by a comparison of the content produced by a study of two year-long self-analytic groups (Dunphy 1964).

This long period of quiet development of methods was brought to a conclusion with two markers. The first, which marked the end of the old, was the publication of my first summary framework of what I now call the theory of social-interaction systems: *Personality and Interpersonal Behavior* (Bales 1970).

The second marker, which ushered in a new era of change, was the fact that demand for the previously very popular self-analytic group course fell off, due in part,

I think, to backlash in reaction to the student revolution, which had hit its peak at Harvard in 1968.

## Multiple-Level Observation of Groups

More than the store fronts in Harvard Square were "trashed" in the student revolution of 1968. During the Vietnam War, in many students' minds, taking a course like my self-analytic-group course, where the instructor talked hardly at all and the students talked all the time about whatever they wanted to, was desirable "revolutionary" activity. But by 1970 or so, student interest in revolutionary activities was definitely on the ebb tide.

Moreover, the solidarity of the faculty of the Department of Social Relations had been irrevocably damaged in the revolution of 1968. There was a painful polarization of the faculty over whether to support a course that had sprouted somewhere in the dark, out of sight like a mushroom, as a result of revolutionary sentiment among the students. This course, "A Radical Critique of American Society," had suddenly become very large and very visible. The polarization of the faculty over this course was the beginning of the end for the Department and Laboratory of Social Relations.

Meanwhile, twenty-five years had passed since the founding of the Department, a period long enough to experience the erosion of a generation turnover in the faculty. Evolutionary selection was working its way on the founding values of the Department as an organization. To make a long and painful story as short as possible, I will simply report that the Department and Laboratory of Social Relations finally died as an entity in 1972.

As a part of all this aftermath, money essential to funding the five or so teachers for the course in self-analytic groups was withdrawn. I cut down to only one section of the course, designed the observation and feedback to be done in rotation by teams of students in the course itself, and put to work in a more serious way still the methods of observation, computation, and feedback I had developed during the previous period. The course became not only an academic self-analytic group, but also a training course in technical methods of observation and computer analysis, with student-team production and presentation of interpretive feedback reports.

These were very different conditions. They gave additional impetus to the further development and perfecting of the technical side of methods for the study of groups and the presentation of feedback. Over a period of about nine years from 1970, with the aid of a considerable number of associates and students, I developed a fully fledged complex system of observation and analysis, designed to take full advantage of the computer. It was a second stage of consolidation of what I now call the theory of social-interaction systems. A book resulted, entitled *SYMLOG: A System for the Multiple Level Observation of Groups* (Bales and Cohen 1979).

During this period my principal collaborators were Stephen P. Cohen, Stephen A. Williamson, Gary Alan Fine, Richard B. Polley, Poppy McLeod, Mark Palmerino, Mark Rhodes, Wallace Bachman, Daniel Isenberg, Ronald Breiger, James Ennis, Bonny K. Parke, Howard Swann, Thomas B. Bixby, Joanne Martin, Susan Fiske, Virginia Bales, Eliot Freeman, M. E. Booher, Phyllis Burrows, Robert Rossel, William F. Hill, Manson Solomon, John McLeish, Wayne Matheson, James Park, Myron Wish, Peter Bricker, Mark Masterson, Steven Presser, Jeff Howard, Martine Goddard, Edward Pattullo, Daniel Pershonok, Martha Stark, Stewart Pizer, Barbara Masser, Chen Sun, Scott Bradner, John Powers, Daniel B. Hogan, Paul D. Edelman, David Tressemer, Reeve Vanneman, Marc Poumadere, Marcie Lobel, Sharon Lobel, Irene Goodman, and Wendy Barnes.

I am indebted to thousands of students who were in my groups, and to probably several hundred academic collaborators, including researchers from other universities, who have helped in various ways, only some of whom I have explicitly mentioned here. I am immensely grateful to them all.

I have dedicated the present book to the founders of the Department and Laboratory of Social Relations at Harvard. They were my teachers and mentors. They provided the institutional nest that I occupied so happily and for so long. This organization, with its many activities, was immensely productive while it lasted, but unfortunately it did not survive a generation turnover of the faculty. Its demise is no doubt a part of my concern with the effectiveness and survival of groups and organizations.

## Spread of Research

By the mid-1970s, my original method, Interaction Process Analysis, had come to the attention of Peter Orlik, a social psychologist at the University of Saarbruecken, and his colleague, Johann Schneider. They came to my shop to learn more about developments in Interaction Process Analysis, and the founding of SYMLOG. A great deal of work in both theory and method began and still continues with them and their colleagues in Saarbruecken, and with Rudolf Fisch at the University of Konstanz. Schneider and Orlik's translation of the book, *SYMLOG*, introduced it to social psychologists in Germany (Schneider and Orlik 1982).

Researchers in Saarbruecken and Konstanz who have made contributions include, in addition to Peter Orlik, Johann Schneider, and Rudolf Fisch: Dieter Beck, Claudia Backes, H. Barrois, M. Baus, B. Sandig, Ulrike Becker, Hans Dieter Daniel, R. Darstein-Bach, P. Faisst, I. Fromm, W. Goetzmann, D. Lessel, A. Grieser, M. Hentges, Y. Herzog, G. Hutschenreuter, Andre Köhler, R. Kolber, C. Korzilius, M. Koster-Seidl, S. Muennich, F. Lessel, B. Loehle, U. Metzger, G. Mueller, Iris Novak, Ulric Scharpf, R. Becker, H. Zimmer, R. Stiefken, H. Struchholz, O. Vogelgesang, and Klaus Wunder. I will never forget my debt to these pioneers, from whom I have learned much.

## *Retirement*—and Beyond

My formal retirement occurred in 1986. In 1988 Richard B. Polley, A. Paul Hare, and Phillip Stone published a collection of articles on experiments in application by academics, called *The SYMLOG Practitioner*. This collection launched a flood of publications about the new system into what Harvard students called "the real world."

Authors in that collection include Richard Polley, Philip Stone, Marc Poumadere, Claire Mays, Robert Koenigs, Margaret Ann Cowen, Saul Kutner, Ruth Kirsch, Peter Fassheber, Beatrix Terjung, Johann Schneider, Ulrike Becker-Beck, Wallace Bachman, Jorge Correia Jesuino, Mark P. Kriger, Louis B. Barnes, Daniel B. Hogan, Bonny K. Parke, Joseph J. Hattink, Pim B. M. Hattink, Volker Tschuschke, Paul David Edelman, Mark Palmerino, Patricia Dean Skinner, Christopher T. Rupert, and A. Paul Hare. These academic explorers in the real world gave me great encouragement and the first indications that SYMLOG would work in application outside the academic nest.

## The Real World

In the mid-1970s I was fortunate in the arrival to the social psychology faculty of Robert Koenigs, who, in two large projects in the Boston area, taught me most of what I know about organization development. Meanwhile he learned about self-analytic groups and SYMLOG. This was critical to my next period of work, since it was to be done with him, in the consulting organization, SYMLOG Consulting Group, in which I am still actively engaged in research, development, and theory.

From 1983 to the present, with my two SCG colleagues, Robert J. Koenigs and Margaret A. Cowen, I have collaborated in SYMLOG Consulting Group, a research and training institute for teaching consultants to use the theory and methods I had developed, and which we continued to develop, in the work of team building, leadership training, and organization development (see Koenigs and Cowen 1988). In this context, and with their active intellectual help, I have been able to develop and implement both the theory and its methods much further than I was able to do in an academic context. I have written extensive "expert programs" and computer-selected texts for reports to clients and leaders about the implications of the data they have provided.

Academic collaborators in this context, in addition to Robert Koenigs and Margaret Cowen, have included Sharon Hare, Maria Cristina Isolabella, Louisa Diana Brunner, Paul Hare, Daniel Hogan, Paul Roman, Hiroo Umeno, Mark Palmerino, as well as a number of others in this and other countries. A number of consultants using the method have collaborated in a recent collection of articles about their experiences and discoveries. It is edited by Sharon E. Hare and A. Paul Hare, and entitled *SYMLOG Field Theory, Organizational Consultation, Value Differences, Personality and Social Perception* (1996). The contributors include A. Paul Hare, David J. Carey, Sharon E. Hare, Marilyn Deming, Robert O. Farquhar, George L. Whaley, Robert J. Koenigs, M. Cristina Isolabella, David L. Ford, Arie Nadler, Shmuel Ellis, Amos Rabin, Eric Sundstrom, and G. Douglas Huet-Cox. I am most grateful for the help of these members and close associates of SCG.

For the present book I have been able to take advantage of the large volume of data collected by SCG consultants in their work with individual group members, teams, organizations, and leaders, mostly in business settings. Some of the most crucial findings leading to the new social-interaction systems theory, in its present developed form, have been made possible by the large volume and variety of data resulting from these applications.

The SCG data bank is designed for theoretical academic research, as well as for research to improve applications. At the present writing it contains more than a million data profiles. A data profile is the standard basic unit of data collection, used in many different contexts. It contains numerical ratings on each of twenty-six value-descriptive items in relation to the rater's *Image* of a given object of perception.

The data bank contains data mostly from business settings in the United States, but more recently from similar settings in a number of other countries and cultures, particularly those in Western Europe, but also in smaller samples from Israel, South Africa, Australia, Japan, China, South Korea, the Philippines, and Thailand. This expansion has required us to deal realistically and urgently with the problems of language differences, cultural differences, translations, validation of translated instruments, computer developments to deal with many languages, and continual new tests of the generality and validity of the theory.

Robert Koenigs has provided the samples from the data bank used in the present book. He has planned them, has explored them extensively with me, and is the virtual second author on the parts of the book presenting findings from our work together. We have worked and thought together in perfect harmony for the last fifteen years. Together, we have climbed a peak in theory, measurement, and application that now seems more lofty to me than I could ever have imagined in my early experimental work in the laboratory.

# Bibliography

Adorno, T. W., E. Frenkel-Brunswick, D. J. Levinson, and R. N. Sanford. 1950. *The authoritarian personality*. New York: Harper.

Allport, F. H. 1924. *Social psychology*. Boston, MA: Houghton-Mifflin.

Allport, G. W. and L. Postman. 1947. *The psychology of rumor*. New York: Henry Holt.

Allport, G. W., P. E. Vernon, and G. Lindzey. 1951. *Study of values* (rev. ed.). Boston, MA: Houghton Mifflin.

Altman, I. 1989. "The reemergence of small group research." *Contemporary Psychology* 34: 253–4.

Argyris, C. 1964. *Integrating the individual and the organization*. New York: Wiley.

Aronoff, J. and Wilson. 1985. *Personality in the social process*. Hillsdale, NJ: Lawrence Erlbaum Associates.

Arrow, K. [1951]1963. *Social choice and individual values* (2d ed.). New York: Wiley.

Bachman, W. 1983. A SYMLOG analysis of an Israeli-Palestinian problem-solving workshop. Unpublished paper, Psychology and Social Relations, Harvard University, Cambridge, MA.

———. 1988. "Nice guys finish first: A SYMLOG analysis of U. S. Naval commands." Pp. 133–53 in R. B. Polley, A. P. Hare, and P. J. Stone (eds.), *The SYMLOG practitioner*. New York: Praeger.

Backes, C. 1983. *Konstruktives' Negativ-Verhalten. Zum Problem der sozialen Erwuenschtheit in der Verhaltensbeschreibung*. Diplomarbeit, Universitaet des Saarlandes, Saarbruecken.

Bailey, K. 1994. *Sociology and the New Systems Theory, toward a theoretical synthesis*. Albany, NY: State University of New York.

Balck, F., G. Jantschek, and J.V. Wietersheim. 1991. "Diagnostics with families: A comparison of Faces II and SYMLOG." *Small Group Research* 22 (1): 115–23.

Baldwin, J. M. 1894. *Mental development in the child and the race*. New York: Macmillan.

———. 1897. *Social and ethical interpretations in mental development*. New York: Macmillan.

Bales, R. F. 1941. "The concept 'situation' as a sociological tool." Master's thesis, University of Oregon, Eugene, OR.

———. 1942. "Types of social structure as factors in cures for alcohol addiction." *Applied Anthropology*, April-June, 1–13.

———. 1944. "The therapeutic role of Alcoholics Anonymous as seen by a sociologist." *Quarterly Journal of Studies on Alcohol*, September.

———. 1945a. *The fixation factor in alcohol addiction: An hypothesis derived from a comparative study of Irish and Jewish social norms*. Ph.D. diss., Harvard University. Published by Arco Press, New York, 1980.

————. 1945b. "Social therapy for a social disorder—Compulsive drinking." *Journal of Social Issues* 1(3): 14–22.

————. 1946. "Cultural differences in rates of alcoholism." *Quarterly Journal of Studies on Alcohol* 6(4): 482–98.

————. 1950. *Interaction process analysis: A method for the study of small groups.* Cambridge, MA: Addison-Wesley. Reprinted 1976, University of Chicago Press.

————. 1951. "Some statistical problems in small group research." *Journal of the American Statistical Association* 45: 311–22.

————. 1952. "Some uniformities of behavior in small social systems." Pp. 146–59 in E. Swanson, T. Newcomb, and E. Hartley (eds.), *Readings in social psychology.* New York: Henry Holt.

————. 1953a. "A theoretical framework for interaction process analysis." Pp. 29–38 in D. Cartwright and A. Zander (eds.), *Group dynamics: Research and theory.* Evanston, IL: Row, Peterson.

————. 1953b. "The equilibrium problem in small groups." Pp. 111–61 in T. Parsons, R. F. Bales, and E. A. Shils, *Working papers in the theory of action.* Glencoe, IL: Free Press.

————. 1954. "In conference." *Harvard Business Review* 32(2): 44–50.

————. 1955. "How people interact in conferences." *Scientific American* 192: 31–35.

————. 1956. "Task status and likeability as a function of talking and listening in decision-making groups." Pp. 148–61 in L. D. White, *The state of the social sciences.* Chicago: University of Chicago Press.

————. 1958a. "Motivational engineering: A feat (review of *Alcoholics Anonymous Comes of Age*)." *Contemporary Psychology* August: 230–31.

————. 1958b. "Task roles and social roles in problem-solving groups." Pp. 437–47 in E. Maccoby, T. Newcomb, and E. Hartley (eds.), *Readings in social psychology.* New York: Henry Holt.

————. 1959. "Small group theory and research." Pp. 293–305 in R. K. Merton, L. Broom, and L. S. Cottrell, Jr. (eds.), *Sociology today: Problems and prospects.* New York: Basic Books.

————. 1962a. "Attitudes toward drinking in the Irish culture." Pp. 157–87 in D. J. Pittman and C. R. Snyder (eds.), *Society, culture, and drinking patterns.* New York: Wiley.

————. 1962b. "Conceptual frameworks for analysis of social interaction: Comments on four papers." *Journal of Experimental Education* 30(4): 323–24.

————. 1966. "Comment on Herbert Blumer's paper (on Sociological implications of the thought of George Herbert Mead)." *American Journal of Sociology* 71(5): 545–47.

————. 1968. "Interaction process analysis." Pp. 465–71 in D. L. Sills (ed.), *International Encyclopedia of the Social Sciences* (volume 7). New York: Macmillan and Free Press.

————. 1970. *Personality and interpersonal behavior.* New York: Holt, Rinehart and Winston. (Out of print, now available in Xerox from SYMLOG Consulting Group, 18580 Polvera Drive, San Diego, CA.)

————. 1973. "Communication in small groups." Pp. 208–18 in G. A. Miller (ed.), *Communication, language and meaning, Psychological Perspectives.* New York: Basic Books.

————. 1974. "The conceptualization of family interaction." Paper presented at meetings of American Sociological Association, Montreal, Canada.

————. 1976. "Four frameworks for the study of social interaction. In Symposium on Interaction in Laboratory and Field Settings." *Small Group Behavior* 7(1): 3–6.

————. 1980. *SYMLOG case study kit: with instructions for a group self study.* New York: Free Press.

————. 1981. *SYMLOG consultant's handbook.* Weston, MA: The SYMLOG Training Institute, 61 Scotch Pine Rd.

————. 1983a. *Hints for building teamwork.* San Diego, CA: SYMLOG Consulting Group.

————. 1983b. *How to read a SYMLOG bargraph.* San Diego, CA: SYMLOG Consulting Group.

————. 1983c. *How to read a SYMLOG field diagram.* San Diego, CA: SYMLOG Consulting Group.

————. 1983d. "SYMLOG: A practical approach to the study of groups." Pp. 499–523 in H. H. Blumberg, A. P. Hare, V. Kent, and M. Davies (eds.). *Small groups and social interaction* (vol. 2). Chichester, UK: Wiley.

————. 1983e. *The SYMLOG key to Individual and Organizational Values.* San Diego, CA: SYMLOG Consulting Group.

————. 1984a. "The integration of social psychology." *Social Psychology Quarterly* 47(1): 98–101.

————. 1984b. Texts for "The Bales Report to an Individual." San Diego, CA: SYMLOG Consulting Group.

————. 1984c. Texts for "The Bales Report to Your Group." San Diego, CA: SYMLOG Consulting Group.

————. 1984d. Texts for "Yourview," an interactive computer program. San Diego, CA: SYMLOG Consulting Group.

————. 1985. "The new field theory in social psychology." *International Journal of Small Group Research* 1(1): 1–18.

————. 1987. *Behavior observation guide.* San Diego, CA: SYMLOG Consulting Group.

————. 1988a. "A new overview of the SYMLOG system: Measuring and changing behavior in groups." Pp. 319–44 in R. B. Polley, A. P. Hare, and P. J. Stone (eds.), *The SYMLOG practitioner.* New York: Praeger.

————. 1988b. *Overview of the SYMLOG system: Measuring and changing behavior in groups.* San Diego, CA: SYMLOG Consulting Group.

————. 1988c. "Preface: SYMLOG—The present state of applications." Pp. xiii–xxi in R. B. Polley, A. P. Hare, and P. J. Stone (eds.), *The SYMLOG practitioner.* New York: Praeger.

Bales, R. F. and E. F. Borgatta. 1955. "Size of group as a factor in the interaction profile." Pp. 396–413 in A. P. Hare, E. F. Borgatta, and R. F. Bales (eds.), *Small groups.* New York: Knopf.

Bales, R. F., S. P. Cohen, with assistance from S. A.Williamson. 1979. *SYMLOG: A system for the multiple level observation of groups.* New York: Free Press.

Bales, R. F. and A. S. Couch. 1969. "The Value Profile: A factor analytic study of value statements." *Sociological Inquiry* 39(1): 3–17.

Bales, R.F., A.S. Couch, and P.J. Stone. 1962. "The interaction simulator." *Annals of the Computation Laboratory* (Harvard University) 31: 305–14.

Bales, R.F., M.A. Cowen, and R.J. Koenigs. 1986. *Interpersonal effectiveness profile, a method for reviewing how you expect to be seen by others—with subsequent hints for increasing your interpersonal effectiveness.* San Diego, CA: SYMLOG Consulting Group.

Bales, R.F. and N.A. Flanders. 1954. "Planning an observation room and group laboratory." *American Sociological Review* 19(6): 771–81.

Bales, R.F. and H. Gerbrands. 1948. "The Interaction Recorder: An apparatus and check list for sequential content analysis of social interaction." *Human Relations* 1(4): 456–63.

Bales, R.F. and A.P. Hare. 1965. "Diagnostic use of the interaction profile." *Journal of Social Psychology* 67: 239–58.

———. 1988. "Annotated bibliography of research on SYMLOG." Pp. 351–84 in R. B. Polley, A. P. Hare, and P. J. Stone (eds.), *The SYMLOG practitioner.* New York: Praeger.

Bales, R.F., A.P. Hare, and E.F. Borgatta. 1957. "Structure and dynamics of small groups: A review of four variables." Pp. 391–422 in J. B. Gittler (ed.), *Review of sociology.* New York: Wiley.

Bales, R.F. and D.J. Isenberg. 1982. "SYMLOG and leadership theory." Pp. 165–95 in J. G. Hunt, U. Sekaran, and C. A. Schriesheim (eds.), *Leadership: Beyond establishment views.* Carbondale, IL: Southern Illinois University Press.

Bales, R.F., R.J. Koenigs, and P.D. Roman. 1987. "Criteria for adaptation of SYMLOG rating items to particular populations and cultural contexts." *International Journal of Small Group Research* 3(2): 161–79.

Bales, R.F. and P.E. Slater. 1955. "Role differentiation." Pp. 259–306 in T. Parsons, R. F. Bales, et al., *The family, socialization, and interaction process.* Glencoe, IL: Free Press.

———. 1957. "Notes on role differentiation in small decision-making groups: Reply to Dr. Wheeler." *Sociometry* 20(2): 152–55.

Bales, R.F. and F.L. Strodtbeck. 1951. "Phases in group problem solving." *Journal of Abnormal and Social Psychology* 46: 485–95.

Bales, R.F., F.L. Strodtbeck, T. M. Mills, and M.E. Roseborough. 1951. "Channels of communication in small groups." *American Sociological Review* 16: 461–68.

Barber, W. H. and R.W. Oestreich. 1992. "Socio-psychological effects of developmental writing in introductory psychology." Unpublished paper.

Barrois, H. 1986. *Interaktionsverhalten von Frauen und Maennern in SYMLOG-Gruppen.* Diplomarbeit, Universitaet des Saarlandes, Saarbruecken.

Barrois, H. and J.F. Schneider. 1987. "Interaction behavior of women and men in German SYMLOG groups." *International Journal of Small Group Research* 3(1): 113–18.

Barton, S. 1994. "Chaos, self-organization, and psychology." *American Psychologist* 49 (1): 5–14.

Bartos, O. J. 1985. "Personality and choice of bargaining strategies." Unpublished paper, Department of Sociology, University of Colorado, Boulder, CO.

———. 1989. "Personality in negotiation: A sociological approach." *International Journal of Small Group Research* 5(2): 163–187.

Baus, M. and B. Sandig. 1985. *Gespraechs-Psychotherapie und weibliches Selbstkonzept.* Hildesheim, Germany: Georg Olms Verlag.

Beck, D. 1982. *Die theory der persoenlichen konstrukte* (Kelly 1955) *und der SYMLOG-Ansatz* (Bales and Cohen 1979*): ein versuch der integration.* Diplomarbeit, FR Psychologie, Universitaet des Saarlandes, Saarbruecken.

————. 1986. "The SYMLOG three dimensional space as a frame of reference for the comparison of individual construct systems." *International Journal of Small Group Research* 2(1): 71–76.

————. 1988. "Social differentiation in intergroup cooperation." *International Journal of Small Group Research* 4(1): 3–29.

————. 1992. *Kooperation und Abgrenzung. Zur Dynamik von Intergruppenbeziehungen in Kooperationssituationen.* Wiesbaden, Germany: Deutscher Universitäs-Verlag.

Beck, D. and M. Diehl. 1996. "Advances in small group research: Contributions from German-speaking countries between 1984 and 1995." Paper presented at the Fortieth Kongress of the Deutsche Gesellschaft fuer Psychologie, Muenchen, Germany.

Becker, U. 1986. "Individual tendencies in person perception and the perceiver's self-concept." *International Journal of Small Group Research* 2(1): 77–82.

Becker, U. and D. Beck. 1986. "Zur Ueberpruefung von Guetkriterien des SYMLOG-Fragebogen Leitvorstellungen individuell und organisationsbezogenen Handelns." Arbeitsbericht, Nr. 3, Universitaet Konstanz, Konstanz.

Becker, U. and J.F. Schneider. 1985. "Freie Personenbeschreibung als Datenquelle fuer die Analyse von Sozialverhalten in Kleingruppen." *Gruppenpsychotherapie und Gruppendynamik* 2: 73–83.

Becker-Beck, U. 1986. "Individual tendencies in person perception and the perceiver's self-concept." *International Journal of Small Group Research* 2: 72–82.

————. 1987. *Personwahrnehmung und Sebstkonzept. Zur Beziehung individualer Tendenzen in der Personwahrnehmung zum Selbstkonzept des Wahrnehmenden.* Frankfurt, Germany.: Lang.

————. 1989. "Methods of interaction process diagnosis: An application of sequential analytical methods to SYMLOG codings of group-interactions." *Gruppendynamik* 20(3): 243–57.

————. 1991. "Methodenentwicklung in der Interaktionsprozessdiagnostik: Ein Weiterentwicklung der SYMLOG interaktions Kodierung unter besonderer Beruecksichtigung der inhaltsebene." FR Psychologie, Universitaet des Saarlandes, Saarbruecken.

Becker-Beck, U. and R. Fisch. 1987. "Issues in the sequential analysis of group interaction processes." *International Journal of Small Group Research* 3(2): 198–212.

Becker-Beck, U. and J.F. Schneider. 1988. *Untersuchungen zur psychometrischen Qualitaet des SYMLOG Beurteilungsbogens zum Socialverhalten.* Arbeiten der FR Psychologie, Nr. 128, Universitaet des Saarlandes, Saarbruecken.

————. 1990. "Small group research in German-speaking countries." *Zeitschrift fuer Sozialpsychologie* 21(4): 274–97.

Bennis, W., K. Benne, and R. Chin, eds. 1961. *The planning of change: Readings in the applied behavioral sciences.* New York: Holt, Rinehart, and Winston.

Bion, W. R. 1961. *Experiences in groups: And other papers.* New York: Basic Books.

Bixby, T. D. 1978. "Action and speech-content: Perception in small group interaction." Honors thesis, Psychology and Social Relations, Harvard University, Cambridge, MA.

Blake, R. R. and J.S. Mouton. 1964. *The managerial grid.* Houston, TX: Gulf.

Bobrow, E. S. 1983. "Mother-adolescent daughter interaction and adherence to diabetic regimens." Ph.D. diss. New York University.

Boethius, S. B. 1987. "The view from the middle: Perceiving patterns of interaction in middle management groups." *International Journal of Small Group Research* 3(1): 1–15.

Bogardus, E. S. 1925. "Measuring social distance." *Journal of Applied Sociology* 9: 299–308.

Bonacich, P. 1968. "Specialization and differentiation of leadership in small laboratory groups." Ph.D. diss., Harvard University, Cambridge, MA.

Booher, M. E. 1976. "Effects of role and dominance on attribution and visual conversation behavior." Honors thesis, Psychology and Social Relations, Harvard University, Cambridge, MA.

Borgatta, E. F. 1953a. "The consistency of subject behavior and the reliability of scoring in interaction process analysis." *American Sociological Review* 18(5): 566–69.

———. 1953b. "Interaction of individuals in reconstituted groups." *Sociometry* 16(4): 302–20.

Borgatta, E. F. and R. F. Bales. 1953. "Task and accumulation of experience as factors in the interaction of small groups." *Sociometry* 16(3): 238–52.

———. 1956. "Sociometric status patterns and characteristics of interaction." *Journal of Social Psychology* 43: 289–97.

Borgatta, E. F., R.F. Bales, and A.S. Couch. 1954. "Some findings relevant to the great man theory of leadership." *American Sociological Review* 19(6): 755–59.

Bormann, E. 1972. "Fantasy and rhetorical vision: The rhetorical criticism of social reality." *Quarterly Journal of Speech* 58: 396–407.

Bower, B. 1995. "Return of the group; people may have evolved to further collective as well as individual interests." *Science News* 148: 328–30.

Breer, P. and E. Locke. 1965. *Task experience as a source of attitudes.* Homewood, IL: Dorsey Press.

Brehm, J. 1966. *A theory of psychological reactance.* New York: Academic Press.

Breiger, R. L. and J.G. Ennis. 1979. "Personae and social roles: The network structure of personality types in the small group." *Social Psychology Quarterly* 42(3): 262–70.

Brennan, J. S. 1982. "SYMLOG: A system for the multiple level observation of groups." *Social Forces* 60(3): 959–61.

Bronstein-Burrows, P. 1981. "Patterns of parent behavior: A crosscultural study." *Merrill-Palmer Quarterly* 27(2): 129–43.

Brown, J. F. 1936. *Psychology and the social order.* New York: McGraw-Hill.

Buckley, W. 1967. *Sociology and modern Systems Theory.* Englewood Cliffs, NJ: Prentice-Hall.

Burgess, E. W. and L.S. Cottrell. 1939. *Predicting the success or failure in marriage.* New York: Prentice-Hall.

Burrows, P. B. 1979. "Parent-child behavior in a sample of Mexican families." Ph.D. diss., Harvard University, Cambridge, MA.

Carey, D. J., with S.E. Hare. 1996. "David J. Carey facilitates three-day teambuilding with police." Pp. 11–25 in S. E. Hare and A. P. Hare (eds.), *SYMLOG field theory*. Westport, CT: Praeger.

Carter, L. F. 1951. "Some research on leadership in small groups." Pp. 146–57 in H. Guetzkow (ed.), *Groups, leadership, and men: Research in human relations*. Pittsburgh, PA: Carnegie.

Case, C. M. 1939. "The value concept in sociology and related fields." *Sociology and Social Research* 23: 404–30.

Casti, J. 1997. *Would-be worlds; How simulation is changing the frontiers of science*. New York: John Wiley and Sons.

Cattell, R., D.R. Saunders, and G.F. Stice. 1951. *The sixteen personality factor questionnaire*. Champaign, IL: Institute of Personality and Ability Testing.

Chansom, N. 1996. "Value orientations of agricultural leaders in farmer associations in Thailand." Ph.D. diss., Graduate Faculty of Liberal and Interdisciplinary Studies, United States International University, San Diego, CA.

Churchill, L. 1961. "Aggression in a small group setting." Ph.D. diss., Harvard University, Cambridge, MA.

Cohen, S. P. 1972. "Varieties of interpersonal relationships in small groups." Ph.D. diss., Harvard University, Cambridge, MA.

———. 1979. "The structure of SYMLOG adjective rating scales." Pp. 396–406 in R. F. Bales, and S. P. Cohen, *SYMLOG*. New York: Free Press.

Cooley, C. H. 1912. *Social organization*. New York: Charles Scribner's Sons.

———. 1922a. *Human nature and the social order* (rev. ed.) New York: Charles Scribner's Sons.

———. 1922b. *Social process*. New York: Charles Scribner's Sons.

———. 1926. "The roots of social knowledge." *American Journal of Sociology* 32: 59–79.

———. 1930. *Sociological theory and social research*. New York: Henry Holt.

Costa, P. T. and T.A. Widiger. 1994. *Personality disorders and the five-factor model of personality*. Washington, DC: American Psychological Association.

Cottrell, L. S. 1942. "The analysis of situational fields in social psychology." *American Sociological Review* 7: 370–82.

Couch, A. S. 1960. "Psychological determinants of interpersonal behavior." Ph.D. diss., Harvard University, Cambridge, MA.

Couch, A. S. and L.F. Carter. 1952. "A factorial study of the rated behavior of group members." Paper presented at meeting of Eastern Psychological Association, March.

Couch, A. S. and D.G. Goodrich. 1952. "Militant radicalism scale." Unpublished document, Harvard University, Cambridge, MA.

Cowen, M. A. 1992. "Team building with SYMLOG." Pp. 65–87 in A. P. Hare, *Groups, teams, and social interaction*. New York: Praeger.

———. 1996. "Forward: Consulting with SYMLOG." Pp. xv–xvi in S. E. Hare and A. P. Hare (eds.), *SYMLOG field theory*. Westport, CT: Praeger.

———. 1997. "The relationship between behavior and value assessments of leader/managers by their coworkers in organizations." Ph.D. diss., Graduate Faculty of Psychology and Family Studies, United States International University, San Diego, CA.

Daniel, H. D. 1985. "Internal consistency of SYMLOG adjective rating scales: A comparison of four studies." Unpublished paper. FR Psychologie, Universitaet Konstanz, Konstanz.

Darstein-Bach, R. 1981. *Erprobung einer Kinderform der SYMLOG-Rating-Methode an einer Schulkindergartengruppe (Fallstudie)*. Diplomarbeit, FR Psychologie, Universitaet des Saarlandes, Saarbruecken.

Davidson, R. A. 1989. "Use of parametric statistics for ordinal data." *International Journal of Small Group Research* 5(2): 201–10.

Davies, A. F. 1980. *Skills, outlooks, and passions*. Cambridge, UK: Cambridge University Press.

Dawkins, R. 1996. *Climbing Mt. Improbable*. New York: W. W. Norton.

de Waal, F. 1996. *Good-natured: The origins of right and wrong in humans and other animals*. Cambridge, MA: Harvard University Press.

Deming M., with S.E. Hare. 1996. "Marilyn Deming promotes leadership effectiveness in a multiphase intervention with a Hawaiian corporation." Pp. 27–40 in S. E. Hare and A. P. Hare (eds.), *SYMLOG field theory*. Westport, CT: Praeger.

Dennett, D. 1995. *Darwin's dangerous idea*. New York: Simon and Schuster.

———. 1996. *Kinds of minds; Toward an understanding of consciousness*. New York: Basic Books.

Dewey, J. 1898. "The reflex arc concept in psychology." *Psychological Review* 3: 357–70.

———. 1933. *How we think*. New York: D. C. Heath.

Diehl-Becker, A. 1987. "Comparison of a German and an American version of a SYMLOG-atlas on Every-day descriptions of behavior." *International Journal of Small Group Research* 3(2): 213–19.

Dion, K. L. and C.R. Evans. 1992. "On cohesiveness: Reply to Keyton and other critics of the construct." *Small Group Research* 23(2): 242–50.

Dollard, J. 1935. *Criteria for the life history*. New Haven, CT: Yale University Press.

Dunphy, D. C. 1964. "Social change in self-analytic groups." Ph.D. diss., Harvard University, Cambridge, MA.

———. 1968. "Phases, roles, and myths in self-analytic groups." *Journal of Applied Behavioral Sciences* 4: 195–226.

Dunphy, D. and R. Dick. 1981. *Organizational change by choice*. Sydney, Australia: McGraw-Hill.

Dunphy, D. and D. Stace. 1990. *Under new management, Australian organizations in transition*. Sydney, Australia: McGraw-Hill.

Durkheim, E. [1893]1960. *The division of labor in society*. Glencoe, IL: Free Press.

Edelman, P. D. 1983. "Values and interpersonal conflict." Ph.D. diss., Harvard University, Cambridge, MA.

Edelman, P. D. and A. Maddocks. 1985. "Steps to finding the right players for an employee-owned team." *Employee Ownership*. Westborough, MA: National Center for Employee Ownership.

Edelman, P. D. and M. Palmerino. 1988. "SYMLOG in marketing research." Pp. 271–80 in R. B. Polley, A. P. Hare, and P. J. Stone (eds.), *The SYMLOG practitioner*. New York: Praeger.

Eigen, M. and R. Winkler. 1965. *Laws of the game: How the principles of nature govern chance* (trans. from the German, 1982, A. Knopf). Princeton, NJ: Princeton University Press.

Ennis, J. G. 1980. "The structure of interaction in five SYMLOG groups: A block-model study of cores and peripheries." Ph.D. diss., Harvard University, Cambridge, MA.

Ernst, M. M. 1989. "Interactions of the protagonists and their auxiliary egos in psychodrama: Process analysis and comparisons using the SYMLOG interaction scoring." *International Journal of Small Group Research* 5 (1): 89–118.

Etzioni, E. 1965. "Dual leadership in complex organizations." *American Sociological Review* 30: 688–98.

Eubank, E. 1932. *The concepts of sociology*. New York: D. C. Heath.

Eysenck, H. J. 1954. *The psychology of politics*. London, UK: Routledge and Kegan Paul.

Faisst, P. 1981. *SYMLOG-Theorie. Einige wissenschaftstheoretische Anmerkungen zu den Konzepten Sprache und Handlung*. Diplomarbeit, FR Psychologie, Universitaet des Saarlandes, Saarbruecken.

Farago, S. 1983. "A study of the relationship between birth order and position in the family social hierarchy in families with and without a moderately mentally handicapped child." Ph.D. diss., School of Education, Health, Nursing and Arts Professions, New York University, New York.

Farquhar, R. O., with S.E. Hare. 1996. "Robert O. Farquhar combines organizational and individual feedback with the executive committee of a scientific research unit." Pp. 41–56 in S. E. Hare and A. P. Hare (eds.), *SYMLOG field theory*. Westport, CT: Praeger.

Farrell, M. P., M. H. Schmitt, and G.D. Heinemann. 1986. "Informal roles, rituals, and styles of humor in interdisciplinary health care teams: Their relationship to stages in group development." *International Journal of Small Group Research* 2(2): 143–62.

———. 1988. "Organizational environments of health care teams: Impact on team development and implications for consultation." *International Journal of Small Group Research* 4 (1): 31–53.

Fassheber, P. and B. Terjung. 1985. "SYMLOG rating data and their relationship to performance and behavior beyond the group situation." *International Journal of Small Group Research* 1(2): 97–108.

———. 1988. "SYMLOG team diagnostics as organizational development." Pp. 99–115 in R. B. Polley, A. P. Hare, and P. J. Stone (eds.), *The SYMLOG practitioner*. New York: Praeger.

Feger, H. 1985. "Structures of interaction in small groups." *International Journal of Small Group Research* 1: 109–21.

Festinger, L. 1954. "A theory of social comparison processes." *Human Relations* 7: 117–40.

———. 1957. *A theory of cognitive dissonance*. Evanston, IL: Row, Peterson.

Fiedler, F. E. 1967. *A theory of leadership effectiveness*. New York: McGraw-Hill.

Fine, G. A. 1976. "A group space analysis of interpersonal dynamics." Ph.D. diss., Harvard University, Cambridge, MA.

———. 1986. "Behavioral change in group space: A reintegration of Lewinian Theory into small group research." *Advances in Group Processes* 3: 23–50.

Fisch, R. 1985. Handanweisung zur Ermittlung von Leitvorstellungen des Verhaltens in Gruppen und Organisationen nach dem SYMLOG-Verfahren. (Translation, unpublished) FR Psychologie, Universitaet Konstanz, Konstanz.

Fisch, R., H.-D Daniel, and D. Beck. 1991. Kleingruppenforschung—Forschungsschwerpunct und Forschungstrends. *Gruppendynamik* 22(3):237–61.

Flugel, J. C. 1921. *Psychoanalytic study of the family.* London, UK: Hogarth Press.

Ford, D. L. 1996. "Management of diversity: An assessment of cross-race managerial behaviors and implications for minority managers' career development." Pp. 111–26 in S. E. Hare and A. P. Hare (eds.), *SYMLOG field theory.* Westport, CT: Praeger.

Freud, S. [1915] 1965. *New introductory lectures in psychoanalysis.* New York: Norton.

Fromm, I. 1981. *Ein Vergleich der Selbstkonzepterhebungs-Methoden von Orlik und Bales.* Diplomarbeit, FR Psychologie, Universitaet des Saarlandes, Saarbruecken.

Gibbard, G. S. 1981. "A framework for the integration of social psychology." *Contemporary Psychology* 26(1): 14–15.

Gleick, J. 1987. *Chaos, making a new science.* New York: Penguin Books.

Goetzmann, W. and D. Lessel. 1980. *Trainingseffekte in SYMLOG-Gruppen. Veraenderung einiger sozialpsychologischer Kennwerte.* Diplomarbeit, FR Psychologie, Universitaet des Saarlandes, Saarbruecken.

Goetzmann, W., J.F. Schneider, and P. Orlik. 1982. *Beurteilung von SYMLOG-Kodierleistungen: Einstandardisiertes Verfahren zur Trainingskontrolle.* Arbeiten der FR Psychologie, Nr. 82, Universitaet des Saarlandes, Saarbruecken.

Goodman, I. F. 1984. "The relationship between the perceptions of family interaction and of television's role in the family." Ph.D. diss. in Education, Harvard University, Cambridge, MA.

Graham, Q. 1984. "The relationship between style of leadership and organizational culture: An exploratory study." Ph.D. diss., George Washington University.

Graumann, C. F. 1979. Die Scheu des Psychologen vor der Interaktion. Ein Schisma und sein Geschichte. *Zeitschrift fur Sozialpsychologie* 10: 284–304.

Greenberg, C., E. Sloane, and J. Woodson. 1971. "Interaction patterns of families with a suicidal adolescent." Master's thesis, School of Social Work, University of Southern California, Los Angeles, CA.

Grieser, A. 1984. *Selbstkonzept und Anorexia nervosa. Ein Beitrag zur Validierung des Selbstkonzeptgitters.* Diplomarbeit, FR Psychologie, Universitaet des Saarlandes, Saarbruecken.

Gruenfeld, L. W. and T.R. Lin. 1984. "Social behavior of field independents and dependents in an organic group." *Human Relation* 37(9): 721–41.

Gualtiert, J. J. 1983. "Transition to parenthood: A study of its effects on the perception of stressfulness of life events, self-esteem, social-support, and marital relationship." Ph.D. diss., State University of New York, Buffalo, NY.

Hampden-Turner, C. and F. Trompenaars. 1997. *Mastering the infinite game.* Oxford, UK: Capstone Publishing.

Hare, A. P. 1957. "Situational differences in leader behavior." *Journal of Abnormal and Social Psychology* 55: 132–35.

———. [1962]1976. *Handbook of small group research.* New York: The Free Press.

———. 1973. "Theories of group development and categories for interaction analysis." *Small Group Behavior* 4(3): 259–304.

———. 1982. *Creativity in small groups.* Beverly Hills, CA: Sage.

———. 1985a. "The significance of SYMLOG in the study of group dynamics." *International Journal of Small Group Research* 1(1): 38–50.

———. 1985b. *Social interaction as drama: Applications from conflict resolution.* Beverly Hills, CA: Sage.

———. 1985c. "Creativity and conformity during Egypt-Israel negotiations." *International Journal of Small Group Research* 1(2): 122–30.

———. 1986. "Expressive and anti-conforming behavior and subgroup formation on the Raft Acali." *International Journal of Small Group Research* 2(2): 197–209.

———. 1989. "New Field Theory: SYMLOG research, 1960–1988." *Advances in Group Processes* 6: 229–57.

———. 1992a. *Groups, teams, and social interaction.* New York: Praeger.

———. 1992b. "SYMLOG analysis." Pp. 125–41 in A. P. Hare, *Groups, teams, and social interaction.* New York: Praeger.

———. 1996a. "A brief history of SYMLOG: In headlines and footnotes." Pp. 193–200 in S. E. Hare and A. P. Hare (eds.), *SYMLOG field theory.* Westport, CT: Praeger.

———. 1996b. "SYMLOG Field Theory." Pp. 1–8 in S. E. Hare and A. P. Hare (eds.), *SYMLOG field theory.* Westport, CT: Praeger.

Hare, A.P. and R.F. Bales. 1963. "Seating position in small group interaction." *Sociometry* 26(4): 480–6.

Hare, A.P. and H.H. Blumberg. 1988. *Dramaturgical analysis of social interaction.* New York: Praeger.

Hare, A. P., H.H. Blumberg, M.F. Davies, and M.V. Kent. 1994. *Small group research: A handbook.* Norwood, NJ: Ablex.

———. 1996. *Small groups: An introduction.* Westport, CT. Praeger.

Hare, A. P., E.F. Borgatta, and R.F. Bales, eds. 1965. *Small groups: Studies in social interaction.* New York: Alfred A. Knopf.

Hare, A. P. and J. Hare. 1996. *J. L. Moreno.* London, UK: Sage.

Hare, A. P., S.E. Hare, and R.J. Koenigs. 1996. "Implicit personality theory, social desirability, and reflected appraisal of self in the context of new field theory (SYMLOG)." Pp. 175–92 in S. E. Hare and A. P. Hare (eds.), *SYMLOG field theory.* Westport, CT: Praeger.

Hare, A. P., R.J. Koenigs, and S.E. Hare. 1996. "Perceptions of observed and model values of male and female managers." Pp. 127–36 in S. E. Hare and A. P. Hare (eds.), *SYMLOG field theory.* Westport, CT: Praeger.

Hare, A. P., H.M. Kritzer, and H.H. Blumberg. 1979. "Functional analysis of persuasive interaction in a role-playing experiment." *Journal of Social Psychology* 107: 77–88.

Hare, A. P. and D. Naveh. 1985a. "Conformity and creativity: Camp David, 1978." *Small Group Behavior* 17(3): 243–68.

———. 1985b. "Creative problem solving: Camp David Summit, 1978." *Small Group Behavior* 16(2): 123–38.

Hare, S. E. 1990. "Implications for culture learning and management training: A comparison of Chinese and American work-related value orientations and a study of switcher managers in the Southern California hospitality industry." Ph.D. diss., Graduate School of Education, University of California, Los Angeles, CA.

———. 1996a. "Implications for cross-cultural management training: A comparison of Chinese and American managers." Pp. 87–101 in S. E. Hare and A. P. Hare (eds.), *SYMLOG field theory.* Westport, CT: Praeger.

————. 1996b. "SYMLOG consulting materials." Pp. 201–30 in S. E. Hare and A. P. Hare (eds.), *SYMLOG field theory*. Westport, CT: Praeger.

Hare, S. E. and A.P. Hare, eds. 1996. *SYMLOG field theory: Organizational consultation, value differences, personality and social perception*. Westport, CT: Praeger.

Hattink, J. A. 1985. "SYMLOG in the classroom." *International Journal of Small Group Research* 1(2): 176–81.

Hattink, J. A. and P.B.M. Hattink. 1988. "Teacher's leadership and pupil's behavior: Influencing the orbital movement." Pp. 245–68 in R. B. Polley, A. P. Hare, and P. J. Stone (eds.). *The SYMLOG practitioner*. New York: Praeger.

Heider, F. 1946. "Attitudes and cognitive organization." *Journal of Psychology* 21: 107–12.

Heinicke, C. M. and R.F. Bales. 1953. "Developmental trends in the structure of small groups." *Sociometry* 16: 7–38.

Hendrick, I. 1934. *Facts and theories of psychoanalysis*. New York: Alfred A. Knopf.

Hentges, M. 1983. *Trainingsfilme fuer Act-Kodierungen in SYMLOG*. Diplomarbeit, FR Psychologie, Universitaet des Saarlandes, Saarbruecken.

Herzog, Y. 1982. *Zum Konzept des Images im SYMLOG-Ansatz*. Diplomarbeit, FR Psychologie, Universitaet des Saarlandes, Saarbruecken.

Hobbes, T. 1655–1946. *Leviathan: or, the matter, forme, and power of a commonwealth, ecclesiastical and civil*, ed. M. Oakeshott. Oxford, UK: Blackwell.

Hogan, D. B. 1983. "Personality assessment and managerial performance: A comparison of the Behavioral Event Interview, SYMLOG General Behavior Description Form, and other assessment measures in predicting job outcome." Ph.D. diss., Harvard University, Cambridge, MA.

————. 1988. "The SYMLOG leadership profile as a predictor of managerial performance." Pp. 191–210 in R. B. Polley. A. P. Hare, and P. J. Stone (eds.), *The SYMLOG practitioner*. New York: Praeger.

Hollander, E. and R. Hunt. 1972. *Classic contributions to social psychology*. New York: Oxford University Press.

Holmes, J. 1986. "Beyond the group situation: The political dimension of SYMLOG value-space." *International Journal of Small Group Research* 2(2): 163–71.

Horney, K. 1939. *New ways in psychoanalysis*. New York: Norton.

Hosking, D. and I. Morley. 1985. "SYMLOG and leadership effectiveness." *Bulletin of the British Psychological Society* 38: 4.

Hoskovec, J. 1982. "SYMLOG: A system for the multiple level observation of groups." *Ceskoslovenska Psychologie* 26(2): 202.

Hurley, J. R. 1991. "Self-acceptance, acceptance of others, and SYMLOG: Equivalent measures of the two central interpersonal dimensions?" *Journal of Clinical Psychology* 47(4): 576–82.

Hutschenreuter, G. 1979. *Verlaufsuntersuchung einer stationaeren Gruppentherapie mit dem SYMLOG-Verfahren*. Diplomarbeit, FR Psychologie, Universitaet des Saarlandes, Saarbruecken.

Ichiyama, M. A. 1988. "Analysis of reflected appraisal using SYMLOG rating data." *International Journal of Small Group Research* 4(2): 181–98.

Ichiyama, M. A. and B.W. Reddy. 1987. "Assessment of small group dynamics: The SYMLOG system." Pp. 185–208 in W. B. Reddy and C. C. Henderson, Jr. (eds.),

*Training theory and practice*. Arlington, VA: NTL Institute for Applied Behavioral Science.

Isenberg, D. J. 1981. "Individual differences in social-knowledge structures." Ph.D. diss., Harvard University, Cambridge, MA.

———. 1986a. "Group Polarization: A critical review and meta-analysis." *Journal of Personality and Social Psychology* 50:1141–51.

———. 1986b. "Individual differences in social-knowledge structures." *International Journal of Small Group Research* 2(2): 113–33.

Isenberg, D. J. and J.G. Ennis. 1981. "Perceiving group members: A comparison of derived and imposed dimensions." *Journal of Personality and Social Psychology* 42(2): 293–305.

Isolabella, M. C. 1992. "Cross-cultural comparison of managers' team membership and leadership value orientations." Ph.D. diss., Graduate Faculty of the School of Human Behavior, United States International University, San Diego, CA.

———. 1993. "Lavorare in team." *Sviluppo e Organizzazione* 139: 17–28.

———. 1997. "Current and future leadership styles in nine European countries: Indications of postmodern trends." Pp. 142–50 in F. Avallone, J. Arnold, and K. de Witte (eds.), *Quaderni di psicologia del lavoro: Feelings work in Europe*. Milano, Italy: Edizioni Angelo Guerini e Associati.

———. in press. "Il conflitto e la cooperazione." Pp. 97–130 in G. Costa and R. C. D. Nacamulli (eds.), *Manuale di organizzazione Aziendale* (volume 3). Torino, Italy: UTET.

Isolabella, M. C., with S.E. Hare. 1996. "North American and Italian managers' views of effective leadership and teamwork: A cross-cultural perspective." Pp. 103–9 in S. E. Hare and A. P. Hare (eds.), *SYMLOG field theory*. Westport, CT: Praeger.

Jacobs, J. [1992] 1994. *Systems of survival*. New York: Vintage Books.

Jaffe, E. D. and I.D. Nebebzahl. 1990. "Group interaction and business game performance." *Simulation and Gaming* 21(2): 133–46.

James, W. 1890. *Principles of psychology*. New York: Henry Holt.

Jameson, S. H. 1937. "Introduction to social interaction." Unpublished manuscript, University of Oregon, Eugene, OR.

Janis, I. L. 1972. *Victims of groupthink: A psychological study of foreign policy decisions and fiascos*. Boston, MA: Houghton Mifflin.

———. 1982. *Groupthink: Psychological studies of policy decisions and fiascoes*. Boston, MA: Houghton Mifflin.

Jesuino, J. C. 1985. "The assessment of leaders by SYMLOG." *International Journal of Small Group Research* 1(1): 87–8.

———. 1988. "The use of SYMLOG in the study of organizational socialization." Pp. 155–72 in R. B. Polley, A. P. Hare, and P. J. Stone (eds.). *The SYMLOG practitioner*. New York: Praeger.

Jones, E. E. 1953. "The role of authoritarianism in the perception and valuation of a prospective leader." Ph.D. diss., Harvard University, Cambridge, MA.

Kaneklin, C. and M.C. Isolabella. 1995. "Le emozioni nelle organizzazioni." Pp. 125–36 in F. Avallone (ed.), *La metamorfosi del lavoro*. Milano, Italy: Franco Angeli.

Kaneklin, C., M.C. Isolabella, and A. Bruno. 1996. Linguaggio e intervento psicosociologico. *Psicologia del Lavoro* 100:55–62.

Kassebaum, G. G. 1958. "Value orientations and interpersonal behavior: An experimental study." Ph.D. diss., Harvard University, Cambridge, MA.

Kassebaum, G., A. Couch, and P. Slater. 1959. "The factorial dimensions of the MMPI." *Journal of Consulting Psychology* 23:226–36.

Kauffman, S. 1995. *At home in the universe*. Harmondsworth: Viking.

Kecharananta, N. 1994. "Value orientations of Thai managers in privatizing state enterprises and the private sector." Ph.D. diss., Graduate Faculty of Liberal and Interdisciplinary Studies, United States International University, San Diego, CA.

Keller, M. E. 1980. "SYMLOG: A system for the multiple level observation of groups." *Personnel* 57(2): 78.

Kelly, L. and R.L. Duran. 1985. "Interaction and performance in small groups: A descriptive report." *International Journal of Small Group Research* 1(2): 182–92.

———. 1986. "A replication of Parke and Houben's study of group types." *International Journal of Small Group Research* 2(2): 186–96.

Keyton, J. 1988. "Comment on Evans and Dion: Still more on group cohesion." *Small Group Research* 23(2): 237–41.

Keyton, J. and J. Springston. 1990. "Redefining cohesiveness in groups." *Small Group Research* 21(2): 234–54.

Klimekfritzges, T. 1981. "SYMLOG: A system for the multiple level observation of groups" and "SYMLOG Case study kit with instructions for a group self study." *Personnel Psychology* 34(1): 201–3.

Kluckhohn, C. 1954. "Values and value-orientations in the theory of action: An exploration in definition and classification." Pp. 388–433 in T. Parsons and E. A. Shils (eds.), *Toward a general theory of action*. Cambridge, MA: Harvard University Press.

Kluckhohn, F. 1950. "Dominant and substitute profiles of cultural orientation." *Social Forces* 28(4).

Koenigs, R. J. 1996. "Leadership can be taught." Pp. 73–83 in S. E. Hare and A. P. Hare (eds.), *SYMLOG field theory*. Westport, CT: Praeger.

Koenigs, R. J. and M.A.Cowen. 1988. "SYMLOG as action research." Pp. 61–87 in R. B. Polley, A. P. Hare, and P. J. Stone (eds.), *The SYMLOG practitioner*. New York: Praeger.

Koffka, K. 1928. *The growth of the mind*. New York: Harcourt, Brace.

———. 1935. *Principles of gestalt psychology*. New York: Harcourt, Brace.

Köhler, A. 1980. *Programme zur Aufarbeitung und Auswertung von SYMLOG-Daten.* Arbeiten der FR Psychologie, Nr. 71, Universitaet des Saarlandes, Saarbruecken.

———. 1986. "Seven years with SYMLOG: A review of research." *International Journal of Small Group Research* 2(1): 83–9.

Köhler, W. 1927. *The mentality of apes*. New York: Harcourt, Brace.

Kolber, R. 1984. *Struktur und Inhaltsanalyse von Selbstkonzeptgitter. Ein Vergleich zwischen Alkoholikern und Studenten*. Diplomarbeit, FR Psychologie, Universitaet des Saarlandes, Saarbruecken.

Korzilius, C. 1981. *Zur Beziehung zwischen Selbstkonzept und sozialem Verhalten in einer studentischen Selbstanalysegruppe*. Diplomarbeit, FR Psychologie, Universitaet des Saarlandes, Saarbruecken.

Korzybsky, E. T. 1933. *Science and sanity*. New York: Science Press.

Koster-Seidl, M. and S. Muennich. 1985. *Selbstkonzept und soziales Umfeld von*

*Alkohol- und Heroinabhaengigen.* Diplomarbeit, FR Psychologie, Universitaet des Saarlandes, Saarbruecken.

Kressel, N. J. 1987. "SYMLOG and behavior therapy: Pathway to expanding horizons." *Small Group Behavior* 2(1): 83–9.

Kriger, M. R. and L.B. Barnes. 1984. "Deep structures and dynamic processes: A multi-method analysis of a high performance organization in a declining industry." Unpublished paper, College of Business Administration, Northeastern University, Boston, MA.

———. 1988. "Executive leadership networks: Top management group dynamics in a high-performance organization." Pp. 173–190 in R. B. Polley, A. P. Hare, and P. J. Stone (eds.). *The SYMLOG practitioner.* New York: Praeger.

Kroeger, F., A. Drinkmann, W. Herzog, and E. Petzold. 1991. "Family diagnostics: Object representation in families with eating disorders." *Small Group Research* 22(1): 99–114.

Kroeger, F., A. Drinkmann, J. Schneider, M. Schmidt-Rinke, and E. Petzold. 1989. "Familiendiagnostik: Standardisierte Methoden und systemische Therapie? SYMLOG als Versuch eines Brueckenschlages." *Gruppenpsychotherapie und Gruppendynamik* 25: 110–26.

Kutner, S. S. 1984. "SYMLOG: A system for the multiple level observation of groups" and "SYMLOG case study kit." *Social Work With Groups* 7 (1): 99–102.

Kutner, S. S. and R.D. Kirsch. 1985. "Clinical applications of SYMLOG: A graphic system of observing relationships." *Journal of the National Association of Social Workers* 30(6): 497–503.

———. 1988. "Enhancement of professional performance in clinical settings through the use of self ratings." Pp. 89–98 in R. B. Polley, A. P. Hare, and P. J. Stone (eds.), *The SYMLOG practitioner.* New York: Praeger.

Kutner, S. S., R.D. Kirsch, and D.E. Cournoyer. 1989. "The impact of the therapist's family of origin on work with client systems." *International Journal of Small Group Research* 5(2): 188–200.

Lang, W. 1982. "A factor analytic study of selected group-relevant personality traits." Ph.D. diss., Department of Educational Psychology, University of Calgary, Alberta, Canada.

Lawrence, H. V. 1992. "The effects of training in feedback on managers' attributional bias and perceived effectiveness of their work in groups." Ph.D. diss., Virginia Polytechnic Institute and State University, Blacksburg, VA.

Leary, T. 1957. *Interpersonal diagnosis of personality.* New York: Ronald.

LeBon, G. 1895–1896. *The crowd: A study of the popular mind.* London: T. Fisher Union.

Leik, R. 1963. "Instrumentality and emotionality in family interaction." *Sociometry* 26: 131–45.

Lessel, F. 1984. *Synchronisationsanalyse der Leiter-Mitglieder-Interaktion in SYMLOG-Gruppen.* Diplomarbeit, FR Psychologie, Universitaet des Saarlandes, Saarbruecken.

Levinger, G. 1964. "Task and social emotional behavior in marriage." *Sociometry* 27: 443–48.

Levinson, D. J. and P.E. Huffman. 1955. "Traditional family ideology and its relation to personality." *Journal of Personality* 23: 251–73.

Lewin, K. 1935. *A dynamic theory of personality.* New York: McGraw-Hill.
———. 1936. *Principles of topological psychology.* New York: McGraw-Hill.
———. 1951. *Field theory in social science.* New York: Harper.
Lewin, K., R. Lippitt, and R.K. White. 1939. "Patterns of aggressive behavior in experimentally created 'social climates.'" *Journal of Social Psychology* 10: 271–99.
Lewin, R. 1992. *Complexity, life at the edge of chaos.* New York: Macmillan.
Lilli, W. 1986. "Von den Schwierigkeiten einer systematischen Gruppenbeobachtung." *Zeitschriftfuer Socialpsychologie* 17(1): 55–9.
Lobel, M. 1982. "The effects of amphetamine and methaqualone on human social interaction." Honors thesis, Psychology and Social Relations, Harvard University, Cambridge, MA.
Lobel, S. A. 1984. "Effects of a sojourn in the United States: A SYMLOG content analysis of in-depth interviews." Ph.D. diss., Harvard University, Cambridge, MA.
———. 1988. "A SYMLOG content analysis of in-depth interviews: Perceptions of Scandinavian visitors to the United States." *International Journal of Small Group Research* 4(2): 123–41.
Locke, J. 1690. *Two treatises of government* (ed. P. Laslett). Cambridge, UK: Cambridge University Press.
Loehle, B. 1982. *Die Operationalisierung des Wertkonzeptes bei Bales und Rokeach. Ein theoretischer und empirischer Vergleich.* Diplomarbeit, FR Psychologie, Universitaet des Saarlandes, Saarbruecken.
Losada, M. and S. Markovitch. 1990. "Groupanalyzer: A system for dynamic analysis of group interaction." *Proceedings of the Twenty-third Annual Hawaii International Conference on System Sciences,* pp. 101–10.
Losada, M., P. Sanchez, and E. Noble. 1989. *Effect of collaborative technology and feedback on interactive sequences in meetings* (Tech. Rep. No. CMI-89-019). Ann Arbor MI: EDS, Center for Machine Intelligence.
Lustig, M. W. 1983. "SYMLOG: A system for the multiple level observation of groups." *Quarterly Journal of Speech* 69(2): 226–27.
———. 1987. "Bales's interpersonal rating forms: Reliability and dimensionality." *Small Group Behavior* 18(1): 99–107.
Magnussen, D. and N.S. Endler, eds. 1977. *Personality at the crossroads: Current issues in interactional psychology.* Hillsdale, NJ: Van Nostrand.
Mainzer, K. 1994. *Thinking in complexity, The complex dynamics of matter, mind, and mankind.* Berlin, Heidelberg, Germany: Springer-Verlag.
Matheson, W. 1972. "An independent validation of Bales's concept of 'social psychological space.'" *Alberta Journal of Educational Research.*
Mays, C. M. and M. Poumadere. 1989. "Decentralizing risk analysis in large engineered systems: An approach to articulating technical and socio-organizational dimensions of system performance." *Risk Analysis* 9(4): 453–61.
McClelland, D. C. 1961. *The achieving society.* Princeton, NJ: Van Nostrand.
———. 1975. *Power: The inner experience.* New York: Wiley.
McClelland, D. C., J.W. Atkinson, R. A. Clark, and E.L. Lowell. 1953. *The achievement motive.* New York: Appleton.
McDougall, W. 1908. *An introduction to social psychology* (30th ed.) London, UK: Methuen. Paperback edition 1963 by Barnes and Noble.

————. 1920. *The group mind* (2d ed.). New York: G. P. Putnam's Sons.

McLeod, P. L. 1985. "The impact of attitudes and social cognition on interpersonal conflict in small groups." Ph.D. diss., Harvard University, Cambridge, MA.

McQuade, J. T. 1983. "A comparison of interaction in single-parent and intact families." Ph.D. diss., Fordham University.

Mead, G. H. 1934. *Mind, self, and society*. Chicago: University of Chicago Press.

————. 1938. *The philosophy of the act*. Chicago: University of Chicago Press.

Mehrabian, A. 1980. *Basic dimensions for a general psychological theory*. Cambridge, MA: Oelgeschlager, Gunn, and Hain.

Melvin, D. 1953. "An experimental and statistical study of two primary social attitudes." Ph.D. diss., University of London.

Merlo, M. C. G., H. Schwallbach, and F. Kroeger. 1991. "Changes in social perception during family therapy of young schizophrenics." *Small Group Research* 22(1): 124–35.

Metzger, U. 1982. *Veraenderung des Selbstkonzepts und der Personwahrnehmung durch eine Ausbildung bei der Telefonseelsorge*. Diplomarbeit, FR Psychologie, Universitaet des Saarlandes, Saarbruecken.

Mills, T. M. 1953. "Power relations in three person groups." *American Sociological Review* 18: 351–57.

————. 1954. "The coalition pattern in three-person groups." *American Sociological Review* 19: 657–67.

Moreno, J. L. 1934. *Who shall survive? A new approach to the problem of human interrelations*. Washington, DC: Nervous and Mental Disease Publishing Company.

Morgan, W. R. 1975. "Bales's role theory: An attribution theory interpretation." *Sociometry* 38(4): 429–44.

Morris, C. 1956. *Varieties of human value*. Chicago: University of Chicago Press.

Moscovici, S. and M. Zavalloni. 1969. "The group as a polarizer of attitudes." *Journal of Personality and Social Psychology* 12: 125–35.

Mueller, G. 1984. *Die Gruppenentwicklung und die soziale Kompetenz des Gruppenmitgliedes—systemtheoretisch betrachtet. Eine Aufarbeitung systemtheoretischer Literatur (besonders auch ausserpsychologischer Herkunft) und deren Bewertung in Hinblick auf das SYMLOG-Gruppenkonzept*. Diplomarbeit, FR Psychologie, Universitaet des Saarlandes, Saarbruecken.

Murray, H. A. et al. 1938. *Explorations in personality*. New York: Oxford University Press.

Myers, D. and H. Lamm. 1976. "The group polarization phenomenon." *Psychological Bulletin* 83: 602–27.

Nadler, A., S. Ellis, and A. Rabin. 1996. "Political leaders in the SYMLOG space: Perceptions of right- and left-wing leaders by right- and left-wing constituencies." Pp. 137–51 in S. E. Hare and A. P. Hare (eds.), *SYMLOG field theory*. Westport, CT: Praeger.

Navarre, D. 1981. "Posture sharing in the interview diad." Ph.D. diss., State University of New York, Buffalo, NY.

Newell, A. and H.A. Simon. 1972. *Human problem solving*. Engelwood Cliffs, NJ: Prentice-Hall.

Nowak, I. and U. Scharpf. 1985. *Analysen des Interaktionsprozesses im pro-*

*tagonistzentrierten Psychodrama—Eine explorative Beobachtungstudie mit SYMLOG.* Diplomarbeit, FR Psychologie, Universitaet Konstanz, Konstanz.

Nowak, W. 1987. "'SYMLOG as an instrument of 'internal' and 'external' perspective taking: Construct validation and temporal change." *International Journal of Small Group Research* 3(2): 180–97.

Nye, J. L. and D.R. Forsyth. 1991. "The effects of prototype-based biases on leadership appraisals: A test of leadership categorization theory." *Small Group Research* 22(3): 360–79.

Ogden, C. 1923. *The meaning of meaning.* New York: Harcourt, Brace.

Ogilvie, S. 1987. "The undesired self: a neglected variable in personality research." *Journal of Personality and Social Psychology* 52: 379–85.

Orlik, P. 1978. A two-component formula for transforming SYMLOG interaction scoring data. Unveroeffentlichtes Manuskript. FR Psychologie, Universitaet des Saarlandes, Saarbruecken.

———. 1979. "Das Selbstkonzept als Bezugsrahmen sozialer Kognitionen." *Zeitschrift fuer Socialpsychologie* 10: 167–82.

———. 1986. "The self-concept as a vector subsystem in the social life space." *International Journal of Small Group Behavior* 2(1): 18–32.

———. 1987. "Ein semantischer Atlas zur Kodierung alltagssprachlicher Verhaltensbeschreibungen nach dem SYMLOG-Raummodell." *International Journal of Small Group Research* 3(1): 88–111.

———. 1989a. "SYMLOG: Another new look in the coming years: Or, the long road to theory-guided research." *Gruppendynamik* 20(2): 221–41.

———. 1989b. "Theoriegeleitete beobachtung von Gruppendynamik." *Zeitschrift fuer Sozialpsychologie* 20(3).

Orlik, P. and R. Becker. 1980. *Ein alternatives Modell zur Berechnung individueller Wahrnehmungsabweichungen bei SYMLOG-Daten.* Arbeiten der FR Psychologie, Nr. 66, Universitaet des Saarlandes, Saarbruecken.

Orlik, P. and J.F. Schneider. 1977. *Interaktionsdiagnostik. Ein Rahmenkonzept zum Training der diagnostischen Kompetenz von Beobachtern sozialer Interaktionen.* Arbeiten der FR Psychologie, Nr. 43, Universitaet des Saarlandes, Saarbruecken. (Reprinted in L. Schmidt, ed., *Lehrbuch der klinischen Psychologie,* pp. 280–305, 1978; 2. Aufl., 1984: pp. 190–205. Stuttgart: Enke.)

———. 1981. *On SYMLOG: Second interview with Robert F. Bales.* Arbeiten der FR Psychologie, Nr. 72, Universitaet des Saarlandes, Saarbruecken.

———. 1989. "SYMLOG (Systematic-Multiple-Level-Observation-of-Groups): Theory guided observation of groups (Editorial)." *Gruppendynamik* 20(3): 219–20.

Osgood, C. E., G.J. Suci, and P.H. Tannenbaum. 1957. *The measurement of meaning.* Urbana, IL: University of Illinois Press.

Ostmann, A. 1992. "On the relationship between formal conflict structure and the social field." *Small Group Research* 23(1): 26–48.

Palmerino, M. 1987. "An exploratory study of perceptual unification and polarization in SYMLOG." Ph.D. diss., Harvard University, Cambridge, MA.

Park, R. E. and E.W. Burgess. 1930. *Introduction to the science of sociology.* Chicago: University of Chicago Press.

Parke, B. K. 1985. "A field adaptation to the SYMLOG adjective rating form suitable for children." *International Journal of Small Group Research* 1 (1): 89–95.

Parke, B. K. and H.C. Houben. 1985. "An objective analysis of group types.' *International Journal of Small Group Research* 1(2): 131–49.

———. 1988a. "Analyses of subgroups and clusterings within groups: Attaining knowledge of the social interaction potential." *International Journal of Small Group Research* 4(2): 143–58.

———. 1988b. "The group diagramming method in the classroom." Pp. 213–44 in R. B. Polley, A. P. Hare, and P. J. Stone (eds.). *The SYMLOG practitioner*. New York: Praeger.

———. 1988c. "A rationale and mathematically justifiable method for group diagram expansions." *International Journal of Small Group Research* 4(2): 169–79.

Parsons, T. 1937. *The structure of social action*. New York: McGraw-Hill.

———. 1951. *The social system*. New York: Free Press.

———. 1968a. "Social interaction." Pp. 429–40 in D. L. Sills (ed.), *International Encyclopedia of Social Sciences*. New York: Macmillan and Free Press.

———. 1968b. "Utilitarianism, sociological thought." Pp. 229–55 in D. L. Sills (ed.), *International Encyclopedia of Social Sciences* (volume 16). New York, Macmillan and Free Press.

Parsons, T. and R.F. Bales. 1953. "The dimensions of action space." Pp. 63–109 in T. Parsons, R. F. Bales, and E. A. Shils, *Working papers in the theory of action*. Glencoe, IL: Free Press.

———. 1955. *Family, socialization, and interaction process*. Glencoe, IL: Free Press.

Parsons, T., R.F. Bales, and E.A. Shils. 1953a. "Phase movement in relation to motivation, symbol formation, and role structure." Pp. 163–269 in T. Parsons, R. F. Bales, and E. A. Shils, *Working papers in the theory of action*. Glencoe, IL: Free Press.

———. 1953b. *Working papers in the theory of action*. Glencoe, IL: Free Press.

Parsons, T. and Shils, E. A. 1954. *Toward a general theory of action*. Cambridge, MA: Harvard University Press.

Perry, R. B. 1909. *The moral economy*. New York: Charles Scribner's Sons.

———. 1926. *General theory of value*. New York: Longmans, Green.

Pettigrew, W. 1967. "Social evaluation theory." Pp. 241–311 in D. Levine (ed.), *Nebraska symposium on motivation*. Lincoln, NE: University of Nebraska Press.

Pflum, G. D. 1982. "The effect of conflict, quality, and time on information use and small group behavior in evaluative decision-making situations." Ph.D. diss., University of Nebraska, Lincoln, NE.

Plutchik, R. and H.R. Conte. 1997. *Circumplex models of personality and emotions*. Washington, DC: American Psychological Association.

Polley, R.B. 1979. "Both sides of the mirror: Small groups and subjectivity." Ph.D. diss., Harvard University, Cambridge, MA.

———. 1983. "Dimensions of political reality." *Journal of Applied Social Psychology* 13 (1): 66–77.

———. 1984. "Subjectivity in issue polarization." *Journal of Applied Social Psychology* 14(5): 426–50.

———. 1985a. "The diagnosis of intact work groups." *Consultation* 4(4): 273–83.

———. 1985b. "A general theory of polarization and unification." *International Journal of Small Group Research* 1(2): 150–61.

———. 1986. "Rethinking the third dimension." *International Journal of Small Group Research* 2(2): 134–40.

————. 1987a. "The consultant as the shaper of legend." *Consultation* 6(2): 102–18.

————. 1987b. "The dimensions of social interaction: A method for improving rating scales." *Social Psychology Quarterly* 50(1): 72–82.

————. 1988. "Group field dynamics and effective mediation." *International Journal of Small Group Research* 4(1): 55–75.

————. 1989a. "On the dimensions of interpersonal behavior: A reply to Lustig." *Small Group Behavior* 20(2): 270–78.

————. 1989b. "The oral tradition: Reflections in the spoken word." *Small Group Behavior* 20(4): 389–405.

————. 1991. "Group process as diagnostic: An introduction." *Small Group Research* 22(1): 92–98.

Polley, R. B. and J. Eid. 1990. "Leadership training on the Bergen Fjord: A case study and evaluation." *Group and Organization Studies* 15(2): 192–211.

Polley, R. B., A.P. Hare, and P.J. Stone, eds. 1988. *The SYMLOG practitioner: Applications of small group research.* New York: Praeger.

Polley, R. B. and P.D. Skinner. 1988. "Delinquency, individualism, and socialization." Pp. 281–300 in R. B. Polley, A. P. Hare, and P. J. Stone (eds.), *The SYMLOG practitioner.* New York: Praeger.

Polley, R. B. and P.J. Stone. 1988. "An introduction to SYMLOG." Pp. 1–13 in R. B. Polley, A. P. Hare, and P. J. Stone (eds.), *The SYMLOG practitioner.* New York: Praeger.

Poumadere, M. 1981. *Le SYMLOG comme nouveau paradigme de la psychosociologie: Logique et contradictions.* Unpublished monograph, Institut SYMLOG de France, 8 rue du Moulin de Cachan, 94320 Cachan, France.

————. 1983. *Image et role du formateur—Passages d'une elaboration groupale.* Unpublished monograph, Institut SYMLOG de France, 8 rue du Moulin de Cachan, 94320 Cachan, France.

————. 1984. "Interventions SYMLOG dans les organisations." *Le Journal des Psychologues* 22 (June).

————. 1985a. "Pratiques de sécurité et relations de travail dans un centre de production nucleaire." *Proceedings of the first national topical meeting of the French Association of Technicians, Engineers, and Occupational Medicine* (A.F.T.I.M.), 30 rue de Conde, 75006 Paris, France.

————. 1985b. "SYMLOG et les valeurs de l'organisation." In R. Reitter and B. Ramanatsoa (eds.), *Pouvoir et Direction.* Paris: McGraw-Hill.

Poumadere, M. and C. Mays. 1986. "Interview with Robert F. Bales." *Le Journal des Psychologues*, Marseille.

————. 1988. "SYMLOG and organizational consulting: The meaning of measurement." Pp. 29–60 in R. B. Polley, A. P. Hare, and P. J. Stone (eds.), *The SYMLOG practitioner.* New York: Praeger.

Powers, J. P. 1980. "The effects of cognitive feedback: The visual representation of the family social interaction field and individual perceptual field diagrams, derived from behavioral ratings given by family members, upon unusual perceptions among family members, locus of family conflict, solutions to family conflict, and family solidarity needs." Unpublished pre–dissertation research project. Boston College, Boston, MA.

Presser, S. 1968. "Gretchen, Lilly, Carla, Suzy, Mariah, and Diane: A study of six women in a self-analytic training group." Honors thesis, Harvard University, Cambridge, MA.

Rhodes, M. A. 1986. "The SYMLOG space as a representation of the multiple level psychological field." Ph.D. diss., Department of Psychology, Harvard University, Cambridge, MA.

Richardson, F. L. W. 1978. "The elusive nature of cooperation in leadership: Discovering a primitive process that regulates human behavior." Chapter 4 in E. M. Eddy and W. L. Partridge (eds.), *Applied anthropology in America*. New York: Columbia University Press.

Roberts, B. and F.L. Strodtbeck. 1953. "Interaction process differences between groups of paranoid schizophrenic and depressed patients." *International Journal of Group Psychotherapy* 3:29–41.

Roman, P. D. 1986. "College student perceptions of effective/ineffective teachers." *International Journal of Small Group Research* 2(2): 210–18.

Ronchi, D. 1982. "Final report of the training and consultation project, New York City Labor-Management Committee Program." Unpublished paper, Department of Communication, Ohio State University, Columbus, OH.

Rosenthal, R. and R. Rosnow. 1969. *Artifact in behavioral research*. New York: Academic Press.

Rosnow, R. L. 1981. *Paradigms in transition: The methodology of social inquiry*. New York: Oxford University Press.

Rousseau, J. J. 1762. *The social contract* 1961. London, UK: Dent.

Royce, J. 1894. *The world and the individual*. New York: Macmillan.

Rupert, C. T. 1984. "Relationship criticism: A study of the possibilities and limitations of the application of Robert F. Bales's SYMLOG and Interaction Process Analysis to Scriptural criticism." Ph.D. diss., Institute of Christian Thought, University of St. Michael's College, Toronto, Canada.

———. 1988. "SYMLOG in the service of literary analysis." Pp. 301–18 in R. B. Polley, A. P. Hare, and P. J. Stone (eds.), *The SYMLOG practitioner*. New York: Praeger.

Rywick, T. 1987. "SYMLOG rating form reliability." *International Journal of Small Group Research* 3(1): 119–25.

Sansolo, J. 1969. "Trainer style and group reaction: An analysis of trainer comments in t-groups and its relation to the learning and satisfaction of group members." Ph.D. diss., Harvard University, Cambridge, MA.

Savage, G. T. 1984. "Negotiation in small group decision-making: An ethnographic and conversational analysis of the process of dialogue in labor-management committee meetings." Ph.D. diss., Ohio State University, Columbus, OH.

———. 1985. "The use of conversational analysis as an interpretive foil for participant observer research on small groups." *International Journal of Small Group Research* 1(2): 193–202.

Sbandi, P. and A. Vogl. 1973. "Das dreidimensionale Gruppenmodell von R. F. Bales." *Gruppendynamik* 4: 181–92.

Scanzoni, J. 1983. "SYMLOG: A system for the multiple level observation of groups." *American Journal of Sociology* 88(4): 814–16.

Schantz, D. 1986. "The use of SYMLOG as a diagnostic tool in drug-related problems on the job." *International Journal of Small Group Research* 2(2): 219–24.

Scharpf, U. and R. Fisch. 1989. "The destiny of suggestions in group decision-making proposals: A contribution on the analysis of content aspects of interaction in group decision-making." *Gruppendynamik* 20(3): 283–96.

Scheinerman, E. 1996. *Invitation to dynamical systems.* Upper Saddle River, NJ: Prentice-Hall, A. Simon and Schuster.

Schneider, J. F. 1977. *Behind and in front of the one-way-mirror. An interview with Robert Freed Bales.* Arbeiten der FR Psychologie, Nr. 46, Universitaet des Saarlandes, Saarbruecken.

———. 1978a. Interview mit Robert Freed Bales. Hinter und vor der Einwegscheibe. *Gruppendynamik* 9: 42–59.

———. 1978b. "Methoden der Interaktionsforschung." Pp. 31–56 in B. Minsel and W. K. Roth (eds.), *Soziale Interaktion in der Schule.* Muenchen, Germany: Urban und Schwarzenberg, Bd. 5.

———. 1979. "Systematische mehrstufige Beobachtung von Gruppen: Bericht ueber ein Beobachtungs- und Lehrkonzept von R. F. Bales." Zusammenfassung fuer die 21. Tagung experimentell arbeitender Psychologen, Heidelberg.

———. 1983. "Beobachtung von Gruppenprozessen." Pp. 381–85 in D. Frey and S. Grei (eds.), *Sozialpsychologie. Ein Handbuch in Schluesselbegriffen.* Muenchen, Germany: Urban und Schwarzenberg.

———. 1984. "SYMLOG als ein Rahmenmodell zur Durchfuehrung und Evaluierung von Interventionen in Gruppen und Organisationen." Pp. 221–44 in H. J. Kurtz, A. Marcotty, and R. T. Stiefel, *Neue Evaluierungskonzepte in der Management-Andragogik.* Muenchen, Germany: Edition Academic.

Schneider, J.F. and U. Becker. 1985. "SYMLOG in der Gruppentherapieforschung: Einige theoretische und methodische Ueberlegungen." Pp. 279–99 in D. Czogalik et al (eds.), *Perspektiven der Psychotherapieforschung: Einzelfall, Gruppe, Institution.* Freiburg, Germany: Hochschul Verlag.

Schneider, J.F. and U. Becker-Beck. 1988. "Delivery and reception of feedback in academic SYMLOG groups: A problem analysis." Pp. 117–29 in R. B. Polley, A. P. Hare, and P. J. Stone (eds.), *The SYMLOG practitioner.* New York: Praeger.

Schneider, J. F. and P. Orlik. 1982. *SYMLOG: Ein System fuer die Mehrstufige Beobachtung von Gruppen.* Stuttgart, Germany: Klett-Cotta.

Schneider, J. F., M. Schneider-Dueker, and U. Becker-Beck. 1989. "Sex roles and social behavior: On the relation between the Bem Sex Role Inventory and the SYMLOG Behavior Rating Scales." *Journal of Social Psychology* 129(4): 471–79.

Schneider, J. F. and E. Zimmer. 1978. *Zur faktoriellen Validitaet einer deutschen Bearbeitung des SYMLOG-adjective-rating-sheet.* Arbeiten der FR Psychologie, Nr. 59, Universitaet des Saarlandes, Saarbruecken.

Schneider-Duker, M. 1989a. "Role as a unit of observation in psychodrama-research: For example, the development of a group." *International Journal of Small Group Research* 5(1): 119–30.

———. 1989b. "Rollenwahl und Gruppenentwicklung im Psychodrama. Ein empirische Untersuchen an Therapie und Selbsterfahrungsgruppen." *Gruppendynamik* 20: 259–72.

Seeman, M. 1996. "The elusive situation." Paper presented at Social Psychology Meetings of American Sociological Association.

Seibert, S. and L. Gruenfeld. 1992. "Masculinity, femininity, and behavior in groups." *Small Group Research* 23(1): 95–122.

Senn, D. 1988. "Myopic social psychology: an overemphasis on individualistic explanations of social behavior." *Journal of Social Behavior and Personality* 3: 45–52.

Shaw, M. and. P. Constanzo. 1982. *Theories of social psychology.* New York: McGraw-Hill.

Sherif, M. 1936. *The psychology of social norms.* New York: Harper.

Silvermann, I. 1977. "Why social psychology fails." *Canadian Psychological Review Psychologie Canadienn* 18:353–8.

Simmel, G. 1902. "The number of members as determining the sociological form of a group." *American Journal of Sociology* 8:1–46, 158–96.

Sjoevold, E. 1995. "Groups in harmony and tension: the development of an analysis of polarization in groups and organizations based on the SYMLOG method." Ph.D. diss., Universitetet I Trondheim, Norway.

Skardal, O., E. Lind, J.V. Gjoen, E. Moser, T. Smordal, S.T. Nyhus, and M.B. Moser. 1986. "The interactional effects of personality and gender in small groups: A missing perspective in research." *International Journal of Small Group Research* 2(2): 172–85.

Slater, P. E. 1955. "Role differentiation in small groups." *American Sociological Review* 20: 300–10.

Small, A. W. 1905. *General sociology.* Chicago: University of Chicago Press.

Smith, A. 1853. *The theory of moral sentiments* (Copyright 1969, 1976). Indianapolis, IN: E. G. West, Liberty Classics.

Smith, M. B. 1972. "Is experimental psychology advancing?" *Journal of Experimental Social Psychology* 8: 86–96.

Smith, M. B., J.S. Bruner, and R.W. White. 1956. *Opinions and personality.* New York: Wiley.

Smitherman, H. 1979. "Group learning and personality." *College Student Journal* 13(3): 251–55.

Sniderman, R. L. 1992. "The use of SYMLOG in the evaluation of effectiveness of a management development program." Ph.D. diss., California School of Professional Studies, Los Angeles, CA.

Solomon, M. J. 1977. "An impressive validation of systematic multiple level observation of groups." Unpublished paper. Psychology and Social Relations, Harvard University, Cambridge, MA.

———. 1981. "Dimensions of interpersonal behavior: A convergent validation within a cognitive interactionist framework." *Journal of Personality* 49:15–26.

Sorokin, P. 1937. *Social and cultural dynamics.* Chicago: American Book Company.

———. 1956. *Fads and follies in modern sociology and related sciences.* Chicago: Henry Regnery.

Steiner, I. 1974. "Whatever happened to the group in social psychology?" *Journal of Experimental Social Psychology* 10: 94–108.

Stiefken, R. 1984. *Die Auswertung freier Selbst- und Fremd-beschreibungen mit Hilfe von SYMLOG und der Inhaltsanalyse nach Bromley als Alternative zu den ueblichen Verfahren der Erfassung von Selbst- und Fremdwahrnehmung.* Diplomarbeit, FR Psychologie, Universitaet des Saarlandes, Saarbruecken.

Stiles, W. B. 1980. Comparison of dimensions derived from rating versus coding of dialogue. *Journal of Personality and Social Psychology* 38(3): 359–74.

Stockton, R. 1981. "SYMLOG: A system for the multiple level observation of groups." *Psychiatry* 44 (2): 184–86.

Stogdill, R. M. 1974. *Handbook of leadership: A survey of theory and research.* New York: Free Press.

Stone, P. J. 1988. "SYMLOG for skeptics." Pp. 15–26 in R. B. Polley, A. P. Hare, and P. J. Stone (eds.), *The SYMLOG practitioner.* New York: Praeger.

Stone, P. J., D.C. Dunphy, M.S. Smith, and D.M. Ogilvie. 1966. *The general inquirer: A computer approach to content analysis.* Cambridge, MA: MIT Press.

Stout, S. A. 1979. "A study of the structure of health values." Doctor of Public Health diss., Department of Health Administration, University of North Carolina, Chapel Hill, NC.

Strodtbeck, F. L. 1950. "A study of husband-wife interaction in three cultures." Ph.D. diss., Harvard University, Cambridge, MA.

———. 1951. "Husband-wife interaction over revealed differences." *American Sociological Review* 16: 468–73.

———. 1954. "The family as a three-person group." *American Sociological Review* 19: 23–29.

———. 1968. "The influence of sex of child and social class on instrumental and expressive roles in a laboratory setting." *Sociology and Social Research* 52: 7–21.

———. 1984. "Difficult decisions behind the originality of SYMLOG." *Social Psychology Quarterly* 47 (1): 95–98.

Strodtbeck, F.L. and R. Mann. 1956. "Sex-role differentiation in jury deliberations." *Sociometry* 19: 3–11.

Struchholz, H. 1979. *Die SYMLOG-Konzeption von Bales am Beispieleiner einer akademischen Selbstanalysegruppe. Eine Fallstudie.* Diplomarbeit, FR Psychologie, Universitaet des Saarlandes, Saarbruecken.

Sucato, V. S. 1976. "Short-term and long-term service: An Interaction Process Analysis." Ph.D. diss., Rutgers University.

Sulloway, F. 1997. *Born to rebel.* New York: Pantheon Books.

Sumner, W. G. [1906]1959. *Folkways.* New York: Dover.

Sundstrom, E., R.J. Koenigs, and G.D. Huet-Cox. 1996. "Personality and perceived values: Myers-Briggs Type Indicator and coworker ratings on SYMLOG." Pp. 155–73 in S. E. Hare and A. P. Hare (eds.), *SYMLOG field theory.* Westport, CT: Praeger.

Swann, H. and R.B. Polley. 1985. "On forming impressions from observed behavior: Two postulates and five parameters." *International Journal of Small Group Behavior* 1(2): 206–14.

Swensen, C. H. 1981. "SYMLOG: A system for the multiple level observation of groups." *Journal of Personality Assessment* 45(1): 99–100.

Tepp, G. A. 1992. "Interactional effects resulting from new member entry into existing groups." Ph.D. diss., Graduate Faculty of the School of Human Behavior, United States International University, San Diego, CA.

Thomas, D. S., ed. 1929. *Some new techniques for studying social behavior.* New York: Columbia University, Teachers College.

Thomas, W. I. 1909. *Source book for social origins*. Chicago: University of Chicago Press.

———. 1924. *The unadjusted girl*. Boston, MA: Little, Brown.

———. 1937. *Primitive behavior*. New York: McGraw-Hill.

Thomas, W. I. and F. Znaniecki. [1918–20]1958. *The Polish peasant in Europe and America*. New York: Dover.

Thrasher, F. M. 1927. *The gang*. Chicago: University of Chicago Press.

Thurstone, L. L. 1919. "The anticipatory aspect of consciousness." *Journal of Philosophy* 16: 561–69.

———. 1947. *Multiple factor analysis*. Chicago: University of Chicago Press.

———. 1949. *The Thurstone temperament schedule*. Chicago: Science Research Associates.

Thurstone, L. L. and E.J. Chave. 1937. *The measurement of attitude*. Chicago: University of Chicago Press.

Toennies, F. [1887]1957. *Community and society* (Gemeinschaft und Gesellschaft). C. P. Loomis, trans. East Lansing, MI: Michigan State University Press.

Tolman, E. C. 1932. *Purposive behavior in animals and men*. New York: Century.

Tootell, G., L. Mason, J.M. Taraldson, M. Barnhill, and P. Prather. 1986. "The independence of norms in small groups." *International Journal of Small Group Research* 2(1): 43–59.

Tosato, D. and L.D. Brunner. 1996. *Efficienza producttiva e cultura organizzativa nelle imprese orafe*. Arezzo, Italy: Associazione Intercamerale di Coordinamento per lo Svilluppo dell'oreficeria, Argenteria e Affini.

Tressemer, D. 1974. "Observing social interaction: Methodological models." Paper presented at meetings of American Psychological Association, New Orleans, LA.

Tschuschke, V. 1988. "Interaction behavior of borderline patients in analytic group therapy." Pp. 261–68 in R. B. Polley, A. P. Hare, and P. J. Stone (eds.), *The SYMLOG practitioner*. New York: Praeger.

———. "Therapeutic effectiveness and outcome in group-psychotherapy." *Gruppenpsychotherapie und Gruppendynamik* 25(1): 60–78.

Vallacher, R. and A. Nowak. 1994. *Dynamical systems in social psychology*. San Diego, CA: Academic Press.

Van Velsor, E. and J.B. Leslie. 1991. *Feedback to managers volume II: A review and comparison of sixteen multi-rater feedback instruments*. Greensboro, NC: Center for Creative Leadership.

Vanneman, R. D. 1974. "Industrial organization during development: A personality and social structure approach." Ph.D. diss., Harvard University, Cambridge, MA.

Vogelgesang, O. 1977. *Die psychologischen Typen C. G. Jungs und die Gruppenrollen von R. F. Bales. Ein theoretischer und praktischer Vergleich*. Diplomarbeit, FR Psychologie, Universitaet des Saarlandes, Saarbruecken.

Voss, P. 1984. "SYMLOG: A System for multilevel group observation." *Zeitschrift fur Psychologie* 192(2): 201–3.

Waagen, C. L. 1982. *The development of group identity through language use*. Ph.D. diss., Pennsylvania State University, State College, PA.

Waldersee, R. and G. Eagleson. 1996. *The efficacy of distributed leadership in implementing change*. Sydney, Australia: Center for Corporate Change, Australian Graduate School of Management in the University of New South Wales.

Waters, M. 1994. *Modern sociological theory*. London, UK : Sage.

Whaley, G. L. 1987. "SYMLOG: A microcomputer-based management development tool." *Northern California Executive Review* (fall): 6–13.

———. 1989. "SYMLOG field diagram of contemporary well-know personalities." *International Journal of Small Group Research* 5(2): 211–20.

Whaley, G. L., with S.E. Hare. 1996. "George L. Whaley predicts the potential for a successful merger of two small engineering service firms." Pp. 57–71 in S. E. Hare and A. P. Hare (eds.), *SYMLOG field theory*. Westport, CT: Praeger.

Wiener, V. and E. Fogelman. 1982. "Conflict management in the family: A SYMLOG analysis of upwardly mobile, lower-class, urban families." Unpublished paper, Department of Psychology, City University of New York, New York.

Williamson, S. A. 1977. "Developmental patterns in self-analytic groups." Ph.D. diss.. Harvard University, Cambridge, MA.

Winter, G. 1952. "Value-orientations as factors in the organization of small groups." Ph.D. diss., Harvard University, Cambridge, MA.

Wish, M. 1976. "Comparisons among multidimensional structures of interpersonal relations." *Multivariate Behavioral Research* 11: 297–324.

Wish, M., R.G. D'Andrade, and J.E. Goodnow. 1976. "Dimensions of interpersonal communication: Correspondence between structures for speech acts and bipolar scales." *Journal of Personality and Social Psychology* 33: 409–20.

Wish, M., M. Deutsch, and S.J. Kaplan. 1976. "Perceived dimensions of interpersonal relations." *Journal of Personality and Social Psychology* 33:409–20.

Wiswell, A. K. and H.V. Lawrence. 1992. "The effects of training in feedback on managers' perceived effectiveness of their work groups." Paper presented at HRD Professor's Network Conference.

Witmer, N. T., S.B. Pond, III, and C.T. Love. 1984. "Small group process: Comparison of memory ratings with observational scoring." *Group and Organization Studies* 9(2): 221–40.

Woodworth, R. S. 1939. "Situation-and-goal set." *American Journal of Psychology* 50:149–60.

Wright, R. 1994. *The moral animal: The new science of evolutionary psychology*. New York: Pantheon Books.

Wunder, K. 1985a. *Ratings und Interaktionssignierung im SYMLOG-Ansatz. Ein Methodenvergleich im Hinblick auf Konsistenz, Sensitivitaet und Validitaet*. Diplomarbeit, FR Psychologie, Universitaet Konstanz, Konstanz.

———. 1985b. "SYMLOG and exchange theory." Unpublished course paper, Department of Psychology, State University of New York, Buffalo, New York.

———. 1987. "A comparison between ratings and scorings in the SYMLOG approach." *International Journal of Small Group Research* 3(1): 126–38.

Wunder, K. and R. Fisch. 1991. "Weitere Qualitaetsprufen des SYMLOG-Verhaltensfragebogens, ein Stichprobenvergleich." FR Psychologie, Universitaet Konstanz, Konstanz.

Wundt, W. 1896. *Outlines of psychology*. Leipzig, Germany: Wilhelm Englemann.

Zipf, G. K. 1949. *Human behavior and the principle of least effort*. Reading, MA: Addison-Wesley.

Znaniecki, F. 1925. *The laws of social psychology*. Warsaw, Poland: Gebethner and Wolff.

———. 1934. *The method of sociology*. New York: Farrar and Rinehart.

# Index of Names

# Index of Topics

Ability, differences of in groups, 174

Acceptance of Authority (Factor I, Bales and Couch), 144

Acceptance of Authority versus Opposition to Authority, 216. *See also* U-D dimension

Acceptance of the Task Orientation of Established Authority versus Rejection of the Task Orientation of Established Authority, 137. *See also* U-D dimension

Acceptance versus Non-acceptance of authority, 7, 11–12. *See also* U-D dimension

Acceptance, differentiation of, and liking or disliking, friendliness or unfriendliness, 134

Achievement, differentiation of, 135

Achievement Training, McClelland's method of, 146

ACT (actual, for other), Image of, rating question, 33, 327

Actions: impelled by values, 132; and reactions, 131; value significance of, 132

Activity Factor (Dimension III, Osgood), 142

Activity (Factor I, IPA studies), measurement of, 167, 168

Acts: first acts and next acts, 240–43; initiated, 130, 131; of leadership, 138; received, 130; serial order of, 225; types of, 131; unit act, 188–91, 192, 194–95

Affectivity, in social interaction, 149

Affects, factor-analytic studies of, 78

Agreement with acceptance of authority (Factor I, Bales and Couch), 112, 113; and authoritarianism, 112

Agreement with equalitarianism (Factor III, Bales and Couch), 112–13

Agreement with individualism (Factor IV, Bales and Couch), 113

Agreement with need-determined expression versus value-determined restraint (Factor II, Bales and Couch), 112, 113

Agrees (IPA Category 3), 225–26, 236, 237, 239, 241; Best Liked and high levels of, 252; Idea specialist and low levels of, 252; third phase of group process and rising rates of, 123. *See also* Interaction Process Analysis

Air defense network, laboratory simulation of, 229–31, 236

Air Force: laboratory simulation of air defense network, 229–31; training and division of labor, 231; training and inculcation of values, 231

Alienation, and unification in the field, 149

Alpha Male, 174

American business: culture of organizations in, 279; culture values of, 56–58; current culture of, 294; and individualism, 58; Optimum Bar-graph profile, suitability for, 98

American Psychological Association, 135

American Sociological Society, 303

Anarchist, values of, 47

Anti-authoritarian values, of democratic individuals, 88

Anti-authority Opposition (Area 10, Value Area Overlay), 64, 68; and REJ, 68

Anti-group Opposition (Area 9, Value Area Overlay), 64, 68, 69; and EXP, 74; and REJ, 68

Approval by authority, differentiation of, 135

Polarization and unification: on Field Diagram, 45, 49; of father and elder son versus later-born sons, 302; of members, 46; similarity across groups, 50; of subgroups, 77; theory of, 16; in value systems, 50; of values, 218

Polarization-Unification Overlay. *See* Overlay (Polarization-Unification)

Polish peasants, Thomas and Znaniecki's study of letters to, 193

Political actor, vector as, 60

Political attitudes: factor-analytic studies of, 203; Eysenck and Melvin's studies of, 143–44; Melvin's studies of, 143

Positive reactions (IPA Problem Area), 225; and Best Liked member, 252; frequencies of, 225–26, 236–37; and negative reactions, 243–45. *See also* Interaction Process Analysis

Positive-Negative. *See* P-N dimension

Potency Factor (Dimension II, Osgood), 142

Power: and dominance, 196–97; and resources, 277; versus merit, 196–97; and values, 90

Prediction, Intercorrelation Space as a model for, 48

Prejudice: Field Diagram and development of, 67; in race relations, 164; and values of religious conservatism, 108

Primate behavior, Goodall's study of, 173

Problem solving (group decision): Dewey's steps in, 159; and differentiation of values, 271; and divergence of three major vectors, 232; inevitable differentiation during, 214; group size in studies of, 332; groups, 119, 131, 148; Most Effective Profile portrayal of, 288; need for, 133; and observation of groups, 195, 332, 333; phases in 159, 233–38; problems in, 161–63; problems of, 207–8; and problems of dominance, 208; and problems of group solidarity, 208; resources required for, 209–10; and status order, 174; steps in, 229–33; and tendency to keep talking, 231–32; traditional

accounts of, 161; and unit act, 192; value conflict and success in, 87; and value priorities in, 91

Problems of control (IPA system problem), 228–29, 238. *See also* Interaction Process Analysis

Problems of evaluation (IPA system problem), 228, 238. *See also* Interaction Process Analysis

Problems of orientation (IPA system problem), 228, 233, 238. *See also* Interaction Process Analysis

Problems of social order, 183, 184; 268–72; of dominance, 208; and CUR, 279; of group solidarity, 208; of problem solving, 207–8; and selection of values, 268; solution shown in EFF, 260; solutions and third-person perspective, 186, 187; of task, 207–8

Psyche, Freud's theory of, 185

*Psychoanalytic Study of the Family* (Flugel 1921), 144

Psychological Clinic, Plympton Street, 331

Psychological Determinants of Interpersonal Behavior (Couch's dissertation), 334

Psychological need, to survive 269–70

*The Psychology of Politics*, by Eysenck, 334

Psychometric measurement, 135

Questions (IPA Problem Area), 225; and attempted answers in interaction process, 246; as feedbacks, 246; frequencies of, 225–26; 245–46; and negative reactions, 245, 246; and role redefinition, 246; and status, 246. *See also* Interaction Process Analysis

Race relations, 164: prejudice in, 164; conflict in, 164

Radcliffe College, research subjects from, 111

Radical Opposition Core (Area 11, Value Area Overlay), 64, 67, 68; and EXP, 74; and REJ, 68

RAND Corporation, 229

Rating form, 7; for behavior, 12, 37; conversion of responses to vectors,